CRYPTANALYSIS

A STUDY OF CIPHERS AND THEIR SOLUTION

(formerly published under the title ELEMENTARY CRYPTANALYSIS)

HELEN FOUCHÉ GAINES

DOVER PUBLICATIONS, INC. NEW YORK

Library of Congress Catalog Card Number: 57-203

International Standard Book Number
ISBN-13: 978-0-486-20097-2
ISBN-10: 0-486-20097-3

Manufactured in the United States by LSC Communications
20097330   2017
www.doverpublications.com

PREFACE

The word *cryptography*, properly speaking, embraces the entire field of secret writing, while that branch of the subject dealing with the solution and reading of cryptic messages is generally referred to as *cryptanalysis*.

Works on the subject of secret writing are comparatively numerous, if not always easily available, but works devoted purely to the analysis of such writing and the solving of its cryptograms have, until recently, been so rare as to be almost non-existent for the general reader.

Today we have two particularly excellent works, but both in foreign languages: *Cours de cryptographie*, by General Marcel Givierge, and *Manuale di crittografia*, by General Luigi Sacco. In English, we find a more elementary work, *The Solution of Codes and Ciphers*, by Louis C. S. Mansfield (Maclehose, London), which, the writer has been told, is to be a first volume. As to America's contribution, we seem to find only small books such as Colonel Parker Hitt's *A B C of Secret Writing*, covering three ciphers, or Colonel H. O. Yardley's *Yardleygrams*.

There are, however, many works which deal most interestingly with the analysis and decryptment of some one particular cipher. Most of these are short works, published in magazines or incorporated into books of a general nature, and nearly always the one cipher dealt with is that type of simple substitution which appears with separated words in the puzzle sections of our current magazines and newspapers.

One well-known gem of cryptanalysis, equal to any modern specimen, can be found in the story, *The Gold Bug*, by Edgar Allan Poe. This, too, deals with the simple substitution cipher just referred to, but covers a case in which word-divisions are absent. Poe has also left us an essay called *Cryptography*.

Rosario Candela's recent book, *The Military Cipher of Commandant Bazeries*, shows the unraveling of one particular cryptogram which, for many years, had baffled the best efforts of all amateurs, and, it is rather suspected, of some few who were not amateurs. The book contains a chapter on general cryptanalysis, and also some cryptograms for solution.

Secret and Urgent, by Fletcher Pratt, is primarily a history of secret writing (a most interesting one, by the way), but contains also a number of examples of cryptanalysis; it also shows a table which the writer has never before seen in published form: a list of English trigrams (three-letter sequences) and the frequency with which they are used in the language. Other examples of decryptment may be found in the Macbeth translation of Langie's genial little book, *De la cryptographie;* the appendix to this translation contains the coveted Playfair demonstration, prepared by Lieutenant Commander W. W. Smith of the United States Navy.

Just why so absorbing a subject has been so neglected in a world full of puzzle lovers is hard to understand, especially since the analytic writer, in addition to entertainment, has something to offer of a more serious nature. It is true that trained cryptanalysts are not greatly in demand in peacetime, and that our present corps of cryptographers has a personnel more than ample for providing necessary codes and ciphers, scientifically selected to fit their individual purposes, and safeguarded with suitable protective devices. Yet of what value is the most excellent of ciphers if, at the time of direst need, this cipher, with all of its safeguards, must be placed in the hands of even one man who cannot appreciate its intrinsic value or imagine a need for extra precautions? At any rate, we make our feeble attempt to reach this " one man." May he learn, at least, that there are reasons for his instructions! In the planning of the present treatise, all purely historical aspects of secret writing were neglected, and many well-known ciphers whose interest is chiefly historical or literary have either been omitted or given but cursory treatment. Certain other ciphers, representative of types, have been treated at whatever length seemed advisable for bringing out principles; and, with each type discussed, a generous number of cryptograms has been provided, on which the student will be able to test his skill as he learns. The student who masters these fundamentals will be acquainted with the principal forms of cipher, and will be able to solve cryptograms prepared by means of these ciphers provided the cryptograms are of adequate length and based on a language which he understands, or of which he is able to secure understandable specimens. Within limits, he should also be able to analyze and solve such cryptograms without being told in advance what the cipher is. This, we believe, is the kind of text-book desired by the many who desire information about " ciphers."

Its material, compiled by members of the American Cryptogram Association, has had to be gathered from a great many sources, both within the organization and elsewhere, making it impossible, at times, to give credit where credit is due. Our chief indebtedness, however, is to M. E. Ohaver for a series of articles published during the years 1924 to 1928 in the former Flynn's Magazine and most unfortunately no longer obtainable from the publishers. Further acknowledgment should be made to Colonel Parker Hitt, whose *Manual for the Solution of Military Ciphers,* though not available for general distribution, can usually be consulted in large public libraries. We have also borrowed liberally from foreign sources, and members of the association have most generously contributed the results of their original research. For this collaboration and co-operation, the writer is particularly grateful.

CONTENTS

CHAPTER I

GENERAL INFORMATION

The subject which we are about to study is the analysis and solution of *cipher*, though not including *code*, which is a very special form of cipher demanding something more than elementary knowledge; nor shall we enter at all into the subject of *invisible inks*, certainly a most important aspect of secret writing, but belonging to the province of chemistry rather than to that of cryptanalysis. *Cipher machines*, also, are not within our present scope.

The term *cipher* implies a *method*, or *system*, of secret writing which, generally speaking, is unlimited in scope; it should be possible, using any one given cipher, to transform any *plain text* whatever, regardless of its length and the language in which it is written, into a *cryptogram*, or single enciphered message. The process of accomplishing this transformation is called *encipherment;* the opposite process, that of transforming the cryptogram into a plaintext, is called *decipherment*.

The word *decrypt*, with its various derivatives, is being used here to signify the process of *solving* and reading cryptograms without any previous knowledge as to their *keys*, or secret formulas; thus the word *decipher* has been left to convey only its one meaning, as mentioned above: the mechanical process of applying a known key. Our word *decrypt*, however, is an innovation borrowed from the modern French and Italian writers, and is somewhat frowned upon by leading cryptologists.

The word *digram* is being used to indicate a two-letter sequence; similarly, we have *trigrams, tetragrams, pentagrams*, etc., to indicate sequences of three, four, five, etc. letters.

Ciphers, in general, fall into three major classifications:
1. Concealment Cipher
2. Transposition Cipher
3. Substitution Cipher

Minor types, such as "abbreviation," are sometimes included, though, to the writer, these have never seemed to be truly of a cryptographic nature.

In *concealment cipher*, the true letters of the secret message are hidden, or disguised, by any device whatever; and this type of cipher, as a general rule, is intended to pass without being suspected as the conveyor of a secret communication.

In *transposition cipher*, the true letters of the secret message are taken out of their text-order, and are rearranged according to any pattern, or *key*, agreed upon by the correspondents.

In *substitution cipher*, these original text-letters are replaced with substitutes, or cipher-symbols, and these symbols are arranged in the same order as their originals. There may, of course, be combinations of types, or combinations of several forms belonging to a single type.

The aristocrat of the cipher family is *code*. This is a form of the substitution cipher which requires the preparation, in advance, of a *code book*. A series of terms likely to be used in future correspondence (that is, words, phrases, and even sentences) is first gathered into a vocabulary, or "dictionary"; and beside each of these terms is placed a substitute known as a *code group*, or *code word*. These substitutes may be groups of letters, or groups of digits, or actual words selected from ordinary language. Very common words or expressions are usually provided with more than one substitute; and nearly always there are substitutes provided for syllables and single letters, so as to take care of all words not originally included in the vocabulary.

No code presents any real security unless the code symbols have been assigned in a thoroughly haphazard manner. This means that any really good code would have to be printed in two separate sections. In one of these, the vocabulary terms would be arranged in alphabetical order, so that they could be readily found when enciphering (*encoding*) messages; but the code groups would be in mixed order and hard to find. In the other section, the code groups would be rearranged in straight alphabetical (or numerical) order, so as to be readily found when deciphering (*decoding*), and the vocabulary terms would be in mixed order. Just what is meant can be seen in Fig. 1, showing fragments from an imaginary code book.

Figure 1

ENCIPHERMENT SECTION		DECIPHERMENT SECTION	
Vocabulary Term	Code Symbol	Code Symbol	Vocabulary Term
A	9001, 2114, 3000*	1120	Assenting to your
Aachen	8463	1121	Horse
About	1119, 0034*	1122	Meet me
About time for	5434	1123*	Come; Paris
Armored car	1125	1124	Th-
Assenting to your	1120	1125	Armored car

*) When a plaintext term has more than one symbol, these are called homophones. Polyphones are symbols which may have more than one meaning.
The terms encoding, decoding are usually preferred to enciphering, deciphering.

A code of this kind, with symbols assigned *absolutely at random*, provided it is carefully used (never without re-encipherment) and a close guard kept over the code books, represents perhaps the maximum of security to be attained in cryptographic correspondence; and security, of course, is of prime importance in the selection of a cipher for any practical purpose.

But in considering the relative merits of the various ciphers, it is always necessary to take into account many factors other than security, each cipher being evaluated in connection with the purpose for which it is wanted: Under what conditions must the encipherment and decipherment take place? How must the cryptograms be transmitted? How much of the enciphered correspondence is likely to be intercepted? What *degree* of security, after all, is absolutely imperative?

A commercial, or other, firm, having a permanent base of operations, and in little danger of being blown to bits by an enemy shell, would not consider the first of these questions from the same angle as the War Department; and the War Department, though considering all of them from several different angles of its own, would still not consider them from the same viewpoint as the State Department.

If messages are to be sent by mail, or by hand, or by telephone, or pasted on a billboard, it is conceivable that a cipher which doubles or trebles their length could still be a practical cipher. For transmission by telephone, the presumption is that the cryptogram must be pronounceable, or, certainly, audible. For written communication, individual purposes have been served by means of pictures.

But when the cryptograms are to be sent by wire or radio, it must be possible to convert them into Morse symbols, either letters or figures, but not intermingled letters and figures. Here, length must be considered, involving questions of time, expense, and the current telegraphic regulations. Moreover, it is conceded that a meaningless text will not be transmitted with absolute accuracy, and a cryptogram which is to be sent by this means must not be of such a nature that ordinary errors of transmission will render it unintelligible at the receiving office.

A factor of particularly grave importance in the selection of a cipher to fit a given purpose is the probable amount of enciphered material which is going to fall into the possession of unauthorized persons. A criminal, who has had to send but one brief cryptogram in a lifetime, might reasonably expect that it will remain forever unread, no matter how weak the cipher. A commercial firm, transmitting thousands of words over the air, is more vulnerable; and the diplomatic office, or the newspaper office, which makes the mistake of publishing almost verbatim the translations of cryptograms which have been transmitted by radio, and thus has surely furnished the cipher expert with *a cryptogram and its translation,* might just as well have presented him with a copy of its code book.

As to just what constitutes the " perfect " cipher, perhaps it might be said that this description fits any cipher whatever which provides the degree of security wanted for an individual purpose, and which is suited in other respects to that individual purpose. Even a basically weak cipher, in the hands of an expert, can be made to serve its purpose; and the strongest can be made useless when improperly used.

In the present text, we are likely to be found looking at ciphers largely from a military angle, which, apparently, has a more general interest than any other. In time of war, the cryptographic service, that is, the encipherment and transmitting service, is suddenly expanded to include a large number of new men, many of whom know nothing whatever of *cryptanalysis*, or the science of decryptment. Many of these are criminally careless through ignorance, so that, entirely aside from numerous other factors (including espionage), it is conceded by the various War Departments that no matter what system or apparatus is selected for cipher purposes, the enemy, soon after the beginning of operations, will be in full possession of details concerning this system, and will have secured a duplicate of any apparatus or machine. For that reason, the secrecy of messages must depend upon a changeable key added to a sound basic cipher.

Speed in encipherment and decipherment is desirable, and often urgent; and the conditions under which these operations must often take place are conducive to a maximum of error. The ideal cipher, under these conditions, would be one which is simple in operation, preferably requiring no written memoranda or apparatus which cannot be quickly destroyed and reconstructed from memory, and having a key which is readily changed, easily communicated, and easily remembered. Yet the present tendency, in all armies, seems to be toward the use of small changeable *codes,* which are written (printed) documents; and, for certain purposes, small mechanical devices.

An enormous number of military cryptograms will be transmitted by radio and taken down by enemy listeners, and even the ordinary wire will be tapped. It is expected that the enemy will intercept dozens, and even hundreds, of cryptograms in a single day, some of which will inevitably be enciphered with the same key. With so much material, knowing the general subject matter, and often exactly what words to expect, or the personal expressions invariably used by individuals, it is conceded that he will read the messages. All that is desired of a cryptogram is that it will resist his efforts for a sufficient length of time to render its contents valueless when he finally discovers them. By that time, of course, the key will have been changed, probably several times, and even the cipher.

With these general facts understood, we may first dispose hastily of the concealment cipher, after which we will examine at greater length the two legitimate types, the transpositions and the substitutions.

CHAPTER II

Concealment Devices

Concealment writing may take a host of forms. Perhaps its oldest known application is found in the ancient device of writing a secret message on the shaved head of a slave and dispatching the slave with his communication after his growing hair had covered the writing. Or, if this appears a little incredible, the ancients have left us records of another device considerably more practical: that of writing the secret message on a wooden tablet, covering this with a wax coating, and writing a second message on top of the first.

In the middle ages we meet a development called *puncture cipher;* any piece of printed matter, such as a public proclamation, serves as the vehicle, and the cipher consists simply in punching holes with a pin under certain letters, so that these letters, read in regular order, will convey the desired information. It is said that this kind of concealment writing was resorted to in England at a comparatively recent period, to avoid the payment of postage. Postage on letters was very high, while newspapers were permitted to travel free, and the correspondents sent their messages very handily by punching holes under the letters printed in newspapers. Where the sender of a message may also control the preparation of the printed vehicle, any desired letters can be pointed out by the use of special type forms, misspelled words, accidental gaps, and so on.

But concealment cipher is not necessarily confined to written and printed matter. Ohaver, in his " Solving Cipher Secrets," demonstrated the conveyance of messages in the shapes and sizes of stones in a garden wall, or in the arrangement of colored candies in a box; and we read, in fiction, of many similar devices, such as a series of knots tied in a string, or beads strung in imitation of the rosary. Again, we hear of cases in which the arrangement of stamps on envelopes is made to represent the terms of a miniature code. All such devices are, of course, combination-cipher rather than pure concealment, since the stones, candies, and so on, must first be made the substitutes for letters or code terms.

A method of pure concealment, said to have been used by Cardinal Richelieu, involved the use of a *grille.* Grilles are made of cardboard, sheet-metal, or other flat material, and are perforated with any desired number, size, and arrangement of openings. The Richelieu grille, of approximately the same size and shape as the paper used for correspondence, could be laid over a sheet of paper so as to reveal only certain portions, and the secret message was written on these. The grille was then removed and the rest of the sheet was filled in with extraneous matter in such a way as to present a seemingly continuous text. The legitimate recipient of this message, having a duplicate grille, simply laid this grille over the sheet of paper, and read his message through the apertures.

Concealment cipher goes by various names, as *null cipher, open-letter cipher, conventional writing, dissimulated writing,* and so on, not always with a difference in meaning, though " conventional writing " does convey somewhat the idea of a tiny code. (In this, casual words have special meanings.)

The name " null cipher " derives from the fact that in any given cryptogram the greater portion of the letters are null, a certain few being significant, and perhaps a few others being significant only in that they act as indicators for finding truly significant letters. To illustrate what is usually meant: Say that your very good friend, Smith, first complains about a radio which he has bought from your neighbor, Johnson, then asks you to take Johnson the following note: " Having trouble about loudspeaker. Believe antenna connected improperly, but do whatever you can." By reading the final letter of each word, you will find out what Smith actually had to say to Johnson: GET READY TO RUN.

That is the null cipher reduced to its elements, though naturally it can be more skillfully applied. Significant letters may be concealed in an infinite variety of ways. The key, as here, may be their positions in words, or in the text as a whole. It may be their distance from one another, expressed in letters or in inches, or their distance to the left or right of certain other letters (indicators) or of punctuation marks (indicators); and this distance, or position, need not be constant, or regular. Sometimes it is governed by an irregular series of numbers.

Similar devices are applied to whole words. We agree, say, that in whatever communications we send to our accomplice, only the third word of each sentence is to be significant. Desiring to send him the order, STRIKE NOW, we write him as follows: " The building *strike* is worrying our friends quite a lot. It has *now* extended to this part of the city."

A purely concealment cipher may be enveloped in apparent ciphers of other types. The true message is concealed, as usual, in a dummy message, and the whole is enciphered in one of the legitimate systems. It is then hoped that the decryptor, satisfied with having solved the dummy, will look no further. Even more effective would be the device of concealing the message in what appears to be a cryptogram, but is not. It is easy to string letters together in such a way as to make them resemble most convincingly a transposition cryptogram, and in this case it would be hoped that the investigator's full attention would be given to the hopeless task of decrypting the dummy.

Concerning the decryptment of concealment cipher, we regret to say that cryptanalysis has little help to offer. Fortunately, most of these ciphers depend absolutely on the belief that they will not be recognized as cipher, and once they are so recognized, they present no resistance. In those few cases where the secret message is not at once obvious, it is sometimes useful to arrange the words (or sentences) in columns, or in rows, for a closer inspection.

Figure 2

```
I N S P E C T
D E T A I L S
F O R
T R I G L E T H
A C K N O W L E D G E
T H E
B O N D S
F R O M
F E W E L L
```

We have, for instance, an apparent memorandum in which the awkwardness of the wording, or some other factor, has drawn our attention to the possibility of cipher: " Inspect details for Trigleth — acknowledge the bonds from Fewell." We arrange these words in column form, aligned by their initials, as in Fig. 2, and the third column promptly gives up the secret message STRIKE NOW.

The words of sentences can, of course, be treated in the same way, and where the alignment from the left gives no results, letters or words can be aligned from the right, or from the center. If columns give no results, diagonals can be inspected, or a zig-zagging line between one column and another.

Experience counts for most, and extensive reading is a vast help. Having seen methods in use, or read the descriptions of methods, we know of some definite thing to look for. Then, too, some of the concealment ciphers have transposition characteristics. This would be the case with the Legrand cipher, which is of the type called " open letter."

This cipher used a numerical key, which, in turn, was based on a keyword in what seems today a rather odd manner: A keyword CAT, made up of the 3d, 1st, and 20th letters of the alphabet, gives the key 3 1 2 0. Before concealment takes place, a series of word-positions is marked off, and these vacant places are numbered (o to 9, or 9 to o), continuing to repeat the ten digits until there are enough of the digits 3, 1, 2, and o to accommodate the words of the secret message. This message is then written, word by word, below its digits, beginning with the first digit 3, then going on to find a digit 1, then a digit 2, then a digit o, then another digit 3, and so on. After the secret message is written into its place, all of the blank positions are filled with connective matter, as in the case of Cardinal Richelieu's grille-writing. Our later study of transpositions will show approximately how we should go about reading this, once we suspect its use.

So far, we have been considering pure concealment. Many of the classic ciphers, fundamentally of the concealment type, are also substitution ciphers, and their decryptment would follow substitution methods. Of these, perhaps the best known is Bacon's biliteral cipher, summed up in Fig. 3.

Figure 3

BACON'S BI-LITERAL ALPHABET

A	aaaaa	IJ	abaaa	R	baaaa
B	aaaab	K	abaab	S	baaab
C	aaaba	L	ababa	T	baaba
D	aaabb	M	ababb	UV	baabb
E	aabaa	N	abbaa	W	babaa
F	aabab	O	abbab	X	babab
G	aabba	P	abbba	Y	babba
H	aabbb	Q	abbbb	Z	babbb

S	T	R	I	K	E
baaab	baaba	baaaa	abaaa	abaab	aabaa

N	O	W
abbaa	abbab	babaa

Hold OFf uNtIl you hEar frOm mE agAin. wE
May cOMpROmIse.

Lord Bacon's cipher presupposes that the encipherer may so control the preparation of his published work that he may prescribe the type to be used for each printed letter, and it is claimed that he actually used his cipher for the preservation of historical secrets, including that of his own parentage. Two fonts of type are required, the letters of one font differing (very slightly) from those of the other font. These we may speak of as the A-font and the B-font, and each letter of the alphabet is given a substitute composed of A's and B's, as shown in full in the figure. Before a message, as STRIKE NOW, can be concealed, it must be expressed in A's and B's, five of these for each of its letters, as shown, so that a message of 9 letters attains a length of 45. For its concealment, we may use any text whatever whose length is 45 letters, for instance, one whose obvious meaning is the contrary of the secret one: " Hold off until you hear from me again. We may compromise." The first five letters, HOLDO, are to represent S, the next five, FFUNT, are to represent T, and so on; and the sole purpose of the A's and B's is to point out the kind of type which must be used in printing the corresponding letters. In the encipherment of the figure, letters taken from the A-font are indicated by lower-case and those of the B-font by capitals, though it is understood that no such emphatic difference is contemplated in the cipher.

While the average modern person would have no opportunity for employing Lord Bacon's cipher as described, he has access to an unlimited number of vehicles other than type-difference. Anything, in fact, may serve the purpose, so long as the material is available in two distinguishable forms and in sufficient quantity.

Our message of 29 *A*'s and 16 *B*'s could be expressed with a deck of playing cards if aces and face-cards are considered to represent *B*'s. It could assume the form of a fence with 45 palings, in which the *B*-palings are crooked, damaged, or missing. Ohaver once made use of a cartridge belt in which the *A*-loops contained cartridges and the *B*-loops were empty. There is an excellent opportunity here, too, for the compiling of "fake" cryptograms, with *A*-letters and *B*-letters distinguished as vowels and consonants, or by the part of the normal alphabet from which they have been taken.

With a biliteral or binumeral alphabet which requires 26 groups, we cannot have fewer than five characters to the group without making groups of different lengths. But another well-known cipher alphabet, devised by the Abbé Trithème for use in much the same way, is triformed, and thus permits that the group-length be reduced to three. The Trithème (Trithemius; Trittemius) alphabet, expressed in digits 1-2-3, was approximately that shown in Fig. 4.

Figure 4

A TRI-NUMERAL ALPHABET

A	111	J	211	S	311
B	112	K	212	T	312
C	113	L	213	U	313
D	121	M	221	V	321
E	122	N	222	W	322
F	123	O	223	X	323
G	131	P	231	Y	331
H	132	Q	232	Z	332
I	133	R	233	&	333

This alphabet has had many applications, including the use of colored candy previously mentioned. One contributor to Ohaver's column submitted a cryptogram of the open-letter type in which the digits 1, 2, 3, were indicated in the *number of syllables* of the successive words. A sentence, "Can you be sure of sufficient assistance from Mayberry?" indicates the digits 1 1 1, 1 1 3, 3 1 3; and, if the alphabet of Fig. 4 is the one in use, represents the letters *A C U*. This is of particular interest in that it is easily done without involving the awkward turns of language that so often betray the concealment cipher. (This same contributor, a Mr. Levine, evolved another cipher, accomplished by an arithmetical process, by which it was possible to make a cryptogram convey two separate messages!)

Many writers have shown alphabets of the biform and triform types applied to open-letter communications by making the significant factor the *number of vowels* contained in successive words. Thus, the sentence given above yields a series 1, 3, 1, 2, 1, 4, 4, 1, 4. Using a biform alphabet, these are usually considered simply as odd and even; with a triform alphabet, some disposition must be made of numbers larger than 3.

The subject is fascinating, and the literature of cryptography is rich with examples. However, we need not delve further into what, after all, is only the stepchild of a legitimate science. The matter of telegraphic transmission alone will bar these ciphers for most general purposes, or the fact that a cipher once betrayed will never serve again. Then, too, the censorship combats it by cutting out or rearranging or changing words, causing the open letter (or telegram) to convey only the information which it purports to convey.

Concealment cipher has, of course, the unique virtue of being able to convey messages under circumstances which make it seem that no communication has passed, and we have hardly touched upon the fact that the short message, prior to its concealment, may have been a well-enciphered one. But we rather suspect that, for the end desired, invisible inks are more convenient and practical.

1. By PICCOLA.

On peut être Napoleon sans être son ami, mes enfants!

2. By B. NATURAL.

FOR SALE! Spring coats. All fine Scotch serge, for ensembles. Stoat trimmed, fashioned right. Black shirred lining, striped. Effective for brides. Act quickly. - Abraham Batz, 522 Broad, Telephone Exchange 7104-R.

3. By TITOGI.

How about releasing Tony, the gang chief? He don't lie, and is not the true slayer either. Let us be friends. I am all right. Ed Lehr.

4. By TRYIT.

To those friends considering it is always news, but all filled ciphers disturb happiness with varied answers!

5. By PICCOLA.

Do not send for any supplies before Monday, at earliest. Order once only, as men in charge are feeling sore about your threat to encourage the mutiny at Ford's. - Wilson.

6. By PICCOLA. (Why not, indeed?)

```
A W I T H   A N Y S E   N D P O R   I T Y O U   M U S T B   E F E A R
T H E C A   N H I T T   R Y A B O   U R E O U   T I S E C   H I Y O U
A N D M Y   T I O N C   U P O R E   A S K T O   C A N D Q.
```

CHAPTER III

TRANSPOSITION TYPES

Transposition has already been explained as a form of cipher in which the letters of a message are disarranged from their natural order in accordance with any pattern, or key, agreeable to the correspondents. The fact that *any* plan may be followed will suggest the possible ramifications as to detail. Transpositions are, in fact, found in every conceivable degree of complexity. They are not even unanimous in their demand that there be two separate operations in the preparation of a cryptogram: (1) the writing down of the plaintext letters, and (2) the taking off of these letters.

Generally speaking, these ciphers follow two types, the regular (geometrical, symmetrical), and the irregular. The strictly geometrical type, sometimes called *complete-unit* transposition, is based on one comparatively small *unit*, or *cycle*, repeated over and over, every unit having exactly the same number of letters and exactly the same disarrangement as the rest. This type always demands an exact

Figure 5

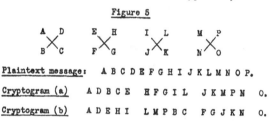

Plaintext message: A B C D E F G H I J K L M N O P.

Cryptogram (a)   A D B C E   H F G I L   J K M P N   O.

Cryptogram (b)   A D E H I   L M P B C   F G J K N   O.

number of units, and when a plaintext message is not evenly divisible into units, it must either be cut down to fit, or lengthened by the addition of extra letters called *nulls*. Some of these keys are actual geometrical figures, such as triangles, diamonds, hexagons, etc., or conventional designs like crosses. Any figure of this kind provides a number of cells, or points, for the *writing in* of letters, and thus will serve as a mnemonic device, or key.

The two operations of writing-in and taking off may be governed by any agreed ruling, though the second of these must be made to result in five-letter groups if the cryptogram is to be transmitted by wire or radio. Fig. 5, in which an imaginary message has been represented as *A B C D E* ....., shows only one of the many ways in which a simple cross could be used as the key for the writing-in operation, together with only two of the many cryptograms which could be taken off from this one arrangement. This figure shows also, in its two cryptograms (a) and (b), two fundamentally different plans for the taking off of transpositions. The unit here is 4, the first unit containing the letters *A B C D*, the next unit *E F G H*, and so on. In cryptogram (a), the letters of every unit are still standing together in a group, while in cryptogram (b), the letters of any one unit have been mixed with letters of other units. In this latter case, the two correspondents will have to agree upon a certain number of crosses per line; otherwise, they run the risk of having to decrypt each other's cryptograms.

The most popular of the geometrical figures appears to be the square, with or without a series of numbers 1 to 25, 1 to 36, and so on. Any device or game, which will provide a square, is likely to be seized upon as the source of a transposition key. We find two widely-known examples of this in the " magic square " and the " knight's tour."

A magic square, as most of us understand this term, is made up of a series of numbers, such as 1 to 25, 1 to 36, which are so arranged in their cells (positions) that the added numbers of any row, column, or diagonal, will always give the same total. A square of given size will provide more than one magic square arrangement; and these numbers, being a series, constitute an *order*, which, once it can be remembered or reconstructed, will serve either for writing in or for taking off a unit of 25, 36, etc., letters.

The *knight's tour* is based on the chessboard, a unit of 64 cells. In the game of chess, where each piece has certain prescribed moves, the piece called the knight must move diagonally across a 2 x 3 oblong. The " tour " consists in starting the

Figure 6

1	4	53	18	55	6	43	20
52	17	2	5	38	19	56	7
3	64	15	54	31	42	21	44
16	51	28	39	34	37	8	57
63	14	35	32	41	30	45	22
50	27	40	29	36	33	58	9
13	62	25	48	11	60	23	46
26	49	12	61	24	47	10	59

knight at one corner and carrying him completely over the 64 cells of the chessboard, causing him to touch every square exactly once without having made any other move than the one allotted to him. Fig. 6 will show one of the many such tours which have been published. Such designs will serve either for writing in or for taking out. In either case, the text is made to contain exactly 64 letters or a multiple thereof. For writing in, the first letter is placed in the cell corresponding to No. 1, the next letter in the cell numbered 2, and so on. For puzzle purposes, the 64 letters are usually left standing in the form of a square. As cipher, they would be taken off, by rows, or by columns, or otherwise. Or the 64 letters may first be written in simple order into the form of a square, and then taken out one by one following the route of the knight.

Other ciphers of the regular type merely employ a unit of so many letters, to be arranged in some specified order, generally in accordance with a numerical key. If, say, the unit has a length of six letters, which we will represent as *A B C D E F*, and the specified order for these is 6 2 1 4 3 5, this unit may be transposed to read *F B A D C E*. Each unit will be transposed to have exactly this pattern, except that semi-occasionally we find a final unit slightly different from the others, owing to the fact that nulls were not added to complete its length (Accurately speaking, this transfers the cipher to the " irregular " class). Units, once transposed in this way, may continue to stand intact, one after another; or they may remain intact, merely exchanging places with one another; or the cipher may be so planned that they do not remain intact, as was the case with our cryptogram (b) of Fig. 5.

Often, two ciphers will differ from each other only in the method by which their cryptograms are produced; oftener, there will be an actual difference, but one which is purely superficial. For instance, we have just mentioned a plaintext unit

A B C D E F as having been transposed with a key 6 2 1 4 3 5 to result in the order *F B A D C E*. Identically the same numerical key, used in another way, will transpose this unit in the order *C B E D F A*. The two resulting cryptograms would be different, but the *kind* of cryptogram would not.

An extremely common form of complete-unit transposition is that indicated in Fig. 7, where a short message, LET US HEAR FROM YOU AT ONCE CON- CERNING JEWELS QQ (38 letters plus 2 *nulls*), has been written into an oblong, or *block,* in one order and taken off in another. Both the writing in and the taking off follow a *route,* rather than a key and, for that reason, the cipher is often spoken of as *route transposition,* rather than *rectangular transposition.*

Three of the many possible *routes* are shown in the three (partial) cryptograms of the figure. In this connection, the American popular terminology seems to favor *horizontals* and *verticals,* rather than " rows " and " columns." The writing in or

Figure 7

```
L E T U S          Cryptograms:
H E A R F
R O M Y O    (a)  By descending verticals, from the left:   L H R U C
U A T O N
C E C O N         C N E E E   O A E E G   L T A M T   C R J S U, etc.
C E R N I
N G J E W    (b)  By alternating verticals from the right, top:
E L S Q Q
                  S F O N N   I W Q Q E   N O O Y R   U T A M T, etc.

(c)  By diagonals:  L H E R E   T U O A U   C A M R S   C'E T Y F   N E C O O, etc.
```

the taking out of a text is said to be done by *straight horizontals,* or by *reversed horizontals* (backward), or by *alternate* (or *alternating*) *horizontals* (written alter- nately in both directions). Similarly, we find *ascending,* or *descending,* or *alternate verticals;* and again the *diagonal* routes will be described as *ascending, descending,* or *alternate.* The route may also be a *spiral* one, and in this case it is said be *clock- wise* or *counter-clockwise.*

For all of these routes, the point of beginning is nearly always one of the four corners, except in the case of the two *spiral* routes, which are just as likely to begin with a central letter, particularly when the rectangle is a square. Colonel Parker Hitt, in his *Manual for the Solution of Military Ciphers,* shows the same series of letters written into forty different blocks, always beginning at one of the four corners.

Rectangular transposition, when used as cipher and not simply as a puzzle, requires that one dimension of the oblong be fixed, the other dimension being en- tirely dependent on the length of the message to be conveyed. In the figure, the pre-arranged width of the block, called its *key-length,* was 5, and the filling of the block required 8 complete units. These were written one by one as simple bits of plaintext, and were then broken up in the method of taking off. Occasionally it will be the vertical dimension of the block which is fixed, and the plaintext will be written in by columns, beginning at the left or at the right. But there is so little difference in the results of the two procedures that a decryptor may solve and read a cryptogram without learning which of the two was actually followed. Ordinarily, it is the simple operation which comes first, the writing in of intact units one after another. Sometimes the opposite is true, the operation of writing in being made very complex, so that the whole block is the unit, the taking off being done by simple rows or columns. Frequently both operations are complex. This kind of transposition belongs rather to the category of puzzles than to cipher; any reason- ably intelligent person can decrypt it, knowing what it is. However, it has not infrequently been applied to serious purposes, and a decryptor, encountering an unknown transposition, would not overlook the possibility of simple rectangular encipherment.

Decryptment, here, is merely a matter of trying out the known routes, and it would never be actually necessary to write out the entire forty-plus blocks, or even half of these, for any one rectangle. The decryptor begins by counting the letters of his cryptogram and factoring the number of these, to find out what oblongs are possible. A 36-letter cryptogram, for instance, might mean dimensions 6 x 6, or dimensions 4 x 9. It could, conceivably, represent dimensions 3 x 12, or 2 x 18. But key-lengths are hardly ever shorter than 5, or as long as 18. He would seize upon the square as the object of his first investigation, writing the cryptogram into that block by various known routes, and also *reading* by various known routes, diagonally, horizontally, vertically, backward, or upside down, until he begins to find words. As a rule, this does not take him very long; often the very efforts of an encipherer to achieve complexity will result in an easier task for the decryptor. However, a spiral will sometimes give trouble.

<u>Figure 8</u>

```
A       E       I
   B  D    F  H  J
      C       G       K.........etc.
```

<u>Taken off</u>: A E I & B   D F H J &   C G K...

The examples appended to this chapter are all of the complete-unit type, and require little knowledge of cryptanalysis for their solution.

Passing on to irregular types, we find these in all degrees of difficulty, from the very simple " rail fence " to the formidable " U. S. Army " double transposition.

The " rail fence " family is outlined sketchily in Fig. 8. The writing in of the plaintext follows a zig-zag route, downward by so many letters, then upward to the line of beginning, as indicated by the series *A B C* ....., and the taking off of the cryptogram is done by straight lines. In explanation of the character &, this has been used here as a signal to show the ends of the straight lines. No such signal is needed if a proper understanding exists between correspondents as to the construction of the " fence " and the length of it which may occupy one line of writing; and in some cases the straight lines are all equal in length.

In Fig. 9, we have a suggested *grille-transposition*, of a kind described by Mario Zanotti as " indefinite." This kind of grille, we believe, is the invention of General Sacco. To picture it complete, we may imagine a flat surface, such as a piece of cardboard, marked off into squares, having dimensions 12 x 6, and turned sidewise. Assuming this to be shown in full, we are looking at 12 *columns*, and each column has 6 of the small squares, or cells. To convert this piece of cardboard into an encipherment grille, we clip out three squares from each one of its 12 columns, always in the most haphazard manner possible. The resulting grille will thus have 36 openings, and, if placed over a sheet of paper (preferably also marked into cells), enables us to transpose the first 36 letters of a message by writing them one at a time into the 36 apertures in some one order and taking them off in another. The original plan was the reverse of the usual: write the letters by columns and take them off by rows.

In the figure, a 9-letter message, STRIKE NOW, has been written into the first three columns of such a grille and, taken off by rows, comes out in the order *N, SO, TI, K, RE, W*. While the figure shows this cryptogram regrouped in the usual fives, the original method, as prescribed with the device, would have grouped it in threes, that is, to correspond with the number of apertures per column. This

Figure 9

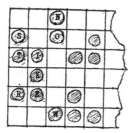

Cryptogram: N S O T I K R E W.

would facilitate the operation of decipherment, which is as follows: Count the number of letters in the cryptogram *and divide this number by 3,* in order to find how many columns were used. Cover (or ignore) the unused portion of the grille, write the cryptogram by straight horizontals into the uncovered portion, then read, or copy, by descending verticals. The recipient of the present cryptogram, for instance, finds nine letters, divides this number by 3, thus ascertaining that three columns were used, covers up the other nine columns, then, proceeding by straight horizontals, places one cryptogram-letter wherever he sees a hole. Having thus restored all letters to their proper columns, he has the plaintext message before him. It will be noticed that an encipherer uses only the number of columns that he needs. His last column does not have to be completed with nulls, as in the case of complete-unit ciphers.

As this grille has just been described, its full capacity is 36 letters, and it has a repeating cycle of that length, presuming that, after the transposition of the first 36 letters, another 36-letter unit is to be transposed by the same grille standing in the same position. But this grille, reversed, provides a new pattern; and the opposite side of the grille provides two additional patterns. These positions may be numbered, thus providing for the encipherment of 144 letters, even assuming that the positions are to be used in 1, 2, 3, 4 order and without varying the method of use. Add to this that the cryptographic offices may have provided half-a-dozen different grilles to be used interchangeably and not always in exactly the same way, and it becomes plain that such an encipherment, in the hands of an operator who knows his business, could be made to furnish a very effective form of transposition.

Zanotti, and others, have also described mechanical devices of a patentable type for accomplishing very involved transpositions. The principle on which most of these operate can be seen in Fig. 10. A certain number of pointers, or narrow sliding rulers, all carrying the same progression of numbers, are so attached to a framework that they can be set, by means of a numerical key, to project at irregular lengths over a sheet of quadrille paper cut to fit into the frame. Thus, each pointer indicates a certain number of empty cells, as nine on the first line, six on the next, and so on. In the example of the figure, presuming that each pointer carries only ten numbers, and that the full number of these pointers is seven, the numerical key would be the column of numbers at the extreme left: 2-5-0-7-3-4-7. The message

Figure 10

```
2 1 / L  E  T  U  S  H  E  A  R
5 4 3 2 1 / F  R  O  M  Y  O
0 9 8 7 6 5 4 3 2 1 / U
7 6 5 4 3 2 1 / A  T  O  N
3 2 1 / C  E  C  O  N  C  E  R
4 3 2 1 / N  I  N  G  J  E  W
7 6 5 4 3 2 1 / E  L  S  Q
```

here is written in the usual horizontals, with a null (not strictly necessary) completing the last line. It could be taken off by columns: *L, EC, TEN, UFCI*, etc. The decipherer, having a duplicate apparatus, would set this according to the prearranged key, copy the cryptogram by columns, and read it by rows. The exact method, of course, can be varied.

Some attempt has been made, too, to evolve cipher machines which will produce effective transpositions, but our understanding is that these have never been accepted as worthwhile. The accomplishment of transposition by mechanical means is far from new. In fact, the oldest transposition cipher of which we have any record was accomplished by means of the Lacedaemonian *scytale*. The Spartan general, departing for foreign conquests, carried with him a rod, or scytale, of exactly the same diameter as one retained by the administration. When it was desired to communicate matter of a confidential nature, the sender, using a narrow strip of parchment, wound this carefully around his scytale with edges meeting uniformly at all points, and wrote his message lengthwise of the rod. When the strip was unrolled, the message appeared as a series of short disconnected fragments, one letter, or two letters, or portions of one or two letters. It was presumed that no person would be able to read the message without being possessed of a duplicate scytale on which to rewind the strip. We are left to suppose that this presumption was justified by fact, though the decryptor of today would make short work of such a system. The scytale, we believe, is the oldest known cipher of any kind, and is still serving today as the emblem of the *American Cryptogram Association.*

Before leaving types, it should be mentioned that any of the transpositions ordinarily used for disarranging single letters can also be used for the transposal of entire words. The popular name for this is " Route Cipher " — possibly because it is rather cumbersome to accomplish by any other than a " route " transposition.

We have said little concerning *decipherment*. This, in practically all cases, is a mere matter of performing inversely the two encipherment operations. For either process, the operator begins by setting down his key or design, or adjusting his mechanical device in the agreed manner. The encipherer " writes in " a plaintext, and " takes off " a cryptogram; the decipherer " writes in " a cryptogram, and " takes off " (or reads) a plaintext. If the encipherer, by agreement, has written the text in rows and taken it off by columns, then the decipherer must do the reverse: write his text by columns and take it off by rows.

Before entering into the subject of *decryptment,* the student should acquaint himself with the significance of the various tables appended to this text, in order that he may consult these or similar tables for information as to *frequencies,* and *sequence.* Every written language has its individual characteristics in these two respects, and, to learn just what these are for each language, various cryptologists have, from time to time, counted the letters, the short words, the combinations, and so forth, often on extremely long texts, afterward arranging these data in the form of charts, or tables, or lists. Two such counts are never duplicates, and there may be a noticeable difference, say, between results obtained from literary text and those obtained from military or telegraphic text; yet results for any one language are surprisingly uniform. Finding, for instance, an unexplained cryptogram in which a count of the letters shows that about 40% of these are vowels (with or without *Y*), we may classify it, not only as a transposition, but as one enciphered in English or German, since one of the Latin languages can hardly be written with so low a vowel percentage. Then, if we note the occurrences of the letter *E,* and find that this makes up about 12% of the total number of letters, we may discard the possibility of German, in which the letter *E* is far more likely to represent 18% of the text. Or, if the vowel percentage is high enough to point to one of the Latin languages, French would be distinguished from the others by the outstanding frequency of its letter *E*, sometimes as great as that of the German *E*, while the Spanish, Portuguese, or Italian language will not always show it as the leading letter, its place having been taken by *A*. In the Serb-Croat language, the letter *A* always predominates, and in Russian the letter *O*.

As to sequence, and considering English combinations only, certain digrams, such as *TH, HE, AN*, etc., very consistently predominate over all others. These almost never show identical percentages in any two digram counts (as the single letters sometimes will), and seldom, if ever, are ranked in exactly the same order, aside from the fact that *TH* invariably comes first. But in all counts, the same fifty to sixty digrams (out of 676) are always found at the top of the list. Thus the Meaker digram chart differs from similar charts made by many others; yet *any* digram chart is the most valuable weapon we have for attacking a cipher. The Carter contact chart contains the same general information expressed in another way for special use in transpositions. (This was not figured from the Meaker chart, but from an earlier one by Ohaver, made on the same kind of text.)

One very useful phase of frequency data is seen in the group percentages. Single letters, especially in short texts, may vary greatly from their normal percentages, while certain classes, taken as a whole, maintain a fairly constant percentage no matter how short the text. Such classes, or groups, listed under the general heading of *English Frequency and Sequence Data,* can be memorized as having roughly approximate percentages: Vowels, 40%; selected high-frequency consonants, 30%; extreme low-frequency group, 2%; the five most frequent letters, mixed, 45%; the nine most frequent letters, 70%. This final group of nine letters, *E T A O N I S R H*, hardly ever varies appreciably; the shorter groups will sometimes vary as much as 5% one way or the other.

Very useful in *code* decryptment is a list of the commonest words. Trigrams have also been investigated, the favorite positions of individual letters in their own words, average word-length, *patterns,* and endless other information, some of which is indispensable, and some merely convenient. It will not be possible, in the space at our disposal, to point out all of the uses to which this kind of information can be put; the student is urged to take his cue from the occasional short references made in connection with examples.

All ciphers are decrypted by the *general methods* suitable to their type, and a transposition cryptogram may involve *factoring, examination of the vowel distribution,* and *anagramming,* either singly or in combination. These are best explained in connection with examples, which may themselves have *special methods,* and we have selected for general discussion four ciphers, two belonging to the complete-unit type and two to the irregular. A careful study of the methods used in individual cases should furnish the student with a basis for analyzing other ciphers and evolving other special methods to suit particular cases.

Concerning the paper work, which, admittedly, is onerous in most forms of cipher investigation, much reference may be found, in the matter which follows, to " paper strips." These are old stand-bys. Most decryptors prefer to do all of their work on cross-section (quadrille) paper, since the writing of the letters into cells enables them to obtain an accurate spacing both laterally and vertically, and this paper is easily cut apart along the separating lines. But for the kind of cryptograms we are likely to see here, many persons prefer to work with a set of anagram blocks. These can be prepared at home from cardboard squares, or may be bought in sets with frequent letters represented in approximately the correct proportions.

7. By TITOGI.

T S S N I   H A Y S T   I N T P I   S E R O O   I A A S N.

Also this: S H C V I   E O L E A   E W E R M.

8. By G. A. SLIGHT.   (Something found in every school-book - IF found!)

T G H M R   R I A Y E   X N U E E   S D E X S   H M T I D   E Q U O A   Y R O A U

N P U E T   G T I T E   S Y S N O   A Q N X A   T U A D S   I S H X.

9. By PICCOLA.

W I N T A   H D A E S   W H L E T   Y L W A I   L H O Q L   A S S S A   S Q.

10. By NEMO. (Magic Square).

L E A S U   L T S G M   S L O E I   E O I M E   A R N S A   S R C D E   K I U S U

H E M A Q   L Y S P R   M E O A.

11. By THE ADMIRAL.

B S P N T   E A E F T   V V O A N   E Y A P U   Z S E T P   T H M N A   T A E E R

S D S S K   P S J E S   T Y S E A   L R H I A   S K S N T   T E Y W O   F T H M W

Y K E F E   N N H C I   E H H U M   I H I T E   O H G E S   U C G D I   O O W E A

S A S N E   R H M A A   S S L E R   G S M N E   D T H K E   M L U A E   T V M F O

R A I W P   A Y A M A   E Y A D.

12. By THE ADMIRAL.

A A F R S   R T N E A   R B N E E   O H S R L   T I A P D   U E O S I   I T T A T

G L F O T   S O U S H   H E P N Y.

13. By DAN SURR.   (Received from General Headquarters following a skirmish).

F A A T R   M N O A T   I L V I S   Y G U C F   F I O O E   P S N K L   T O I N V

R T T O A   H N D N E   E R E N N   B M P U N   P O R R K   A U O M E   A N A I E

T S S B N   R G T G S   T T I E E   I C T H R.

14. By PICCOLA.   (This is serious advice!)

F F L T A   A R N I E   U O R N T   O T D L A   N R W S O   I A T T E   Y B A N T

M E H S K   O G R Z E   P S R E I   O A O A M   S S S M A   L P I L Y   S.

15. By FRA-GRANT.   (This might have been a little easier. Still - ?)

Q Y T E Y   O F U B U   Q E H I H   T E C H T   H S A U A   O N S I T   I T T T I

E T T E L   L S E A P   L T N T.

CHAPTER IV

GEOMETRICAL TYPES — THE NIHILIST TRANSPOSITION

In the preceding chapter, we glanced at the most elementary form of *columnar transposition:* a text is written into a block by rows and taken off by columns in such a way that even though all or part of the columns may be reversed in direction, these columns are always left standing one after another in regular order. Columnar transposition becomes less crude when the order for taking off the columns is an irregular one, governed by a changeable numerical key, the length of this key governing also the width of the rectangle. This process can be examined in Fig. 11. In this figure, the numerical key, 4 1 6 5 3 2 7, was first derived from a *keyword*, HALIFAX, according to the following very common plan: The two *A's*, taken from left to right, receive the first two numbers; the third number, in the

Figure 11

Usual Plan for Transposing
Columns

```
H  A  L  I  F  A  X
4  1  6  5  3  2  7

L  E  T  U  S  H  E
A  R  F  R  O  M  Y
O  U  A  T  O  N  C
E  C  O  N  C  E  R
N  I  N  G  J  E  W
E  L  S  X  X  X  X
```

Cryptogram: E R U C I   L H M N E

E X S O O   C J X L A   O E N E U,etc.

absence of *B, C, D,* and *E,* is assigned to *F;* and so on, following the alphabetical rank of the letters present, and taking repeated letters from left to right. The presence of seven numbers implies seven columns, and it is said that the *key-length* is 7. When a text has been written into a block of that width, with a key-number standing above each column, these columns can be taken off in the order shown by the numbers, and not in regular sequence.

The key, used exactly as described, is a " taking off " key, and this is the common way of using one. It can, however, be used for " writing in " the successive units, placing the first letter of a given unit beneath number 1, the second letter beneath number 2, and so on until the seventh letter has been written below number 7, afterward beginning with the first letter of another unit below number 1 again. Under this plan the first unit of our figure, *L E T U S H E,* would have been *written in* in the order *U L H S T E E.* Since all units would follow exactly the same pattern, the resulting *columns* would be identical with those of the present block; the only essential difference would be that the new columns are already transposed, and can be taken off in straight order. The two resulting cryptograms, however, would not be the same. The unit which was *written in* in the order *U L H S T E E,* would have been in the order *E H S L U T E* had the method been that of *taking out* (or " off "). The Nihilist transposition is ordinarily accomplished by " writing in," and its numerical key is applied to *both columns and rows.* Thus its major unit is a square, and the seven-letter keyword HALIFAX, applied to both dimensions of a rectangle, demands a unit of 49 letters, while the shorter word SCOTIA, key-length 6, requires a unit of 36 letters.

Theoretically, this cipher is a *double transposition,* requiring two successive operations as shown in Fig. 12. But in practice, these two transpositions can take place simultaneously as pointed out in Fig. 13. The operator, having laid out his key-numbers at top and side of his square, begins his writing in the cell at which the column headed by number 1 crosses the row headed by number 1. He *writes in* his first unit, proceeds to the row numbered 2 for the writing in of his second unit, then to the row numbered 3, and so on, taking rows in the order shown by the numbers at the left, and placing the letters of his unit by following the numbers across the top. Thus, with only a little concentration, he has the entire major

Figure 12

Nihilist Plan

(a) **Transposal of Columns**

```
S  C  O  T  I  A
5  2  4  6  3  1

S  E  U  H  T  L    (Let us h)
R  A  F  O  R  E
A  Y  U  T  O  M
A  N  E  B  C  O
E  U  J  W  T  O
X  L  X  X  S  E
```

(b) **Transposal of Rows**

```
            S-5   E  U  J  W  T  O
            C-2   R  A  F  O  R  E
            O-4   A  N  E  B  C  O
            T-6   X  L  X  X  S  E
            I-3   A  Y  U  T  O  M
            A-1   S  E  U  H  T  L  (Let us h)
```

(c) **Cryptogram:** E U J W T   O R A F O   R E A N E

B C O X L   X X S E A   Y U T O M   S E U H T   L.

unit at one continuous writing. The decipherer, too, having restored his cryptogram unit to its block and written his two series of numbers, may read, or copy, continuously. The decipherer, in fact, uses the exact method which would produce a Nihilist cryptogram if a key were used in the " taking out " manner. What we have described is the encipherment of a single major unit; and all cryptograms must contain an exact number of these major units.

The second operation, that of taking off the cryptogram, is not always done by straight horizontals as we have shown this under (c) of Fig. 12. This, of course, is the expected way; but the Nihilist square is quite frequently taken off by some other one of the forty-odd routes possible to rectangular transpositions. The decipherer, knowing this route, merely writes his units back into their blocks; but the decryptor is often faced with a preliminary problem of discovering how they were taken off. Sometimes he must also discover how many units a cryptogram contains.

To understand how such problems are solved, it is necessary to pause and consider the make-up of ordinary written plaíntext. English vowel-percentage, as mentioned, is about 40%, and practically never varies out of its limits 35%-45%. Each 40 vowels are fairly *evenly* distributed throughout their 100 letters. Take any English text whatever, not composed of initials or otherwise distorted, and, beginning where you please, mark it off into ten-letter segments and count the vowels in each of the segments. You will find that the majority of these have **exactly** the normal number of vowels, which is 4. Others will have 3 or 5, which, though outside of the limits 35%-45%, are the closest variations possible. It will be a rare segment indeed which contains fewer than 3 vowels or a greater number than 5. But suppose, having marked off such a text into ten-letter units, or segments.

we take each of these segments individually and mix up the order of its letters, though still allowing it to stand where it is. And suppose, having done this, we erase the original division-marks and, beginning at some point in the midst of a former segment, we again mark off a series of ten-letter units, and count the vowels of these new segments. This time, we are just as likely as not to find seven or eight vowels in one segment and none at all in the next, depending on just what we did to the old units, and still we have not actually mixed the units; we simply have our division marks in the wrong places. Imagine, then, how the vowel distribution can vary when a transposition is one so planned as to break up units and scramble their letters.

This fact of uniformity in vowel distribution is of enormous assistance in dealing with the simpler transpositions. For instance, it may be that what we want to know is the length of the units, and that what we have is a cryptogram of 144 letters, which could be a single square, or a series of 36-letter squares, or even a series of

Figure 13

```
  5 2 4 6 3 1       5 2 4 6 3 1        5 2 4 6 3 1

5                 5                  5
2                 2 . A . . . E      2 R A F O R E
4                 4                  4
6                 6                  6
3                 3                  3 . Y . . . M
1 . E . . . L     1 S E U ñ T L      1 S E U H T L
```

16-letter or 9-letter squares. We may start at the beginning of this cryptogram and mark it off into equal segments of any length we like, afterward counting the vowels per segment. If every segment shows approximately a 40% vowel count, the chances are that we have a series of intact units, each one merely transposed within itself; but if one segment shows 50%, another 30%, another 28%, and so on, we may be quite sure that our division marks are in the wrong places.

Returning, now, to the Nihilist cipher, suppose we consider the make-up of its major unit, that is, of any one block. This major unit is a series of minor units, and each of these minor units, at the time of encipherment, was written by itself on its own line. In the beginning, it was a small fragment of plaintext, presumably conforming closely to a 40% vowel count. It is true that we placed it on the line in transposed order, but we did not remove any of its letters or add any new letters. Even in the transposal of the lines themselves, we merely removed a number of intact units from one place to another. There has never been a time, throughout the entire encipherment, when we took any letter out of its original minor unit and put it with some other unit. Thus, as we first see our completed Nihilist square, we still have, on each horizontal line, a small fragment of an English sentence in which all of the original vowels are still present. If such a block is now taken off by straight horizontals, it is no more than a series of intact units. To break up these units, we must at least take it out by verticals; and they will, of course, be much more thoroughly mixed when taken out by diagonals or spirals.

The decryptor, hoping for the best, writes his cryptogram into a square (or series of squares) by straight horizontals and counts the vowels per horizontal line. If his block is wide, he may estimate the actual number of vowels represented by 40%; if it is narrow, he may only roughly approximate the number; but in either case what he hopes to see is *evenness of distribution*. More than half of his units must be exactly normal, and any which are not exactly normal must show the smallest variation possible. If he finds that this is the case, he assumes that his block arrangement is the encipherer's original square, with only the minor possibility that half of his lines may be written in the wrong direction. If his distribution is not uniform, he counts the vowels per *column* so as to find out what kind of distribution he would get from a vertical arrangement (ascending or descending). If this, too, fails to show him a uniform vowel distribution, he writes out a new block by the route of alternating verticals (or gets this count from his first block; this is possible, though a little confusing). Afterward, he may go on to the diagonals and spirals until finally he reaches the arrangement in which more than half of his horizontal lines show a 40% vowel count, and the rest a minimum variation.

Now let us consider a concrete example of decryptment. The (purely imaginary) history of the cryptogram shown as Fig. 14 is meager. It was taken from the body of an unnamed man, killed in attempting to dynamite a bridge in an American town called Baysport.

To begin with, the cipher appears to be transposition. Its cryptogram shows 37½% of vowels, very close to the number expected of English or German. It is

Figure 14

```
I Y W B B   O R T A F   T I X D G   S S E G H   N A T O O   I T O X T   L U T R E

L X F A Y   S D R C H   T O M E D   E I O V I   K F T V T   L A E U.
```

too short to provide any reliable distinction between these two languages, but the source of the cryptogram points to English. Again, the encipherer, although he has grouped his message in the usual fives, has neglected to complete his final group with a null, and from this we judge that 64 letters is the actual length of the message. The fact that 64 is a *square* is promptly noticed. But it is also the sum of several smaller squares, and the unit might be 16. To investigate this possibility, we may mark the cryptogram off into four equal segments of 16 letters each, and count the vowels per segment. The normal number of vowels in a 16-letter segment should be about 6, and segments of this length are long enough to afford reliable information, so that we may promptly discard the possible unit 16 when we find that the first segment shows 5 vowels (31%), the second, 7 vowels (44%), and the remaining two, respectively, 4 and 8. Such a distribution does not prove that the unit 16 is a total impossibility, because many things are not average in single examples, but it is an extremely bad one and would never be accepted. On the other hand, a satisfactory distribution does not prove absolutely that a given unit-length, or block arrangement, is correct. Here, had there been no question of the ever-present *square*, we might have been led astray by the unit 32, which divides the vowels of the present cryptogram into two equal halves. In this connection, we can only say that the decryptment of any cipher, even the simplest, will at times include a number of wanderings which we shall have to overlook in demonstrating principles.

Assuming, then, that the large unit, 64, is correct, we must get it back into its block — presumably square — in the encipherer's original arrangement. Fig. 15 shows the same cryptogram written into two different blocks. For an 8-letter unit, the normal number of vowels is about 3 (actually 3.2). In block (a), a count taken on the horizontal lines shows half of the units normal, two of the others with the smallest possible variation, and two greatly outside the 35%-45% limits. When the unit is so short, and when the line containing only one vowel may be the one which was completed with nulls, and most particularly when we have no other units to act as a check, we cannot confidently discard a block of this kind. In practice, we might waste some time giving it a trial, or we might look for something better. Notice that its distribution is " ragged." We expected to find *even* distribution, with *more* than half of the units exactly normal. This block (a) is the simple horizontal arrangement. To find out what the simple vertical arrangement would give us, we have only to examine the columns of this. Here the count is obviously bad.

In block (b), we have one of the diagonal rearrangements from which two sets of vowel counts can also be taken. Here, the horizontal lines have given us exactly what we hoped for: Evenness of distribution, more than half of the units normal, and only one unit outside of limits. This, almost surely, is the encipherer's original block, in which every line contains one intact unit.

From our meager history of the case, we do not, of course, know that this is specifically the Nihilist cipher. It becomes a case of considering the various ci-

Figure 15

(a)	Horizontal Rearrangement, With TWO Vowel-Counts		(b)	Diagonal Rearrangement, With TWO Vowel-Counts	
	I Y W B B O R T	3		I W O F G N O L	3
	A F T I X D G S	2		Y B A D H T E R	3
	S E G H N A T O	3		B T X G I R D E	2
	O I T O X T L U	4		R I E O T S M V	3
	T R E L X F A Y	3		T S O U Y O O T	5
	S D R C H T O M	1		S T L A T I F L	2
	E D E I O V I K	5		A T F H E K T E	3
	F T V T L A E U	3		X X C D I V A U	3
	4 3 2 3 1 3 4 4			3 1 4 3 4 2 4 3	

phers with which we happen to be acquainted, and a *columnar* transposition of the general kind shown in Fig. 11 is an exceedingly common case. Moreover, a series of juggled columns is suggested here in the fact that intact units are standing on their own lines and still have not resulted in plaintext.

In Fig. 16, we have the successive steps which would be taken in order to investigate this probability. At (a), the diagonal rearrangement of our cryptogram, selected as the most likely of those which were examined, has been repeated with its eight columns set wide apart, and consecutively numbered for identification. These presumed columns are now cut apart, and thus we have eight paper strips which can be moved about and rearranged in various manners in the hope of causing words to form on some of the lines.

Since we lack that most powerful of decrypting tools, a *probable word*, we are forced to begin with probable letter-sequence. If the magic letter *Q* were present, we should look for a companion *U*, and after that for a vowel to follow *QU*. But this, too, is lacking.

Familiarity with English digrams (or, in the case of the beginner, an inspection of the digram chart or the list of digrams) shows that *TH* is by far the most frequent combination used in the language, and that *HE* and *HA*, also including an *H*, are very prominent among the leaders. Further than this, the list of trigrams informs us that both *THE* and *THA* are of outstanding frequency. Of the four letters included, three are so frequent, and appear in so many different combinations, as to be confusing; but *H*, though belonging to the high-frequency group, does not appear in many *different* combinations, and is less frequent than the other three.

Looking, then, for *H*, we find it twice in our present cryptogram, once on the

second row and once on the **seventh**; and, since the seventh row shows two *T*'s and
the second only one *T*, suppose we try the second row, placing together the two
columns (strips) which are headed by the numbers 6-5 in order to set up a digram
TH on the second row, as shown at (b).

Figure 16

(a)

1	2	3	4	5	6	7	8
I	W	O	F	G	N	O	L
Y	B	A	D	H	T	E	R
B	T	X	G	I	R	D	E
R	I	E	O	T	S	M	V
T	S	O	U	Y	O	O	T
S	T	L	A	T	I	F	L
A	T	F	H	E	K	T	E
X	X	C	D	I	V	A	U

(b)

6	5
N	G
T	H
R	I
S	T
O	Y
I	T
K	E
V	I

(c)

6	5	7	....	6	5	7	4	...	1	6	5	7	4
N	G	O		N	G	O	F		I	N	G	O	F
T	H	E		T	H	E	D		Y	T	H	E	D
R	I	D		R	I	D	G		B	R	I	D	G
S	T	M		S	T	M	O		R	S	T	M	O
O	Y	O		O	Y	O	U		T	O	Y	O	U
I	T	F		I	T	F	A		S	I	T	F	A
K	E	T		K	E	T	H		A	K	E	T	H
V	I	A		V	I	A	D		X	V	I	A	D

(d)

6	5	3	....	6	5	3	4	...
N	G	O		N	G	O	F	(Abandoned in
T	H	A		T	H	A	D	
R	I	X		R	I	X	G	favor of c.)
S	T	E		S	T	E	O	
O	Y	O		O	Y	O	U	
I	T	L		I	T	L	A	
K	E	F		K	E	F	H	
V	I	C		V	I	C	D	

The formation of this digram *TH* on the second row has automatically set up
a digram *NG* on the top row, a digram *RI* on the third row, and so on; and we find,
upon examining these newly-formed digrams, that the whole series is made up of
good English combinations. Thus, it looks as if our combination 6-5 is correct, and
we will proceed with a possible *HE* or *HA*, attempting to complete a trigram *THE*
or *THA* on the second row.

Both *E* and *A* are present on the second row, and we may observe at the steps
marked (c) and (d) in the figure just what would be the result of adding strip 7
or strip 3. At first glance, it appears that combinations 6-5-7 and 6-5-3 are about

equally probable. But it so happens that both set-ups have formed a sequence *YO* on the fifth line, suggesting *YOU;* and when the only *U* on that line is tried in both places, it becomes evident that combination 6-5-7-4 is going to give better results than combination 6-5-3-4, where we find poor sequences like *KEFH*. At this point, or earlier, a decryptor will probably proceed on the left side of his set-up, completing the syllable *ING* and the series of column-numbers 1-6-5-7-4, as shown. When this setting together of columns automatically brings out on the third row a sequence *BRIDG*, we have our first suggestion of a *probable word*, since the man who had this cryptogram on his person had just attempted to blow up a *BRIDGE*. After this, all is plain sailing; the necessary *E* happens to be on the same line, and even if it were not, we have only three strips left, and these may be placed by trial. Thus our eight paper strips arrive at the stage indicated on the left-hand side of Fig. 17.

Figure 17

		Strips in order								Adjustment of rows							
	2	1	6	5	7	4	8	3									
1	W	I	N	G	O	F	L	O		2....	B	Y	T	H	E	D	R	A
2	B	Y	T	H	E	D	R	A		1....	W	I	N	G	O	F	L	O
3	T	B	R	I	D	G	E	X		6....	T	S	I	T	F	A	L	L
4	I	R	S	T	M	O	V	E		5....	S	T	O	Y	O	U	T	O
5	S	T	O	Y	O	U	T	O		7....	T	A	K	E	T	H	E	F
6	T	S	I	T	F	A	L	L		4....	I	R	S	T	M	O	V	E
7	T	A	K	E	T	H	E	F		8....	X	X	V	I	A	D	U	C
8	X	X	V	I	A	D	U	C		3....	T	B	R	I	D	G	E	X

"Taking-out" Key: $\dfrac{2\ 1\ 6\ 5\ 7\ 4\ 8\ 3}{1\ 2\ 3\ 4\ 5\ 6\ 7\ 8}$ "Writing-in" Key: $\dfrac{1\ 2\ 3\ 4\ 5\ 6\ 7\ 8}{2\ 1\ 8\ 6\ 4\ 3\ 5\ 7}$

If we have previously met the Nihilist transposition, we can see now what the cipher is, and, if it is a true Nihilist, we can finish the reconstruction *by decipherment with the key*. To do this, we simply number the rows from 1 to 8 and then disarrange these rows so that their numbers will reproduce the series of column numbers. This is shown on the right-hand side of Fig. 17, where the plaintext is easily read: " By the drawing of lots, it falls to you to take the first move. Viaduct bridge." The gentleman required three nulls, and thriftily made use of them as punctuation. If we have not previously met the Nihilist encipherment, or if this cryptogram is of a kindred type but governed by two separate keys, one for columns and another for rows, the only difference is that we may have to experiment a little with rows before finding their correct order.

In completing our solution, we have obtained a key, 2 1 6 5 7 4 8 3, shown in the series of column-numbers, and should other cryptograms be intercepted having the same key as the first, we need merely decipher them with our key. It is, however, a " taking out " key, while the Nihilist, as we have seen, is ordinarily *written in*. Having either of the keys, we may find the other easily enough as suggested in the figure. Simply " number the numbers " and put them back in serial order. The new set of numbers, now disarranged, will show you the other key. It would not be impossible for the student who is a good guesser to find the keyword on which our present writing-in key was based. This kind of work, with paper strips, is much more rapid than it probably seems, and is often done at random. The keen eye needs no digram list for the spotting of *HT*, merely reversed, with *GN* above it.

Speaking now of the ordinary columnars (Fig. 11), one minor point should perhaps be brought to the attention of the very new student. Quite often, a digram, such as the *QU* of Fig. 18, is not written on a single line, and it may be necessary to match this valuable digram in the manner shown at (b) of that figure, coming out in the end as at (c). In such event, we can later on transfer columns 5-6-7 to the other side of the block, raising them all by one position. (Column numbers, in this case, are for reference only.) The same would not apply to a Nihilist block in which the whereabouts of the " next " row is unknown; the diagram *QU* would have to be abandoned in favor of something else.

Figure 18

(a)	(b)	(c)

```
(a)                      (b)              (c)

1 2 3 4 5 6 7              1              1 2 3 4
- - - - - - -           7  -             - - - -
                       -   T             5 6 7
T H I S I S Q          Q   U             - - -   T H I S
U I T E T R U          U   E                     I S Q U I T E
E B U T W E D          D                         T R U E B U T
                                                 W E D
```

We mentioned briefly, too, the possibility of finding alternating horizontals, so that only half of the rows can be " anagrammed " together. Such minor problems, and they are numerous, can all be ironed out easily enough once the student is familiar with his type, and columnar transposition, encountered frequently and in all sorts of disguises, is surely the most fascinating of all types. In Chapter *VI* we are to meet it again, this time with an incomplete rectangle.

16. By PICCOLA. (Ordinary columnar).

```
O E E H E    A T F L S    V A S Y C    I O A E D    Q O H D F    M C M T C    P O G E O

R E U G M    I E F U O    G C Y W G    D Q U U I    A L S I E    R M O R M    R R A T O  A Q.
```

17. By KRIS KROST. (Nihilist).

```
T C I G R    H N L A G    T L I S A    A O M O R    N R I M N    M E T R N    K S A O E

I S D L E    I K H H H    E R D F T    A S O I E    T I H N E    B T K E.
```

18. By MERLIN. (Nihilist. Its keyword has been used as a word-spacer).

```
T O L F P    T E E R B    I V O P S    N R E W O    R L I T T    E S E N E    T O O H O

F H H E H    N Y H I O    P F O S T    G I P H E    I E E T K    I N U I B    N R A A Y

R R E E W    L S T H T    E E R D T    S E A I R    S R E A E    R R E P E    U E U R S

S U I R R    O F E S T    R P O P A    O R R B E    E O N T T    E E R T A    H E R A R

L A D I O    E E Z E L    Y A O A Y    M S L U L    W I Y N N    O O S S T    G T S H L

W E Y M D    M E A R E    E U R I Y    T P P R N    Y N T Y O.
```

19. By SLEEPY. (Nihilist "route-cipher").

Wants Little Wish Should Long Muster But The Man And Gold Wants If Me Many Below Mint For Not A So And Nor Of More With Score In Song Wants Were I That Told Exactly Are Here A Long 'Tis Many 'Tis My But Each Still Little Would SoJ

20. By TITOGI. (Ordinary columnar).

T W E I S   I A H O D   S P O D E   R I T O N   J E U T A   I A S Y S   H N T S T
K D N R S   W U.

21. By PICCOLA. (Ordinary columnar).

T E E P H   B M E F E   B N T U X   A V E H A   R D W X I   E L N C V   E V R O I

T A F U L   B O R O N   T H M T M   U E F S H   O E T T L   E D A K E   E G D N L

E E N N I   O O E B E   E E R S T   N R Y D C   N X O N O   E N E X.

(And now try this. Probable word: EXAMPLE).

H E L K L   T I P N W   H S E S I   A X S R R   E E A C M   C P L T L   T E O S D

R A O E E   X T I H Y   E U H N G   E M Y T A   S L M A A   D S C.

CHAPTER V

Geometrical Types — The Turning Grille

The well-known *turning grille,* also known as the *rotating,* or *revolving* grille, is said to have been originated by an Italian, Girolamo Cardano (or Cardan). Such grilles can be prepared from any substantial material capable of being made into sheets and marked into cells, and may take the form of any geometrical figure which happens to be equilateral. The number of cells to be clipped out, so as to form apertures for the writing of letters, is based on the shape of the grille, as: one-third of the total number for a triangle, one-fourth for a square, and so on; and the writing of the letters is done on a section of paper of the same size and shape as the grille, and preferably ruled off into cells which correspond to those of the grille. After such a grille has been placed on its corresponding section of paper, and a letter has been written through each aperture, the grille is *turned* a certain number of degrees to a new position on the same section of paper, so as to cover from sight the letters already written, and expose another series of blank cells for the writing of new letters; and this continues until the grille has taken its full number of positions and every cell has been accounted for on the section of paper beneath it. The preferred grille is a square, based on square cells, and takes four positions. Usually it is based on an *even number* of these cells; otherwise, the full number of cells is not evenly divisible into quarters, leaving an extra central cell which has to be omitted or specially dealt with.

The grille called " Fleissner," after an Austrian cryptologist, Eduard Fleissner von Wostrowitz, is the perfected Cardan grille as described by Jules Verne in his story, " Mathias Sandorf." Colonel Fleissner's grille is a square, taking four positions, and is always based on an even number of cells. In preparing this grille, it is easy enough to select apertures at random in such a way that each one governs its own four cells on the paper beneath, causing each of these to be uncovered exactly once. But concerning the preparation of the grille, there is a phase which affects the value of the cipher itself: unless the grille can be constructed at will, in accordance with a key which is " easily changed, communicated, and remembered," it requires the keeping on hand of a material apparatus which can be stolen or copied, or which cannot be destroyed in case of emergency.

There are, of course, many ways in which a key could be applied. The method used here is one published several years ago by Ohaver, and can be studied in Fig. 19. First, as shown at (a), we have a quick mechanical method for selecting apertures that cannot conflict. The square is divided into four quarters, and each quarter, treated as if it were the one occupying the upper left-hand corner, receives its consecutive cell numbers, 1 to 9 (or 1 to 4, 1 to 16, 1 to 25, 1 to 36, etc.). If the route of writing-in is made exactly the same for all four of the quarters, it becomes possible to clip *one each* of the numerals 1, 2, 3, 4, 5 . . . . etc., taken absolutely at pleasure, and each resulting aperture will expose only its particular four cells. This can be seen at (b).

The grille shown at (b), however, was based on the key-phrase FRIENDLY GROUPS, and the method can be studied at (c), following Ohaver's plan, even to its minute details. The fact that the square is based on 6 is told in the initial letter of the key-word, *F*, 6th letter of the alphabet. This key-word must yield nine letters, one for each proposed aperture in the grille. A short word, such as FRIEND, can be lengthened by a partial repetition, as FRIENDFRI, while a longer word is cut off after its ninth letter, as it was in Fig. 19. This literal key is next converted to a numerical key, as explained in the preceding chapter, and the nine resulting numbers are divided as evenly as possible into four sections. Finally, considering the four quarters of the grille in some definitely agreed rotation, each section of key-numbers will show what numerals are to be clipped from a given quarter. In the figure, the numerals 3 and 8 were clipped from the first quarter, numerals 5 and 2 from the second — proceeding in a clockwise direction, — numerals 7 and 1 from the third quarter, and numerals 6, 9, and 4 from the remaining quarter.

Figure 19 - Preparation of a Grille

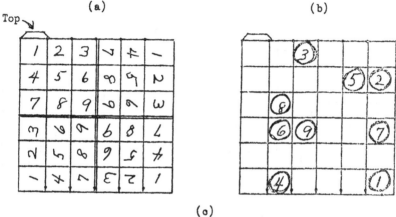

(a)   (b)

Top

(c)

F R I E N D L Y G
3 8.5 2.7 1.6 9 4   1st Q: 3,8;   2d; 5,2;   3d: 7,1;   4th: 6,9,4

Another method for selecting cells, proposed by Edward Nickerson, dispenses with numerals, using in their places the letters of a key-word which must be without repetitions, as FRIENDLY G happens to be. If these nine letters, all different, be written into the nine cells of each quarter, following exactly the same route in each case, it becomes possible to clip one each of the letters *F, R, I, E, N, D, L, Y, G*, taken wherever desired. The choice can be made as follows: Taking the four quarters of the grille in the agreed rotation, follow the normal alphabet, clipping *A*, (when present,) from the first quarter, *B*, (when present,) from the second quarter, *C*, (when present,) from the third quarter, and so on. Or, to insure a more even distribution, rearrange the nine letters in alphabetical sequence: *D E, F G, I L, N R Y*, and divide as in the former plan, clipping *D* and *E* from the first quarter, *F* and *G* from the second, and so on. While it is possible to provide key-phrases of sixteen letters, without repeating, it is probably more convenient to take whatever number of letters is needed from a key-mixed alphabet of the following type: F R I E N D L Y G O U P S A B C . . . . . . W X Z *f r i e* . . . . . .

In Fig. 20, at (a), (b), (c), (d), we have a detailed picture of the operation of this grille on the 36-letter plaintext unit: MISFIRE ON VIADUCT JOB X RUSH INSTRUCTIONS. One definite edge of the grille must be designated as the top, and there is a right and a wrong side. Taking precautions in these respects, we place the grille over a sheet of paper and mark its outline with a pencil (or otherwise make sure of maintaining this one location). We write the first nine letters as at (a), and give the grille a quarter-turn to the right. We add the second nine letters as at (b) — where the newly-written letters are the capitals; the others, in lower case, are presumed to be hidden from sight by the solid portion of the grille. Another quarter-turn makes ready for the next nine letters (c), and a remaining quarter-turn completes the revolution (d). The writing-in, at all times, is *straight ahead*: cells taken from left to right, and lines taken from top to bottom.

Figure 20 - Four Stages of Enoipherment

(a)

	M				
			I	S	
	F				
	I	R			E
	O				N

(b)

		m			
V		I	A	i	s
	f	D			U
	i	r			e
				C	
T	o	J		O	n

(c)

B		m		X	
v		i	a	i	s
R	f	d	U	S	u
	i	r		H	e
I	N			o	
t	o	j	S	o	n

(d)

b	T	m	R	x	U
v	C	i	a	i	s
r	f	d	u	s	u
T	i	r	I	h	e
i	n	O	N	o	S
t	o	j	s	o	n

In the Jules Verne story, the three units of his cryptogram were left standing in their blocks. Verne's heroes were clever enough to unearth a ready-made grille, and, by laying this, in its four successive positions, above each of the three blocks, were able to read the message through the apertures. Today, such blocks would be taken off in five-letter groups, and possibly by a devious route. A little concealment can be afforded, too, by completing the last five-letter group with nulls, or, better, by adding these nulls at the beginning of the cryptogram. It is also possible to make the final 36-letter unit *incomplete* by blanking out its bottom cells before putting in the letters.

A grille can be used in other ways. Negligible changes can be produced in its cryptograms by altering the customary order of its four positions. A more substantial change is introduced by departures from the straight horizontal direction of the writing-in. It is possible to revolve the paper instead of the grille, setting the letters right-side-up at the time of their taking off. And in all of these cases, the grille is still serving as an instrument for *writing-in;* there would be corresponding cases in which it is used as an instrument for *taking out* the letters of a prepared block. Each variation, perhaps, would require its own separate analysis before its individual inherent weaknesses could be spotted and used as the basis for a special method. If the student, after observing some special methods applied to ordinary grille encipherment, cares to try his hand at analyzing some one of its variations, we suggest that he take a series of numbers, 1 to 36, 1 to 64, etc., and carry these through a complete encipherment to see what becomes of each one.

Grille transposition, like the Nihilist, involves a major unit composed of minor units. But here, the four minor units are never left intact, and if the type of encipherment is not known in advance, the decryptment of a single block will give somewhat more trouble than the decryptment of a single Nihilist block, for the reason that the decryptor usually exhausts the simpler possibilities before trying the complex. With grille encipherment known, or suspected, we have a cipher bristling with points of attack.

The strictly horizontal writing-in of each minor unit has had to be done within a fairly short compass, and no two consecutive letters of this unit can have been placed very far apart without causing other letters to draw closer together. Their average distance apart is four cells. For the decryptor, this actual distance apart of letters is made shorter by his knowledge that for each letter considered, there are three others which cannot have been written into the same unit with it, *and that he knows definitely what these three letters are.*

Particularly interesting is the assistance he receives from the symmetrical pattern into which the letters of his four units are written; position 3 is position 1 reversed, and position 4 is position 2 reversed. Thus, having tentatively selected the letters of a probable word, or fairly long sequence, he can check the correctness of his observations by examining another sequence which would automatically build up, traveling in the opposite direction, in the reverse position of the grille.

For a clear understanding of these matters, suppose we consider the decryptment of the block just enciphered, on the assumption that we suspect the presence there of the word VIADUCT. Fig. 21 shows a 6 x 6 block carrying consecutive cell-numbers, which are also the serial numbers of the cryptogram letters, as these appear in a separate block beside the first. It is understood that our first move would be that of ascertaining whether or not the seven letters of this word are all present. It must be remembered, too, that a long word is not necessarily altogether in one unit; the grille might have been turned before the word was completed.

In the present case, however, our first letter, *V*, is found near the top of the square, and only once, so that if the word VIADUCT is present, a substantial portion of it must have been written before the grille was turned. We expect to find letters *I, A, D, U,* and so on, following the letter *V* in just that order, and without any very great distance between any two of them; and if, approaching the bottom of the square, we find it necessary to proceed backward for *U, C,* or *T,* then the grille was surely turned before that *U, C,* or *T,* was written.

Now, considering together the two blocks of Fig. 21, we find that our first letter, *V,* occupies cell No. 7. In imagination, we revolve a grille in which the only aperture has been cut in cell 7, and find that this aperture exposes the cells numbered 5, 30, and 32. These three cells, then, were surely covered from sight when the letter *V* was written into cell 7, and regardless of what the letters are that occupy these three cells, it is definitely impossible that any one of the three could have been used in the same minor unit with the V of cell 7. Looking for a letter I, we find several within a very short range. But the block contains only one A, and since we cannot proceed backward after selecting the I, the position of A (cell 10) tells us that only the I of cell 9 is possible. We accept, then, the I of cell 9, and, again revolving an imaginary grille with its only aperture cut in cell 9, we eliminate the letters found in cells 17, 28, and 20. Similarly, accepting A of cell 10, we eliminate whatever letters are occupying cells 23, 27, and 14. So far, none of the letters eliminated have been wanted for the development of the word VIADUCT; but notice that the fourth letter, D, found only once in the block, occupies cell 15, thus eliminating the letters of cells 16, 22, and 21, one of which is U, the next letter needed. Thus, we are not forced to make a decision as between the U of cell 16 and the U of cell 18.

Figure 21

1	2	3	4	5	6		B	T	̶R̶	R	̶U̶	U
7	8	9	10	11	12		V_7	C	I_9	A_{10}	I	S
13	14	15	16	17	18		R	̶R̶	D_{15}	̶	̶	U_{18}
19	20	21	22	23	24		T_{19}	̶	̶R̶	I_{22}	̶R̶	E
25	26	27	28	29	30		I	N	O_{27}	N_{28}	C	S_{30}
31	32	33	34	35	36		T	̶O̶$_{32}$	J	̶	O	N

We have put together, then, the letters $V\ I\ A\ D\ U$ in the only manner which is possible at all, and their cell-numbers, taken in order, are 7-9-10-15-18. If the grille is reversed, these same openings, named in the same order, will uncover cells 30-28-27-22-19; these new cells, however, will not be seen in reverse order; they will be in straight order like their letters. If, then, our sequence $VIADU$ is correct, the five letters found in cells 19-22-27-28-30, taken in normal order, should form an acceptable English combination. A glance at the right-hand block of Fig. 21 will show that this check-sequence is $T\ I\ O\ N\ S$.

When we selected V, we automatically selected S of cell 30 as its check-letter. When we added I on the right-hand side of V, we obtained with it the N of cell 28 on the *left* side of S, giving the check-digram as NS, entirely acceptable. With A, we added the O of cell 27, giving the check-trigram as ONS, still acceptable; and so on to $IONS, TIONS$. Our complete word VIADUCT produces the check-sequence $UCTIONS$. It must not be objected that the fact of having only one each of letters V, A, D, has too greatly facilitated the search. This is an entirely legitimate expectation in a case where we deal with one unit, and the decryptor, when possible, chooses his probable word with this in mind. In the absence of a probable word, we are never without probable sequences: the list of frequent trigrams, and the various common affixes, such as *-TION, -MENT, -ENCE, -ABLE, CON-, PRE-*, etc. For the first three or four letters, where decisions are sometimes uncertain, it is more satisfactory to work directly on the square (prepared in ink), so that impossible cells may be canceled in pencil, and the pencil marks erased when wrong; but once well started, a paper or celluloid grille can be prepared to fit the block, and the chosen cells actually cut out as they are selected. Having found seven out of nine apertures, we may, if we like, turn the paper grille and experiment with its other two positions. The letters, in this case, will show gaps in sequence, and may indicate by these gaps just where the new openings ought to be cut. With one full unit determined, we have the grille for reading the others. The only remaining problem would be that of deciding the exact sequence of these four units, with their context as a guide.

For the case in which it is necessary to begin with letter-sequences, particularly if driven back to the digram list, the device shown in Fig. 22 may prove of considerable assistance: The cryptogram is written in both directions, and thus pairs

Figure 22

1	2	3	4	5	6	7	8	9	10	11	12	13	14	15	16	17	18
B	T	M	R	X	U	V	C	I	A	I	S	R	F	D	U	S	U
N	O	S	J	O	T	S	C	N	O	N	I	E	H	I	R	I	T
36	35	34	33	32	31	30	29	28	27	26	25	24	23	22	21	20	19

19	20	21	22	23	24	25	26	27	28	29	30	31	32	33	34	35	36
T	I	R	I	H	E	I	N	O	N	C	S	T	O	J	S	O	N
U	S	U	D	F	R	S	I	A	I	C	V	U	X	R	M	T	B
18	17	16	15	14	13	12	11	10	9	8	7	6	5	4	3	2	1

every letter with its check-letter, so that check-sequences here would be written backward. This idea is adapted from General Givierge's *Cours de cryptographie*.

Working with digrams is tedious, but will, in the end, give results. Considering, for instance, Fig. 22, its first letter is B. Of letters standing immediately to the right of B, the first one which would form a good digram with it is the R of cell 4. But consideration of a possible digram BR, cells 1-4, shows the check-digram as JN, cells 33-36, and this latter digram is so rare in the language that Meaker did not find it even once in his 10,000-letter text. The next letter known to have an affinity for B is the U of cell 6, but a possible digram BU, cells 1-6, cannot be considered, for the reason that cells 1 and 6 are uncovered by the same opening in the grille. The distance away of the next letters to which B is partial proves frightening, and B is abandoned (it is actually followed by the X of cell 5).

Beginning over, with T of cell 2: The first frequent digram noticed is TR, cells 2-4, and shows the check-digram as JO, cells 33-35. We accept this at once, be-

Figure 23

```
R R T H A O     U E E O S B     A G D E A E
A V E B K U     N E S F D I     A N K S S S
T A D P E B     R A N S U K     O D X F D N
C R E A R R     N J A T I Y     G O A O A R
A O I L I D     X T U S O B     R A A N L E
T S G T E P     L M A O T V     H R A X E X
```

cause the letter J must presumably be followed by a vowel, and the only vowel immediately available is this particular O. To extend the accepted TR, we require a vowel. The first one is U, cell 6, and extends the check-digram to TJO, cells 31-33-35, acceptable if T is the final letter of a word. To extend the supposed trigram TRU, we experiment with C of cell 8 and obtain a check-sequence CTJO, cells 29-31-33-35, which is still encouraging. We must know, of course, that no two of the chosen cells are in conflict with each other. The unit we have partially reconstructed is the second one of Fig. 20, and the check-sequence is the fourth unit.

A method somewhat resembling the foregoing consists in writing another block beside the first, in which the letters of the cryptogram are strictly in reversed order. The pattern of the check-sequence will then follow exactly that of the sequence under examination, merely with its letters in reverse order. Still a further suggestion was made by Herbert Raines: In the preparation of the two blocks, one in straight order and the other in reverse order, the writing should be done vertically, with all columns containing four letters. The symmetry can still be found, and any two consecutive plaintext letters are more nearly at their original distance apart — the average 4.

So far, we have been dealing with an isolated unit. In Fig. 23 we have a longer cryptogram, suspected of being a reply to the first. We have set it up in its three blocks, expecting to decipher it with the same grille, but find that something is wrong. To see quickly how the presence of several units

Figure 24

Straight			Reversed		
7	8	9	28	29	30
A	V	E	L	I	D
N	E	S	S	O	B
A	N	K	N	L	E

modifies the case, suppose we consider some sequence, right or wrong, which is easily examined, such as the *AVE* on the second row of the first block. Regardless of what the transposition is, if all three of these units are enciphered alike, each of the additional blocks contains a corresponding trigram in exactly the same location as the one under consideration; here we have *NES* in the second block and *ANK* in the third. But if the transposition is specifically that of the grille, each one of the three trigrams *AVE, NES, ANK*, has a check-trigram in its own block. Thus we have the six trigrams listed with their cell-numbers in Fig. 24. Since all of these are acceptable, we should, in practice, be encouraged to accept them; thus, it may be well to say here that, in dealing with all ciphers these false beginnings will quite frequently pitch the decryptor headlong into a solution, through no act of wisdom on his own part.

Now, in order to arm ourselves against the larger grilles, which are somewhat more troublesome, and for investigation of cryptograms which may or may not have been accomplished with a grille, suppose we take a look at Ohaver's mechanical method — that is, his use of paper strips. Picturing any block of 36 cells, numbered consecutively as we saw these in Fig. 21, let us imagine that there is a grille placed over this block, and that this grille has only one opening. If the cell that shows is No. 1, then, at the first turn of the grille, we uncover cell No. 6; at the next turn, cell No. 36; and, at the final turn, cell No. 31. We will call this series of cell-numbers an *index*, and say that the index for this particular aperture is 1-6-36-31. In the first block of the new cryptogram, the letters which follow this index are *R O P T*. In the second block, the same index governs the letters *U B V L*, and, in the third block, *A E X H*. But if the single opening in our hypothetical grille has exposed cell No. 2, then its *index*, discovered in the same way, is 2-12-35-25, and the corresponding letters, in the three blocks of this cryptogram are, respectively, *R U E A, E I T X*, and *G S E R*. Similarly, each one of the other seven apertures possible in this quarter of the grille has an index, expressible in cell-numbers, and governs a certain series of letters in each cryptogram block. If the grille is the Fleissner, the index for any aperture, in a grille of any size, will always contain four numbers, and will govern four letters per block.

If the grille is a 16-letter one, there will be only four of these indices, beginning in cells 1, 2, 5, 6. If it is a 36-letter grille, there will be nine, beginning in cells 1, 2, 3, 7, 8, 9, 13, 14, 15. A 64-letter grille will have 16, beginning in cells 1, 2, 3, 4, 9, 10, 11, 12, 17, 18, 19, 20, 25, 26, 27, 28; and so on to grilles of 100, 144, etc., letters. After one grows accustomed to the swastika-like route of the open cell, such indices are not at all difficult to prepare at the moment of need; however, many solvers prefer to make them up in sets, once for all, and have them ready as they happen to be wanted. As to the finding of the four letters per block which follow any one index, it is sufficient to remember that the cell numbers, arranged in the manner shown, are also the serial numbers of the letters belonging to any one unit. Thus it is not necessary to write the units into their squares; we need merely number the letters of a unit from 1 to 36, and select those having the desired serial numbers.

Returning, now, to our cryptogram: Our unit appears to be 36, since a division of this kind distributes the vowels uniformly; and a unit of 36 may have been produced with a grille. If so, this grille had 9 apertures, and we need 9 paper strips, one for each aperture. On each strip we are to have: the four index numbers, the four corresponding letters from the first block, the four corresponding letters from the second block, and the four corresponding letters from the third block. But since, in each case, the first three cell-numbers or the first three letters *must be repeated,* our strip will actually contain seven numbers and twenty-one

Figure 25

Preparation of Slips

Index.......	1	2	3	7	8	9	13	14	15
	6	12	18	5	11	17	4	10	16
	36	35	34	30	29	28	24	23	22
	31	25	19	32	26	20	33	27	21
	1	2	3	7	8	9	13	14	15
	6	12	18	5	11	17	4	10	16
	36	35	34	30	29	28	24	23	22

Block 1......	R	R	T	A	V	E	T	A	D
	O	U	B	A	K	E	H	B	P
	P	E	T	D	I	L	R	R	A
	T	A	C	S	O	R	G	I	E
	R	R	T	A	V	E	T	A	D
	O	U	B	A	K	E	H	B	P
	P	E	T	D	I	L	R	R	A

Block 2......	U	E	E	N	E	S	R	A	N
	B	I	K	S	D	U	O	F	S
	V	T	O	B	O	S	Y	I	T
	L	X	N	M	T	J	A	U	A
	U	E	E	N	E	S	R	A	N
	B	I	K	S	D	U	O	F	S
	V	T	O	B	O	S	Y	I	T

Block 3......	A	G	D	A	N	K	O	D	X
	E	S	N	A	S	D	E	S	F
	X	E	X	E	L	N	R	A	O
	H	R	G	R	A	O	A	A	A
	A	G	D	A	N	K	O	D	X
	E	S	N	A	S	D	E	S	F
	X	E	X	E	L	N	R	A	O

letters. These nine strips are prepared all in one set-up, the details of which can be examined in Fig. 25. In Fig. 26, the strips of Fig. 25 have been cut apart and rearranged in such a way as to bring out plaintext on the top row of every block; this is, of course, the first *full* row, as pointed out in each case by the four asterisks. It will be noticed that the top row of cell-numbers is arranged in strictly ascending order (our strictly horizontal route of writing-in). If the third row be now examined (as pointed out by two asterisks), it is found that this, too, carries plaintext, merely written backward, and that here the cell-numbers are arranged in strictly descending order.

Now, to read the cryptogram: Each full row of numbers includes all cell-numbers belonging to some one of the four units, and any one of these four rows of numbers is a key to the grille, since it shows exactly what cells were uncovered when the corresponding unit was written in. To obtain the grille, we have only to select some one row of numbers, as 12-36-10-16-34-9-26-32-13, and clip out these particular cells in a square numbered as we saw it in Fig. 21. The student who cares to know what " instructions " were being sent might also satisfy his curiosity as to whether or not this new cryptogram could have been deciphered rather than decrypted.

Figure 26

One Correct Adjustment of Slips

```
                                      9                13
                 1          3         17   8   7    4
     2    6   14   15   18     28   11   5   24
    12   36   10   16   34     20   29  30   33    ****
    35   31   23   22   19      9   26  32   13    **
    25    1   27   21    3     17    8   7    4
     2    6   14   15   18     28   11   5   24    **
    12   36   10   16   34          29  30
    35        23   22

                              E     V    A            T
                              E     L    K    A        H
             R            T   L     R    I    A        R
     R   O   A   D   B     R  E     E    O    D        G    ****
     U   P   B   P   T     T  E     E    O    S        T
     E   T   R   A   C     T  E     E    V    A        H    **
     A   R   I   E   T     B  L     L    K    A        R
     R   O   A   D   B     T  I     I         D
     U   P   B   P   T
     E       R   A             S                       R
                               U    E    N             O
             U            E    S    S    D    N        Y
     E   B   A   N   K     K   J    S    O    S    B   A    ****
     I   V   F   S   O     O   S    S    T    M    B   R
     T   L   I   T   N     E   U    U    E    N        O    **
     X   U   U   A   E     K   S    S    D    S        Y
     E   B   A   N   K     O   O                  O    B
     I   V   F   S   O
     T       I   T             K                            O
                          D    N    N    A    A             E
             A            D    O    S    A                  R
     G   E   D   X   N     N   O    L    E    A             A    ****
     S   X   S   F   X     X   K    K    A    R             O
     E   H   S   A   O     G   D    A    N    A             E    **
     R   A   A   A   D     D   N    N    S    A             R
     G   E   D   X   N         L    S    A    L             R
     S   X   S   F   X              L    E
     E       A   O
```

Concerning the grille cryptograms which follow, it seems not impossible that the student who has seen his principles applied only to a unit of 36 might find some difficulty in adjusting them to grilles of other sizes. A tip, then, on Example 22: Instead of the regulation nulls, its single unit was completed with a common Spanish phrase beginning with Q. And if it still resists: the author's own name was used as the key for constructing the grille.

In adjusting his paper strips (when this is the method he prefers) it makes no particular difference what plan he follows, so long as it works. Some decryptors prefer to concentrate altogether on the strictly ascending series of cell-numbers, allowing letters to form their own sequences. Others will always have before them the set-up of squares, noting there some possible letter-sequence, finding (by means of their cell-numbers) the strips which contain these letters, and then observing results in other blocks. If the given strip cannot be found, then the cell must be already in use.

The shortest road is that of the probable word. For instance, the set-up shown as Fig. 26 was actually initiated by the solver at the letter J of the second block, this being a rare letter and almost invariably followed by a vowel. Of the several vowels immediately in sight (in the square) the correct one was promptly suggested by the sequence so plainly in sight, OB, suggesting the word JOB, one already used by these people in discussing their mysterious activities. The corresponding cell-numbers, 20-29-30, were found to be on three separate strips — a necessary condition — and when placed together brought out the straight sequences RID and OLE, with reversed sequences AVE, NEU, and AND. Another very probable word was suggested by the check-sequence AVE ($HAVE$), and the necessary *H* was found with cell-number 33, bringing solution to the point suggested roughly in Fig. 27, where attention was promptly focussed on the tetragram *RIDG*, suggesting *BRIDGE*, another word previously used. There were two strips carrying the desired *E*, but both refused to fit; and here the cell-numbers came into play. The last one found, 33, was large and suggested that its letter, *G*, might be the last letter of a unit; afterward, the building was continued on the left, with *B*.

Figure 27

Straight					Reversed			
20	29	30	33		17	8	7	4
R	I	D	G		E	V	A	H (Have)
J	O	B	A		U	E	N	O (one u)
O	L	E	A		D	N	A	E (e and)

22. By PICCOLA. (Probable word: CRYPTOGRAMS).

T S T H E   T T U S H   O E D G F   R D O E O   G R I S A   A M S N M   Q E U G I

B R I E L   N O S T H   S I C L S   E T S W A   T H A B R   Y P A E.

23. By DAMONOMAD and POPPY. (Probable word: RIGHT FLANK).

A E K D S   P V T O O   N N A A O   N R O N P   R O C T I   E H T R E   H N E T I

A F G S R   H T N I L   O V T E F   F A L M K   I E C L A   A S N M.

24. By DAMONOMAD and POPPY. (Probable word: SPECIAL MESSENGER).

E Y U I S   S N S F P   A O P E R   I S C O A   M N R A I   R G A A T   A L I M N

E G E E I   S O S N O   S A D N B   E I T N O   N G U E P   R H T E E   W S R U A

S S K V Y   F I T O N   O U E Y S   O C M W O   T N S T E   U O B D G.

25. By SAHIB.

R N I I I   N G T F L   A I L N N   D E E T D   R V E U S   E S T H R   E I G E Y

F I A N O   U R R D L   G Y T N H   A E O N R   N E K C D   E E I S E   Y B S E F

W Y P G R   L O L O E   U O F H P   A T V E R   E H E R A   E D G M I   T R H N E

E I S Y T   Q T S I I   S A U S G   I E A I C   A S L L K   L L T T X   H V H E A

R X A X.

26. By NEMO.

I K O T H   N N E H N   E E I R C   R A G E L   O R N O H   K T W T C   H O H E I

E S S W W   T N E T R   H A R E O   L S P L A   A G E A E   R L D B R   Y E U I T

R T R E N   I D T H E   I A D E I   E N D P D   A B R A E   C R K E M   T A O A U

T O T S Y   N B P E S   N U H E S   R A H E S   U P D.

27. By DAN SURR.

OLTLA LIGER TIVHE LLERK 1EAE1 JFEIY YOOUU

STHEA VASGY ASAWC KEPLU EZTIZ OSIT.

28. By PICCOLA. (This is not a grille. It's a serious matter!)

HSOES NPTAE TOHIS TWLED TTFAI BTYUY OTCEO

11TRC YSBTR AHBTE 1DOUS CIUOK ROQN.

CHAPTER VI

IRREGULAR TYPES — COLUMNAR TRANSPOSITION

Square units, in actual use, are less convenient than those rectangular encipherments in which only one dimension of the block is restricted, thus permitting that a single key govern messages of many different lengths. We have a more practical cipher in the columnar transposition of Chapter *IV*, and this can be rendered somewhat safer if care be taken to avoid completing the rectangle. The preparation of such a block is illustrated in Fig. 28, where the key-word PARADISE is being used to encipher the following text: REGRET CHANGE IN SYSTEMS BUT THOUGHT ADVISABLE ACCOUNT INCREASED VOLUME SENT BY AIR.

First, let us understand the purpose of the four nulls. It is customary, when cryptograms are to be transmitted by wire or radio, to make them evenly divisible into five-letter groups. This usually means the addition of from one to four nulls, and since the nature of the cipher makes it inadvisable that additional letters be added to the enciphered cryptogram, any desired nulls must be added in the block before the columns are taken off. Another precaution usually recommended is the avoidance altogether of key-lengths which are divisible by 5, so that an encipherer is practically never compelled to add a complete five-letter group in order to leave his rectangle incomplete. It might be added that our use of letters *XXXX* is for emphasis only; a better series would be one of the nature *AAEO*.

Figure 28

```
P A R A D I S E
6 1 7 2 3 5 8 4

R E G R E T C H
A N G E I N S Y
S T E M S B U T
T H O U G H T A
D V I S A B L E
A C C O U N T I
N C R E A S E D
V O L U M E S E
N T B Y A I R X
X X X . . . . .
```

The decipherer's only problem is illustrated in Fig. 29. Knowing the key, the decipherer knows that there must be eight columns. The number of letters, 75, divided by 8, results in 9, with remainder 3; thus, the short columns are to contain nine letters, and there will be three which contain ten letters. He lays out an 8 x 10 block, cancels the last five cells, writes his key-numbers across the tops of the columns, and then begins to copy letters, filling the column numbered 1, then the column numbered 2, and so on, finally reading his message by straight horizontals.

Figure 29

```
P A R A D I S E
6 1 7 2 3 5 8 4

— — — — — — — —
— — — — — — — —
. . . . . . . . . . . . . .
. . . . . . . . . . . . . .
— — — — x x x x x
— — — — — — — —
```

The cryptogram from this block is shown as Fig. 30, and illustrates the manner in which the decryptor will number the letters of practically all cryptograms in order that he may quickly locate any desired letter, or learn, by subtraction, the distance apart of any two letters. The decryptor, of course, does not know how many columns the cryptogram contains, and even after he finds out the key-length, he still does not know exactly the point at which any one column ends and another begins.

This form of transposition is among the most fascinating of decryptment problems, and we shall look at it from several angles. The simplest case is that in which the decryptor correctly assumes the presence in his cryptogram of some word or phrase whose length is greater than that of the key; if this probable word is long enough, he is able to learn, not only the key-length, but the order in which to write his columns. Our present cryptogram, for instance, has key-length 8, and contains

Figure 30

The Cryptogram Prepared for Examination

```
    5         10        15        20        25        30
E N T H V  C C O T X  R E M U S  O E U Y E  I S G A U  A M A H Y

   35         40        45        50        55        60
T A E I D  E X T N B  H B N S E  I R A S T  D A N V N  X G G E O

   65         70        75
I C R L B  X C S U T  L T E S R
```

two nine-letter words, ADVISABLE and INCREASED. These two words, repeated in Fig. 31, will show what happens when a word is long enough to overlap the block. With the word ADVISABLE, the final E falls below the initial A, and when this column is taken off, the letters A E will stand in sequence in the cryptogram. Similarly, the word INCREASED will provide, in the cryptogram, a digram I D. Should the decryptor suspect the presence of either of these words, he would look at once for sequences of this kind in his cryptogram, and the presence of AE (or ID) would tell him that the key-length is probably 8, which is the distance apart of the two letters in his probable word.

Figure 31

```
6 1 7 2 3 5 8 4
. . . . . . . .
. . . . . . . A
D V I S A B L E
. . . . . . . I
N C R E A S E D
V O L U M E . .
```

The ideal case is that in which the probable word is long enough to furnish more than one of these overlapping letters, as shown in Fig. 32 in connection with the " word " INCREASED VOLUME. Suppose that we have suspected the presence of this expression in our cryptogram, and have ascertained that the necessary letters are present for forming it. We consider its letters one by one, in the order I, N, C, R . . . . and go through the cryptogram, underscoring (or otherwise noting) all cases in which the given letter is followed immediately by another of the letters found in the same probable " word." But, in considering any one letter, say the letter N, we ignore such sequences as NT, NB, NX, whose second letters, T, B, X, do not occur in the expression INCREASED VOLUME. Fig. 33 shows exactly what digrams of this kind can be found in connection with letters I, N, C, R, E, and also the distance (or distances) apart of the two given letters as found in the probable word. Notice that in connection with every letter there is one digram in which this distance is 8, the correct key-length of our present cryptogram. And when these digrams are selected from the tabulation, and set up vertically with top letters in the order I N C R E, the lower five letters prove up in the order D V O L U. In actual work, the tabulation must sometimes be made, though ordinarily it will suffice to start directly with the " proving up."

Figure 32

```
I N C R E A S
E D V O L U M
E
I N C R E A S E
D V O L U M E
I N C R E A S E D V
O L U M E
```

Now let us go ahead and solve the cryptogram, as shown in Fig. 34. We will assume, to begin with, that our cryptogram has been prepared at the top of a sheet, and that our various trials are being made on the blank space beneath it. We will assume also that, having discovered key-length 8, we have divided this cryptogram roughly into eight segments, three of which contain ten letters and the rest nine.

First, we are in possession of a series of embryo columns, shown at (a), and these can be set up without looking at the cryptogram at all. Having done this, we turn to the cryptogram, find each one of the sequences again, and lengthen the columns of our beginning block by adding to each pair of letters a few of the letters which immediately precede and follow it. Thus, our block begins to build up as at (b); and, for each time that a partial column is set up in (b), the segment which contained it is promptly circled out of the cryptogram itself, which now begins to assume the appearance indicated at (c). Thus some words have automatically formed on the new lines which tell us plainly that the final column must contain a sequence *L T E*, followed by *S* or *W*, and the appearance of the cryptogram tells us plainly where to look for it; the final segment is the only one having enough letters to furnish another nine- or ten-letter column.

At stage (c), we are practically in possession of the numerical key, and to show this, the cryptogram segments have been numbered. The first one, containing *V C C O T X*, has been set up in the partial block as column 3; thus the third column of (b) should have key-number *1*. The second segment, containing *S O E U Y E*, has been set up as column 5, showing that the fifth column of (b) should have key-number *2*. And so on with the rest, until the eight key-numbers are standing in the order 4-6-1-7-2-3-5-8. This is shown at (d), and directly below this, at (e) is the

Figure 33

Letter Examined & Sequences Found	Distance Apart In Word		
I	IS	6	
	ID	8	
	IR	3	
	IC	2	
N	NS	5	
	NV	8	
C	CO	8	
	CR	1	
	CS	4	
R	RE	1 4 11	
	RA	2	
	RL	8	
E	EM	9	(6)*
	EU	8	(5)*
	EO	6	(3)*
	ES	2	

(*) Distances from the second E

Proving up: I N C R E . . .
(8)   D V O L U

enciperer's original key. It can be seen that we are now in very much the same position as the legitimate decipherer; by making a few trials, each time shifting one key-number from the left side to the right, we need do little more than decipher. Usually, however, it is quicker simply to go on and rough. out the block we have already started, and then make the necessary adjustments, approximately as shown in Fig. 35. Having noted, in the cryptogram, that there are some unused letters,

Figure 34

Investigating the Key-length. 8

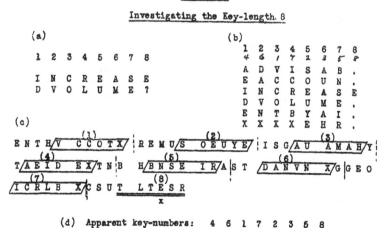

(a)

```
   1  2  3  4  5  6  7  8

   I  N  C  R  E  A  S  E
   D  V  O  L  U  M  E  ?
```

(b)

```
   1  2  3  4  5  6  7  8
   4  6  1  7  2  3  5  8
   A  D  V  I  S  A  B  .
   E  A  C  C  O  U  N  .
   I  N  C  R  E  A  S  E
   D  V  O  L  U  M  E  .
   E  N  T  B  Y  A  I  .
   X  X  X  X  E  H  R  .
```

(c)

```
        (1)                  (2)                  (3)
E N T H/V  C C O T X/ R E M U/S   O E U Y E/ I S G/A U   A M A H/Y
     (4)                  (5)                  (6)
T/A E I D   E X/T N B   H/B N S E   I R/A S T  /D A N V N   X/G G E O
   (7)                  (8)
/I C R L B   X/C S U T   L T E S R
                              x
```

(d) Apparent key-numbers: 4 6 1 7 2 3 5 8

(e) True key-numbers: 6 1 7 2 3 5 8 4

E N T H, on the left side of segment 1, we assume temporarily that all other unused letters belong to the segment which follows them, and add them all, indiscriminately, at the top of the block. Where this is shown, at the left side of Fig. 35, the true key-numbers, as found in the cryptogram, have been added above the original reference numbers, and similarly with the adjusted block on the right.

With the block roughed out, and knowing that a cryptogram of 75 letters using key-length 8 cannot have columns of any other length than 9 and 10, the first obvious maladjustment is seen in column 1 (key 4), which has only 8 letters. Since this is the 4th segment of the cryptogram, its remaining letter (or its remaining two letters) will have to be found at the end of the third segment or at the begin-

Figure 35

Forming and Adjusting a Tentative Block

4	6	1	7	2	3	5	8		4	6	1	7	2	3	5	8
1	2	3	4	5	6	7	8		1	2	3	4	5	6	7	8
		E	G	R		T	C			R	E	G	R	E	T	C
	A	N	G	E	I	N	S		H	A	N	G	E	I	N	S
Y	S	T	E	M	S	B	U		Y	S	T	E	M	S	B	U
T	T	H	O	U	G	H	T		T	T	H	O	U	G	H	T
A	D	V	I	S	A	B	L		A	D	V	I	S	A	B	L
E	A	C	C	O	U	N	T		E	A	C	C	O	U	N	T
I	N	C	R	E	A	S	E		I	N	C	R	E	A	S	E
D	V	O	L	U	M	E	S		D	V	O	L	U	M	E	S
E	N	T	B	Y	A	I	R		E	N	T	B	Y	A	I	R
X	X	X	X	E	H	R			X	X	X	X				

Column 1 must have another letter, top. (Found at bottom of Column 6).
(4)   (3)

Column 6 must then have another letter, top. (Found at bottom of Column 5).
(3)   (2)

Column 7, bottom, then shows an extra letter, which must be transferred to
(5)

    Column 2, top. When these transfers have been made, as shown on
    (6)

the right, all that remains is to transfer the short column (1)
(4)

to the right-hand side of its block, raising it by one position.

ning of the fifth (keys 3 and 5), that is, at the bottom, or at the top, respectively, of the columns originally set up as columns 6 and 7. The selection of *H* from the bottom of column 6 leaves this column too short, while the top row of the block shows a gap in sequence, and evidently needs the *E* at the end of the second segment. The lone *R* which remains at the bottom of column 7 is then erased and written at the top of column 2, and thus we arrive at the adjustment shown on the right side of the figure, where the only remaining operation will be that of transferring the misplaced nine-letter column to its own side of the block. This final adjustment shows us the segments of the cryptogram in their key order: 6-1-7-2-3-5-8-4.

Having seen the ideal case, the student will understand how the less perfect example would be handled, or the case in which the probable word is not long enough to overlap at all. For the latter, he would attempt to find some word like CRYPTOGRAM, in which there are letters such as *C,Y,P,G,M,* not likely to appear more than once or twice in a short text. We need not discuss this latter case, since we are to see something very much like it before the present chapter ends.

Now, as a preliminary to those cases in which we are unable to find a probable word, suppose we turn to the back of the book, and make an inspection of the tool chest. First in importance, and valuable in ciphers of all kinds, is the digram chart which O. Phelps Meaker has been kind enough to prepare especially for this text. To learn how often he encountered any given digram in his 10,000-letter count, note its first letter in the horizontal alphabet, at the top of a column, then note its second letter in the vertical alphabet, at the beginning of a row, and observe the figure which occupies the cell at the intersection of this column and row. If the digram is *TH*, its frequency was 315; if the digram is *JN*, the cell is blank. This does not mean that the digram *TH* will appear exactly 315 times in any other 10,000-letter text, or that *JN* will never be found (occurring, say, as initials). It merely shows that the digram *TH* is of remarkably high frequency, while a digram *JN* is so rare that it practically never appears. The most commonly occurring digrams of this chart have been listed on another page in the order of decreasing frequencies. A list of the principal reversals is also given, with other data which will be found useful in the majority of ciphers. Meaker's digram chart shows also the frequencies found for single letters in the same text. These are shown at the extreme right, and were obtained by adding the figures found on the 26 rows of the chart proper. When such counts are made, every letter in the text is considered to be the first letter of a digram, and no attention is paid to the separations between words. Thus the single-letter frequencies can be found by totalling either the columns or the rows, which, except for minor discrepancies, will check against each other.

So much for *frequencies*. Now let us take a closer look at *sequence*. Certain letters, ordinarily those of lowest frequency, are peculiar in their *contacts* with other letters. The shining example, in most languages, is the letter *Q*, followed, almost 100% of the time, by *U* plus another vowel; and if it seems, in the present text, that the significance of *QU* is being overlooked, this is simply because the individuality of this digram, like that of the German *CH* (*CK*), is so well advertised that even the novice encipherer finds a way to avoid using it. It is impossible, however, to avoid all letters having individual preferences. We still have *J* and *V*, practically sure to be followed by vowels, and *Z*, almost as sure. We have *X*, nearly always preceded by a vowel, but more often followed by a consonant. If these are missing from the cryptogram, we may have letters like *K*, *B*, and *P*, which confine an enormous percentage of their contacts to vowels; or to vowels and liquids; or to letters from the high-frequency group *E T A O N I R S H*. Even among the high-frequency letters themselves we find that *H* is followed about 75% of the time by either *E* or *A*, and that it is preceded largely by *T*, with *S*, *C*, and *W* as the next favorites; or we find that *N* is inordinately fond of vowels on its left, though with some preference for consonants on its right. All information of this kind is present in the digram chart, and usually is known to the decryptor without recourse to a chart.

For the beginner, however, who might like to have it in a more visible form, another chart, of a kind which we believe has never before been published, appears on page 220. This is F. R. Carter's contact chart, on which every letter of the alphabet has been listed in the center of the page, with its favorite contact-letters beside it. The arrangement here is from the center outward; the letters shown on the left of any given letter are those which most often precede it, with percentages as found in Ohaver's digram chart; letters shown on the right are those which most often follow, with percentages from the same digram chart. This information was not completed to the end for every letter, since the only information wanted is the actual preferences of each letter, or the fact that it has none. However, the outermost columns will show the complete percentages of vowel and consonant contacts for all letters as these were found in one 10,000-letter text. With such a chart before us, it becomes very easy, in the absence of *Q*, and other particularly vulnerable letters, to make good use of whatever letters we happen to have; and it is hoped that this new " contact chart " will prove sufficiently valuable to justify Carter's labor in having compiled it for us. As to the other data in the appendix, the student will do well to look it over. The list of trigrams is that of the Parker Hitt Manual, where *THE* was shown as having been found 89 times in 10,000 letters, the others graduating downward to *MEN*, found 20 times. Now let us return to our columnar transposition.

Figure 36

Key-length	Columns, 75 Letters
Key 5:	(Impossible under system)
Key 6:	3 columns of 13
	3 columns of 12
Key 7:	5 columns of 11
	2 columns of 10
Key 8:	3 columns of 10
	5 columns of 9
Key 9:	3 columns of 9
	6 columns of 8
Key 10:	(Improbable under system)
Key 11:	9 columns of 7
	2 columns of 6
(Etc.)	

When a digram *QU* is actually present in a text, or when it is fairly certain that some other digram may be present, such as the *YP* of CRYPTOGRAM (that is, one composed of two infrequent letters), it is possible to discover (or limit) the key-length by observing the distance apart of these two letters in the cryptogram. To approximate such a case, using the foregoing cryptogram (Fig. 30), we will make use of the digram *VI*, and, in order to be brief, we will assume that the letter *V*, position 5, is the only one in the cryptogram, and that the only *I*'s present are those at positions 46 and 61. In one case the interval which separates *V* from *I* is 41, and, in the other, 56. As a preliminary step, we may discard all key-lengths which are factors of 75: 3, 5, 15, 25. In addition, we may discard, for the time being, the key-lengths 10, 20, etc., which are multiples of 5. Of those left, any very short length, as 2 or 4, is very improbable. We may consider, then, possible key-lengths of 6, 7, 8, 9, 11, etc., as far as we care to take them.

To make ready for the investigation, we first prepare a sheet of the kind shown as Fig. 36, where each possible key-length has been used as a divisor in order to learn the column-lengths for each one in a 75-letter cryptogram.

Now let us picture any text written into any block, as in Fig. 37, where long columns have five letters and short columns have four. Considering any digram in the text, as *QU* at the beginning, its two letters are separated by exactly one column of length, provided the letters are counted straight down the columns and columns are taken in one straight direction, or provided the counting is done strictly upward with columns always taken in one direction. In the case of *QU*, this column of separation is a long one (five letters), while, in the case of *AF*, on the right-hand side of the block, it is a short one (four letters), but in both cases it is a full column. This is true, also, of the digram *FE*, which is on two different lines, presuming that, having counted all the way to the end of the last column, we start again with the first. If both letters are in short columns, the interval which separates them is that of a short column, and if both are in long columns, this interval is that of a long column. But if one letter is in a long column and the other in a short column, the separating interval may be long or short, according to whether the columns are taken in straight order or in reverse order.

Figure 37

```
Q U I T E A F  *
E W F A N S W
I L L B E D E
L I G H T E D **
T O S E E
```

*) From F in a short column to E in a long column is an interval of 5; but from E to F is an interval of 4.

**) From T to E is an interval of 5; from E to T is an interval of 4.

If the columns of Fig. 37 should be cut apart, and placed in some other order, then other columns might be placed between the one containing Q and its neighbor containing U, but these would be *full columns*, never fractional columns, so that the interval from Q to U would always be an exact number of full columns.

This is what happens in columnar transposition. If the digram *VI*, which we intend to consider, was actually present in the original encipherment block, then, in the cryptogram, its letters V and I are separated by an exact number of columns, long or short or mixed. Also, if the column containing V was taken off first, the distance from V to I may include the full number of long columns permitted by the key-length, but must fall one short of including all of the short columns; but if the I comes first, the opposite is true. Now, assuming that the only V's and I's in our cryptogram are those appearing at positions 5, 46, and 61, we find that if the first of the I's is considered, the distance from V to I is 41, while, if the other is the one considered, then this distance is 56. We will investigate, first, the interval 41.

If V and the first I stood in sequence in the encipherment block, either as *VI* or as *IV*, then the interval 41 represents a certain number of complete columns, and if the digram was *VI* (since the *V*-column was evidently taken off first), this interval 41 must not include the full number of short columns, but may include the full number of long ones.

Consulting Fig. 36, we find that key-length 6 calls for columns having 12 and 13 letters, and it is impossible to divide an interval 41 into columns of such lengths. The key-length 7 calls for columns having 10 or 11 letters, of which only two columns may have the shorter length; an interval 41 can be divided into the right lengths, but only if three of the columns are short. Thus, if the first I is the correct one, the key-lengths 6 and 7 are totally impossible, as is also key-length 8. The key-length 9, however, calls for columns having 8 and 9 letters, of which six have the shorter length. An interval 41 can be divided to produce four short columns and one long column. Again, the key-length 11 calls for columns having 6 and 7 letters, of which two columns may be short; and an interval 41 will provide five long columns and one short column. These two key-lengths, then, 9 and 11, are possible, presuming that the first I is the one which actually followed V. When the other I, interval 56, is investigated in the same way, it is found that the only key-lengths possible are 8 and 11.

So that if the digram *VI* is present at all, the key-length must be 8, 9, 11, or something longer. Since the key-length 11 is possible in both cases, this is the one which tempts; when it fails, the remaining two can be tried. The student may decide for himself whether a trigram *IVI* is possible, considering the distance apart of the two I's. It will be readily understood how this method, in combination with the one first explained, could be used, say, in a cryptogram where the suspected word is CIPHER, with the low-frequency letter P occurring only once.

Totally aside from analysis, there are many ways in which the key-length can become known, or suspected. If the correspondence is a military one, it may have been learned by espionage, perhaps through careless talk on the part of an enlisted man; or, because of careless habits on the part of the authority providing the keys, in having confined himself always to certain lengths. Knowing the key-length is two-thirds of the battle. It enables us, as in our former case, to mark off the cryptogram into its approximate column-lengths, making it easier to know the approximate whereabouts of any several letters supposed to form a sequence. It even enables us to prepare a block, which, cut apart to form paper strips, will effect a mechanical solution almost as easily as in the case of the completed unit. Such a block, for our foregoing cryptogram (Fig. 30), can be studied in Fig. 38, and is explained as follows: An 8-unit key, used on a 75-letter text, calls definitely for three 10-letter columns and five 9-letter columns, and these columns have become eight segments in the cryptogram. If all three of the long columns were taken off first, then the arrangement shown at (a) has every letter in its proper column. And if all three of these were taken off last, then the arrangement shown at (b) has every letter in its proper column. With blocks shown for the two extreme cases, it can be seen that the block at (c) is a combination-block, in which one of

Figure 38

Preparation of Strips for a Known Key-length

(a) **Long Columns at Left**

```
E  R  I  T  B  S  G  C
N  E  S  A  H  T  E  S
T  M  G  E  B  D  O  U
H  U  A  I  N  A  I  T
V  S  U  D  S  N  C  L
C  O  A  E  E  V  R  T
C  E  M  X  I  N  L  E
O  U  A  T  R  X  B  S
T  Y  H  N  A  G  X  R
X  E  Y
```

(b) **Long Columns at Right**

```
E  X  Y  A  X  I  X  X
N  R  E  H  T  R  G  C
T  E  I  Y  N  A  G  S
H  M  S  T  B  S  E  U
V  U  G  A  H  T  O  T
C  S  A  E  B  D  I  L
C  O  U  I  N  A  C  T
O  E  A  D  S  N  R  E
T  U  M  E  E  V  L  S
            N  B  R
```

(c) **Combination Block**

```
1  2  3  4  5  6  7  8
         a  x  i
      y  h  t  r  x
   x  e  y  n  a  g  x
E  R  I  T  B  S  G  C
N  E  S  A  H  T  E  S
T  M  G  E  B  D  O  U
H  U  A  I  N  A  I  T
V  S  U  D  S  N  C  L
C  O  A  E  E  V  R  T
C  E  M  X  I  N  L  E
O  U  A  T  R  X  B  S
T  Y  H  N  A  G  X  R
X  E  Y
```

(d) **Matching Strips**

the two extremes has been superimposed upon the other, so that every column in block (c) shows every letter which it could possibly have contained. By concealing the letters of the " cap," we have a duplicate of block (a); and by changing the alignment, so as to bring all of the topmost letters into the same row, we have block (b), with a " cap " attached at the bottom.

Comparing block (c) with the two above it: If the first column of (a) was actually a short one, then its last letter, X, belongs at the top of the second column. The making of this transfer would cause the second column to have eleven letters, so that it would become necessary also to transfer the last letter of the second column to the top of the third; this third column would then have too many letters, and its last letter would have to be transferred to the top of the fourth, which at present has only nine and may have another. But if the second column was also short, then there are two of its letters which belong at the top of column 3. And if this column, too, was a short one, it has three transferable letters at the bottom.

To prepare such a block, first write the cryptogram as at (a), and mark off its transferable (uncertain) letters by the following rule: One for the first column, two for the second, and so on, until the number is *equal to the number of long columns*, which is the maximum number possible. But if the final row is more than half filled, *the maximum will not be reached*, and a check may be made by marking off letters from right to left: zero for the last column, one for the next-to-last, two for the third-to-last, and so backward to the number which equals the number of long columns. Having marked off the transferable letters, form the " bonnet " by copying these, in each case, at the top of the following column, preferably making some clear distinction to show the duplication. For this latter purpose, many solvers use red ink. In this kind of work, as we saw in a previous case, the spacing must be accurate both laterally and vertically, since many of the letters belonging to the same sequence are not found on the same row. A few of the strips cut from block (c) have been matched at (d), where the beginning was made from the common suffix -*ABLE*. The duplicated letters *A H Y* have shown up plainly, partly by the style in which the letters are written, and partly, too, by the fact of consecutive column-numbers, 3 and 4. This same thing is true of the letters *X T N*, column-numbers 4 and 5. These numbers, it must not be forgotten, are also the serial numbers of the cryptogram segments, and thus are the key-numbers. With the eight strips correctly matched, and any misplaced columns transferred to their own side of the block, the strip-numbers as they stand across the top will reproduce the numerical key.

The matching of strips is generally a purely mechanical process, in which impossibilities are not considered. However, having before us a block (a) or (b), it is possible to apply the principle used with our former digram *VI*, and find out in advance whether certain letters found on two strips can possibly have stood in sequence. Nor is the cutting apart of the strips really necessary; it is merely a convenient method for dispensing with mental effort.

Now suppose we consider this same cryptogram on the theory that its key-length cannot be determined, or restricted to certain possibilities. Our first step is to select, somewhere in the cryptogram, a segment which is to be set up vertically on a sheet of paper to act as a *trial column*. If we select it from the body of the cryptogram, we shall have to make it a rather long segment, since we are uncertain as to whether it represents one column or parts of two. We should do this, however, if the body of the cryptogram shows *Q*, or any other letter or series of letters likely to be vulnerable. Otherwise, we know definitely that one of the columns begins with the first letter of the cryptogram, and that another column ends with the final letter of the cryptogram, and one or the other of these two segments is usually chosen, preferably the one containing the largest number of vulnerable letters. If we have a probable word, and find that its letter *P*, or *M*, or *G*, is the only one in the cryptogram, we select the segment which contains this *P*, or *M*, or *G*.

Wherever the trial segment is taken, there is always the question as to how many letters ought to be included. In Fig. 39, the decryptor has decided to take the beginning segment of the cryptogram, and has started with 15 letters. He has written beside it another 15-letter segment, chosen because of *NG, HO, VI*, and is attempting to tell, by the

Figure 39

Figure 39

Tests, in Attempting to Judge Column-Length

E G	20	(15)
N G	75	(83)
T E	94	(74)
H O	46	(42)
V I	19	(14)
C C	12	(6)
C R	7	(12)
O L	17	(36)
T B	14	(8)
X X	-	(-)
R C	14	(7)
E S	145	(115)
M U	13	(7)
U T	45	(35)
S L	6	(9)

(First column of figures is taken from Meaker's chart; the second is from Ohaver's).

appearance of his digrams, and their frequencies as taken from two different digram charts, just about how far his digrams are uniformly good. If the nulls in use are actually *XX*, he knows immediately that this is the end of his two columns; otherwise, his digrams are acceptable throughout. If he sets down beside each digram its frequency as taken from Meaker's chart, he might decide that his digrams are

Figure 40

(The numbers assigned to these set-ups merely indicate the order in which the second segments were taken).

1		8		9		10		11			2		3	
E U	7	E Y	17	E B	11	E X	17	E G	20		E S		E O*	
N S	51	N T	110	N N	9	N G	75	N G	75		N O		N E	
T O	111	T A	56	T S	32	T G	1	T E	94		T E		T U	
*H E	251	*H E	251	*H E	251	*H E	251	*H O	46		H U		H Y*	
V U	-	V I	19	V I	19	V O	6	V I	19		V Y*		V E	
C Y	-	C D	-	C R	7	C I	15	C C	12		C E		C I	
C E	55	C E	55	C A	44	C C	12	C R	7		C I		C S*	
O I	13	O X	-	O S	37	O R	113	O L	17		O S		O G	
	488		508		410		490		290					

(1)		(8)		(9)		(10)		(11)	
	488		508		410		490		290
H E	251	H E	251	H E	251	H E	251	H O	46
	237		257		159		239		244

Ranked in the order: 8, 11, 10, 1, 9

. . . .

Same Test, Using Mr. Ohaver's Digram Frequencies:

1		8		9		10		11	
E U	6	E Y	24	E B	24	E X	14	E G	15
N S	47	N T	97	N N	8	N G	83	N G	83
T O	92	T A	64	T S	27	T G	-	T E	74
*H E	305	*H E	305	*H E	305	*H E	305	*H O	42
V U	-	V I	14	V I	14	V O	9	V I	14
C Y	1	C D	-	C R	12	C I	19	C C	6
C E	46	C E	46	C A	36	C C	6	C R	12
O I	15	O X	1	O S	35	O R	99	O L	36
	512		551		461		535		282

(1)		(8)		(9)		(10)		(11)	
	512		551		461		535		282
H E	305	H E	305	H E	305	H E	305	H O	42
	207		246		156		230		240

Ranked in the order: 8, 11, 10, 1, 9 (as before).

2	3
E S	E O*
N O	N E
T E	T U
H U	H Y*
V Y*	V E
C E	C I
C I	C S*
O S	O G

4	5
E E	E I
N U	N S
T Y	T G*
H E	H A
V I	V U*
C S*	C A
C G*	C M*
O A	O A

6	7
E S	E H*
N G	N Y
T A	T T
H U	H A
V A	V E
C M*	C I
C A	C D*
O H*	O E*

(Set-up No. 2 would have been tested.)

good as far as *UT*, depending somewhat on the letters represented in our *XX*. Using Ohaver's frequencies, he would feel sure that his digrams are good as far as *OL*. In many cases the frequencies shown for the lower digrams will grow so erratic as to be plainly unlikely; and in other cases, more difficult than the present one, a check on the probable column-length can be had by preparing a similar set-up for the end-segment of the cryptogram, in which the lower digrams are excellent, while those extending upward may grow erratic. This decryptor is safe, however, in accepting as much or as little of the length as he likes; there will be a more definite line of demarcation when he attempts to write beside these a third column of 15 letters. The only cases which ever give trouble are those in which a short text has been enciphered with a long key. Key-lengths, generally speaking, hardly ever run outside of limits 5 to 15, that is, lengths which come from single words. Thus a tentative key-length 10, 11, 12, lying half-way between these extremes, is always safe to try. The key-length 10, applied to 75 letters, gives columns of 7 or 8, and, in the discussion which follows, the tentative column-length was fixed at 8 letters.

Usually these trials are made by setting up the trial column (in pencil) several times in succession, so that several of the possible combinations can be seen side by side, in order to determine which is best. Sometimes this can be decided by simple observation. Otherwise, the combinations can be subjected to a digram test. This is made by setting down beside each digram, as formed by each pair

Figure 41

1		2		3		4	
Y E	12	D E	39	R E	148	E E	39
E N	120	E N	120	A N	172	O N	145
I T	88	X T	1	S T	121	I T	88
S H	30	T H	315	T H	315	C H	46
G V	-	N V	4	D V	4	R V	5
A C	39	B C	-	A C	39	L C	8
U C	17	H C	2	N C	31	B C	-
A O	2	B O	11	V O	6	X O	1
	308		492		836		332

• • • • •

Same Test, Using Mr. Ohaver's Digram-Frequencies:

1		2		3		4	
Y E	8	D E	64	R E	139	E E	57
E N	101	E N	101	A N	168	O N	162
I T	90	X T	4	S T	119	I T	90
S H	40	T H	377	T H	377	C H	53
G V	1	N V	1	D V	1	R V	6
A C	35	B C	-	A C	35	L C	1
U C	11	H C	-	N C	34	B C	-
A O	2	B O	13	V O	9	X O	1
	288		560		882		370

of columns, its frequency as taken from a digram chart. These figures are then added in each of the set-ups, and the supposition is that the combination furnishing the highest frequency-total will be the correct one, provided this high total has been produced by all of its digrams collectively, and not by some one or two individual digrams. With short columns, such tests are never conclusive, but with as many as ten or twelve digrams they are nearly always dependable, and even with only five or six digrams they will often select a correct combination.

It was decided here to choose as the trial column the first eight letters of the cryptogram: *E N T H V C C O*. This column is filled with consonants, indicating that those which follow or precede it might contain a number of vowels; and of the six consonants present, practically every one could be called a " vulnerable " letter, or, as we say in the Association, a " clue-letter." If we wish, for instance, to choose a column which will fit well on the right-hand side of this trial column, we can search the rest of the cryptogram for two consecutive vowels to 'follow, respectively, *H* and *V*, and these two vowels we should expect to find followed, either immediately or at interval 2 by some letter (usually a high-frequency one) which will follow at least one of the *C*'s. This kind of pattern, unfortunately, was found eleven times. In practice, we should probably abandon it rather than copy down

Figure 42

Trigram Observation

1	2	3(*)	4	5
REU	REY	REB	REX	REG
ANS	ANT	ANN	ANG	ANG
STO	STA	STS	STG	STE
THE	THE	THE	THE	THO
DVU	DVI	DVI	DVO	DVI
ACY	ACD*	ACR	ACI	ACC
NCE	NCE	NCA	NCC*	NCR
VOI	VOX*	VOS	VOR	VOL

(*) Acceptance of combination 3 would
entail shortening columns.

and test eleven combinations; here, however, the eleven set-ups can all be seen in Fig. 40, accompanied by serial numbers to show the order in which their second columns were taken from the cryptogram. Some of these have not been tested. Of the five retained, particular attention is called to the fact that the one having the very lowest total is actually the correct one, as may be seen by turning back to the encipherment block. But when a single row of corresponding digrams (*HE* in the first four set-ups and *HO* in No. 11), has been subtracted throughout, it is seen that No. 11 moves upward toward its proper rank, having now the second highest total. In practice, it might even be selected in preference to No. 8, which grows erratic after its fifth digram (frequencies of 0, 55, 0). But the column-length 5, in practice, is not unlikely, so that a test made on the right-hand side of our trial column has not been at all conclusive.

Postponing the decision, then, let us take a fresh sheet of paper and make some tests for columns which can be fitted on the left-hand side of our trial column. Here, we find that the best " clue-letters " are *N* and *H*, standing at interval 2. To precede *N*, we should like to find one of the vowels of which it is so fond, and to precede *H*, we hope to find either *T* or one of the letters *S, C, W*. That is, we hope to find a pattern in the rest of the cryptogram in which some vowel, other than *Y*, is followed at interval 2 by one of the letters *T,S,C,W*. This time we find only four segments, and when the test is made for these, as shown in Fig. 41, the resulting totals point decisively to the correct combination, which is No. 3. Notice, in both of these tests, that results are identical whether the frequency-figures are those counted by Meaker or those counted by Ohaver: In the test of Fig. 40, the five combinations (using either chart) are ranked in the order 8, 11, 10, 1, 9, while the test of Fig. 41 has ranked its four combinations in the order 3, 2, 4, 1. Selecting, then, combination No. 3 of Fig. 41, let us return to the doubtful tests of Fig. 40 and attempt to effect a combination between our No. 3 and some one of the five previously considered worth retaining. Thus we can make an observation of trigrams, as shown in Fig. 42.

Figure 43

/E N T H V   C C O/T X   R E M U S   O E U Y E   I S G A Y   A M A H Y

T A E I D   E X T N B   H B N S E   I/R A S T   D A N V/N   X/G G E O

I C R L/B   X C S U T   L T E S R

Here, we must be guided by our judgment, since trigram tests, even with figures available, would never be feasible on columns of this length. The acceptance of No. 3, evidently, would mean the cutting of our column-length to 5 letters, which, as we have said, is not at all unlikely in an actual case. The two highest tests from Fig. 40, however, are those included in Nos. 2 and 5. With reference to No. 2, where the right-hand digrams have the higher total, it is not impossible that the trigrams *ACD* and *VOX* were actually in use, or that the set-up should be

Figure 44

```
(a)            (b)             (c)              (d)
A R E G        A R E G R       A R E G R E      X A R E G R E T
H A N G        H A N G E       H A N G E I      C H A N G E I N
Y S T E        Y S T E M       Y S T E M S      S Y S T E M S B
T T H O        T T H O U       T T H O U G      U T T H O U G H
A D V I        A D V I S       A D V I S A      T A D V I S A B
E A C C        E A C C O       E A C C O U      L E A C C O U N
I N C R        I N C R E       I N C R E A      T I N C R   A S
D V O L        D V O L U       D V O L U M      E D V O L U M E
                                                ...S
                                                ...R
                               (e)
```

```
E N T H V   C C O/T X   /R E M U S   O E U/Y/E   I S G A U   A M/A H Y

T A E I D/   E X/T N B   H B N S E/   I/R A S T   D A N V/N   X/G G E O

I C R L/B   X C S U T   L T E S R
```

```
(f)                  (g)                  (h)
X A R E G R E T      X * R E G R E T      * * R E G R E T    C H
C H A N G E I N      C H A N G E I N      C H A N G E I N    S Y
S Y S T E M S B      S Y S T E M S B      S Y S T E M S B    U T
U T T H O U G H      U T T H O U G H      U T T H O U G H    T A
T A D V I S A B      T A D V I S A B      T A D V I S A B    L E
L E A C C O U N      L E A C C O U N      L E A C C O U N    T I
T I N C R E A S      T I N C R E A S      T I N C R E A S    E D
E D V O L U M E      E D V O L U M E      E D V O L U M E    S E
S E N T B Y * I      S E N T B Y A I      S E N T B Y A I    R X
R X X X             R X X X *             R X X X X
                                         6 1 7 2 3 5   8 4
                                         .....(Key).......
```

cut, above the trigram *ACD;* but No. 5 is the one which *carries word-suggestions all the way to the end.*

With the adding of other columns, which can be done on either side of the set-up, further digram tests can be made (taken only on the two extreme right-hand or left-hand columns), but in most cases no further tests are needed. Considering, for instance, that No. 5 is the combination tentatively accepted, we need a segment from the cryptogram containing the *U* which ought (apparently) to follow *THO*, then the *S* or *C* which ought (apparently) to follow *DVI;* that is, we want to find a sequence *US* or *UC* in the rest of the cryptogram; and this (apparently) should be followed by two vowels in succession, to fit after the sequences *ACC* and *NCR.* In other words, we know exactly what kinds of letters ought to make up the column which can be added on the right side of combination 5, and even the specific letters. Or, if it is the left side on which we have chosen to fit the new column, we need a segment containing the *A* of the apparent *ADVI*, followed at interval 2 by the vowel, probably *I*, which ought to precede a trigram *NCR*.

In Fig. 43, the three segments of set-up No. 5 have been circled out of the cryptogram (to prevent further use of their letters), and the segment chosen to fit on the left side of set-up No. 5 has been underscored, ready to be circled out in case it is found to fit. It is now possible to see the suggested nine-letter words, ADVISABLE and INCREASED, the guessing of which would permit us to apply the easy method first described.

With or without these guesses, the rest of the solution, as outlined in Fig. 44, is now plain sailing. At (a), the underscored segment of Fig. 43 is in place. At (b), the column containing the desired *US* and following vowels has been set up on the right, where we seem to need the *E* or *A* of ADVISE or ADVISABLE, followed immediately by the *U* or *R* of ACCOUNT or ACCORD. At (c), we have found the segment, and at (d) (usually earlier), we are introduced to the actual lengths of our columns.

Figure 45

The OHAVER CV-VC Test:

RATEB	OWSTT	EETOP	UUIMC	YUACG
AIOIA	OBSTB	BAKAR	YYEDT	UWYNT
NNFKG	FJSOT	WYQAR	IROIH.

TT		TO	cv	TM		TE	cv
WO	cv	WP		WC		WD	
YP	vc	YU		YY		YT	vc
(QU)		(QU)		(QU)		(QU)	
AU		AI		AA		AW	vc
RI	cv	RM		RO	cv	RY	cv
IM	vc	IC	vc	IG	vc	IN	vc
4		2		2		5	

The following is the original cryptogram used by Mr. Ohaver for demonstration:

TVYIE	TRROR	EHNIA	EUDSR	IEONI
ORENA	EEORP	TEALO	LTSUH	LHQNO
UCADD	CSAAE	TDVFU	GNNYC	YI.

(Reprinted from Detective Fiction Weekly of October 8, 1927, with permission of The Frank A. Munsey Company).

This latter can be seen by looking at the cryptogram (e), where all segments, as soon as selected, have been circled out. In finding a column which would complete the very evident word SYSTEM and, at the same time, furnish a letter suitable to precede *HA*, we find that this is the end-segment of the cryptogram, and would leave only two letters — far fewer than the number needed for furnishing another column.

At (f), we have extended the rest of the columns by two (and one) letters, except that there is a gap in sequence on the next-to-last line. At (g), we have transferred the letter which will fill this gap, leaving a misplaced *X* at the top; and, at (h), we have placed this *X* where it belongs and are now ready to transfer the two misplaced columns and recover the key. This key, as before, is found by numbering the segments of the cryptogram, and assigning these key-numbers to the correct columns in the adjusted block. It is usually possible to go further, and learn the long words on which such keys might have been based.

Concerning digram-tests, Ohaver suggests another which is more quickly made than the frequency test, and which the writer, so far, has found fully as reliable. Using " C " for " consonant " and " V " for " vowel," he speaks of this as his VC-CV or " mixed " test. A digram like *HA* is a *cv* digram, one like *AT* is a *vc* digram, and others are *vv* and *cc* digrams. His theory is this: Since almost two-thirds of the digrams used in the language will be of *mixed* formation, that is, either *vc* or *cv* digrams, it stands to reason that the set-up containing the largest number of " mixed " digrams would probably be the correct choice. The student may look it over in Fig. 45.

As to possible variations, a cipher with a new name is not necessarily a different cipher. Fig. 46 shows a cipher originated many years ago by the cryptologist

Figure 46

The Myszkowsky Cipher

(a)   **Keyword:** CURTAINS

```
C  U  R  T  A  I  N  S  C  U  R  T  A  I  N  S  C  U  R  T  A
4 19 11 16  1  7  9 14  5 20 12 17  2  8 10 15  6 21 13 18  3
R  E  G  R  E  T  C  H  A  N  G  E  I  N  S  Y  S  T  E  M  S
```

Cryptogram: E I S R A   S T N C S   G G E H Y   R E M E N   T.

(b)   **Keyword:** PARADISE

```
P  A  R  A  D  I  S  E  P  A  R  A  D  I  S  E  P  A  R  A  D
14  1 17  2  7 12 20 10 15  3 18  4  8 13 21 11 16  5 19  6  9
R  E  G  R  E  T  C  H  A  N  G  E  I  N  S  Y  S  T  E  M  S
```

Cryptogram: E R N E T   M E I S H   Y T N R A   S G G E C   S.

E. Myszkowsky, and advertised by its inventor as non-decryptable. The key-word here is repeated often enough to furnish one key-letter for each text-letter, nulls being added, when necessary, to prevent the complete unit which would result if key-word and text were allowed to end at the same point. This long series of key-letters is then treated as a single word, and is converted to a numerical key in the usual way, all *A*'s receiving the first numbers, all *B*'s the next numbers, and so on. The message of the figure is very short: REGRET CHANGE IN SYSTEMS. Try enciphering this in the ordinary columnar transposition, using first the key-word CURTAIN, which contains no repeated letters, and afterward the key-word PARADISE, which has a repeated letter *A*. In the second case, what happens to the two columns belonging to the *A*-numbers? Suspecting a Myszkowsky encipherment, how could you go about unscrambling the two? Suppose there were three?

Fig. 47 plays another variation on the columnar theme. This cipher, originated by a member of the *American Cryptogram Association,* follows the rules of columnar transposition in all respects except that pairs alternate throughout with single letters (The text is: CHIEF WANTS YOU TO INTERVIEW SMITH). Can you pick out at a glance the really vulnerable feature of this cipher, and formulate a special method for its solution?

Figure 47

The "AMSCO" Cipher (A.M.Scott)

```
R    A    C    K    E    T
5    1    2    4    3    6

CH   I    EF   W    AN   T
S    YO   U    TO   I    NT
ER   V    IE   W    SM   I
T    HX
```

Order for taking off:

I YO V HX / EF U IE /...

Cryptogram: I Y O V H   X E F U I.....

29. By NEMO. (A military message).

A O T O I   N E H T C   T O T L I   I A W G E   L P R V L   R I I R I   U A D E O
W L R R R   L C M E O   N P E P T   A V T S O   H O E E N   L S N P S   S B Y T S
L R O P D   R G E T S   S T S Y A   W N E.

30. By PICCOLA. (Hostilities?)

T A M L R   I T E D W   E E D H H   N P W O S   W R S H C   N O I E D   O H I L T
C S T N I   W A A R C   D H H D A   I E T P T   R L R O W   A S E E T   A K F P W
G M A T X   E K A H D   P I L E O   F H W G I   N H A K S   F S S A A   A H E H N
D H H E H.

31. By AMSCO. (The "AMSCO" Cipher).

N W L E L   N T L C S   L W D L Y   L N S O O   I D F I N   R U C H A   L N D C B
S I D E A   I T E T I   K S T B E   E O U T J   A T I L I   A C O R E   A Y E E G   A O.

32. By PICCOLA. (Can you recover this nice long keyword from the numbers?)

Y K I E T   N T H H E   X I A E N   U B A K E   E W S C S   I H T N L   N E N E A
K I E O B   O L I E E   A M C I F   T I N A H   S K A N I   D L G S O   E E I T T
S W H L L   E U A D H   F S H A B   E O E N O   A N O S C   P H S N O   D H T X R
N H R E A.

33. By PICCOLA. (An easy Myszkowski. Probable words: SOLVE, CIPHER, COLUMN).

V I N S C   F E A E O   O H S E F   H L H E U   N S T N C   L T S L C   I A E S H
R H S I R   E R M T S   E T E P D   T O I N M   R T T H T   T L R U B   E.

34. By PICCOLA. (Nothing like a bit of "philosophy" - oyeah?)

E L O S W   E A H X P   N N T R N   H L W I E   G E I G E   A E Q A G   L E A R R
Q L O N K   E S Q L O   R N X A R   S P X S E   E A E I P   A G L R E   P R Y M T
H N K S E   I X X A Y.

35. By PICCOLA. (Not so easy; still, it's just another columnar).

H R O T E   T E T E H   I W E O T   T D A O D   K G D T C   E R A I W   O S Y N H
Y R H T W.

CHAPTER VII

GENERAL METHODS — MULTIPLE ANAGRAMMING, ETC.

In the past few chapters, we have been looking at all of the general methods for decryptment of transpositions. We have seen the use of *factoring*, which determines, for the geometric cipher, what key-lengths are possible, and, for the irregular one, what key-lengths are not. *Vowel-distribution* has enabled us, in some cases, to determine the length of major units, or has assisted in the restoration of minor units to their original intact groups. *Anagramming* has been seen throughout: the matching of letters and columns with or without the application of language statistics.

So far, we have been materially assisted by advance knowledge as to what the cipher is. Where the type is unknown, and cannot be promptly identified, and assuming, of course, that the decryptor has no probable words, transpositions, taken as a whole, present confusing problems in the very multiplicity of their possibilities. General Givierge, in his *Cours de cryptographie*, remarks of this case that novices, as a rule, display a tendency to recoil from the cryptogram as if uncertain "which end to pick it up by." He adds that the best advice he can give is to pick it up *somewhere* and do *something*, rather than be satisfied to sit all day long and admire the cryptogram!

As to how a type may sometimes be identified, the difference between the regular and irregular types is ordinarily suggested by the number of letters contained in the cryptograms. Irregular types, intended for practical purposes, are nearly always seen in complete five-letter groups, where the geometric cipher usually results in a broken group at the end of its cryptogram. This, of course, is never mandatory upon the encipherer; it merely happens because the only persons making use of such ciphers are those who do not realize the advisability of doing otherwise.

Among the irregular types, a columnar formation can usually be spotted by the "bunching" of vowels at intervals throughout the cryptogram. Then, too, we are still to see those cases in which the exact type of the cipher may not become apparent until after solution is well started.

It is usually well, when a new system is encountered, to analyze it and find out what the transposition finally does to the letters. This can be done by preparing actual cryptograms in which the plaintext letters are serially numbered; or, if the question of vowel-distribution is not involved, by using the serial numbers without the letters, as suggested in a previous chapter. Many ciphers, of course, will not require even this amount of analysis, even though their type, accurately speaking, is irregular. For example, the one shown as Fig. 48, whether or not its rectangle is to be completed, is merely another *route*, so that once having seen it, we might try to follow this route again. But the student who cares to give this cipher his careful consideration must notice that its longer cryptograms would be full of reversed plaintext segments; that these would grow longer and longer with a constant rate of increase, and would always alternate with incoherent segments which, in their turn, would grow shorter and shorter; also that these incoherent segments, if set up as columns, would show plaintext.

The complete-unit cipher, generally speaking, can hardly present any real complexities. Consider, for instance, the following variation on a Nihilist encipherment, which was proposed by Geo. C. Lamb, the author of Chapter *X*: The key-length, to begin with, must be divisible by 3, but this is not used for writing-in.

The plaintext is written into its block, not in straight order, but following a *route* which begins in the upper left corner and goes forward for the first three letters, drops down to the second line and runs backward for the next three letters, drops to the third line to run forward for another three, and so on back and forth until the first three columns have been filled with trigrams written alternately forward and backward. It then moves over to the second three columns, beginning this time at the bottom and " snaking " upward to the top. For the third three columns it moves downward again, and so on until the square block has been filled. After this very devious primary transposition, the unit is taken off by means of the key, on the Nihilist principle of transposing both columns and rows with the same key.

We believe that the resulting cryptogram could prove puzzling to any cryptanalyst who has met the cipher for the first time. It is true that he has, in the original square, a large number of intact minor units, provided he can restore them.

Figure 48

Cipher Requiring Little Analysis

```
1   2   3   4   5...

T | H | W | S | E
S   I   O   E   .
D   L   U   E   .
B   O   T   M   .

←   .   .   .
```

Plaintext: THIS WOULD SEEM TO BE...

Cryptogram: T H W S E   S I O E....

But these units are very tiny, and the several of them which stand on any one row are not continuous among themselves; thus his vowel-distribution, while approximately normal, would probably not satisfy his expectations. If, however, having failed to find a more satisfactory block arrangement, he attempts to match columns (it being remembered that he is accustomed to reading in all sorts of directions in order to discover plaintext fragments), he will most certainly discover the trigrams and trace their route. Afterward, however, having met and analyzed the cipher, it would probably occur to him to look for exactly this complexity whenever he discovers that he is dealing with a square whose key-length is divisible by 3. We have mentioned before the assistance which may be had from the mere knowledge that a certain method exists.

Complete-unit ciphers, of course, may be troublesome, but their complexities are necessarily confined to one small area. An irregular cipher, on the other hand, usually involves the entire text, and its complexities may be real. In this class we occasionally find ciphers in which a single cryptogram is impossible to break; and we find others in which the eventual solution of one cryptogram will not instantaneously provide the key to another enciphered exactly like it. Such ciphers are well worth analyzing, for surely, somewhere, they have their weaknesses; and most certainly any two cryptograms enciphered exactly alike should be decipherable with the same key.

The cipher shown in Fig. 49 is of the double-columnar type known in this country as the " United States Army " double transposition, and has, in fact, been authorized for use, under suitable conditions, in the military service of more than one country. As may be seen from the figure, this cipher is, in all respects, the columnar transposition of the preceding chapter accomplished twice in succession on the same text (decipherment being, as usual, the reversal of the encipherment process).

The same rules apply here, as in the single columnar transposition, to the use of nulls, and to the advisability of avoiding the key-length which is a multiple of 5. It goes without saying that the block should never, under any circumstances, be allowed to work out as a square; this, in substance, would be the block unit of the Nihilist cipher. While the figure shows a primary cryptogram, taken off from the upper block, this, in practice, is never actually done. The columns of the upper block are always transferred direct to the rows of the lower one, and only the columns of the lower block are taken off as an actual cryptogram. In preparing this cryptogram, both blocks should be laid out at the same time; otherwise, there is danger that the operator may apply the first transposition and forget the second,

Figure 49

The "United States Army" Double Transposition

1st Encipherment

```
P  A  R  A  D  I  S  E
6  1  7  2  3  5  8  4

R  E  G  R  E  T  C  H     Primary Cryptogram
A  N  G  E  I  N  S  Y
S  T  E  M  S  X  X  X     (Not usually
X                          taken off)
```

2d Encipherment   ENT, REM, EIS, HYX,

```
P  A  R  A  D  I  S  E     TNX, RASX, GGE, CSX.
6  1  7  2  3  5  8  4

E  N  T  R  E  M  E  I
S  H  Y  X  T  N  X  R
A  S  X  G  G  E  C  S     Final Cryptogram:
X
```

N H S R X, G E T G I, R S M N E, E S A X T, Y X E X C.

thus sending out a simple columnar transposition which carries the key to all of his other cryptograms. This cipher, as may be seen, has its points. Yet it will have been noticed that its use for military purposes was not authorized without restrictions.

The special hazards of military correspondence have already been mentioned: the huge volume of interceptable cryptograms; the ever-present knowledge as to probable subject-matter and more-than-probable words, including numbers and dates; the personal habits of individual operators; above all, the fact that much of the enciphering is necessarily done by operators who are not, in the first place, trained for their work, and who, very often, must perform this work rapidly under conditions which are far from conducive to clear thinking. These, however, are chiefly the hazards of the firing line. Back of the lines, where hazards are reduced, there may be a chance that a cryptogram will not be intercepted at all. It becomes possible, for many purposes, to make use of a cipher in which a single cryptogram, though probably read in the end, will resist the decryptor for the necessary length of time, several hours or several days. The double columnar transposition can be very resistant, especially when the key is long and the columns short, and can be made even more complicated by carrying it through still a third block, perhaps using a different key with each new block.

Why, then, would it not be possible to use such a cipher for general communication? To this, there are two answers. For transposition cipher, taken as a whole, has two very serious drawbacks.

First, a transposition, in order to be a good one, must be a transposition of the whole text, and not a series of short individual transpositions. Thus, it becomes possible that an error, either in the encipherment or in the transmission, will not be confined to one small area, but will garble the whole message. In this way, we have not only the delay during which the legitimate decipherer is attempting to decrypt his own message, but, should he fail, the danger which lies in having it repeated. The decryptor who has been provided with both the correct and the incorrect version of a same cryptogram, is often able to figure out both the system and the key.

The other drawback is the danger which lies in the fact of so very many cryptograms. These, originating at many different sources, and all enciphered with the same key, will invariably include many of *identically the same length*. The nature of transposition cipher makes it inevitable that when any two texts of exactly the same length are enciphered with the same key, they will follow exactly the same route. The first letter in both messages will be transferred to exactly the same serial position in both cryptograms; the second letter in both will be transferred to another same serial position, and so on. If we are able to match correctly any two or three letters in one of the cryptograms, the two or three corresponding letters of the other cryptogram will also be correctly matched and will serve as a check. This being the case, any two or more cryptograms which are found to have the same length can be written one below another so as to place corresponding letters in the form of columns, and the problem is reduced to one of *geometric* columnar transposition.

With ciphers of the complete-unit type, the same thing can be done having several of the major units. We have, say, a single cryptogram accomplished with a Fleissner grille, and taken off by spirals. It may be that nulls were added in the final group, or at the beginning, or the final unit may have been left incomplete (by blanking out the unwanted portion of the final grille-block). In spite of these possibilities, the unit-length, known to be a square based on an even number, can be determined — *or assumed* — and the placing of the several units one below another provides columns made up of corresponding letters. It is even possible, at times, to apply this process, with suitable modifications, to several cryptograms whose length is only approximately the same. It has been done, for instance, with cryptograms from Sacco's indefinite grille, mentioned in Chapter *III* (General Sacco himself has explained the modifications). Such a process is ordinarily referred to as *multiple anagramming*, and we have already seen, in the case of the grille, how it may be modified so as to take full advantage of any inherent weaknesses when the cipher is known.

For discussion of the general case, suppose that we have intercepted a number of cryptograms (seen, by their letter-frequencies, to be transpositions), and that among these we have been able to find five in which the length is 25 letters. Since all of these have been coming from the same two stations, and within a comparatively short period of time, it seems reasonable to suppose that at least a portion of them have been enciphered with the same key, and, upon this assumption, we have written the five cryptograms one below another so as to set up the 25 columns shown in Fig. 50. We wish now to rearrange the 25 columns in such a way as to bring out plaintext on every row, or, failing that, on some of the rows. Once the set-up has been prepared, we may arrive at our goal by any road that suits our fancy. The majority of solvers will simply cut the columns apart and start matching strips at random; and this, probably, is a good enough method, especially when columns are so short. The writer, personally, prefers to leave the set-up intact, at any rate until solution is well started, trying out in pencil the various possible column-combinations, and circling out accepted columns from the set-up in the same way in which segments were circled out of cryptograms in the preceding chapter.

Figure 50

A series of five cryptograms prepared as columns:

1	2	3	4	5	6	7	8	9	10	11	12	13	14	15	16	17	18	19	20	21	22	23	24	25
C	D	D	N	C	A	A	R	T	H	L	O	I	K	A	O	E	R	T	L	S	N	A	N	O
D	A	I	T	E	L	O	C	W	A	I	U	X	D	N	T	Y	M	I	N	M	O	E	Y	O
B	T	O	A	T	T	U	T	O	C	F	L	I	Y	K	X	N	E	I	O	S	B	F	Y	Y
T	A	R	O	T	O	R	E	I	L	N	A	O	H	R	I	O	N	M	D	S	R	J	Y	S
W	E	K	L	N	C	H	T	S	T	S	I	E	G	E	I	H	O	O	P	D	T	N	A	O

For those who like method, we repeat a suggestion which has already been made: Many columns are usually present in such a set-up which contain *more than one* of the " clue-letters," as here, for instance, column 14 is practically made up of them. Such a column makes a good point of beginning, since we may search the set-up, not for some single letter, but for a pattern made up of several. For column 14, specifically, we might examine the top row of letters, pausing whenever we come to one of those letters frequently preceding K, and examining the rest of its column to find out what letter would have to precede H on the fourth row. We may fail with the first such column, but not with all.

Another particularly good method, and one which might work in the present case in spite of the very brief columns, is that of finding the particular column which contains the first letters of all the messages. Well over half of the initials used in the language will be found in the group $T A O S W C I H B D$, and with a frequency in somewhat that order. Any column made up entirely of these particular letters may be the one which begins the messages; and when this can be found, it pays to remember that a vowel is practically always present among the first three letters of each message.

As to finding the end-segment, it seems that this would be of little value except in those cases where final groups are not completed. However, the letter E has a great fondness for final positions, with terminals restricted largely to the group $E S T D N R Y O$; and it is also true that many encipherers make a habit of completing their final groups with such letters as X and Q.

Aside from the general case, each individual case carries clues of its own, and the finding of these must depend upon the detective ability (or experience) of the decryptor. Here, for instance, we find that the letter K has appeared three times in only 125 letters of text. This letter, normally, has one of the lowest frequencies in the language, and often is not found at all in 125 letters of text. Finding it three times, then, rather suggests the presence of some one word, a word so important to the subject-matter that it has been used in three different messages.

When considering the letter K, the first combination which comes to mind is a digram CK preceded by a vowel; and the letter C, also, is not a letter which we expect to find in confusing numbers. When an examination of the set-up shows that, for each of the K's, there is a C present on the same row, we are inclined to accept the hypothesis of a repeated word. In practice, we should pick out the three columns containing K, place beside each one a column which will set the digram CK together, and *build on all three combinations simultaneously* to the point at which the supposed word appears or is proved non-existent. Following out only one of these, let us consider column 14, where K is on the top row. On this row we find that C has appeared twice. Both of the C's are tried with K, as shown in Fig. 51; we find that both combinations will provide acceptable digrams, but there is little doubt as to which we would select. Combination 1-14 is merely acceptable, while

combination 5-14 provides a very accurate description of the column which would
fit best on its left. There should be a vowel on the top row, to precede *CK*, and
another on the bottom row, to precede *NG*. After that, perhaps another vowel
should be found on the fourth row, to precede *TH*, or perhaps, in this case, an *S*,
since the list of frequent trigrams includes a sequence *STH;* and, finally, something
suitable to precede *TY*, which appears to be a syllable, but may belong to two different words. The five columns which will meet these requirements have been
added in Fig. 52. In this figure, two combinations may be discarded,
because of trigrams *KTY* and *YTY*. The others appear acceptable.
At this point, however, the sequence *XTY* of combination 16-5-14
begins to draw attention because of its very few possibilities
(SIXTY, NEXT YEAR, etc.), making it likely that one of these
will quickly select or discard the entire combination. For building
SIXTY, row 3 of the set-up contains two *I*'s and one *S*. The two
I's, columns 13 and 19, when inspected visually, are found to bring
out, on the top row, the two sequences *I O C K* and *T O C K*, while the *S*, column
21, brings out, on the top row, another *S*, which would extend these, respectively,
to read *S I O C K* and *S T O C K*, the latter surely the more acceptable. The results of these additions, with subsequent development, can be examined in Fig. 53.
The completion of the word SIXTY has brought out also: STOCK, *MITED*,
SMITH, DOING. The presence of the word STOCK suggests extending the se-

Figure 51

1-14	5-14
C K	C K
D D	E D
B Y	T Y
T H	T H
W G	N G

Figure 52

12-5-14	13-5-14	15-5-14	16-5-14	25-5-14
O C K	I C K	A C K	O C K	O C K
U E D	X E D	N E D	T E D	O E D
L T Y	I T Y	K T Y	X T Y	Y T Y
A T H	O T H	R T H	I T H	S T H
I N G	E N G	E N G	I N G	O N G

quence *MITED* to read **LIMITED**, and the addition of two more columns on the
left brings out another *CK*, suggesting another appearance of the word STOCK.
The chances are that we have already been building on this other word STOCK,
but if not, we may build it now to the point shown in the figure, where the top row
suggests RAILROAD STOCK, the third row, FIFTY TO SIXTY, and the second
may or may not suggest MEXICO. Thus we are well on our way to solution, and

Figure 53

11	8	25	6	3	21	19	16	5	14
L	R	O	A	D	S	T	O	C	K
I	C	O	L	I	M	I	T	E	D
F	T	Y	T	O	S	I	X	T	Y
N	E	S	O	R	S	M	I	T	H
S	T	O	C	K	D	O	I	N	G

have not once had recourse to a long prepared list of probable words: *division, regi-
ment, battalion, attack, advance, report, forward, artillery, ammunition, communication, enemy, signal, retreat, troops,* and so on.

Naturally, there are times when the matching of the columns, for one reason or
another, proves troublesome. We are thrown off by errors, by the presence of nulls,
initials, abbreviations, etc., or by the encipherer's use of cover-up devices, such as
the writing of *YH* instead of *TH*. Or we find that the handling of many paper
strips, caused by message length, is awkward and confusing. But if, in the eyes
of the decryptor, there is any good reason for finding out the contents of such messages, he can always succeed, even with only two letters per column.

So far, nothing has been said about helping ourselves to the serial numbers of

the columns, which, during the rearrangement of letters, are automatically forming in a certain sequence across the top of the set-up. Regardless of the cipher, it
can do no harm to examine these, and find out what information, if any, they are
able to give. In some cases, they will provide us with both the system and its key,
enabling us to throw away the strips and start deciphering. Suppose, for instance,
we have correctly matched sixteen columns, and find their numbers in the following order: 31-10-24-37-17-3-32-11-25-38-18-4-33-12-26-39. A careful examination
shows that the numbers are running in sets of six. After the first six are passed, the
next six have repeated them with an increase of 1, and another six appear to be
forming up which will repeat them with an increase of 2. We may verify this by
finding the columns which have numbers 19-5-34-13, etc., and, if the set-up continues to show plaintext, we know that we are dealing with a simple columnar transposition. Notice that if the above series were marked into segments of six numbers
each, and the segments placed one below another, we should have *six columns,* each
one made up of numbers which are consecutive. Thus, we may sometimes learn
from a series of numbers: (1) the system, which is straight columnar transposition;
(2) the key-length, which is 6; and (3) the key itself, which, taking the six numbers
according to size, is 5-2-4-6-3-1, possibly with the wrong numbers coming first,
though it happens that in this case they do not. This is our old friend SCOTIA,
used on forty numbers, in case the student cares to verify it.

The trail of the columns is not so plain where a second transposition has done
something to the first. But it is still present; the most complex of ciphers has
method of some kind, provided we can find it. Consider, for instance, the series of
numbers, 11-8-25-6-3-21-19-16-5-14, which has been forming in Fig. 53. Examination here shows pairs of consecutive numbers, 11-8, 6-3, and 19-16, all having the
same numerical difference of 3; that is, the plan of our present encipherment, whatever it is, has, on three separate occasions, caused some plaintext digram to appear
in the cryptogram reversed, and with its letters three positions apart. Irrespective
of the type of transposition, this constant numerical difference of 3 might be found
again; perhaps we can set some two columns together correctly simply by *reproducing this numerical difference* in the two column-numbers. A glance ahead at the
next figure will show that we actually could, by setting together columns 12-9 or
columns 20-17. Where we cannot discover a repeated numerical difference, perhaps
we can discover a progressing difference, or some other signs of regularity.

Now, returning to the particular case, let us pass on to Fig. 54, in which the
matching of the 25 columns has finally been completed, and make a careful comparison between the two numerical series 12-9-10-15 and 20-17-18-23. What can
these represent but the *fragments of four columns,* belonging to a *first encipherment
block,* which have been laid down along the *rows* of a *second encipherment block,*
and taken out in slices? And since the lineal distance apart of any pair of numbers, as 12 and 20, is seen from the figure to be six positions, it would be possible, by
writing the series of numbers in lines of six numbers each, to place each pair of
corresponding numbers in a same column. The trail, usually, is not so wide, but
there is little doubt here that we have been dealing with a case of double columnar
transposition in which the key-length of the original block was 6. We shall come
back to this in a moment.

Suppose, now, we give our attention to the various series of numbers which appear in Fig. 54, and make sure that we understand what they are. The numbers running across the tops of the columns were, originally, the *serial numbers of cryptogram letters* (or columns). When we restored these letters to their plaintext order,
we disarranged their serial numbers, causing these to come out in the order 1-7-24-
22-12-9, etc. This series, then, is made up of *cryptogram serial numbers.* But it is
also a *key,* since it shows us exactly the order in which we might *take off a plaintext*

in order to form a cryptogram. It is a key of the Myszkowsky type, according to which every letter in the text has its individual key-number, as we saw in Fig. 46 (imagine that encipherment accomplished twice in succession). We do not desire, however, to take off plaintext. And, to use this same key on a cryptogram, we should have to use it in the *writing-in* manner; that is, first lay out the series of key-numbers, and then, taking the cryptogram letters in their 1-2-3 order, place them, one by one, below their key-numbers. But once the plaintext has been restored, the *plaintext letters* (or columns) *may also have serial numbers,* and these new serial numbers, in the figure, have been added at the bottoms of the columns. Should we now restore these columns to the order in which we found them, that is, to their cryptogram order, each column taking with it its new serial number, we should find, running across the bottom of the set-up, another mixed series of num-

Figure 54

The Columns of Figure 50, After Solution by Multiple Anagramming:

```
1  7 24 22 12  9 10 15  4  2 20 17 18 23 13 11  8 25  6  3 21 19 16  5 14

C  A  N  N  O  T  H  A  N  D  L  E  R  A  I  L  R  O  A  D  S  T  O  C  K
D  O  Y  O  U  W  A  N  T  A  N  Y  M  E  X  I  C  O  L  I  M  I  T  E  D
B  U  Y  B  L  O  C  K  A  T  O  N  E  F  I  F  T  Y  T  O  S  I  X  T  Y
T  R  Y  R  A  I  L  R  O  A  D  O  N  J  O  N  E  S  O  R  S  M  I  T  H
W  H  A  T  I  S  T  E  L  E  P  H  O  N  E  S  T  O  C  K  D  O  I  N  G

1  2  3  4  5  6  7  8  9 10 11 12 13 14 15 16 17 18 19 20 21 22 23 24 25
```

(Plaintext serial numbers, added at bottoms of columns)

(Appearance of the plaintext serial numbers, if the above columns should be restored to their cryptogram order)

```
1 10 20  9 24 19  2 17  6  7 16  5 15 25  8 23 12 13 22 11 21  4 14  3 18
```

bers in the order 1-10-20-9-24, etc., which is a different order from that of the cryptogram numbers, and this new series is made up of *plaintext serial numbers.* This is the other key, having the same relationship to the first as that explained in connection with the short Nihilist key. Applied to the plaintext, it would have to be used in the *writing-in* manner; used on the cryptogram, it serves for *taking-off.* Thus we are able to recover from our reconstructed plaintext two long keys, either one of which will serve to decipher additional cryptograms, *but only on condition that these new cryptograms contain exactly 25 letters.*

If, then, we hope to decipher cryptograms of other lengths, which originally were enciphered with exactly the same key as our present five, it is still necessary that we take one or the other of these long Myszkowsky-type keys and reduce it to the short columnar form. The theory on which this is done should not be at all difficult to understand if it be kept in mind that both of our long keys are actually the serial numbers of letters, and that each individual serial number accompanied its letter throughout the encipherment process. This will explain any references which are made to FIRST and SECOND encipherment blocks, with their respective columns and rows. Whichever of the long keys we decide to reduce, our first objective, always, is that of determining the *length* of the shorter key; after that we restore its *order.*

The first process, summed up in Fig. 55, was originally published, so far as the writer knows, by M. E. Ohaver, and makes use of the cryptogram numbers which were the first series obtained. The discovery of the shorter key-length is made by searching the set-up for some numerical difference (between any two numbers whatever) which is repeated by corresponding pairs of numbers at some regular interval. For convenience in making the search, Qhaver suggests that the mixed cryptogram numbers be written, with uniform spacing, on two strips of paper, in one case repeated. One strip can then be moved along beside the other so as to place pairs of numbers in actual contact. It is immaterial what numerical difference is used; the

Figure 55

Finding the Original Short Key from the CRYPTOGRAM Serial Numbers - M.E.OHAVER

Finding the key-length:

```
1  7 24 22 12   9 10 15   4   2 20 17 18 23 13 11   8 25   6   3 21 19 16   5 14.
1  7 24 22 12   9 10 15   4   2 20 17 18 23 13 11   8 25   6   3 21 19 16   5 14  1  7
         x  .  .  .  .  .  x                                         (Repeat series)
```

A difference of 1 occurs again at the interval 6. The two

series 9-17 and 10-18 are fragments of columns from the **first**

encipherment block. The key-length necessary for placing

either pair in a same column is 6.

Replacing cryptogram numbers in first encipherment block:

```
(As PLAINTEXT)...  1   7  24  22  12   9
                  10  15   4   2  20  17
                  18  23  13  11   8  25
                   6   3  21  19  16   5
                  14
```

COLUMNS of the FIRST encipherment block are converted to ROWS of the SECOND:

```
(a)                          (b)                     (c)
   1 10 18  6 14                 1 10 18  6 14 22       1 - 3 - 5 - 2 - 4 - 6
  22  2 11 19/ 7 15 23   3       2 11 19  7 15 23       ——————————————————
     12 20  8 16                 3 12 20  8 16 24       1   10          6
  24  4 13 21/ 9 17 25   5       4 13 21  9 17 25       2    .          7
                                 5                      3               8
                                                        4               9
                                                        5
At (a) the columns of the first block are      (C  O  S  M  O  S)
arranged so as to make the cryptogram numbers  At (c) the order is
run consecutively in each of the new columns.  shown in which the columns
At (b) this block has been adjusted, so as     of (b) would be taken off.
to form six columns.                           This order is the KEY.
```

difference 1 pointed out in the figure seemed a little more visible than others. This difference 1 has been noted between the numbers 9 and 10, and the next difference 1 has been found *six positions away* between the numbers 17 and 18, but is not found again between the numbers 25 and 6, which stand at the next interval of six positions. This may be a clue, but it is not what we had hoped to find. The clue is strengthened, however, by the observation that a difference of 5 occurs just at the right of the original difference 1, and is also repeated at the lineal interval 6.

To find a good clear example, using the strips as they stand, let us go back toward the left, and look for a difference 2. We find it first between the numbers 24 and 22; exactly six positions away, we find it again between the numbers 4 and 2;

another six positions, and we find it between the numbers 13 and 11; still another six positions, and we find it for the fourth time between the numbers 21 and 19. Thus we have two series of numbers, 24-4-13-21 and 22-2-11-19, which run parallel to each other with their numbers always separated by interval 6. Sequences of this kind came from the *columns of a first encipherment block*, and can all be placed back in these columns by re-writing the mixed cryptogram numbers in lines of *six numbers each*. Sometimes we find such columns broken to bits, as would be the case should we continue moving the strip until we have completely exhausted the possibilities for difference 1; and we never find them complete, since these columns of the first encipherment block were taken out in irregular order and written continuously upon the rows of a *second encipherment block,* and after that were sliced through in the taking out of columns from the second block. We found traces of them once before, where a difference of 8 was found throughout four consecutive pairs of numbers 12-20, 9-17, 10-18, 15-23, always at an interval of 6 positions.

The key-length, then, is 6, and the cryptogram numbers (in their plaintext order) if written into a block of that width, will reproduce the first encipherment block. From this, we wish to carry the numbers, column by column, into their second encipherment block, from which they may then be taken out, again by columns, in such a way as to bring them back to their cryptogram order 1-2-3. If this is to happen, the numbers must run consecutively in the new columns, and the number 1 must be on the top line. We select, then, from the restored plaintext block, the column which contains the number 1, then the column containing the number 2, and so on, writing these columns horizontally on the rows of the new block, in such an order as to make the numbers consecutive in every column. This may or may not require the adjustments indicated in the figure at (a) and (b). When block (b) is completely adjusted, the order in which it would be necessary to take its columns so as to produce the cryptogram numbers in their original 1-2-3 sequence, is the order of the original short key. Our key-word COSMOS, incidentally, could have been better chosen.

In Ohaver's process, we have taken the *cryptogram numbers* and *enciphered* them. By the process of General Givierge, summed up in Fig. 56, we do the opposite: we take the *plaintext numbers,* in their cryptogram order, and *decipher* them, so as to bring them back to their correct plaintext order 1-2-3. For learning the key-length, General Givierge endeavors to find that number which, when added or subtracted throughout the series of numbers, will most often cause one of its segments to repeat another. The portions which repeat are the columns, or partial columns, not from a first encipherment block, but from a *second,* since the process here is to follow out a decipherment. In the figure, the left-hand block (not strictly necessary) represents the plaintext, written as a cryptogram, and the one on the right represents it in what is known to have been its first encipherment block. To develop the second block: either take columns from the right-hand block and lay them on the rows of the central one in such an order that its columns can be taken out to form the cryptogram; or, write the cryptogram arrangement into the columns of the central block in such an order that its *rows* will show the columns of the plaintext block on the right. The order in which columns must be taken from the right-hand block to form the central one (or that in which columns must be taken from the central block to reproduce the cryptogram arrangement) is the order of the original short key. The condensed presentation here is also drawn from the writings of M. E. Ohaver. General Givierge, who seems first to have published the method, was chiefly concerned with exposing the possibilities of *analysis,* as applied to numbers generally, and explains to us the reason of the increase 6 which betrays the key-length in the plaintext series of numbers. The width of the original block being 6, each number is larger by 6 than the one just above it, making every one of the columns an arithmetical progression in which the constant difference is 6. These columns, still retaining their regular increase of 6, are laid down on the rows of a second block, and, for at least a portion of their length, some two or more of them always continue parallel, with progressions of 6 running side by side. Thus the taking out of columns from the second block will, at times, select *one each* from two or

Figure 56

Finding the Original Short Key from the PLAINTEXT Serial Numbers - GIVIERGE

To find the key-length: Try adding (or subtracting) possible key-lengths (4, 5, 6, 7, etc.) to the whole series until some one of these added numbers causes portions of the series to repeat.

```
1 10 20  9 24 19  2 17  6  7 16  5 15 25  8 23 12 13 22 11 21  4 14  3 18
  6  6  6  6  6  6  6  6  6  6  6  6  6  6  6  6  6  6  6  6  6  6  6  6

7 16 26 15 30 25  8 23 12 13 22 11 21 31 14 29 18 19 28 17 27 10 20  9 24
```

The portions which repeat when the correct key-length, 6, is added, are columns, or part-columns, from the SECOND encipherment block.

Plaintext Serial Numbers In CRYPTOGRAM Order:				S E C O N D Encipherment Block						F I R S T Encipherment Block					
/1	10	20	9	1	7	13	19	25	4	1	2	3	4	5	6
24/19	2	17		10	16	22	2	8	14	7	8	9	10	11	12
6/7	16	5		20	5	11	17	23	3	13	14	15	16	17	18
15/25	8	23		9	15	21	6	12	18	19	20	21	22	23	24
12/13	22	11		24						25					
21/4	14	3	18												

The ROWS of the CRYPTOGRAM BLOCK, (approximately of column-length), must be written back into the COLUMNS of the SECOND ENCIPHERMENT BLOCK in such an order that the ROWS of this SECOND encipherment block could have been taken off as a primary cryptogram from the COLUMNS of the FIRST ENCIPHERMENT BLOCK, extreme right, known to be the original order of the numbers.

The original short KEY can then be found by observing (in the central block) the order in which columns have been taken from the right-hand block. That is, find the small numbers which were on the top row; these are standing in the order 1, 4, 2, 5, 3, 6 (a writing-in key), and the columns which are headed by these receive key-numbers in the order 1-3-5-2-4-6.

more different progressions of 6, and the new columns, throughout some portion of their length, will differ from one another by exactly 6, the original key-length.

We have seen, then, the general case in which the " enemy " decryptor, having several cryptograms of the same length, enciphered with the same key, is able to use a purely mechanical method in order to restore the plaintext, and afterward, by observing traces of a known cipher, to extract their key. For the solution of single cryptograms enciphered in complicated systems, the writer knows of no other method than straight anagramming, in which the single letters, accompanied by their serial numbers, are written on individual cardboard squares (or imagined to be so), and the attempt made to match them up. Attention has already been called to some possibilities which may lie in the serial numbers whenever the sequences or probable words are thought to be correctly matched. But with absolutely nothing known or suspected as to source or subject matter, and with nothing discoverable from serial numbers or possible routes (and taking it for granted that any accumulation of letters represented in about the normal frequency-proportions can be made to yield dozens of different solutions), it would hardly seem that the decryptor, even should he find the correct solution, would have a means of distinguishing it from any other.

For the student who may care to struggle with a case of single anagramming, we have appended a problem in Fig. 57, together with a means for finding out the solu-

Figure 57

A Single Cryptogram in Double Columnar Transposition:

L H D L A   O D D H L   H E E U I   X D F P I   U T A E R   O I T Q A   E T E R L

N I E N A   U D K L I   E E H Y N   M S J L C   N H P B O   A D G R N.

The Solution, Enciphered by a Method Mentioned in Chapter III:

M T Q P I N A I E N E I T H R G E K D U U D L L I R I H F R T E C L O L N J

L A S H A A U Y D O E E L N E N D H P D H D E A B Q.

tion and perhaps even the key-word. It has come from the Philadelphia headquarters of a band of revolutionists, and our stool-pigeon tells us that the leaders of this movement are to be called together for consultation during the coming summer.

The finding of a *key-word,* after recovery of the numerical key, is not, of course, necessary to the decipherment of further cryptograms. However, this recovery will afford us the same convenience which it gave to the encipherer; that is, a simple mnemonic device for reproducing the numbers at will. And to recover the actual original key-word may, at times, provide some insight into the habits or mental make-up of the person who selected it, and who may select others like it, or might, conceivably, make use of this same key-word in some other kind of encipherment. If the key is short, it is practically always possible to recover more than one word; but with long keys, we seldom, if ever, recover more than the one word on which the numbers were actually based. In this connection, however, it must be remembered that key-words are not necessarily taken from any one language; thus, their recovery becomes largely a matter of combined information, intuition, guesses, trials, and determination, so that an exact method for accomplishing it is hard to give. But, presuming that key-numbers have been derived in the usual way, those which are small are, in general, likely to have derived from the earlier portion of the alphabet, which contains *A, E, I.* So long as they increase toward the right, they may continue to represent a same letter, and when they do, this letter is usually a vowel. When an increase occurs on the left, the new number has certainly derived from a new letter, coming later in the alphabet. Whatever the language, then, it is very easy to determine the two extreme alphabetical limits outside of which no one of the letters can possibly be found.

This can be seen at (a) of Fig. 58. The numbers 1, 2, 3, might all have derived from *A,* but the number 4 cannot have derived from a letter coming earlier in the alphabet than *B.* Similarly, the numbers 4, 5, might, by possibility alone, have derived from *B;* the numbers 6, 7, 8, might all have derived from *C,* the numbers 9, 10, from *D,* and, finally, the number 11, from no letter earlier than *E.* When these earliest possible limits have been established for every key-number, and it is seen that the range is five letters, then the last five letters of the alphabet, V,W,X,Y,Z, may be used to establish the limits at the other end of the alphabet. It is seen now, that the key-number 6, must have derived from some letter between C and X, inclusive, and similarly with the others. But when we come to the particular case, it becomes necessary to make assumptions; for instance, were these numbers derived from a common English word or from a Russian proper name? The person who selected it, so far as we know, is accustomed to speaking English, and in all of his past cryptograms we have been able to recover common English words rather than proper names. Assuming, then, as at (b) of the same figure, that we are to

Figure 58

(a) Limits:

```
6   9   1   4  11   7  10   2   3   8   5
C   D   A   B   E   C   D   A   A   C   B

X   Y   V   W   Z   X   Y   V   V   X   W
```

(b) Assumption of English word:

```
6   9   1   4  11   7  10   2   3   8   5
                A                   A   B   L   E

(F  (M   A   C  (N  (F  (M   A   B   L   E
 L   Y       D   Z   L   Y
             E      (New limits)
```

recover his usual common English word, we set down A as a possible letter for the key-numbers 1 and 2. But when we arrive at the number 3, we see that we cannot assign here a third A, since common English words of this length do not contain a doubled A. The earliest letter possible, then, is B, and, upon noting the consecutive letters AB at this particular point, we think at once of the common English terminal sequence -$ABLE$.

To find whether this is possible, we make sure that the new letters, L E, alphabetically considered, do not run contrary to their supposed numbers, 8 5. Then, having accepted these four letters as entirely possible and likely, we work back to the missing number, 4, and find, now, that it has new limits; it must have derived from E, D, or C, and from nothing else, and of these, we are inclined to discard E, which would give a sequence AE. We then work back to other missing numbers, 6 and 7, and find that these, too, have acquired new limits; they must be found somewhere between F and L, inclusive. All numbers which follow 8 have attained a new limit in the earlier portion of the alphabet, but not in the latter portion. These are all shown in (b). At this point, any knowledge at all of English prefixes will suggest what the first two letters are and will narrow the limits still further. The student, perhaps, has already guessed the word.

Of the keys which follow, (a) and (b) were derived from English words, one of which has been used in the present chapter. The remaining four are derived from proper names, respectively (c) German, (d) Italian, (e) Spanish, and (f) French.

(a) 1-9-2-4-11-3-7-8-6-10-5.

(b) 2-7-8-3-4-1-6-5-9-10.

(c) 2-5-11-3-9-13-6-12-8-1-4-7-10.

(d) 9-1-10-6-5-2-8-7-4-3.

(e) 2-11-3-6-7-9-1-5-8-4-10.

(f) 5-1-4-6-2-3-9-8-7.

36. By TITOGI.

(a)   U O Y M E   E T E N A   W H T I M   C I C T I   J I U S O   G N H Y F.

(b)   Y T M I L   L E M L E   W U A A J   T W O N F   O R T A H   L H T G I.

(c)   R O P U L   E A E E B   A H F T K   O D T S C   I L T T M   R Y T I H.

(d)   U M H T S   E U O K S   I H W T R   A H C I O   W A O H T   Y O S S Y.

(e)   E C E R L   T A D A R   M R E A O   G P O Y M   E E A A T   N I B S A.

(f)   R E U O T   K N A E H   E H H L Y   W D E L E   E E E O M   N W S L L.

(g)   I H L P U   H T T G I   Y T T A S   N E R T E   O R Y T A   H N J D S.

(h)   E S E F K   A C A P E   E O L S A   M E J N S   T E O M S   L E O T I.

(i)   T E N E W   O H S K I   I N S G T   M O O H T   A A T H U   E U T O B.

(j)   H T P R A   H L E R E   E R E T A   T L E E H   S T T T E   H B N B S.

37. By EFSEE.

(a)   I U E G N   M O W H X   T A N O I   P D I L S   F P I A R -

(b)   F N E E T   X I E T O   N O T S M   G R T R Y   V G P A C -

(c)   S F U F N   I C E Q E   S C U N R   I L T M Y   I O I P T -

(d)   B T E E S   N B I H I   E T L N X   O E S N R   E I E G T.

38. By SIR ORM. (This has a keyword!)

T A S H L   E C P W E   T C I H A   O T N R A   O O H L W   D O Y I L   E O H R L

E V A T E   A O M N L   E V N W I   W I E I H   S M H E T   H N W O I   O L S V I

I F S S O   W A S O T   F I L E H   N M G O F   I E R A L   O C G N N.

39. By DAMONOMAD. (And he calls this a "Nihilist" !)

A H N S E   S T I H D   I S O M E   A T H I O   O H D I O   U T T I K   M I E S O

F G S N E   R W U G T   S G Y I S   L A T I T   T A A N H   O G E N Y   L A W E A

L E R T M   I W T O E   D.

40. By FRA-GRANT. (A military message sent by General Calamity to Major Catastrophe).

T E H A N   E M G S L   L I W S N   E T T A C   K Y E I A   A E B P S   O U R P E

M O C E E   T U N R I   S T E R S   A F O E T   O R T D A   E R T E F   D I N C A

S E R E T   T U O P W   A R U R E   F F O Y A   E E D F O   R D R C R.

No. 40 can be decrypted by the multiple-anagramming of its units. Afterward,
if you are unable to reconstruct the system, No. 41 will tell you all.

41. By PICCOLA. (Single block - completed unit - with columns transposed. The
key to this transposition may amuse you, provided you can
reconstruct it in letters!)

A O U U P   D M C A N   I O G T R   S A A Y N   K N C A B   M N A O A   T L E C B

Q S D O R   E E W W D   N C K E E   S T S H N   I E T E U   H K N I P   D I T Y F

U X G I V   L T A I P   H R C S N   R R E H S   B M E E A   R M T A I   U T E W O

P I R S M   H O O E V   R W F N X   S D A H I   E T S S U   F C N N E   E S N F S

E O O L T   U A E A O   F T V L T   E E O E C.

<u>42.</u> By TITOGI and PICCOLA. (General information - nothing more).

(a) I H S E W   D O X H D   H T S E O   E H R N E   C T O O A   G A R S A

N O E A O   S O H U W   R T C A U   R E N T T   O M S O C   N Y N P G   S H A P P

N F S N E   R T E H E   P M A W S   M E G I A   E A P O R   Y D T A A   S S A F M

I H S R C   H E C W N   E I T A T   R X E I S   O A C F A   T I C E N   I R T E U

Y H T E R   T S R S E   L S T E G   P A H R W.   (b)   S R H J I   A X E C A

N E Y P K   A N D A T   S D L I L   A S L N T   G E A D Y   E B L Y T   S C C I D

T C S G A,   M C E E N   W A T I E   A E N H L   A B D Y A   G H C H E   G I H O I

L P O N P   A S E D N   T T W E S   Y E F I M   L A R E R   H N E D I   O T E L R

O S I T D   S S R I S   N I R R F   S S P E C   T R E I F   B G O M R   X S E N A

H A R N L.   (c)   A E G Y B   A T Y N S   R I D T O   O S D N E   Y E E E O

G N I U U   T W S N L   H E I I S   C G H H W   D R R U W   E A H E T   K C T W V

O E H H I.

<u>43.</u> By TITOGI. (Keerful, Si! All is not gold that glitters).

C T I H N   A I E S O   R M F Y E   E C T H U   W I S L A   E D K R L   B E R N M

J I T S D   A N D O O   H T V A T   H T E R Y   G A U N O   T S A P E   M O E S U

R I L T E   D I E O N   E N R C A   F I N P O   L H O E A   G R B X S.

<u>44.</u> By ALII KIONA. (Nou hooda thawt it uvvim?)

E N W N O   T N S E N   Y U H O I   K H N O E   W A O T I   U S S A L   B W S F R

M I E I D   I H R W N   T F N D S   E E O T U   E Y B N O   T E W E Z   E E D I B

A E R Y I   P L R N P   Z R S M U   T A S O I   S U S D T   D T R N H   N O A S A   F E Z.

CHAPTER VIII

SUBSTITUTION TYPES

Substitution cipher presupposes the selection of a set of symbols which can represent the letters or words of messages. As to what these symbols may be, there is practically no limit; we meet substitution in our every-day life: the dots and dashes of the Morse alphabet, the pot-hooks of shorthand, the combinations of Braille, and so on; and we hear of its use in the sign-language of Indians and Gipsies, or in the drum-language of the African jungle. These, of course, are not cipher, yet in each case the plain language has been replaced with symbols. Considering the use of symbols for cipher purposes, there are doubtless many among us who played, as children, with the alphabet of the " Masonic " cipher, based upon a design like the one used for ticktacktoe. Lord Bacon's alphabet has already been mentioned. The use of printers' symbols, and similar characters, can be seen in the works of Edgar Allan Poe. Charles I of England is said to have used a cipher alphabet in which letters were represented by a series of dots, placed in certain positions with reference to the line of writing. An endless number of queer symbols is met with in fiction, such as the use of the little dancing men by Sir Arthur Conan Doyle. Cipher alphabets of the nature mentioned do not produce ciphers in any way different from those produced by substitution with letters and numbers; as a matter of fact, the decryptor who must deal with a cryptogram made up of arbitrary signs usually begins the work by making a substitution of his own, replacing each unfamiliar symbol with some one letter (or number). We will confine our discussion, then, to those characters which are transmissible by Morse.

Substitution ciphers may be classified under four major types, each having its subdivisions and variations, and its intercombinations with other types:

1. *Simple substitution* (also called *monoalphabetic substitution*) makes use of only one cipher alphabet.

2. *Multiple-alphabet substitution* (also called *double-key substitution, polyalphabetic substitution,* etc.) makes use of several different cipher alphabets according to some agreed plan.

The term " multisubstitutional " is sometimes applied to the multiple alphabet cipher, but more correctly refers to a certain form of the simple substitution cipher, in which the single alphabet is so designed as to provide optional substitutes for all or part of the letters.

3. *Polygram substitution* provides a scheme by means of which groups of letters are replaced integrally with other groups, which may be of letters or of numbers.

4. *Fractional substitution,* which requires a certain type of cipher alphabet, breaks up the substitutes for single letters, and subjects these fractions to further encipherment. More often than not, the result is a combination cipher, rather than a purely substitutional one.

CHAPTER IX

Simple Substitution — Fundamentals

Simple substitution is ordinarily defined as a cipher in which each letter of the alphabet has one fixed substitute, and each cryptogram-symbol represents one fixed original. When this cipher is used for puzzle purposes, as we find it in our newspapers and popular magazines, the substitutes (which are invariably letters of the alphabet) may be chosen at random, and the cryptograms must follow certain arbitrary rulings which are designed to make them " fair ": Word-divisions and punctuation must follow religiously those of the original text; a certain minimum of length must be provided; no letter may act as its own substitute; foreign words are not permissible; and so on. Aside from the observance of such rules, however, no holds are barred; the constructor of such a cryptogram, totally unconcerned with the meaning of his plaintext (except that it must have one), sometimes gives his chief attention to distorting the normal language characteristics in an effort to baffle the analyst, and often will carefully search his dictionary for words like *yclept, crwth, syzygy, pterodactyl, ichthyomancy,* not infrequently producing a plaintext which is almost as incomprehensible as its corresponding cryptogram. Our study here will be confined to the simple substitution cipher as applied to normal English text.

When a substitution key (a pair of alphabets) is being used for cipher purposes, the letters which make up the cipher alphabet cannot be chosen at random; the key must be of such a nature that any one of the several correspondents, desiring to make use of it, will have it at his disposal. Word-divisions are usually concealed, or, occasionally, falsified. Punctuation, if used at all, must don the apparel worn by the rest of the text; no limitations can be placed on length, and no word whatever can be barred, where the intention is that of conveying actual messages; and it is not at all uncommon to find that one or more letters are serving as their own substitutes.

In discussing keys, we will make some arbitrary rulings of our own, but only in the interests of clarity. We will assume, for all cases, that the two necessary alphabets are always written horizontally, as several are shown in Fig. 59; that wherever the two complete alphabets appear, the upper of the pair is always the one in which plaintext letters must be found, so that the lower one is always the cipher alphabet. Thus, whenever the two alphabets are written out in full, the substitute for any given plaintext letter will be the letter standing immediately below it; and the original of any cipher letter will be the letter standing just above it. Wherever it seems advisable to show a distinction, the cipher letters will be expressed as capitals and the plaintext letters will appear in lower case.

Among the oldest cipher alphabets ever used for practical purposes are those of the type called " Caesar," one such alphabet having been used by Julius Caesar, and another by Octavius. As may be seen at (a) of Fig. 59, this type of cipher alphabet is no more than a simple *shifting* of the normal alphabet to a new point of beginning. Using this particular example, the word " Caesar " will be enciphered as *F D H V D U;* or, if the word *R Y H U* is found in a cryptogram, it deciphers as " over."

At (b) of the same figure, we have a pair of *inverse* normal alphabets. Here, it is not necessary to specify that one of the pair is a plaintext alphabet and the other a cipher alphabet; whenever a plaintext alphabet is merely reversed and allowed to serve as its own cipher alphabet, the encipherment becomes *reciprocal;* that is, whenever *Z* is the substitute for *A*, then *A* will also be the substitute for *Z*, and so for other letters. Thus, we need not write down more than half of the key shown at (b); and, in any other case of reciprocal alphabets, only enough of it to make sure that we have all 26 of the letters; after that, we may find them where we please, both for encipherment and for decipherment. Simple reciprocal alphabets are also ancient. The one just mentioned, and also the one shown at (c), are both said to have been used in parts of the Bible. The two inverse alphabets of (b) may, of course, be *shifted* with reference to each other; that is, one or the other may be caused to begin at any desired letter, just as is done with the ordinary alphabet in deriving one of the " Caesars." It is also possible, as indicated at (d), to divide the

Figure 59

Some Simple Substitution Keys

(a)
A shifted, or "Caesar," alphabet:

```
Plaintext:  a b c d e f g h i j k l m n o p q r s t u v w x y z
CIPHER:     D E F G H I J K L M N O P Q R S T U V W X Y Z A B C
```

(b)
A pair of inverse alphabets:

```
A B C D E F G H I J K L M N O P Q R S T U V W X Y Z
Z Y X W V U T S R Q P O N M L K J I H G F E D C B A
```

Other examples of the RECIPROCAL alphabet:

```
(c)  A B C D E F G H I J K L M      (e)  C U L P E R A B D F G H I
     N O P Q R S T U V W X Y Z           Z Y X W V T S Q O N M K J

(d)  A B C D E F G H I J K L M      (f)  C U L P E R A B D F G H I
     T S R Q P O N Z Y X W V U           J K M N O Q S T V W X Y Z
```

normal alphabet into its two halves, and shift one of the halves; in this case the encipherment would be reciprocal whether or not the shifted portion runs in reverse order. At (e) and (f), we have mixed (or interverted) alphabets which, though crude, are more in line with modern practice than those which precede them, since both of these are based on the key-word CULPEPER.

The usual plan for deriving cipher alphabets from key-words is as follows: First, all repeated occurrences of any same letter, such as the second *P* and the second *E* of the word CULPEPER, are discarded. The unrepeated letters of the key-word, as *C U L P E R*, are placed at the beginning of the cipher alphabet, and the rest of the 26 letters are made to follow these, usually in their normal alphabetical order. If an adequate key-word be chosen, for instance the word UNCOPYRIGHTABLE, a well-mixed alphabet results; but, in order to have a cipher alphabet which is truly incoherent, and hard for the decryptor to reconstruct, we may write this already-mixed alphabet into block form and subject it to a transposition of some kind. Several examples of this may be examined in Fig. 60. In example (a), the repeated letters of the key-word have merely been discarded, while example (b) retains these two positions in order to produce more and shorter columns, with three different lengths. In both cases, the columns of the block have been taken out by descending verticals to form cipher alphabets (a) and (b), but the transposition may follow any desired route or other process. Example (c) suggests further uses for key-words. Still another process (not shown) consists in writing the key-numbers above a block, exactly as in example (c), and allowing them to govern the *lengths of rows.* In the writing-in of the alphabet, normal or mixed, the first row of letters is made to end under key-number 1, the second row under key-number 2, and so on, so that the completed block contains rows of different lengths; it may then be taken off by columns, or otherwise. Numerous other devices exist, but it should be plain from the foregoing that we have an unlimited field in which to derive well-scrambled cipher alphabets, so that there is no need whatever for forming one at random and later being unable to set it up again.

Figure 60

Some Methods for Forming a Keyword-Mixed Alphabet

Keyword: CULPEPER

(a)

```
C U L P E R
A B D F G H
I J K M N O
Q S T V W X
Y Z
```

(b)*

```
C U L P E * * R
A B D F G H I J
K M N O Q S T V
W X Y Z
```

*)(An OHAVER Method).

(c)

```
C U L P E P E R
1 8 4 5 2 6 3 7
A B C D E F G H
I J K L M N O P
Q R S T U V W X
Y Z
```

(a)

Plaintext:	a b c d e f g h i j k l m n o p q r s t u v w x y z
CIPHER:	C A I Q Y U B J S Z L D K T P F M V E G N W R H O X

(b)

Plaintext:	a b c d e f g h i j k l m n o p q r s t u v w x y z
CIPHER:	C A K W U B M X L D N Y P F O Z E G Q H S I T R J V

(c)

Plaintext:	a b c d e f g h i j k l m n o p q r s t u v w x y z
CIPHER:	A I Q Y E M U G O W C K S D L T F N V H P X B J R Z

For the *encipherment* of substitution cryptograms, the plaintext is first written out in full with enough space between its lines to allow for the later insertion of cryptogram-letters. The correct substitute for each letter is then written below it, after which, these substitutes are nearly always marked off into five-letter groups, and the groups are taken off on another sheet to form the finished cryptogram. It is sometimes recommended that plaintext and cipher letters be written in two differ-

Figure 61

"Running Down the Alphabet"

Cryptogram:	Y B P R O B Q L...
	Z C Q S P C R M...
	A D R T Q D S N...
Plaintext:	B E S U R E T O...

ent colors, so as to avoid any risk of taking off portions of plaintext along with a cryptogram.

For *decipherment*, the plan is the same, except that the cryptogram is written first, and the two alphabets of the key exchange their functions. Often, when the cipher alphabet in use is so incoherent that its letters are not quickly found, the decipherer will prepare for himself a special *decipherment key*, in which he places the letters of his cipher alphabet in straight alphabetical order, and allows the plaintext alphabet to grow mixed.

In taking up the *decryptment* of simple substitution, we may dispose summarily of the Caesar alphabets by pointing to Fig. 61. If we suspect that one of these has been used, we may verify the suspicion by taking some ten-or-fifteen-letter segment of the cryptogram, and, with each of its letters as a beginning, extend the ten or fifteen alphabets, a few letters at a time, until we come to the line which is purely plaintext. This process is popularly known as "running down the alphabet," and whenever it results in a row of plaintext, we may quickly determine the amount of "shift," set up the cipher alphabet, and start deciphering. The same thing is true of a pair of *inverse normal alphabets* which have merely been *shifted with reference to each other*. But in this case, the cryptogram (or that segment of it which is being investigated), *must first be enciphered in the same kind of alphabet*. To explain this, suppose that our cryptogram fragment is *B Y K I L Y J O*. If we encipher this with the pair of inverse alphabets which was shown at (b) of Fig. 59, we obtain a new cryptogram fragment *Y B P R O B Q L*. This new fragment is now a "Caesar," and we may "run it down the alphabet" until we find its plaintext. This particular fragment was done with a pair of inverse normal alphabets in which the lower one began at *C*, instead of at *Z*. Most decryptors, in dealing with any kind of substitution, will make these two tests before trying anything else. When the guess proves correct, a great deal of paper work can be saved.

Concerning decryptment in the case of the less simple alphabets, the true vulnerability of simple substitution can be seen when the word "battalion," enciphered in alphabet (f) of our Fig. 59, becomes *T S B B S M Z E P*. Since each letter of the alphabet may have only one substitute, the pattern of *-atta-* shows up clearly in its enciphered version *-SBBS-*. The decryptor knows instantly what kind of pattern it represents, since the letters *S* and *B* can have only one original each. The frequency with which these two letters have been used in his cryptogram will tell him approximately what their two originals ought to be, and, by making a few trials, he loses little time in arriving at a solution. As a matter of fact, a simple monoliteral substitution, given fewer than a hundred letters of text and no information whatever as to source or subject-matter, can be decrypted purely through the frequencies and other characteristics of its letters; and if, in addition, the original word-divisions have been preserved, we have the lengths and patterns of these words, plus the knowledge that individual letters have their favorite positions in words.

The "Crypt" with word-divisions. — Not infrequently, the cryptogram which retains its word-divisions can be read at sight, without putting pencil to paper, and this regardless of how short it may be. Again, even though based on normal text, it will prove more troublesome; and thus, in dealing with this type of simple substitution, we attack each individual example according to what appears at first glance to be its greatest weakness. The cryptogram shown in Fig. 62, for instance, would be attacked through its many *short words*, probably the simplest of the available methods. The words in question are those numbered 3 (*RD*), 4 (*MD*), 9 (*QYR*), 11 (*RKV*), 13 (*DF*), and 15 (*DN*). Among the two-letter words, it is noticeable that every one of these includes a letter *D*, used indiscriminately as the initial or final letter. We do not need to know much of cryptanalysis to guess that this letter represents the *o* found in such words as *to, no, do, go, of, on, or*. A comparison of the two three-letter words shows that these, also, have a common letter, *R*, which ends one of these words and begins the other. Of all words in English, the commonest is *the*. If *RKV* be assumed as *the*, then *RD*, already thought to contain *o*, will check as *to*, another extremely common word.

Thus we are able to begin work by *tentatively assuming* that the four cryptogram letters *R*, *K*, *V*, and *D*, are the substitutes, respectively, for plaintext letters *t*, *h*, *e*, and *o*. These assumptions are tested by actually making the necessary substitutions directly on the cryptogram, as seen at (a) of Fig. 62. And we may be sure that they are correct when we see the 12th word clearly outlined as *other*. This word gives a new substitution: cipher letter *T* evidently represents *r*, occurring in three

different words; the actual making of this substitution will cause the 8th word to
show a very common ending: *-tter*.

If we now consider the other three-letter word, the 9th of the cryptogram, we
see that QYR cannot represent any one of the common words *not, got, out, yet,* since
the substitutes for *o* and *e* have already been determined. It may, however, represent the common word *but*, especially if we care to investigate the frequency in
the cryptogram of its first letter, Q. This letter has been used only once; and its
assumed original, *b*, is normally of very low frequency, and, in addition, is known
to have a fondness for initial positions. The assumption of this word as *but* gives
us the substitute for *u*, which appears to be Y.

Figure 62

Making Substitutions

(a)
```
        1              2          3      4        5          6              7
  F D R J N U    H V X X U    R D    M D    S K V S O    P J R K    Z D Y F Z J X
    o t              •        t o    o      h e          t h        o

        8          9                  10      11          12      13
  G S R R V T    Q Y R    W D A R W D F V    R K V    D R K V T    D F
    t t e          t        o   t o   e      t h e    o t h e      o

            14        15              16          17
  S Z Z D Y F R    D N    N V O V T S X    S A W V Z R.
    o          t    o        e   e          e   t
```

(b)
```
    ...D F      S Z Z D Y F R    D N...            ...Z D Y F Z J X...
      o n       a c c o u n t    o f               c o u n o . .
      13            14            15                    7
```

In addition to the points mentioned, it is not unusual to find·that short words, by
their very positions with reference to some longer word, will identify a whole sequence, as might happen with the sequence shown at (b) of the same figure. Good
examples of this are: *as well as, as soon as, in order to,* and so on. In this particular case of (b), we began with only the identified *o,* and immediately were able to
identify *t;* this alone should serve for spotting the whole sequence *on account of,*
taking into consideration the doubled *c.* Notice what the identification of the word
account will do toward identifying the 7th word.

Among methods which do not seem indicated in the given example, there is a
very fertile field for research in the examination of *terminal sequences.* When two
or more of the affixes *-tion, -ing, in-,* and *con-* are present in the same text, as they
practically always are, they will serve to identify one another, and may, in addition,
be cross-compared with many of the short words, as *in, on, no, not, into, upon, can.*
The prefix *sub-* may serve to identify the word *but.* There is a whole group *-ment,
-ence, -ance, -ency, -ancy;* another group *pre-, re-, -er, de-, -ed,* etc.; or a good comparison in *be-, -able, -ible,* etc.

Still a third road to solution, especially popular with those who solve the " aristocrats," is found in *pattern words,* that is, words having one or more letters repeated.
The puzzler, examining a dictionary, prepares lists for his permanent use, one
list for each " pattern "; such a list, for instance, would contain PATTERN, FALL-
ING and all other words in which the third and fourth letters are the same and all
others different, another would contain all words having the pattern STATE, DE-
FER, ROBOT, still another all words of the pattern BANANA, ROCOCO, and so
on. The solver, having thus armed himself in advance, begins work by searching his
cryptogram for words having repeated cipher letters, and attempts to identify these

from the proper lists. He may provide himself, also, with non-pattern lists, on which words have given lengths but contain no repeated letters; and with "transposal lists" containing pairs of words (as NIGHT and THING) which use the same letters but not in the same order. It is true that such lists are troublesome to prepare, but they are extremely effective; they will break the most resistant of the "aristocrats" or the shortest example of legitimate cipher.

No matter how resistant the cryptogram, all that is really needed is an *entry*, the identification of one word, or of three or four letters. The experienced solver knows well that persistence will find this entry, and trusts largely to instinct and perseverance; the beginner, however, may feel at a loss for a "system," and, if so, may, perhaps, be able to find suggestions for one in the next few paragraphs.

First of all, in any substitution problem, there should be a counting of the letters in the cryptogram in order to find out their frequencies. This is called a *frequency count*, and is usually accomplished as follows: The decryptor first lays out the normal alphabet — either horizontally or vertically. He then begins with the first letter of his cryptogram, taking letters one by one just as he finds them, and for each time that he finds a letter in his cryptogram, he places a tally mark beside that same letter as found in his prepared alphabet. The result of such a count, taken on the foregoing cryptogram, will be shown further on, when the same cryptogram appears again without its word-divisions.

If the problem seems likely to prove really difficult, there should also be a *contact count*; that is, a list showing every letter, together with the two which have flanked it right and left each time it was used. Such a count is partly shown in Fig. 63. This, like the frequency count, may be prepared either vertically or horizontally; and, just as in making ready for the frequency count, an alphabet may be laid out in advance ready to receive the contact letters, taken from the cryptogram as they happen to be found. Specifically: The letter *F* comes first in the cryptogram; it has no left-hand contact, but is contacted on the right by *D*. We find the *F* of the prepared alphabet, and place beside it its contacts: *-D. The second letter of the cryptogram is *D*, flanked by *F* and *R*. We find the *D* of the prepared alphabet, and place beside it its contacts: *F-R*; and so on to the end of the cryptogram. Some solvers do not prepare an alphabet in advance, but simply put down the main letters as they happen to come across them in the cryptogram. It should be added, too, that the few contacts included in Fig. 63 were taken from the *undivided* cryptogram. When word-divisions exist, and are known to be the correct ones, a great many solvers do not include any contacts which involve two different words. Here, for instance, the second appearance of *D* is shown with contacts *R-M*. These solvers, knowing that this *D* stands at the end of a word, will leave the *M*-contact blank: *R-**

It will be noticed from the figure that the contact-count is, in itself, a frequency

Figure 63

A Favorite Form of Frequency Count Combined With CONTACT Data

A	$\dfrac{D\ S}{R\ W}$	2/4
B		
C		
D	$\dfrac{F\ R\ M\ Z\ W\ W\ V\ T\ Z\ R}{R\ M\ S\ Y\ A\ F\ R\ F\ Y\ N}$	10/11
E		
F	$\dfrac{*\ Y\ D\ D\ Y}{D\ Z\ V\ S\ R}$	5/6
G	$\dfrac{X}{S}$	1/2
(Etc.)		

Concerning the numbers: A has a frequency of 2, and a variety-count of 4. D has a frequency of 10, and a variety-count of only 11. (Yet D, with so little variety of contact is a vowel!)

count; it shows that *A* has been used twice (frequency 2), that *B* and *C* have not been used at all, that *D* has a frequency of 10, and so on. We may also make it a *variety-count,* by noting down beside each letter the number of *different* letters present among its contacts. Ordinarily, the vowels have more variety in their contacts than do the consonants, and take part in more reversals. The uses of contact data will be examined more closely later on.

Now, giving our attention to English frequencies: No matter what frequency table we examine, we always find that the letter *E* tops the list, with a frequency of over 12%. Except in telegraphic text, the letter *T* always has the second frequency, near 10%. After that, the frequency tables will disagree as to whether *A* or *O* should have the third frequency, or whether *I* should come before *N,* or *S* before *R;* but always the same nine letters, *E T A O N I R S H,* will constitute the *high-frequency group* of letters. These particular letters will make up about 70% of any English text, and it is almost impossible to prepare one, no matter how short, without using them in about that proportion, though in the shorter texts, *L* and *D* will sometimes creep up into the high-frequency class, taking the place of *H.* Following the high-frequency group, we find a group of letters which are always of *moderate frequency;* and a third group made up of *low-frequency* letters. Since the frequency tables themselves are not duplicates throughout, we could not expect, even having a 10,000-letter cryptogram, to make substitutions by simply following the frequency table and be absolutely sure of coming out with the correct solution, though we might very nearly do so, and might, to some extent, succeed in doing this with a cryptogram of 2,000 letters. The " aristocrats," however, are arbitrarily confined to lengths which run between 75 and 100 letters. Even without manipulation, a text of this length will not always show *E* as a frequent letter, and may, for some reason, show *Z* or *X* with a fairly high frequency.

However, the " class distinctions " among the letters are always, to some extent, dependable. High-frequency letters, moderate-frequency letters, and low-frequency letters, all tend to be very exclusive. They will exchange frequencies with letters of their own class, but all three classes are disinclined to welcome outsiders. The vowels, also, as we have seen, have their fraternity; if the frequency of *E* is lowered, some other vowel, even *U* and *Y,* will insist upon making up the difference, rather than yield this privilege to a consonant.

The high-frequency group, as mentioned, includes the nine letters *E T A O N I R S H.* Even in this exclusive circle, there are cliques — not ironclad, but clearly noticeable:

Class I. The letters *T O S* appear frequently *both as initial letters and as final letters* in their own words, with terminal *O* confined largely to short words. All three of these are very freely doubled.

Class II. The letters *A I H* appear frequently as *initial letters,* but far less frequently as finals, especially *A I.* Not one of these is readily doubled.

Class III. The letters *E N R* appear frequently as *final letters,* but far less frequently as initials. The letter *E* is very freely doubled; the other two not so often.

The following further observation might be made: When one of these letters changes its class, the least likely exchange is one occurring between classes *II* and *III.*

Now let us return to the foregoing cryptogram and consider the application of this information. A frequency count taken on this cryptogram will show that when its letters are rearranged according to their frequencies, they divide automatically into three rather clearly-defined groups, much like those of the normal frequency table. There are eight letters which outrank the rest, and these, named in the order of decreasing frequencies, are: R, D, V, S, F, Z, K, X. Presumably, then, most of these are substitutes for letters of the class $E\ T\ A\ O\ N\ I\ R\ S\ H$.

If an examination now be made of the terminal letters in the cryptogram, it will be found that, of the eight considered, the letters $R\ D\ F$ have appeared at least once in both positions. These we may label class (a), as being good material for the originals t, o, s. It is found that the letters $S\ Z$ have appeared at least once as initials, but not at all as finals. These we may label class (b), that is, good material for the originals a, i, h, except for a point which will be mentioned in a moment. The remaining three letters, $V\ K\ X$ are found at least once as finals, but not at all as initials; these we will call class (c), good material for the originals e, n, r. Thus, we are enabled to begin our work by noting down the following possibilities:

> (a) $R\ D\ F$ might represent (I) $— T\ O\ S$. (Compare the facts: t, o, n).
> (b) $S\ Z$ might represent (II) $— A\ I\ H$. (Compare the facts: a, c).
> (c) $V\ K\ X$ might represent $(III) — E\ N\ R$. (Compare the facts: e, h, l).

While such a classification is probably never 100% accurate, the writer has still to find a cryptogram (unless among the very badly manipulated " aristocrats ") in which at least part of the assumptions are not correct. We are dealing, however, with the *very short cryptogram*, in which a single occurrence of a letter in a given position can be regarded as of some importance.

Ordinarily, the most frequent letter of (c) will represent e, as it does here. This letter is famous as a final letter, and any printed page will show it at the end of 17 or 18 words in every hundred. There is not so clear a distinction between T and S of class I.

The most vulnerable of the groups, however, is (b). Of the three letters which may be represented here, two are vowels, concerning which we are to hear more, and not one is readily doubled. When Z, tentatively included in this group, is found to have been doubled near the beginning of a word, it is seen to be wrongly classified.

This method, as mentioned, is intended merely as a suggested means for effecting an entry. The correct identification of only four letters, as we have seen, will make enormous inroads into the contents of a cryptogram.

Other points which will at times prove helpful are as follows: In words of three and five letters, the central one is nearly always a vowel, taking it for granted that the words *the* and *and* will never be present in any difficult cryptogram. In the longer words, the favorite positions of the vowels are the two positions which follow the initial letter and the two positions which precede the final letter. The favorite position of I, in fact, is well known as the third-to-last. About half the words used in any written text are of the type called *negative*, or *empty;* that is, the pronouns and auxiliary verbs, and particularly the various kinds of connectives *without which no sentence can be put together*. If your cryptogram is an " aristocrat," you will probably find that most of your prepositions begin with A: *amongst, amidst, adown*, etc. Every sentence contains a verb, and these are more or less limited in their possible terminations. Any letter used only two or three times, and always followed by the same letter, is good material for Q. With what has been said, the student should have no trouble in dealing with the first fifteen " aristocrats " which follow the next chapter. As to the remaining thirty-five of Mr. Lamb's collection, we need say only this: It is impossible to avoid every characteristic of the English language and still write English.

The General Case. — Now let us examine carefully Fig. 64, where the foregoing cryptogram is repeated without its word-separations, and is followed by its frequency and contact data. The various devices indicated in this figure are all of a more or less optional nature. Concerning the preparation of the cryptogram itself, the chief requirement is that it be done in ink, or typewritten, on paper which

Figure 64

5	10	11	3	3	2	1	9	4	4	2	11	10	1	10	6	4	9	6	2	1	3	11	4
F	D	R	J	N	U	H	V	X	X	U	R	D	M	D	S	K	V	S	O	P	J	R	K

5	10	3	5	5	3	4	1	6	11	11	9	3	1	3	11	3	10	2	11	3	10	5	9
Z	D	Y	F	Z	J	X	G	S	R	R	V	T	Q	Y	R	.W	D	A	R	W	D	F	V

11	4	9	10	11	4	9	3	10	5	6	5	5	10	3	5	11	10	3	3	9	2	9	3
R	K	V	D	R	K	V	T	D	F	S	Z	Z	D	Y	F	R	D	N	N	V	O	V	T

6	4	6	2	3	9	5	11
S	X	S	A	W	V	Z	R

Ordinary Frequency Count:

A	B	C	D	E	F	G	H	I	J	K	L	M	N	O	P	Q	R	S	T	U	V	W	X	Y	Z
2			10		5	1	1		3	4		1	3	2	1	1	11	6	3	2	9	3	4	3	5

Contact-Information:

(High-frequency symbols)

R	D	V	S	F	Z	K	X
D.J	F.R	H.X	D.K	..D	K.D	S.V	V.X
U.D	R.M	K.S	V.O	Y.Z	F.J	R.Z	X.U
J.K	M.S	R.T	G.R	D.V	S.Z	R.V*	J.G
S.R	Z.Y*	F.R	F.Z	D.S	Z.D	R.V*	S.S
R.V	W.A	K.D	T.X	Y.R	V.R		
Y.W	W.F	K.T	X.A				
A.W	V.R	N.O					
V.K	T.F	O.T	(Low-frequency symbols)				
D.K	Z.Y*	W.Z					
F.D	R.N		G	H	M	P	Q
Z..			X.S	U.V	D.D	O.J	T.Y

(Moderate-frequency symbols)

J	N	T	W	Y	A	O	U
R.N	J.U	V.Q	R.D*	D.F*	D.R	S.P	N.H
P.R	D.N	V.D	R.D*	Q.R	S.W	V.V	X.R
Z.X	N.V	V.S	A.V	D.F*			

will suffer a great deal of erasure. The placing of its frequency figure above each letter is highly recommended, but not vital. Many solvers will underscore all possible repeated sequences, and will indicate in some other manner all reversals of digrams; others will underscore only the repeated trigrams and longer sequences; and still others do not underscore at all, being content to have all of these repetitions and reversals listed before them in the contact data.

As to the preparation of the contact data, most of the expert decryptors seem to prefer the vertical arrangement of Fig. 63 to the one shown here. But, in simple substitution, a full listing, made for all letters, is not necessary in dealing with the average cryptogram. Usually, it will serve the purpose to make a frequency count first, and then prepare a listing of contacts which includes only chosen letters, those of very high frequency and those of very low frequency; with many cryptograms, no listing at all need be prepared. The contact data, however, are valuable. Each pair of contact-letters actually indicates a trigram. Examining, for instance, the listing under *R:* The first expression, *D.J.*, represents a trigram *DRJ* in which the central letter was omitted in order to conserve time and space. When we find, lower down in the same listing, another letter *D*, we see in this a repeated digram *DR*. Considering the right-hand side of the same listing: When we find *K* used three times, we see this as a digram *RK* used three times. *By finding its duplication, under K* (left side), we are able to see that two of these repetitions are continued as parts of a repeated trigram *RKV*. In the list of contacts for *D*, we find a repeated trigram *ZDY*, which may be traced, under *Y*, as part of a longer repeated sequence, *ZDYF*. It is usually best to underscore these longer repeated sequences on the cryptogram; often, they can be identified from the list of frequent trigrams. But repeated digrams, as a rule, are so numerous as to be in the way when noted on the cryptogram itself. With digrams, only those which are repeated oftenest need be underscored; they can nearly always be identified direct from the list of frequent digrams. The solver, then, prepares his cryptogram and sequence data to suit himself, varying his method according to the difficulty of the given example. With this done, his usual method of solution follows the process popularly known as " vowel-spotting."

The Vowel-Solution Method. — Using this process, the first step is that of separating the vowels from the consonants; the second is that of assigning identities to the selected vowels, and afterward to the most recognizable of the consonants.

For assistance in applying this method, suppose we extract certain information from the digram chart and have this concretely before us in a series of numbered " pointers ":

1. The vowels *A E I O* are normally found in the high-frequency section of the frequency count; the vowel *U* in the section of moderate frequencies, and the vowel *Y* in the low-frequency section.
2. Letters contacting low-frequency letters are usually vowels.
3. Letters showing a wide variety in their contact-letters are usually vowels.
4. In repeated digrams, one letter is usually a vowel.
5. In reversed digrams, one letter is usually a vowel.
6. Doubled consonants are usually flanked by vowels, and vice versa.
7. It is unusual to find more than five consonants in succession.
8. Vowels do not often contact one another. If the letter of highest frequency can be assumed as *E*, any other high-frequency letter which never touches *E* at all is practically sure to be another vowel, and one which contacts it very often cannot be a vowel. (This will apply equally to other vowels, wrongly assumed as *E*.)

With a text of reasonable length, say 150 letters, it is sometimes possible to determine with certainty just which of the cryptogram-letters represent the six vowels; with shorter cryptograms, we can usually find four; sometimes only three. But once the separation has been made, individual vowels can usually be established as follows:

The most frequent one is ordinarily *E*. The one which never touches it is most likely to be *O*. Both of these are very freely doubled, and for that reason are often confused with each other, but seldom with any other vowel. They rarely touch each other.

The vowel which follows *E* and almost never precedes it, is *A*.

The vowel which reverses with it is *I*.

The same two observations will apply to the vowel *O;* but a distinction occurs when the vowel *U* can be found; this vowel precedes *E* and follows *O.*
The only vowel-vowel digrams of any real frequency are *OU, EA, IO.*
Three vowels found in succession may represent *IOU, EOU, UOU, EAU.*

As to identification of the consonants: Those letters still remaining in the high-frequency section of the frequency count will usually include *T N R S H.* Of these, the most easily identified is *H,* which precedes all vowels and seldom follows one; it may be identified often as part of repeated sequences *TH, HE, HA.*

Next to *H,* the most recognizable of the consonants, aside from frequency, is probably *R,* which reverses freely and indiscriminately with all vowels, and has a strong affinity for other high-frequency letters.

The consonant *T* can usually be identified by its frequency, by its tendency to precede vowels rather than follow them, and by its almost inevitable combination with *H* on more than one occasion. It is also notably difficult to distinguish from the vowels.

The letter *N* has characteristics which are to some extent the opposite of those mentioned for *H;* it prefers to follow vowels and precede consonants, and, to a lesser extent, the same is true of *S,* according to some charts. However, *N, S,* and *T* are all readily reversible with vowels, and are sometimes hard to tell apart.

The only frequent reversals of two consonants are *ST-TS* and *RT-TR.*
The doubles *TT* and *SS* are among the most frequent in the language.

Having this information, together with what we know of frequent digrams and frequent trigrams and very common short words, we are well armed against the longer cryptograms. Those which are shorter will give more trouble; but it takes a very short cryptogram indeed to be really resistant.

Our foregoing cryptogram contains only 80 letters.

Figure 65

(Cryptogram Frequencies:)

R	D	V		S	F	Z		K	X
11	10	9		6	5	5		4	4
E	T			A	O	N	I	R	S	H

(Normal Grouping)

To apply " pointers " in this case, let us begin by considering the individual frequencies of the letters *E T A O N I R S H.* Their frequencies per 100, according to our own chart, are about as follows: *E,* 12; *T,* 10; *A,* 8; *O,* 8; *N,* 7; *I,* 7; *R,* 6; *S,* 7; *H,* 5. Thus, when frequency alone is considered, *E* and *T* have a tendency to draw away from the others and form a private high-frequency group of their own. The distinction among the others is not so clear, and not always the same in all tables; we can only say of these that *A* and *O* will always outrank the rest, and will be closely followed by one of the others, usually *N,* and that *H* will always rank last.

Thus, the high-frequency group itself tends to sub-divide more or less clearly into three minor groupings: *E T — A O N — I R S H.* Of these, the first minor group shows one vowel, the second shows two, and the third shows one; the vowels *U* and *Y* are not present.

Now if the eight leading letters of our cryptogram, already listed as *R D V S F Z K X,* be examined in this respect, it is found that these, also, have a tendency toward separation into groups of differing frequency, which more or less correspond to the normal groupings, as indicated roughly in Fig. 65.

Normally, we expect the highest of these subdivisions to contain one vowel and one consonant, specifically E and T. When we find that the corresponding subdivision of the cryptogram contains three letters, the supposition is that one of the vowels, O or A, has moved up into this section; in that case, it has taken part of the frequency of E, making it not at all unlikely that the most frequent letter of the cryptogram will not represent E, and will not, in fact, represent a vowel. And if, as we believe, there are two vowels in the highest section, then we are not likely to find more than one in the central subdivision, especially when we note that it contains only three letters. This would leave the fourth vowel to be found in the third subdivision.

Thus, we have applied pointer No. 1. For the application of pointer No. 2, we turn to the contact data. Comparing first the three letters $R\ D\ V$, and making a careful inspection of all cryptogram letters whose frequency is 3 or lower, we find that, of our three letters, the letter R has 7 contacts with low-frequency letters, the letter D has 9, and the letter V has 8. Thus, the letter R, though having a higher frequency than the other two, has fewer low-frequency contacts than either, and so begins to draw away and assume the aspect of a consonant.

The application of pointers Nos. 3, 4, and 5, provides no satisfactory distinction. But in pointer No. 8, we find a very clear distinction: D and V have touched each other only once, while R has contacted both with a total of six contacts — a great many for a cryptogram of this length.

We decide, then, that R is a consonant, and that D and V are vowels.

Considering the central subdivision, where we expect to find one vowel: Application of pointer No. 2 shows that S has four of the low-frequency contacts, while F has two and Z has only one. Further examination of S by pointer No. 3 shows that it has an unusual variety in its contact-letters. Thus, S would appear to be the vowel here.

As to the third section, there is so little difference in frequency between these letters and some others not included in the high-frequency class, that any distinction found would not be convincing.

The individual cryptogram, however, has happened to contain the sequences $VXXU, SRRV, SZZD, DNNV$. Application of pointer No. 6 confirms our previous selection of D, V, S, as vowels, and suggests that the letter U might also represent a vowel. Since the frequency of this letter is only 2, we cannot feel so confident in drawing conclusions about it; however, a glance at the contact data shows that it has touched four different letters, which is 100% variety, that one of these four letters is an accepted consonant, and that none of the other three, so far, is an accepted vowel (pointers 3 and 8). The chances are that this letter U, with its low frequency, represents y in some such formation as *ally, ully, etty,* etc.

With four vowels tentatively isolated, we are now in a position to apply pointer No. 7, and this we may do by returning to the cryptogram and marking for attention each appearance of each supposed vowel. This is usually done by circling each one with a pencil mark. In Fig. 66, a small letter " v " has served the same purpose, and a few serial numbers have been added for convenience of reference. Now let us examine Fig. 66.

At (a), watching the small " v's," we find a fairly uniform distribution of vowels except for three long segments beginning, respectively, at the 20th, 27th, and 37th letters. For convenience, these have been copied out at (b). The two of these which are longer, and therefore most likely to contain at least one of the missing vowels, are both found to have included Z and J. Of these two letters, Z is one which was previously discarded (from the central section of the high-frequency group) during our preliminary investigation. Examining it again, to make sure, we find it now as a double between two supposed vowels, and having two additional contacts with supposed vowels (pointers 6 and 8). But *J*, we find, has never contacted any supposed vowel; it reverses with a supposed consonant, and shows as much variety as could be expected of a letter appearing only three times.

The acceptance of *J* provides five of the vowels, with frequencies of 10, 9, 6, 2,

Figure 66

```
(a.)
  v     ?   v   v       v     v     v  v   v  v         ?       25
F D R J N U H V X X U R D M D S K V S O P J R K Z

  v         ?       v       v           v         v     v       50
D Y F Z J X G S R R V T Q Y R W D A R W D F V R K

  v  v       v   v   v       v           v     v     v   v 75
V D R K V T D F S Z Z D Y F R D N N V O V T S X S

     v                                                         80
A W V Z R
```

```
(b)   20-25                27-32              37-41

        O P J R K Z          Y F Z J X G        T Q Y R W
          ? t                    ?                  t
```

```
(c)
F D R J N U H V X X U R D M D S K V S O P J R K Z
  e t i     y     o       y t e     e a h o a       i t h

D Y F Z J X G S R R V T Q Y R W D A R W D F V R K
e       i       a t t o       t     e     t     e     o t h

V D R K V T D F S Z Z D Y F R D N N V O V T S X S
o e t h o     e     a       e     t e     o     o     a     a

A W V Z R
  o   t
```

```
(d)
   Preliminary assumptions:   y t e . e a h o a .     t h o e t h o .
   CORRECTIONS:               y t 0 . 0 a h E a .     t h E 0 t h E .
                              ...to go ahead...       ...the other...
```

```
(e)
F D R J N U H V X X U R D M D S K V S O P J R K Z
  o t i     y   e       y t o     o a h e a       i t h
N           F                 G               D W
```

Notify *e**y to go ahead with.......

and 3 — a total of 30 out of an expected 32. In a longer cryptogram, we should probably look for the sixth vowel among those letters having approximately the correct frequency for making up the expected 40%. As to the present case, we should have no trouble selecting it from the five-letter segment at (b); but this would cause us to spot also the short word in which it is used, and our immediate concern is that of spotting vowels only through their known characteristics as vowels. We will assume, then, that the last vowel cannot be found.

The next step demands that we assign to the most frequent of the supposed vowels the value *e*, which happens to be a wrong assumption. Concerning this, it may be well to repeat here something which has already been said: In dealing with the simplest of cryptograms, there is often a short detour into trial and error. Also, the average decryptor, accustomed to the work, and fully aware of what he may expect from only 80 letters of text, will usually pause at this point and make some further observations before filling in any of his substitutions. However, there is value even in the making of wrong substitutions; the actual placing of supposed plaintext values in their supposed positions puts the plaintext possibilities before us *in visual form,* causing us to note easily those very points for which the experienced decryptor examines in advance.

Figure 67

1. F D R J N   U H V X X   U R D M D   S K V S O   P J R K Z   D Y F Z J

   X G S R R   V T Q Y R   W D A R W   D F V R K   V D R K V   T D F S Z

   Z D Y F R   D N N V O   V T S X S   A W V Z R.
                                                     (80 letters).

2. H V X X U   T V W D T   R A Z D Y   F Z J X T   V S O U R   D S Z R N

   S E D T S   Q X U L K   S E V O T   D W W V O   D R K V T   G S R R V

   T Q Y R A   Y M M V A   R P V A K   D Y X O H   V V W K S   G G V T J

   F M S R R   K J A R K   T D Y M K   T J Z K S   T O A L R   K J F H R

   K V U G S   U M T S F   R R K V A   Y Q A J O   U R K S R   U D Y A W

   D H V D N.
            (155 letters. - Total for both cryptograms: 235).

At (c), then, we have made our substitutions. We have assumed that the most frequent vowel, *D*, is representing *e*. Having noted the v-v digrams *DS, VD, VS,* we have selected *S*, rather than *V*, as the substitute for *a*, preferring a digram *oa* (*DS*) to a digram *ao* (*VD*). This leaves the vowel of second frequency, *V*, to represent *o*. This will cause the third of the v-v digrams (*VS*) to represent *oe*, not frequent, but better than the digram *ao* previously mentioned. *J*, then, probably represents *i*, and *U* may represent *y*.

As to consonants, we have assigned the value *t* to the most frequent one, *R*, and there has been no difficulty in identifying *h* in the letter *K*, which three times has followed *R*. But our present cryptogram is too short to provide any clear distinction among letters which might represent *n, r, s.* With the seven substitutions made, as shown at (c), notice how quickly it becomes possible to spot the incongruity of sequences *tho*, more than once, in a short text which contains not a single occurrence of *he* or *ha*. Notice again, at (d), how quickly the mere exchanging of the values *e* and *o* will bring out word-suggestions.

At (e), the first line of the cryptogram is repeated, as it would appear after the making of this exchange. The beginning of the message can almost be read: The first word appears to be *notify*, furnishing two new substitutes. Three more can be furnished in the suggested sequence *to go ahead with.* And here, the word *with* would be tried in any case, because it is a common word, and because the frequency of the letter *P* is suggestive of *w*. Arrived at this point, we begin to notice patterns: *postpone, council, account, matter,* and so on; so that the rest of the solution is largely a matter of filling in framework. In the given example, it would also be noticed that *F* and *N* have resulted from reciprocal encipherment; this may not be the case with other letters, but it presents a possibility which is always well-worth investigating.

Figure 68

Digram Count for the Longer Cryptograms

(First-Letters)

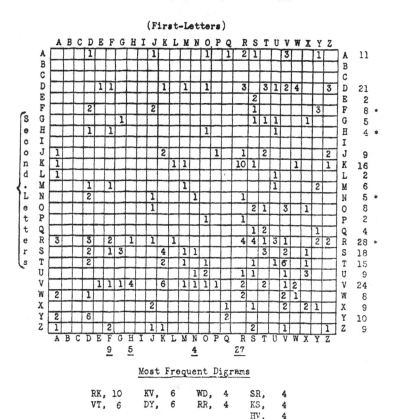

(2nd ↓ / 1st →)	A	B	C	D	E	F	G	H	I	J	K	L	M	N	O	P	Q	R	S	T	U	V	W	X	Y	Z		Total
A			1						1					1		1	2	1			3			1			A	11
B																											B	
C																											C	
D			1	1						1		1		1				3		3	1	2	4			3	D	21
E																		2									E	2
F			2					2										1					3				F	8 *
G									1									1	1	1		1					G	5
H			1		1								1					1									H	4 *
I																											I	
J	1								2					1		1	2									2	J	9
K	1									1	1							10	1		1					1	K	16
L	1																	1									L	2
M			1	1									1					1					2				M	6
N				2				1				1				1											N	5 *
O							1								2	1		3			1						O	8
P										1				1													P	2
Q																		1	2				1				Q	4
R	3			3	2	1	1	1										4	4	1	3	1		2	2		R	28 *
S				2		1	3				4	1	1						3	2	1						S	18
T				2					2	1	1							1			1	6	1				T	15
U														1	2			1	1		1	3					U	9
V					1	1	1	4			6	1	1	1	1			2		2		1	2				V	24
W	2			1														2			2	1					W	8
X										2				1		1		2				2	1				X	9
Y	2			6										2													Y	10
Z	1			2			1	1		1								2			1					1	Z	9
	A	B	C	D	E	F	G	H	I	J	K	L	M	N	O	P	Q	R	S	T	U	V	W	X	Y	Z		

Column totals: <u>9</u> <u>5</u>   <u>4</u>   <u>27</u>

(Left margin, vertically: Second Letters)

Most Frequent Digrams

RK, 10	KV, 6	WD, 4	SR, 4
VT, 6	DY, 6	RR, 4	KS, 4
			HV, 4

The Digram-Solution Method. — This method, representing another of our many debts to M. E. Ohaver, may be used either in conjunction with the vowel method, or independently, as the fundamental method of attack. For a satisfactory demonstration, however, we need more material, and Fig. 67 shows our cryptogram again, together with a suspected reply. Thus we have a length of 235 letters, so that the preparation of contact-notations, which we found sufficient in the preceding case, becomes here an irksome task.

For these longer cryptograms, it is usually best to put all of our data into the form of a *digram-count*, as indicated in Fig. 68. This is most easily done as follows: Using a sheet of cross-section paper, mark off the limits of a 26 x 26 square;

write the normal alphabet across the top, so that each of its letters will govern a column; and write it again along one side, so that each letter will govern a row. For added convenience, these two alphabets may be repeated, as they are shown in the figure. Now, remembering that each letter in the text is the first letter of a digram (except the two which are finals), our two texts, with their total of 235 letters, are to provide a count on 233 digrams. Taking letters one by one, just as they come in the cryptograms, find each letter in the upper alphabet; find, in the side alphabet, the letter which immediately follows it in the cryptogram, and count this digram by placing a tally-mark in the cell at which the column and row governed by these two letters are found to intersect. In the figure, the tally-marks have been replaced with numbers showing their totals. It will be noted that the process described is identically the method which would have been used by Meaker in preparing the digram chart; and, just as in the case of the digram chart, the counting of the digrams has automatically counted the single letters. To obtain their frequencies, we may total either the columns or the rows, taking the larger figure in those few discrepancies caused by initial or final letters. With the chart understood, the digram-method of solution can be shown in a nutshell.

An inspection of this chart enables us to find quickly that the leading digrams are those listed: *RK, VT, KV, DY*, etc. These, almost certainly, are the substitutes for digrams ranking high on the normal list, and many others, having a frequency of 3, are very likely indeed to be substitutes for digrams from that same high-frequency class. Our text, of course, is still short, even with 235 letters, and we do not invariably find, in texts of this length, that the ranking digram (in this case *RK*, frequency 10) is the substitute for *th*, though the chances are, at all times, that it is. And should it prove here that *RK* does not represent *th*, then we may be quite sure that *th* is represented in one of the digrams *VT, KV, DY*, having the next frequency, 6. With the single exception of *RR*, each digram of the nine which are listed below the chart car be checked against three other digrams: Its own reversal; the doubling of its first letter; and the doubling of its second letter. In addition, it may be checked through the individual frequencies of its two component letters. These points of comparison, made for each of the nine leading digrams, have been tabulated in Fig. 69, so that the discussion may be easily followed.

Examining *RK*, assumed to represent *th*: Its reversal, *KR*, has not appeared on the chart, which is satisfactory for a digram of no greater frequency than its supposed original, *ht*. The doubling of its first letter, *RR*, has appeared four times, which is satisfactory for *tt*, one of the leading doubles of our language. The doubling of its second letter, *KK*, has not appeared, which is eminently satisfactory for a digram as rare as *hh*. Its first letter, *R*, has a frequency of 28, the highest in the cryptogram, which is not at all unusual in the case of *t;* and its second letter, *K*, has a frequency of 16, a little high for *h*, but not unsatisfactory. Thus, we find nothing, so far, to contradict the supposition that the digram *RK* is the substitute for *th*. But if *K* represents *h*, it should be possible to find digrams beginning with *K* which will check equally well as the substitutes for *he* and *ha*. We do, in fact, find *KV* and *KS*. But which is which? Examination of Fig. 69 shows that one of these, *KS*, has a reversal, *SK*, frequency 1; but this is not informative, since it would be equally expected of *eh* or *ah*. Further examination shows that *V* has been doubled, which is far more characteristic of *e* than of *a*. Also, the individual frequency of *V*, 24, is the second highest in the cryptogram, and more likely to be that of *e* than that of *a*. Thus we may assume that *KV* represents *he* and that *KS* represents *ha*. This automatically identifies the digram *SR* as *at*. As to *VT*, this, apparently, involves the only reversal of any prominence in the cryptogram. Its first letter has already been identified as *e*, and the outstanding reversal of the language is *er-re*. This is not so certain as in the preceding cases, but the frequency of *T* is satisfactory as that of *r*.

Thus we have identified the letters *t, h, e, a, r*, which is as far as the tabulation has been carried. Having the substitute for *h*, we may now bring in the vowel-solution method through examination of digrams *KD, KJ, KT, KZ;* or continue with the digram-solution method by looking over the field for some of the other *h*-digrams: *sh, ch, wh, ph, gh*, and so on. The first of these should be easily identified by the frequency of *s*, and, in addition to the regular three check-digrams, we might check this against a possible *st*, another of our leading English digrams. With the process explained, we need not go further; the substitution of letters *t, h, e, a, r, s*, will surely break any simple substitution cryptogram. Possibly, enough has not been said as to the use of the trigram list, the consideration of com-

Figure 69

Digram		Doubled Letter		Letter Frequency		Supposed
Original	Reversed	1st	2d	1st	2d	Identity
R K 10	K R...	R R 4	K K...	R_28	K 16	t h
V T 6	T V 2	V V 1	T T...	V 24	T 15	e r
K V 6	V K...	K K...	V V 1	K 16	V 24	h e
D Y 6	Y D...	D D...	Y Y...	D 21	Y 10	?
W D 4	D W 1	W W 1	D D...	W 8	D 21	?
S R 4	R S...	S S...	R R 4	S 18	R 28	a t
K S 4	S K 1	K K...	S S...	K 16	S 18	h a
R R 4	....	....	....	R 28		t t
H V 4	V H...	H H...	V V 1	H 5	V 24	? (-e)

mon affixes, common short words, and so on; but these are all points which the student can best develop for himself.

Another point, however, must not be overlooked: *the long repeated sequences HVXXU, ZDYFZJX, DRKVT, GSRRVT.* Repeated sequences of these lengths will usually come from *repeated whole words*, making it possible, to some extent, to attack the cryptogram by word-division methods. It is, in fact, the repetition of sequences, these and many others, which, in the beginning, has led us to assume that both cryptograms are using the same key. As to the recovery of this key, we need not wait until solution is complete. Even in simple substitution, it is well, during the identification of substitutes, to have before us a sort of skeleton key, in which the plaintext alphabet has been written out in normal order, so that the substitutes, as fast as their identities are discovered, can be placed below their originals.

Thus, having identified as many as twelve letters in our present cryptogram, this skeleton key, or framework, might begin to assume the appearance which is indicated in the upper tabulation of Fig. 70. Here, we are able to note a reciprocal encipherment between *A* and *S, F* and *N, R* and *T,* and *U* and *Y,* suggesting that the whole encipherment may have been reciprocal; if so, we have the identities of four additional substitutes: *O, I, H, E,* representing *d, j, k, v,* respectively. If they are present in the cryptogram, these four substitutions may be tried; but with or without their presence in the cryptogram, they can be added to the skeleton key, as in the lower tabulation of the figure. Notice that when this has been done, the cipher alphabet is beginning to show alphabetical sequences (reversed). We find *H I J K,* and, just before this, *D F,* which is an alphabetical sequence if the letter *E* has been taken out for use in a key-word. Between *DF* and *HIJK* of the cipher alphabet, we need only *G* to fill out the sequence; therefore either *l* or *m* must belong to the key-word; comparing this with what is found at the other end of the sequence, we find that either *L* or *M* would be the substitute for *g*. Between *NO*, we find *V*, evi-

Figure 70

Supposing 12 substitutes to have been identified:

```
Plaintext alphabet:  a b c d e f g h i j k l m n o p q r s t u v w x y z
CIPHER ALPHABET:     S     V N   K J         F D     T A R Y       U
```

Assuming reciprocal substitution:

```
Plaintext alphabet:  a b c d e f g h i j k l m n o p q r s t u v w x y z
CIPHER ALPHABET:     S   O V N   K J I H     F D     T A R Y E     U
                     Q?P?  *  L?            G?      C?B?*      *      T?
                              M?
```

dently misplaced; and, following *O* and preceding *S*, we find two positions which
may be occupied by two of the letters *PQR*, of which *R* has already been placed
(under *t*). That is, where the encipherer has used a key-word-mixed alphabet without troubling to carry it through a transposition process of any kind, we are often
able to build it up again, and make it help us in the solution. This is especially true
if he has used reciprocal encipherment; with the substitutes which may actually be
found in our foregoing cryptograms, a little rearrangement is all that is needed in
order to discover exactly what the original key was. When the cipher alphabet has
been carried through a transposition block, it is not so easy to recover during the
actual process of solution; afterward, however, it is not usually difficult to treat it
by one of the transposition processes, just as if it were a transposition cryptogram
of 26 letters. In the examples which follow, the key-word-mixed alphabets were
used as they stood, though we believe that none of the encipherment was reciprocal.
In one case, however, the plaintext and cipher alphabets were both mixed, according to different key-words, so that the recovery of this key may prove troublesome.

45. By PICCOLA.

```
S C Y J T   O P N R M   J T U E A   W S R O R   O A E P Q   R J C R O   A R M P H

Q K J Q S   R S J H A   X P F K E   A Q R M Y   S R P Q P   M P S E C   A H C A W

S R O P E   E E S H A   Q O P V S   H I R O A   Q P F A E   A H I R O   P H N P Q

R J H T F   U A M C J   M R Y R O   M A A W A   E E B T Q   R W M S R   A S R J H

A I M J T   K U A E J   W P H J R   O A M P H   N Q A A W   O P R Y J   T Q A A L.
```

46. By PICCOLA. (Plaintext and Cipher Alphabets have each a key-word).

```
J C W E H   S N D F S   B N J I V   T E A G V   D H O C Q   Q I Q F R   P H F K Q

E A R F Q   A R F A H   F Q E J C   B N J N H   B E O C B   N L N O V   H B L F Q

J B N A B   L F V H C   A J I V B   N W N S T   B L E A G   V A J N S   R F W N S

Y R V S S   C A E H V   A Q F C J   E A G J N   A W N S O   V B V C Q   Y D C S P

H E H O C   S P E A G   B E O N A   F R L C A   G N E A K   C S O N S   H A C B E

F A C Q X.
```

47. By PALOMITA. (No key-word).

```
B O Y B A   N K I L L   A P K R I   Y A P Y Y   U P B L Y   E R P B P   L G Y G M

H L A B O   Y K J A K   L P Y L H   H J A C R   P O R C Q   U Y N B H   L A B O Y

G N A Z N   Y L H B O   Y K N A N   P R B R W   O J C B R   C Q D N P   K.
```

48. By PICCOLA. (Of these two, one has normal word divisions; the other has not).

W T E I C   H E P P C   A E P T J   W P O Y D   Q P   R M E L U   E I N D E P Q   T C

Q D Q D P C P D   R K G   E P U O P Q D Q   U Q D J I C.   I S Y E   Q   T C P V E M Y R

E W M   E K E C   Q E S P E L   U E I N E ?   P   D Q H U P Q C   G P J   T C V !

E O E E I Q M C I,   P   K J   P E S X Q T E Q M C I   P   K J P D Q D   J I D P U P U

C G   G Y J R Q T   E V E M Y   P   D H K G E P Q F D I S.

49. By PICCOLA.

P B K L A B E I   C D J   D B I   L Y P K   L D   O I X   L Y I   P K   V Y A L ?

A G F Y A M I L K   L Y I K I   D C   A G G   L D   O I X-V D J R K   L Y I   C P B R P B N

X D Q   A J I ?   Q K   J I S P B R K   L Y A L   A B R   M X   Q F   P L   F P E O   L D

I B R   V Y P E Y   O B D V   X D Q   P C   E G I A J   F I J C I E L G X   P K

S I A B P B N   P L K.   A J P K L D E J A L   A B   B D L   P K   L Y P K   B D !

CHAPTER X

THE CONSONANT-LINE SHORT CUT

A Method for Attacking Difficult Cases

By George C. Lamb

Several routine methods have been evolved for special use on the very difficult " aristocrat " — that fascinating form of simple substitution with word-divisions in which the message is of no importance whatever and the encipherer's full attention has been given to manipulation of letter characteristics. Of the several such methods which have proved workable over a long period of years, the author's favorite is the " consonant-line " method, the exact value of which has been tested in a special analysis of 130 very difficult cryptograms. However, it should be stated clearly that no method is a mechanical crypt-solver; these devices merely serve to bring out clues which to the haphazard worker are totally invisible. For discussion, we will consider an example by M. E. Bosley which appeared as No. 19 Aristocrat in *The Cryptogram* for June, 1936. This is shown at Fig. 71.

Figure 71

```
U W Y M N X K A    E H X R B Z    U V X M U W B Z    O Y Z T W H V C X Y A

C Y A U Z    D B R A H V K B A;    Z W S V A H K U Z B K C,    M S C X

C Y X B S,    X V Z Y T R Y C X P.
```

The work must be initiated by isolating a small group of consonants, and the problem of selecting these with certainty is one which for years has baffled the shrewdest solvers of both the National Puzzlers' League and the American Cryptogram Association. Many successful solvers have based their selection on frequency alone, rearranging the letters of a frequency count in the order of decreasing frequency and marking off a section of low-frequency letters which will presumably include only consonants. But the clever manipulator is able to distort frequencies out of all resemblance to the normal table, and here we will base our selection on *variety of contact* — something which the constructor cannot successfully manipulate.

Fig. 72 sums up the entire process. At (a) we have a list of contacts taken in the order of appearance of the letters, and at (b) a rearrangement of the cryptogram letters *in the order of decreasing variety of contact*. Immediately above each letter is its " variety count " and directly above this is its frequency figure. In this set-up, a certain number of letters taken at the extreme right may confidently be marked off as a group of consonants. As to just where the line of demarcation may be set, recent analysis has shown that it is safe to include 20% of the total variety-count. In this case, the sum of all variety-figures is 104, and 20% of this, roughly, is 21. If we begin with *P* at the extreme right and add numbers backward for a count of 21, we find that the line of demarcation falls between *R* and *C*. However, we have at this point four letters, *M, R, C, S*, whose variety-count is uniformly 5, and any two of which might have occupied the places of *C* and *S*. To accept a vowel at this stage would mar the effectiveness of our system, and either we must discard all four of these letters, or we must find a means of differentiation other than their variety of contact. At this point, letter-frequencies come into play.

Examining the set-up just as we have it prepared at (b), note that the two figures just above M are 3-5. This is a "step-up" of 2 points. Note that just above R we have the same two figures 3-5, another step-up. Above C, we find the two figures 6-5, this time a "step-down" of 1 point; and above S we again find 3-5, a step-up. According to years of observation, confirmed by investigation of special cases, a vowel nearly always shows a tendency to step up, while consonants are

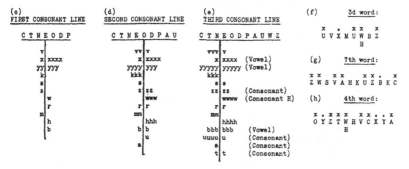

Figure 72

(a) List of Contacts

U_6	W_7	Y_9	M_5	N_2	X_{10}	K_7	A_7	E_1	H_6	R_5	B_8	Z_6	V_8	O_1	T_4	C_5	D_1	S_5	P_1
-W	U-Y	W-M	Y-N	M-X	N-K	X-A	K-	-H	E-X	X-B	R-Z	B-	U-X	-Y	Z-W	V-X	-B	W-V	X-
-V	U-B	O-Z	X-U		H-R	V-B	Y-		W-V	B-A	W-Z	B-	H-C		Y-R	-Y		M-C	
M-W	T-H	X-A	-S		V-M	H-U	Y-U		A-V	T-Y	D-R	Y-T	H-K			K-		B-	
A-Z	Z-S	C-A			C-Y	B-C	R-H		A-K		K-A	U-	S-A			S-X			
K-Z		C-X			C-		B-				Z-K	-W	X-Z			-Y			
		Z-T			Y-B		V-H				X-S	U-B				Y-X			
		R-C			-V							V-Y							
					C-P														

(The figures give the "variety-count," or number of different letters contacted. Reversals may be indicated by circling letters. Note that in dealing with normal word-divisions, we may omit contacts falling between one word and another.)

(b) Basis for Primary Isolation of Consonant-Group:

Letter-frequencies: 8 7 6 5 4 4 6 5 4 7 3 3 6 3 2 1 1 1 1 1
VARIETY OF CONTACT: 10 9 8 8 7 7 7 6 6 6 5 5 5 5 4 2 1 1 1 1 (104)
X Y B V W K A U H Z M R C S T N E O D P

(c) FIRST CONSONANT LINE	(d) SECOND CONSONANT LINE	(e) THIRD CONSONANT LINE	(f)	3d word:
C T N E O D P	C T N E O D P A U	C T N E O D P A U W Z		x . x x x U V X M U W B Z H

(c)
```
C T N E O D P

      v
  x | xxxx
 yy | yyy
  k |
  s |
  z |
    | w
    | r
  m |
  h |
  b |
```

(d)
```
C T N E O D P A U

   vv | v
    x | xxxx
 yyyy | yyy
 kkk  |
    s |
    z | zz
      | www
    r | r
   mm |
    b | hhh
      | b
      | u
    a |
```

(e)
```
C T N E O D P A U W Z

   vvv | v
     x | xxxx   (Vowel)
 yyyyy | yyyyy  (Vowel)
  kkk  |
     s | s
    zz | zz     (Consonant)
       | wwww    (Consonant H)
     r | r
    mm |
  bbb  | bbb    (Vowel)
 uuuu  | u      (Consonant)
     a |        (Consonant)
     t | t      (Consonant)
```

(g) 7th word:
```
x x   x x    x x . x
Z W S V A H K U Z B K C
```

(h) 4th word:
```
x . x x x   x x . . x
O Y Z T W H V C X Y A
H
```

prone to step down. Thus among our four doubtful letters, there are three, M, R, and S, of which one will probably be a vowel. But the remaining letter, C, has the step-down peculiar to consonants; and while a step-down of only 1 point would not be definitely informative when found at the left end of the set-up, it almost certainly indicates in the present position that C is a consonant. Thus, we are able to include seven letters, $C\ T\ N\ E\ O\ D\ P$, in our group of "sure-fire" consonants, but have to dispense with several points of our 21-count.

At (c) we have the beginning stage of the actual investigation, while (d) and (e) are amplifications of the first stage. In these the original consonants are used to determine other consonants, progressing from stage (c) to stage (e). First, the original group of consonants is set down on a sheet of paper, and the space below it is bisected by the consonant-line. Consulting (a), we then find the letters of this group one by one, and all contacting letters which precede any one of them we set down on the left side of the consonant-line, and all those which follow any one of them we set down on the right side, always once for each time that the contacting letter appears. Thus we have stage (c). While we do not often encounter doubled letters in this form of cryptogram, it may be well to say here that while a doubled letter would be counted among the frequencies of letter appearance, its contacts with itself would not be entered on the consonant-line. That is, a doubled *L* would add a frequency of 2 to the general count, but contacts *L-L* would be ignored.

At (d) we have the first step in amplification, for which we are indebted to Chester A. Griffin. If there is any letter in the cryptogram which *does not appear at all in* (c), such a letter is practically sure to be another consonant. In this case we find *A* and *U*, and in (d) these two letters have been added to the consonant group and their contacts placed on the consonant-line. From this point onward, the work becomes more tentative, and, as a detail of operation, Mr. Griffin suggests that further additions to the consonant-line be made in another color of lead; if it then becomes a matter of necessity to erase, only the new letters will be included in the erasing.

Figure 73

```
        1                 2                3                     4
 x x . x x . x x   x . . x . x    x x . x x x . x   x . x x x . x x . . x
 U W Y M N X K A   E H X R B Z    U V X M U W B Z   O Y Z T W H V C X Y A
   h                                      h                 h


        5              6                   7                      8
 x . x x x     x . x x . x x . x    x x . x x . x x x . x x    x . x .
 C Y A U Z     D B R A H V K B A;   Z W S V A H K U Z B K C,   M S C X
                                        h


       9              10
 x . . . .     . x x . x x . x . x
 C Y X B S,    X V Z Y T R Y C X P.
```

Further work includes the application of the " force method." That is, we turn our attention to the cryptogram itself, marking with a small cross, or otherwise, all letters determined as consonants, and placing a dot, or other indication, over all letters determined as vowels. Some vowels become evident as early as stage (c), as here we find both *X* and *Y* freely contacting our preliminary group of consonants, and if confirmation is needed, a glance back at set-up (b) will show that both of these are step-up letters. They may be labeled vowels without hesitation.

As to consonants, there are two clear text letters, *h* and *n*, which, owing to their many contacts with other consonants, and particularly with the low-frequency consonants (as in the digrams *CH, GH, PH, WH, NG, NC, NK, NQ*, etc.), will often show up clearly on the consonant-line. Of these two, *n* will appear largely upon the left side of the line, and *h*, the more reliable of the two, upon the right side. Examining (d) we find *W* and *H* appearing exclusively on the right side of the line, and since, under the rules of the game, no letter may be its own substitute, we may assume here that *W* represents *h*.

Further concerning *h:* An examination of the cryptogram shows that *W* has occurred twice as the second letter of a word, and the second-position is particularly characteristic of *h*. Then, assuming that *W* actually does represent *h*, we have in the seventh word of the cryptogram an intimation that the letter *Z* is also a consonant (since formations like AHEAD, AHA, are very rare, and seldom, if ever, occur in long words). Thus, we have two new consonants, *W* and *Z*, to be added to the consonant-line, with their contacts below, extending operations to stage (e). If desired, the spotted consonants may now be crossed off on the line itself, or merely indicated as in (e). It seems evident from (e), confirmed by (b), that *B* is our third vowel, and the supposition can be strengthened by inspecting the third cryptogram word, which, at this time, will have appeared as in (f). It also appears from (e) and (b), confirmed by the aspect of the tenth cryptogram word, that *R* is a consonant. Similarly, *M*, which, on three appearances, has twice contacted a vowel, may be placed as a consonant. These two new consonants, *R* and *M*, are added to the group of known consonants, and all of their contacts are placed on the consonant-line. Our next victim is *S*, evidently a vowel in spite of (e) because of its position in the seventh cryptogram word (g), which, otherwise, must begin with five consonants in succession. Presuming that a fifth vowel is to be found, the same word suggests either *K* or *H* as the candidate. The choice falls on *H*, according to the fourth cryptogram word (h); and thus continuing the force method with one eye on the consonant-line and the other on the cryptogram, the v-c formation of the cryptogram is finally established as in Fig. 73. Actual identification and solution fol-

Figure 74

```
A text prepared by RUFUS T. STROHM:                    H Y N W B D

OMRI, UNKEMPT HELP, BRISKLY SCYTHED BUCKWHEAT            ee eeee
                                                        t  t
CROP.  PANICKY SKYLARK UPSHOT; BUMPKIN SHOWED            w
                                                        ss
SMIRK.                                                   o  oo
                                                        l  l
Frequency:   8 6 5 4 5 3 4 5 4 6 5 3 4 4 4 3 2 3 2      c
Variety:    10 8 7 7 7 6 6 6 6 6 5 5 5 5 4 4 4 2 1      kkk k
            K P E M R A C I O S H L T U Y N W B D        u  uu
                      x         x x x x x                a
                                                        i  i
                                                        h
Amplification at step (d) adds  P and M.                r
```

low the usual path of patterns, cross-comparison of words, and inspiration, where all systems are subordinate to the solver's own perspicacity . . . or " cipher brains." Chapter *IX* has given some methods for identifying letters from their characteristics, and also mentioned the preparation and use of pattern-word lists.

At this point, it might be well to mention the " vowel-line " method, whose appearance was antecedent to that of the consonant-line. This earlier method was conceived by Erik Boden, and in principle works in reverse to the consonant-line method. Its set-up is like that of the consonant-line except that vowels, instead of consonants, are placed at the top. The contacts made by the determined vowels are listed fore and aft as is done with the consonants in the consonant-line method. The vowel-line shows several letters by certain characteristics . . . a letter appearing exclusively on the left might represent *h*, and one appearing solely on the right can be taken for *n*. The liquids, *l* and *r*, straddle the line about equally. On the supposition that you have located three vowels, the list of contacts on the vowel-line will not include, or only rarely, any other vowels as yet unidentified. A good suggestion is to use the consonant-line as specified, and then follow up with the vowel-line, using the vowels you have *definitely* identified as such. The result will be thus: The letter appearing exclusively to the right of the consonant-line will appear solely on the left of the vowel-line, and vice versa. If such appearances are noted, then you have spotted *h* and *n* . . . . . identified as suggested in another part of this chapter.

The workability of the consonant-line system in unravelling the mysteries of the " Dizzy " crypt is best judged by making a series of preliminary sheets from clear text. In Fig. 74, for instance, we have the solution to one of the most skillfully manipulated cryptograms in the collection of 130. This was prepared by Rufus T. Strohm as No. 17 Aristocrat of the April, 1932, *Cryptogram.* The total variety-count is 104, 20% of which is about 21. The line of demarcation thus falls in the group *H L T U*, each with a variety-count of 5 and no step-down. *H*, with figures 5-5, could be grouped with the remaining letters, giving us *H Y N W B D* as consonants, with *P* and *M* to be added at step (d). We thus include *Y* among our sure-fire consonants, and, in fact, it often is a consonant, but this is a problem no solver

Figure 75

A text prepared by J. LLOYD.HOOD: D C M P B F Q W J K

GARGANTUAN MESTIZO ESCORTS JUNOESQUE NEGRO   aaaa aaaa
                                                         oo ooo
WOMAN ADOWN NIGHT CLUB AISLE.   DARK HUED   eeee
                                                          n n
AMAZON HAD BEAUTIFUL LAPIS-LAZULI PENDANT.   ss
                                                              l
Frequency: 14 9 8 6 10 7 6 6 6 4 4 5 3 3 2 3 2 2 1 1 2 1 1 i i
Variety: 12 11 11 9 8 8 6 6 6 5 5 4 4 4 3 3 3 2 2 2 2 1 1 u uuu
            A E U 1 N O L S T G R D H Z C M P B F Q W J K r
                       x   x x x x x x x x x

Amplification at step (d) adds T, G, H, and Z.

has yet been able to overcome. However, the letter *Y* can usually be spotted by *position.* Note that except for *Y*, every vowel here is a step-up letter.

The above two examples have represented the " tough " case. In Fig. 75, where the text is the solution to a crypt by J. Lloyd Hood published as No. 9 in the February, 1932, *Cryptogram,* we have the average comparatively simple case. The total variety-count is 118, making the isolation count about 23 and throwing the line of demarcation into the group *D H Z*, where *D* is the only step-down letter. Every letter in the isolated group is actually a consonant, and step (d) adds the letters *T G H Z*. On the consonant-line, *A, O*, and to a lesser extent *U*, stand out clearly as vowels. *E* might be mistaken for *H* until we apply the force method, while *I* shows a step-up of three points, in addition to whatever shows up on the cryptogram. So up and at 'em! Edgar Allan Poe spoke truly when he suggested that whatever the human mind can devise, the human mind can also untangle.

NOTE: For additional methods of analytical attack on this kind of cryptogram, the student is referred to the booklet " Cryptogram Solving," by M. E. Ohaver. This can be purchased direct from the author (Columbus, Ohio) for twenty-five cents, or may be purchased from the Frank A. Munsey Company. The textbooks of the National Puzzlers League also include chapters devoted to the solving of cryptograms; further information concerning these may be had by writing to R. T. Strohm, 1328 E. Gibson Street, Scranton, Pa.

H. F. G.

50. By ROBO.

POUYH   IBQUAV   PUKO   M   EGUHAC   MK   KOH   POUKH

OBLJH,   KOHBCBGH   GBBJHNHYK   GHSHUNHC   MA   UAWLGR   KB

BAH   HRH   POUSO   SMLJHC   IYUACAHJJ.

51. By SUE DE NYMME.

"IDFURSF   UJBDOC   UJY   NEGNXDNOWN   IDFU   FUN   CXJKGDOC

JOY   RGGXNKKDBN   AJO   IN   WJOORF   JGGXNWDJFN   FUN

JZZJHDMDFL RZ FUN URONKF JOY CNONXRSK." —RXDNOFJM

JYJCN.

52. By I TAPPA KE.

B HCN FBA IOA CAXW PBXLSBW RAMC MPJ SCCHK.

BLMJI MPBM PJ RK IOAARAN COM CL MPJ SCCHK.

53. By TRYCHS.

ZAXABAPRSANL CDRLT ZNLZDLSERSANL NQ WNWFBRSANL, ZBNTD

FSABAPRSANL NQ SKD BRLU, TWEDRU NQ ALUFTSEV — RBB

UEAXD HABU BAQD RHRV.

54. By DECIBEL.

KTJ UZ WJIWNLUFZA, RNUJW FV NYYWZQFBNUJCP ZAJ IZTWUG

KJJYJW UGNA FU NYYJNWV UZ MJ RGJA CZZDFAH FAUZ FU.

55. By B. NATURAL.

GBAM BP NCLBGMC: — IBAM FDCCDIH HKULC BP DSBD, RBGE

BP BPTBLPL, AGDKC BP RBVSBULP, FLEMH VLEM BP BGGBPDBH.

SKHFLPT LNM BN BP RBHHDKCB, UDN BPTBUMHNBDP BP

NMPPMHHMM, NDDE FBVLCF BP EMPNKVEW.

56. By POSIUS.

SHTOADDCTUD TO SLIHCTICDP LHA XCZA IHALICAD TO SALFA

— IEAR TUXR KCUB ICXX VA LHA DIHTUM AUTNME IT

KHALZ IEAP. — ABPNUB KNHZA.

57. By LIGHTNING.

QFY. NZZDO, YOFLAVU HAVVOF NVVBCVSOY: "FOSAZO RBF

YBCZ AY RFBQ DNKO QFY. HCQZDAVU; BCK BR FOYZOSK

RBF WOF, A YCUUOYK YBCZ GO ONKOV AV YADOVSO!"

58. By BOUNCING BOB.

ACGLCRW BDHMW AHSXGE. "XI EHN TCYD DH WBDCFSXBO

GMWVXD OWMW, EHN ZNBD FW CD SWCBD WXRODE EWCMB

HSV CYV CGGHZACYXWV FE EHNM ACMWYDB."

59. By MISISEEG.

"PC KFJJW LF LPAS YG KF CYNE FH WFYJ LRCS,"

KPRI MYITS, RDOSLSJPLS PHLSJ-IRDDSJ KGSPASJ, PK ES

KSDLSDNSI CPD LF DRDSLW-DRDS WSPJK.

60. By EEGH.

EZVPJHOW HJWZB JZKRCHSPO HRRCHAOF OZAPEFE CSTF
JHWFBRSCCHB JBHVCSPL ZNFB RFBOSHP BAL VISCOW VFHBSPL
BAQQFB OIZFO.

61. By MERLIN.

ABDZYX UYDU ZA VYWZCE FBGH DBVTYCF SJJX YU RBVJ,
JKJC URBGER FBG LZAR URJF LJHJ.

62. By P. A. BEE.

"ZHN TCJP VDTK QHWWQF CLTDRP NDTX; ZHN CLGFP VDTK
QHWWQF WTF LTDRP NDTX." MSHLJ VTQJP ZB VCJFP LCR
GTCA WGF PQTX. LDBEW ITJFP VDTK PSLG HOFCP NDTX!

63. By SHORTY.

ABCDEFB XYGF HXYNEP OF QNHA BDRXA SYB SDPRFAZ
XYNHFKDSF KXY EDTFH VXCURDUR SNBUDANBF CBYNUP FIFBZ
KFFT YB AKY. BYNRX PFAYNB KYNEP ANBU AXF ABDVT.

64. By AH TIN DU.

ABCD ABEFGHJ KGLA: — MKNNDOH PBOLA, FBPDE AMBNNGHJ,
ARBON PBOLA KHL KSSGTDA. PRDH NRDAD SKGE, NOW
XRKON KHL CGLHGJRN BGE.

T I P   O F F S

For the benefit of the beginner a list of "tip-offs" are given below. By comparing these groups, affixes and single letters it is possible to find combinations which fit. For instance: ABC compared with ABCD, ABGA, GA, DHA might result in "the", "then", "that", "at", "not", etc.

50. M, MK, KB, KOH, BAH, MA, PUKO.

51. FUN, IDFU, IN, IDFURSF.

52. B, MPJ, MPBM, PJ, RA-, -RAN.

53. AL-, -SANL, ZNL-, SKD.

54. UZ, FAUZ, FU, -FAH, -UFZA, FV, ZAJ.

55. BP, BP-, -NBDP.

56. IT, TO; IEAR, IEAP, AUTNME.

57. A, AV, -AVU; BR, RBF, RFBQ.

58. DH, CD, CYV, HSV; identify W through its frequency.

59. Note Pattern group; DRDSLW-DRDS.

60. SPL; O; EFE, word 5, last word.

61. Use of J, LJHJ, JKJC, -ZCE, ZA.

62. WGF, QHWWQF, WTF.

63. AXF, KXY, AKY; FIFBZ, YB.

64. -GHJ, KHL.

65. By KING SLY.

KING   NERO   PRVBY   KHNC   AVCL,   FHYYVY   CAVRDLK   CHFN.

DEAF   TFENGY   IC;   DHULY   ERBV   YCHTL.   RIBY   XHFF,

ERTFIKERD   FHYYEL.

66. By THE SHADOW.

FJ   CIGBHQ   KDDH,   LDQ   FJJPHLC   DXXCIGBHQ   CAP.   LDQQDHP

BCCAP: EBQMJ   DXX;   JPHLC   KDDHEBQMJ   BC   QDHP.

67. By "33".

OXVXAKZDKY   KYKOMSQXDI   DIAB   ABOQSXIZW   ZWIALBV   BVXQDO.

DOSQDOXASZ   SZSOPXYQ   YQSOQZBY   BYQLBO,   BOOSQXA   XADIDAZSYQ.

68. By BUBBLES.

SBCWFK   VWUKPI   FCRSX   PFNUKVSB.   VWZGRE   XZKRP   ZBTFV.

WPGU   SFGDJ   DPERBFGP;   VPIFZ   TPASX   JKPVA   IKOBCU   OGPRIV.

69. By DEAN RELAX.

XYZABCD   ZEFZGBAZHDBHI   JBDY   KGLMZOCNHBDZ   OBCXNMZGC   XKPXBQA

KABO   SPKXT   ANHNXPBHBX   FPZNXYGNBX   FGBCAC.

70. By WEHANONOWIT.

ZYXWVXUTSRQUXO   PXWVTW   ZWNZXMXRTL   XOOTKQXRQKT   YNWRQUSORSWT:

ZWNJSUTL   RXIXUTRSV,   ONHTOQX,   YTJTNVX,   JQMQRXOQL,   TR

UTRTWX,   XJ   QIPQIQRSV.

71. By CURLY.

WINIWKB   OWBWO   KRSRKVRV   CRSRC   NWEWN   WCTPXVQBR   XWKWXR.

AWKWARD   TJJRKV   VQPQVDRK   DZKRWD.   KRSRKRPD   BWOVRC   AKWEV,

GWKKQRB   HE   JCTTB   DZKM   BQSQBR.

96   *ELEMENTARY CRYPTANALYSIS*

72. By GALUPOLY.

LKMEGDIMJ, LHFABCGNKEF, LSNJJDI, LBMNKCJ, LBMEFJP MJR

LBTNIG GMVN RDSSDAXTK RNADLBNEDJI SCE AEFLKCIEMLBNE.

73. By SABIO.

WILD PANGRAMS RDMB ALCW EFFRRD HLFEM INJW. HAKNLLO

QLNTNW. INJW TFFRRD NIIRD UGUGVWG, WJGORTX RDMB

PAYWV XDOMAT ROZAVD.

74. By GINHUTS.

OLDMADE OVID SLATILK, ZLOMLX VWXYB, WERK SLMB LERVI,

NLI CLRO EVRS GKTV OTAHB ADGV TVWEY, YBLTO LISWR

RLDEWLEB.

75. By CIPHERMIT.

ABZYC DXXZBF, GYZBHVDX SZBHC, SGYBZTH VRZBS JKZBVXQ

FBZUB YDWZBY, WXZBYF, BZTRV WZBF, RDHCEBYMRZBS, FZBIB,

YBZHF, HBMEVZB; MRZBS YBVYZBIBF QZBXC.

76. By A. D. CODER.

ABCDEFB GHICD CJKLIC MNHHSJ OPCIQG MNJRBD PLFGSPLBR,

EILQ KICDTSCIR KICJRAC HL PLDRSJ GOFBBSIDQCNR.

77. By ROVING VIC.

MOCKMOCK ZPLY KPYO RSRI-RSRI FIPTSU FLIPFLIP. NERTS-NERTS

WICHWICH, SHPYSHPY TCYL, SILLSILL, MREX UPMD XRT.

APTS-ACTS WEPMWERM OLIREZU WPTRE MHIL.

78. By AMSCO.

ABWKGLWB ELTFTELHEG, SENGLMTUG FTELSABWKGLTF, LGBTGXGU

KHLCTHK DHTF BTOG HFATFH DGKESLTU.

79. By M. G. M.

ABCDECBFA, GHDIJKLF, HFBMD, NLHMO IEDHOBF OPPMGHR,

SMPDBIDBO UR VPHD, OMHGUMEONB, SPMDILFFEA.

80. By SIMPLICIUS.

VKJPE PBSCKZ RLHRTGM HJALCGSBR TLCG; RKPHCLRHM

NLMHGJCGAAKMBM; LIUJCGM NJCMJBH KQ CKZGPHM.

81. By KRIPTOBENS.

DYFR SWCX VHZS WMLB TMLB CZYO PHUT WKHT, JKOS

MOSY PHOB, NHTK IKAR AMLW WHCU, DUKT! LMSR LYZV

ECMQ XKOS, DMOT VHNK, VMLB, PUCK! VHDK YZKO, GHLB

UYVS! WHAT BOYS, YOUR LUCK!

82. By PHONEY.

ABCDE FEGHI, GEJBI; KLBGI MDCEH NDEST IEKRD DREIN

UMELV. TLHNR RGHBD HLWJI SRMHN, VESTI JHEKB, XBDJI

LDENB YRDIB; PDRGV ZRDSI, BKLWNI OEDJF WYBEN. CEGOF

EOLBM.

83. By ARROWHEAD.

ABCDEF GHIJK, LMN OPQR, STU VWXY. ZWHTAJ, FBIDEB

FEWCUH VHAXMP, HJQD BHXEJ XHUTA, EQGIF GTJE IHWREJMP.

84. By THE GRIFFIN.

TWDOIUESMA DMPOIREXYK TRXAWEKMLI XRYMUOLSED AMIEXKUGNO

MUTRYOLSDH YMKAGRXEIO GZPRKAESOY WHTOXZGDMA TDEHBXMIWS.

85. By SOUR PUSS.

OYESK PACHYDERMS AOPFL UXFD MHZOY XFBR PLMBS OZPL.

ZUFPLBAGH LBYCF QZDYPX YDLM GZQFBD ADLYJ RZUD.

86. By LIVEDEVIL.

PREVIOUSLY BDACL YOEL YFOCG, FLHCY, EHJJPOVLB GHKRCL,

UCOFMJ APCR EONQ MOIQCHBAPJ.

87. By NEOTERIC.

RXUGUZLQTVFR, CNSQRLQTVFR OTDALN RB MVFTQQRX QSTQ.

TFXUTSLCGSFZJ FTVXLVQNZ FTOSQ GUFLVOU DRTQDRX TRF.

88. By ZERO.

KROLGDB FURZGV ZDWFK BRXWKV VSULQW DORQJ GLUW WUDFN.

VZDUWKB FXEDQ MXQLRU MXELODQWOB ZLQV.

89. By JOKEL.

JPLX VUNKOM MLKDUB FUGHVP VKHCX VUPD FWHMVP; LQUMDPBV,

VWJKPLMNB; ULKFUGIKB, QKDHGP; VUXPLCMJ, AMJPVUD.

90. By LEE ANDER.

CLOUDY BERG-SLHVEC BECTR, UI BECT, FVRAKMY MGRAK-HVEC

BUDNR-VRGL BUZCLI EY BDAAEDA. NEKYDNLC; GEESE PUNFUY;

BETT ESTDNLC.

91. By TRYIT.

LSYKCTLSTRYITAB,   MCDSLMLE,   ZSRBWLX   IUOLSC   UWLAC   BMTUZYLAB

YRUYHU   GTKVBC   KPMDSCASWUWVD   PLANKX   UCLM   WSKCHBXU   WVUBCB

VUITSRPLBD   STUMBLER   JSLP   BHLMDVXU.

92. By DIZZY.

ABCDEFG,   DZEIBJK   LMFDBCN,   MNTLYEA   PRZBGSF   TSBIURP

IECLSBJ,   UKFIZBS,   PNFLARB;   EVLKZRO   PWELMBK   VTXPLNZ

TPXOBZG.

93. By ZANYCODAB.

ODZNERITFNM   VNDRR   BNOFDSK   PNIODRHE   EVMCDTIS   EVANZTOS

FNQRZO   HCRI   PVEOHE.   RZROHIK,   URFRES   CNISLVZTF   AZSBE

HGAZNLS.   QNCTK   OZRUNI   ASFRGSE   GTERLVITEO.

94. By I. D. CIPHER.

JBMDVKJVMBTD   AWTHVQBLTQV   VGLBQWFXH   FXBJWTHVQNM   VCWYBLGX.

BDGWCDWKZ,   DKWYFWKMB   RNMBJCDPCY,   GZCBQWFDP.

95. By NEON.

CDFGH,   JHKLM   NPQLR,   SDTVW   XMZDW   PATVF   LRXBV   CDTWE

QRIGH.   TKHFO   XRDIP   NHILW   EFDQL,   JMUVW   MRPES,   VHFAW

NRAPW.

96. By TWISTO.

FJKXZA,   ETXZQ,   ZCHUQP   QPZUP,   ZLLKUPTW   QBTJPZ   EDGN,

PQZM   BTJMN   QPZDU,   MTUIWXJ   ZXGJUW   ZPFEWU   DUQBTW

IBTQUWHJX.

97. By NUMERO.

BCBDBEBFC   GHIBEK   UGVBQW   BRWPF   OPFQR   STDGPBQ — EFHIKA

YBQWYTZW   BLGUGZR   LKFQCGZUZGTHCYKZI.

98. By WHIZZ BANG.

PGZPAPBPGZP?   AZFHIDEPXOA   AFISTP   YOEN   BPYC   PBFISX   PJDOBK

PKLPOT.   BWXDYOPA   AFEYWI   LOIN   BFKTDEOP   TWRI   WFDI.   BWLF

BLPZR   ESPAD   HZDJOBWK   ZWHPKI.

99. By INVICTUS.

PDOKX   ZEVR   MOLTA.   MPNDR-NEX   NPKWTM   FACHX   PSGTLUR

PGPGEVU   CPUFAD.   CZBPAQEUTCV   TAMR   TAOLPG   BPVUC.   HAEUWD

KONRUYC   RBENZCMR   MVEYOR.

CHAPTER XI

SIMPLE SUBSTITUTION WITH COMPLEXITIES

Concerning the numberless variations and complications which have been applied to the simple substitution cipher, our discussion here will have to be along general lines, with perhaps a brief mention of some analytical principle. Decryptment, for the most part, involves no principles other than those already discussed, and can only be demonstrated on very long texts. All such ciphers, however, will yield readily to the " probable word method," and the student, in considering each case, should not lose sight of the one method which applies equally to all.

If the *probable word* is a pattern word, so much the better; but *every word carries a pattern in the normal frequencies of its letters*. For instance, the word CIPHER, considered in relation to a text of 100 letters, has, roughly, the frequency-pattern 3-7-2-5-12-6; or, considered in relation to a 200-letter text, a pattern which is approximately double the first: 6-14-4-10-24-12. A cryptogram supposed to contain this word may be prepared as recommended in Chapter *IX*, with a frequency-figure written above each letter. The frequency-pattern of the word CIPHER, based on approximately the same amount of text, may then be written on a slip of paper and passed along below the frequency-figures shown for cryptogram-letters, in the hope of finding points at which the two sets of figures are, to some extent, alike. Wherever such points can be found, the suspected word can be assumed to be present there. So long as the method remains that of simple substitution, any substitutes which can be found in this way can have no other originals than those first determined; thus, their substitution throughout the cryptogram will serve to bring out other possibilities.

For the multiple-substitute cases, that is, those cases in which all or part of the letters may have more than one substitute, the frequencies of such letters as *I, H, E, R,* may be left blank (or cut in half, dependent upon just what the cipher is), and only the frequencies of *C* and *P*, standing two positions apart, need be considered. Particularly helpful, in this case, would be a probable word such as CRYPTO-GRAM, in which five infrequent letters are standing at known distances apart. The frequency-pattern of this word, based on 100, can be expressed roughly as *3 - 2 2 - - 2 - - 2,* and the attempt made to find points in the cryptogram at which five letters of somewhat these frequencies are standing at the given intervals apart. The foregoing is based on the supposition that while the encipherer, having several substitutes per letter, will be able to conceal the true frequencies of his high-frequency letters, *there is not much that he can do toward concealing his low frequencies.* He can, of course, produce any frequencies that he likes by swamping his text with nulls; and this, in the hands of a clever operator, can be very effective, especially if the circumstances are such that he can keep his method a secret. But for the average practical purpose, the time consumed in the encipherment, and the increased length of the cryptograms, are highly undesirable features, especially if it be kept in mind that there are many other ciphers than simple substitution. As to attack by analytical methods, the one device which is more likely than any other to prove applicable in all cases is the preparation of a digram count of exactly the kind we saw in Fig. 68. Such a chart will afford the means for studying carefully the *contacts* of any given letter: just what its *variety* seems to be; whether or not this seems disproportionate to its apparent frequency; whether or not it shows a tendency to touch letters of lower frequency, or to be present in reversals; and so on.

Many of these ciphers, however, make use of two letters to represent one. With these, it is the single-letter frequency count which is best made on a chart. That is, the cryptogram is first marked off into its pairs, and these pairs are counted in the same way as that described for digrams. But digrams, in this case, will be represented by four letters, and usually the number of different pairs is so large that the examination of digrams will have to be done by listing. For any cipher whatever in which the substitutes are two-digit numbers, a frequency count taken in chart form is usually far more convenient than one made by listing the numbers in advance. With only the ten digits, the 100 cells can be made larger than the 676 cells needed for letters, and the chart still be small and compact. The pairs of digits would be counted in exactly the same way as so many digrams. With numbers, it is sometimes possible to take the subsequent digram count, also, on a chart. Solution, in many cases, involves pure guess-work. The decryptor, perhaps, has begun his examination by testing his cryptogram for some variation of the " Caesar " encipherment. He has counted the first hundred or so of his letters, and has discovered that his frequency count is not going to be that of an ordinary simple substitution; that is, it is evidently not going to be one which he would be able to mark off into sections of high, medium, and low frequencies (usually with several letters missing), which would certainly be the case had each plaintext letter been replaced always with a given substitute throughout the cryptogram. Perhaps he has then marked his cryptogram into pairs of numbers or letters, and finds that these, also, are not likely to furnish the kind of frequency count which betrays simple substitution or some other cipher with which he is familiar. At this point, he is likely to pause and consider the source of the cryptogram. Is this the work of an expert, or the work of an amateur? Is it worthwhile to make up the statistics? Or shall I try for some one of the novelties which I have met many times before?

One device which is particularly popular with amateurs is that of assigning to each letter the numerical value which represents its serial position in the normal (or reversed) alphabet, A having the value 1, B the value 2, and so on, and afterward representing each plaintext letter with two (or more) others which will express some arithmetical process. For instance, the letter C (value 3) might, in some one of these systems, have the substitute AB (1 plus 2), or the substitute DA (4 minus 1), or the substitute YD (25 plus 4 equals 29; and 29 minus 26 equals 3); and so on to infinity.

Other simple devices, hardly worth calling ciphers, which have been used in the columns of *The Cryptogram* under the title " Simple Substitution with Frills," have included: (1) The use of false word divisions. (2) The simple reversal of an otherwise unmanipulated cryptogram. (3) The use of two given digrams, placed alternately at the ends of words. (4) The use of a new cipher alphabet for each new sentence. The first of these, of course, should have been suspected after examination of the apparent terminal letters. The second, theoretically, ought to be spotted if the method of solution includes a close investigation of digrams. As to the third device, any two digrams, used in the manner described, will attain impossible percentages; our leading digram, *TH,* in normal text, remains fairly close to three or four percent. It was the fourth device, however, which caused the greatest consternation among the younger solvers; in this case, the making of the frequency count will show what the trouble is: It begins very well, with the expected resemblance to a normal count, and suddenly begins to grow erratic.

Not every variation encountered in dealing with simple substitution is employed with the deliberate intention of creating difficulties. Those correspondents, for instance, who select some one letter, as X, and place it after each word as a word-separator, do so because they find it difficult to read their texts unless the word-divisions are present. As to whether or not this device does actually create difficulties: The person who is content to make use of simple substitution as his means of secret communication, is not usually inspired to employ more than one such letter. The length of an English word being somewhat shorter than five letters, any single letter placed religiously after each word will attain a frequency (based on the new length) of not less than 18%, where the letter *E*, at its very maximum, can rarely attain 15%. The decryptor, taking his preliminary frequency count, quickly discovers this one letter of enormous frequency. He might suspect German, or even French, and look for other characteristics of those languages. But having reason to believe that the language is English, he recognizes this letter instantly for what it is; he first makes sure that it is distributed throughout the cryptogram at an average interval of five or six letters, then calmly circles it out and deals with a case of word-divisions.

Figure 76

"Alphabet" for Encipherment of Numbers

```
"Plaintext" ..    1 2 3 4 5 6 7 8 9 0
"CIPHER"   ...    A B C D E F G H I J
```

Text ready for encipherment:

```
WE HAVE  WCBEW  BALES.
```

Considering something of a more practical nature, there is another very common device, used with every conceivable kind of cipher, which is not in the least intended for the purpose of creating difficulties, yet invariably does in short cryptograms. The ordinary practice, when dealing with numbers, necessary punctuation marks, and so on, is to write these out in words: *three hundred twenty five; quote; dollars.* But where a given correspondence is likely to involve a great many of these, so that the ordinary practice is very wasteful, the encipherer is nearly always provided with a little " cipher alphabet " of the general kind indicated in Fig. 76, in which the ten digits, any desired punctuation marks, and any other needed symbols ($, %, @) have each a single substitute. In the " alphabet " of the figure, the number 325 will be enciphered *CBE*. But if this enciphered group *CBE* is always to be cleanly distinguishable from the rest of the text, a means must be found for making this distinction, and this is usually done by reserving some one letter to act solely as an *indicator* and never using this letter for any other purpose. This indicator-letter, as *W*, may then be placed at the beginning and end of the enciphered group *CBE*, and the resulting group, *WCBEW*, may be placed in the plaintext message, ready to receive whatever kind of encipherment is given to the rest of the letters. These groups, used in short cryptograms, can give about the same amount of trouble as would so many nulls. But where cryptograms are longer, with a great many such groups, the decryptor invariably spots them by means of the recurrent indicator. Sometimes one letter is used, and sometimes two (*W*. . .*W*, or *K*. . .*W*); but in either case, the indicator always appears as a pair of correlatives, and wherever the first of the pair is found, its companion is never far away. Some provision must, of course, be made for replacing the indicator letter in the plaintext alphabet. In English, we ordinarily select *J* for any such omission; this is a letter which is rarely used and, on those scattered occasions when it does occur, it can be replaced with *I*. Among the Latins, it is commoner to make use of *K* and *W*; these two letters are not used at all in their native languages, and can be replaced, respectively, with *Q* and *VV*. It is also possible to omit *X*, replacing it with *KS*, or

V, replacing it with *U*. The fact that it is possible to shorten the message alphabet without appreciably impairing the clearness of its messages has given rise to what is probably the most practical of the simple substitution variations: two or three letters, as *J, K, V*, are omitted from the plaintext alphabet, while the cipher alphabet retains its full 26, and in this way some extra substitutes are provided which can be given to the more frequent letters. It is possible to dispense with as many as five letters, replacing *J, K, X, V, W* with *I, Q, QS, U, UU*, and assign the extra substitutes to *E, T, A, O, N*. Fig. 77 illustrates an alphabet of this kind. Here, the letters *I J* are to have the same substitute, and the letters *K Q* are to have the same substitute. This releases two extra substitutes which may be given to *E* and *T*.

Figure 77

```
                                    j q
Plaintext:  a b c d e f g h i k l m n o p r s t u v w x y z E T
CIPHER:     C U L P E R Z Y X W V T S Q O N M K J I H G F D B A
```

Encipherment:
```
            w e m u s t h a v e b e t t e r c o v e r a g e ...
            H E T J M K Y C I B U E A K B N L Q I E N C Z B ...
```

The foregoing is one of those cases in which the decryptor can learn a great deal by taking his frequency count in the form of a digram chart. And he knows, of course, that his cryptogram contains some two letters whose combined frequencies will reproduce the frequency of *E*, or of *T*.

In Fig. 78, we have a " checkerboard " which, primarily, is intended as a *transformation device;* that is, a means for replacing single letters with syllables, and, consequently, for replacing five-letter incoherent groups with ten-letter pronounceable groups; under the European agreement, the price of transmission is the same

Figure 78

```
        L N R S T
                          b  a  t  t  a  l  i  o  n
    A   C U L P E     ER NE UL LU NE AR RI OR NO
    E   R A B D F
    I   G H I J K
    O   M N O Q S              Regrouped:
    U   T V W Y Z
                      ERNEULLUNE ARRIORNO.
```

for both, and the pronounceable groups are less likely to result in transmission errors. The alphabet is first reduced to 25 letters (in this case by the omission of *X*), and is written into a 5 x 5 square. The five vowels, written at one side, will then serve to designate the five rows, while five other letters, written across the top, will designate columns. Any letter found inside the square may thus be pointed out by naming the two letters which will indicate its column and row. In the given example, *A* can be replaced with *EN* or *NE; T* with *UL* or *LU*, and so on.

The fact that two interchangeable substitutes have been provided for each letter of the alphabet has led many persons to use this device, absolutely without modifications, as a simple substitution key. Yet it must be plain that any decryptor, taking his preliminary frequency count, will discover, before going very far, that this count is being made on only ten different letters, and thus can represent only one possible kind of encipherment. A frequency count taken on the pairs, with no distinction made between a given digram and its reversal, will afford the necessary proof; after that, the average decryptor will usually replace the pairs with single letters (or numbers), just as he would in dealing with printers' symbols, or other inconvenient characters. The checkerboards which are actually intended for encipherment purposes ordinarily use digits for pointing out columns and rows.

Where the digits at the side are the same as those across the top, it becomes necessary to observe an order, as column-row, or row-column, and this, using only five digits, is ordinary simple substitution, in which every letter has one substitute. But if the five digits at the side are different from the five written across the top, then the order is immaterial, and any number may be interchangeable with its reversal; that is, 17 or 71 can represent the same letter.

This encipherment might not be spotted so promptly as the case in which only ten letters are present out of a possible 26. But if the count is made on a chart, as recommended at the beginning of the chapter, it is very readily detectible that there are two separate groups of digits, *neither one of which has ever formed any combination within itself*, every number in the cryptogram being composed of one digit from each group. Thus we see plainly the trail which is left by co-ordinates.

Figure 79

The KEY-PHRASE Cipher

(a)

Plaintext:	a b c d e f g h i j k l m n o p q r s t u v w x y z
CIPHER:	O N E W H O H A S P A S S E D O N I S A M O N G U S

(b)

CIPHER.......	O	M	S	S	
May represent:	A	U	I	I	Full
	F	L	L	Fuss
	P	M	M	Fuzz
	V	S	S	Pull
	Z		Z	Puss

Checkerboards, of course, can be used to better advantage. But, before leaving the simple for the complex, we must not overlook the celebrated *key-phrase cipher*, which discards the idea of multiple substitutes in favor of multiple originals! This cipher, shown in Fig. 79, is said to have been used for serious purposes. Its only difference from the ordinary simple substitution lies in the nature of the cipher alphabet, which must be a plaintext sentence, or phrase, containing the necessary 26 letters. The mysterious pronouncement, " One who has passed on is among us," is the earliest example of which the writer has any recollection; those of later years have been largely proverbs, or other familiar sayings: " Journeys end in lovers' meeting "; " Prosperity is just around the C." As any cryptogram-letter may have five or six different originals, it is readily understood why the cryptograms of the key-phrase cipher are seldom seen without their word-divisions; yet, curiously enough, their translations are almost never ambiguous.

As to their decryptment, the student who cares to try the appended example will find that it is hardly more difficult than one of the simpler " aristocrats." The method is about the same for both, keeping in mind that the frequency shown by any cryptogram-letter is either the frequency belonging to one letter or the exact sum of the frequencies belonging to several. Here, however, the reconstruction of the key simultaneously with the identification of substitutes is a very important adjunct to solving; the cipher-alphabet, being pure plaintext, can often be built up long in advance of solution. It might be added that this cipher, with or without word-divisions, is readily distinguished from all others by the make-up of its frequency count, which, as a rule, consists chiefly of the high-frequency letters in unusual numbers.

Passing now to the more difficult cases, we will glance at a few of those ciphers which are truly multisubstitutional; that is, which provide multiple substitutes for all or most of the plaintext letters. This is usually accomplished by the use of two-digit numbers, of which one hundred are possible: 01-02-03. . . . . .98-99-00. These one hundred numbers may be assigned as substitutes to the twenty-six letters, in proportions roughly approximate to their normal frequencies, as suggested in Fig. 80; or most of them may be so assigned, and the rest reserved as substitutes for digits, punctuation, and so on. For security, however, they must never be assigned in regular order, as in the figure, or even by any methodical process, but absolutely in incoherent order. Thus, while the form indicated in Fig. 80 will be convenient enough for encipherment purposes, it is much less so for decipherment, and ordinarily there will be two separate tables, the second of these making it more convenient to find numbers. This *deciphering key* can be prepared as a list, running in numerical order; but a much more usual and convenient method is that of preparing it in the form of a chart; that is, the ten digits are written across the top and along one side of a 10 x 10 square, exactly as if making ready to take a number-count, and the letters, or other characters, are then distributed in the 100 cells so that the correct digits will serve as co-ordinates for pointing them out. Such a key is changeable, but not readily communicated and remembered without written documents; and to overcome this very serious defect, many mnemonic devices have been conceived, of which the following is perhaps the most practical: Simply treat the one hundred numbers as if they were a plaintext message, and encipher the series by any one of the irregular transposition processes.

Figure 80

A	11, 12, 13, 14
B	15
C	16, 17
D	18, 19
E	20, 21, 22, 23, 24
(Etc.)	

The two commonest of the checkerboard keys are shown in Fig. 81. When digits are used, as in (a), an order must be observed in reading the two co-ordinates. The letter *L*, for instance, may have any one of the substitutes 13, 18, 63, or 68, but may not also have their reversals, since these, using the same order, row-column, would all be substitutes for *G*. Using letters, however, it is possible to have two en-

Figure 81

(a)						(b)					
	1	2	3	4	5		A	C	E	G	I
	6	7	8	9	0		B	D	F	H	J
1-6	C	U	L	P	E	K-L	C	U	L	P	E
2-7	R	A	B	D	F	M-N	R	A	B	D	F
3-8	G	H	I	J	K	O-P	G	H	I	J	K
4-9	M	N	O	Q	S	Q-R	M	N	O	Q	S
5-0	T	V	W	Y	Z	S-T	T	V	W	Y	"

tirely different series at top and side, as in (b); in this case, no order need be observed, and the letter *L* may have any one of eight substitutes: *KE, KF, LE, LF, EK, FK, EL,* or *FL*. By including the still unused letters *U V W X Y Z*, it can be arranged to provide yet more substitutes for some of the letters. For either of these cases, the external numbers or letters (preferably in mixed order), could constitute a semi-fixed key — that is, one not changed every day — while the mixed alphabet of the square could be changed as often as desired. Innumerable other keys of this type are found. For the most part, they are based on rectangles of 35, 36, or 40 cells, the extra cells being used for digits, or other desired symbols, and especially for extra appearances of the more frequent letters.

One such key, the Grandpré cipher shown in Fig. 82, uses 100 cells. The filling of the square with ten ten-letter words provides letters in somewhat the normal frequency proportions, and an eleventh ten-letter word, composed of the ten initials, serves as a sort of mnemonic device for stringing the first ten together. The words, of course, must be chosen in such a way as to include all 26 of the letters.

General Sacco, dealing with fractional substitutions (Chapter *XXII*), shows the same idea in a checkerboard which he describes as " frequential." This square is simply filled with letters, used in proportions roughly approximating their normal frequencies; for ready finding, all repetitions of a letter are placed close together, but filled in on diagonals, which, to some extent, will prevent their being represented by consecutive numbers.

Figure 82

The GRANDPRÉ Cipher

In Fig. 83, we have the checkerboard again, with a modification. If the key used is exactly the one of the figure, those letters which are standing on the first three rows may have twelve substitutes each, and those which are standing on the fourth row may have eight. In all of these cases, the substitute for any letter is a pair. But the final row, including here the letters *V W X Y Z*, is not enciphered with a pair of co-ordinates; each letter may represent itself, or each may represent the one on its left or right, but in any case, the substitute is a *single letter*. Thus we have cryptograms in which most of the

	1	2	3	4	5	6	7	8	9	0
1	E	Q	U	A	N	I	M	I	T	Y
2	X	Y	L	O	P	H	O	N	E	S
3	H	A	L	F	O	P	E	N	E	D
4	U	N	B	L	O	C	K	I	N	G
5	M	O	V	A	B	I	L	I	T	Y
6	A	D	J	U	R	A	T	I	O	N
7	T	H	E	O	R	I	Z	I	N	G
8	I	G	N	O	R	A	N	T	L	Y
9	O	W	N	E	R	S	H	I	P	S
0	N	O	V	I	T	I	A	T	E	S

letters are represented by pairs, but a few are not. Such words as *ever, you, with, when, by, have,* and so on, will occasionally occur; or, if not, then the encipherer may insert a few nulls at strategic points. Thus, the decryptor, taking his count purely on pairs, is expected to take some of them correctly and " straddle " the rest. Such a device is described by Givierge, also the following similar device. The cipher alphabet consists only of two-digit numbers, but includes no number coming from the 40's. With all of the 40's omitted, a sequence 44 becomes impossible; and the encipherer, having first prepared his cryptogram, looks it over, and, here and there, inserts a digit 4 beside another digit 4, producing the impossible sequence 44. The decipherer, wherever he sees this, need merely erase one of the 4's, and since the digits,

Figure 83

```
      K L M N O
      F G H I J

A-E-S   A B C D E   b a X t t a l i o n
B-P-T   F G H I K   AG EF Y NR DI SK KU TI CN HQ
C-Q-U   L M N O P        ≡
D-R     Q R S T U
        V W X Y Z
```

in Morse, have their own distinctive symbols, there is no great danger of errors in transmission which the decipherer will be unable to straighten out; but the decryptor, as before, is expected to " straddle." Concerning decryptment, in all of these cases, there is little that we can say here except that, given sufficient material, these ciphers can all be decrypted with comparatively little trouble.* The " straddling " devices, perhaps, would represent the most difficult case, presuming that the decryptor has no probable words and none of the information which comes through espionage or from that even more fertile source, the carelessness of the encipherer. In dealing with one of these, the decryptor, who normally expects a certain amount of uniformity in the frequency counts made from different portions of a same cryptogram, is likely to find that his count is showing altogether new substitutes, or the same substitutes with altogether new frequencies. He suspects, then, that he may

* For a clear and detailed exposition of the decryptment method ordinarily used in multiple-substitute cases, see *Secret and Urgent* (Bobbs-Merrill), page 64 et seq. For dictionary cipher and simple codes, see *The Solution of Codes and Ciphers*, by Louis C. S. Mansfield (Maclehose), page 56 et seq., or *Cryptography* (Langie-Macbeth; Dutton), page 88 et seq.

be " straddling " between two pairs, and tries making his count *in sections* until he finally discovers what letters (or digit) are causing the trouble.

The use of co-ordinates, in those cases where row and column are interchangeable as to order, shows up very plainly when the pair-count has been made on a chart; as previously mentioned for a case of digits, the letters will divide automatically into two groups, neither of which ever forms any combination within itself. With the other case, where an order must be observed, there are not so many substitutes per letter. But in either case, it is possible to *pair the letters* which belong together. Here, for instance, are the letters *E* and *F*. The frequent combinations of both *E* and *F* are always formed with the same letters; and both have avoided the same letters; *these two must have been paired*. Their combinations with *G* and *H* are much more frequent than their combinations with *I* and *J*; thus *G* and *H* must have been paired, and *I* and *J* must have been paired. This combina-

Figure 84

An Example of BOOK CIPHER

4-1	1-5	3-16	4-11	1-3	1-6	2-2	6-21	1-4	3-2	4-25	4-2
3-3	1-1	2-12	5-22	4-10	6-7	6-2	5-6	5-7	2-7	1-2	1-8
6-1	3-7	5-4	3-6.								

(Key "volume": 23d Psalm),

tion *EG* (and its equivalents), has been frequently followed by this other combination (and its equivalents) and so on. When a great many pairs can be considered equivalent to one another, it is possible to begin setting up the checkerboard. Some such devices, of course, are safer than others. But the mere fact that they double the lengths of the cryptograms renders them unfit for any purpose where speed is a requirement; nor can the added time and expense of transmission be tolerated for any purpose whatever unless there is some very definite gain in secrecy.

One great objection to any device offering optional substitutes is that the encipherer himself seems unable to take full advantage of his system. Even having at his disposal five different substitutes for *E*, he falls into the habit of using one of these in preference to the other four; or, determined to avoid this, he uses them meticulously according to rotation, so that when a frequency chart is prepared from his cryptograms, this chart, which is, after all, a *graph*, will show the five uniform frequencies sticking out like a sore thumb. Even *book cipher*, notably secure, however unwieldy in use, has been decrypted because of the encipherer's very human tendency to use a substitute more than once rather than search for a new one among the hundreds at his disposal.

In book cipher, any agreed book, or other written or printed document, will serve as a *key-volume*, so long as it is one that is sure to be at hand when wanted. Words, or letters, can then be represented by a series of numbers usually indicating: page, (column), line, serial position. One letter or one word may thus have a substitute such as 20-1-4-32. An example is provided in Fig. 84, which the interested student may puzzle out for himself. The particular key-volume was issued in 1848, but we think this should cause no trouble. When the key-volume selected happens to be the ordinary dictionary, identically the same cipher becomes known as *dictionary cipher*, which is, to all intents and purposes, a very insecure form of *code*. Perhaps the two names together, book cipher and dictionary cipher, might be said to represent the maximum and minimum degree of safety found in the code family.

We leave undiscussed the subject of those alphabets which are based on phonetics, with digraphs *TH, SH, CH*, having their individual symbols, and each vowel capable of having several. The student who desires to prepare one may find the necessary suggestions in any shorthand manual; his substitutes can be two-digit numbers, and his encipherment may be any one of those intended for the normal alphabet. Having made mention of several processes which, to the younger student, may present frightening possibilities, we hasten to add that the four appended examples are all of a type which he should be able to solve without a great deal of difficulty.

100. By PICCOLA. (Key-Phrase Cipher - intercepted by a "Royalist" spy).

```
N H H K O   H W A   E H M A   U I   H U U H S T   U S A   S T U N   H U
M H N I W A H T.   N H H H S A   D T H H   I A   I I E I A M   H K M
U W A H O L W N   W H T M A M   D S T H A   J T E S U   T O   T K
N W I E W A O O.   O U H K M   W A H M N   U I   H U U H S T   N W T O I K
H K M   W A H A H O A   N W T O I K A W O.
```

101. By PICCOLA. (Probable words: CIPHER, SUBSTITUTION, ALPHABET, etc).

```
D K I U O   C Z P V C   L U Z I Q   U W·Y V B   V I N C D   U U L C U   K U Z I I

U O C Z P   V C L U Z   P Y N U S   Q S C Z I   U L Q T U   K H I C Z   I K L U Z

P Y N N Y   J Q Y L U   P L U Z I   Q J S C U   L U S U E   Y G U Z I   Q I U T Q

N U F S U   Z F L U I   C V F Q S   W Q I I S   U Y S U G   S Q N B L   U G U O V

V Y F S Q   Y I H I Y   I K O H K   U V P T Y   K Q I J U   Y V P P C   E S Y U O

F Q S U L   C Z N Y Z   F K E S Y   Z I U Z I   R Q V V C.
```

102. By PICCOLA. (Probable words: COLLECTION, GALLERIES, FIGURINE, etc).

```
Y C G U T   H M P Y B   X S K R M   G X U F P   C M I B C   J G R M K   X L X S Z

N Q V V U   N I X Q S   Q E E X Z   H M X S R   L E Q M L   C V U D Y   C G R N Q

S E X J U   S K X C V   X S E Q M   T C I X Q   S K Y C I   I Y R K C   S C Z M C

L I Q V U   S E M Q T   K Y R T Q   M Z C S Z   C V V U M   X R L F C   L L U R S

M U N R S   I V B X S   C N U M K   C X S W H   C M I R M   D Y C L L   X S N U J

X L C P P   R C M U J   D T C B O   R X S K Y   X L E U V   V Q F L N   Q V V R N

I X Q S S   Q F X X X.
```

103. By EFSEE. (Probable words: PEOPLE, PERSON, CIRCUMSTANCES, etc).

```
B E C O M   I C I Q U   E X P A Y   O T I A N   S I Z I P   I A N D O   A B U M Y

O R E A N   U S Q U I   M O N I P   M A M A M   I F O X E   G A O K A   Z U K I S

G O V I S   A W A Z A   I T H I N   A I L M O   S U I S H   E A T R U   A L E M O

F A T I C   A G I D O   Y E M B E   Y O L E N   A C O S E   K E E L S   O G I Z A

C O O L S   I D I O R   Q U A Z O   W A G E S   D I B U S   I V I P U   A Z A M E

S I D A R   T A C O·O   Y A P E S   L I A R S   E W O A L   O N I K O   L O M B A

R I L A Z   A L O W I   A V U M A   K A T L O   F I C I N   A I M I L   N A Q U I

M O N I P   S A W O G   A P A V I   H I S U E   C A N O S   M O L E T   A M E K O

W A I V S   I A R T E   Z E I R S   I L A Z E   G A S A M   I V E E P.
```

CHAPTER XII

MULTIPLE-ALPHABET CIPHERS — THE VIGENERE

The theory of polyalphabetical substitution is as follows: The encipherer has at his disposal several simple substitution alphabets, usually 26. He uses one such alphabet to encipher only one letter; for the next letter, he may use another cipher alphabet; for the third letter, a third alphabet; and so on, until some preconcerted plan has been followed out. The earliest known ciphers of this kind, the Porta (1563) and the Vigenère (1586), made use of a chart, or *tableau*, on which all of the available cipher alphabets were written out in full one below another. The Gronsfeld cipher (1655) used a purely mental encipherment plan; but the Beaufort ciphers, arriving two hundred years later (1857), again made use of a tableau, and something of the same idea survives in the use of *strips;* that is, a set of long narrow cards, each card carrying a simple substitution key. Slides, however, must have been in use near the time of Beaufort, since the best-known of the slide-ciphers, the Saint-Cyr, was being taught in 1880 at the French military school from which it takes its name. As to cipher disks, these appear to have been known even in Porta's time, and have passed through many complications, though it has not been a great many years since a very simple disk was in use in our own army. (A drawing of the United States Army Cipher Disk may be seen in Webster's New International Dictionary.)

To know thoroughly any one of these ciphers is to understand the fundamental principles of all, and we are going to base our studies chiefly upon the Vigenère, most perfect of the simpler types, and the basis upon which others have been founded. Fig. 85 shows, in full, the Vigenère tableau, or " alphabet square." The alphabet standing horizontally across the top of this figure is the plaintext alphabet, and serves for the whole tableau. Below this, and parallel to it, are the 26 " Caesar " alphabets, the first one being a duplicate of the plaintext alphabet, while the remaining 25 have been *shifted*, one letter at a time, until the last one begins with *Z*. These are the 26 available cipher alphabets, and each one is named according to its first letter, which is also spoken of as its *key*. Thus, the key-letter *A* points out the *A*-alphabet; the key-letter *B* points out the *B*-alphabet, and so on. The alphabet standing vertically on the left side of the tableau is merely a list of these key-letters, and so is called the key-alphabet. Except where cipher machines are employed, the ordinary plan of encipherment does not make use of the full 26 available cipher alphabets; only a few of these are used, and these few are taken always in a given rotation, so that the cipher becomes *periodic*. If the rotation includes, say, twelve of the cipher alphabets (whether or not these are all different), the cryptograms are said to have a *period of 12*. (The word " cycle " is also used in this connection.) Since each letter of the normal alphabet is the key to one of the Vigenère cipher alphabets, the encipherer, wishing to make use of several different cipher alphabets, is able to remember their sequence by means of a key-word, in which each letter will point out one particular cipher alphabet. If today's key-word is BED, only three cipher alphabets will be used, the *B*-alphabet, the *E*-alphabet, and the *D*-alphabet, and the cryptograms will all have a *period of 3*. But if, tomorrow, the key-word is changed to CONSTANTINOPLE, the complete rotation will include fourteen alphabets, and the cryptograms will have a *period of 14*.

Figure 85

THE VIGENERE TABLEAU

```
  A B C D E F G H I J K L M N O P Q R S T U V W X Y Z

A A B C D E F G H I J K L M N O P Q R S T U V W X Y Z
B B C D E F G H I J K L M N O P Q R S T U V W X Y Z A
C C D E F G H I J K L M N O P Q R S T U V W X Y Z A B
D D E F G H I J K L M N O P Q R S T U V W X Y Z A B C
E E F G H I J K L M N O P Q R S T U V W X Y Z A B C D
F F G H I J K L M N O P Q R S T U V W X Y Z A B C D E
G G H I J K L M N O P Q R S T U V W X Y Z A B C D E F
H H I J K L M N O P Q R S T U V W X Y Z A B C D E F G
I I J K L M N O P Q R S T U V W X Y Z A B C D E F G H
J J K L M N O P Q R S T U V W X Y Z A B C D E F G H I
K K L M N O P Q R S T U V W X Y Z A B C D E F G H I J
L L M N O P Q R S T U V W X Y Z A B C D E F G H I J K
M M N O P Q R S T U V W X Y Z A B C D E F G H I J K L
N N O P Q R S T U V W X Y Z A B C D E F G H I J K L M
O O P Q R S T U V W X Y Z A B C D E F G H I J K L M N
P P Q R S T U V W X Y Z A B C D E F G H I J K L M N O
Q Q R S T U V W X Y Z A B C D E F G H I J K L M N O P
R R S T U V W X Y Z A B C D E F G H I J K L M N O P Q
S S T U V W X Y Z A B C D E F G H I J K L M N O P Q R
T T U V W X Y Z A B C D E F G H I J K L M N O P Q R S
U U V W X Y Z A B C D E F G H I J K L M N O P Q R S T
V V W X Y Z A B C D E F G H I J K L M N O P Q R S T U
W W X Y Z A B C D E F G H I J K L M N O P Q R S T U V
X X Y Z A B C D E F G H I J K L M N O P Q R S T U V W
Y Y Z A B C D E F G H I J K L M N O P Q R S T U V W X
Z Z A B C D E F G H I J K L M N O P Q R S T U V W X Y
```

To make use of a cipher alphabet, say the *B*-alphabet, we may lay a ruler across the tableau in such a way that this one alphabet is pointed out. Then, to encipher any letter, as *S*, we may find this letter, *S*, in the plaintext alphabet at the top, and trace down its column as far as the *B*-alphabet which is being pointed out by the ruler; we find that the substitute, in this alphabet, is *T*. Or, wishing to decipher *T*, we find this letter in the *B*-alphabet and trace upward to the plaintext alphabet in order to find that its original is *S*. While the foregoing explains the principle, it has not been expressed in the usual language. Where we have mentioned the use of the *B*-alphabet, it is much commoner to hear that a certain letter has been enciphered or deciphered " with key-letter *B*," and the usual description of the encipherment will be somewhat as follows: To encipher *S* by *B*, find *S* in the plaintext alphabet, find *B* in the key-alphabet, and use the substitute which is found at the intersection of the *S*-column with the *B*-row. Or: To decipher *T* by *B*, first find the key-letter *B*, trace horizontally to the right as far as the cipher-letter *T*, then trace upward to its original, *S*. This, we believe, is the original description, as explained by Blaise de Vigenère himself, and the original encipherment plan was that indicated in Fig. 86. The message of this figure is SEND SUPPLIES TO MORLEY'S STATION. The key-word, BED, has been repeated often enough to pair one key-

Figure 86

Original Method of VIGENÈRE Encipherment

Key:	B E D B	E D B E D B E D	B E	D B E D B E D	B E D B E D B
Message:	S E N D	S U P P L I E S	T O	M O R L E Y S	S T A T I O N
Cipher:	T I Q E	W X Q T O J I V	U S	P P V O F C V	T X D U M R O

Figure 87

Modern Encipherment

B	E	D		B	E	D		B	E	D
S	E	N		D	S	U		P	P	L
T	I	Q		E	W	X		Q	T	O
I	E	S		T	O	M		O	R	L
J	I	V		U	S	P		P	V	O
E	Y	S		S	T	A		T	I	O
F	C	V		T	X	D		U	M	R
N										
O										

```
       5          10          15          20          25          30
T I Q E W   X Q T O J   I V U S P   P V O F C   V T X D U   M R O X X
```

letter with each text-letter, and these pairs are handled *one at a time:* S is enciphered by *B*, *E* is enciphered by *E*, *N* is enciphered by *D*, and so on, following the original description.

The modern method would be that of Fig. 87. Knowing that a great many letters are going to be enciphered by *B*, a great many others by *E*, and a great many others by *D*, and having no wish to preserve word-divisions, we begin by writing our plaintext into three columns (or by grouping it conveniently), and then encipher at a single writing all of those letters which are to be enciphered by any one same key-letter. That is, we apply one cipher alphabet at a time, as first explained. The modern practice will also require that the cryptogram be taken off in five-letter groups, and that the final group be made complete. This is another of those cases in which the decryptor will number his letters, as shown in the figure. The student who has not previously met the Vigenère cipher is urged to perform the two operations of encipherment and decipherment and thus familiarize himself with the use of a tableau; it is possible that in most of his subsequent reading he will find explanations based on the " columns " and " rows " of a " tableau," when, as a matter of fact, no tableau has been used. To understand how this might be, suppose we take a look now at the Saint-Cyr cipher.

In Fig. 88, we have the principle of the sliding device by means of which this encipherment is accomplished. The Saint-Cyr slide is very easily prepared of cardboard, or of any other flexible and fairly strong material, but may also be prepared of wood, or may be set up for any temporary purpose on two strips of paper. Its details, also, may be varied to suit the operator's own convenience. As shown, however, the upper and single alphabet, which is the plaintext one, is written on a card, and slots will be cut in this card at two points: Just below and to the left of *A;* and just below and to the right of *Z.* This plaintext alphabet is considered stationary.

Figure 88

THE SAINT-CYR SLIDE

```
    A B C D E F G H I J K L M N O P Q R S T U V W X Y Z
A B C D E F G H I J K L M N O P Q R S T U V W X Y Z A B C D E F G H I J..
                                                              (To Y.)
```

The lower and double alphabet, which is to furnish all of the substitutes, is written on a long narrow strip, the two ends of which may be inserted into the slots of the other card. This strip, or slide, may then be moved back and forth at will. However prepared, the spacing must be uniform throughout both alphabets. The Saint-Cyr cipher also makes use of a key-word in which each letter is the key to a cipher alphabet, and which is applied exactly as in Fig. 86 or Fig. 87. To apply the key-letter *B*, we adjust the slide in such a way that the *B* of the sliding alphabet will stand directly beneath *A* of the stationary one. This gives us exactly the same set-up which we used in Chapter *IX* for cases of simple substitution; that is, we have a plaintext alphabet with a cipher alphabet standing just below it; each plaintext letter is standing directly above its substitute, and each substitute directly beneath its original. The cipher alphabet just referred to, in which key-letter *B*, found in the sliding alphabet, is standing directly below the index-letter, *A*, found in the stationary alphabet, is identical with the *B*-alphabet of the Vigenère tableau, and is even called by the same name. Should we move the sliding alphabet, so as to place key-letter *C* directly beneath index-letter *A*, we reproduce the *C*-alphabet of the Vigenère cipher, again called by the same name. In the figure, we have the *E*-alphabet in position, with key-letter *E* standing directly beneath index-letter *A*. And since the sliding alphabet may be placed in 26 different positions, each time reproducing one of the Vigenère cipher alphabets, having the same key and the same name, it appears that our Saint-Cyr " cipher " is merely a duplication of the Vigenère. The chances are, then, that even though we call our cipher by its original name, and even make references to its tableau, our actual work of encipherment and decipherment will have been accomplished by means of the more convenient and rapid Saint-Cyr slide. But where a slide is possible, a *cipher disk* is also possible, and many will prefer to use the disk.

To prepare one of these, we might proceed as follows: First, cut out from cardboard (or other desired material) a pair of disks, one smaller than the other. Divide the peripheries of both disks into 26 equal segments, and write the 26 letters of the alphabet in a circle around both of the peripheries, causing both alphabets to run in the same direction. Place the smaller disk on top of the larger; and, finally, stick a drawing pin through the exact center of both disks, to serve as a pivot. The smaller disk may now be rotated to 26 different positions, so that any desired key-letter can be caused to stand beside index-letter *A* of the outer disk, and will place in position the cipher alphabet of which it is the key. The use of this revolving alphabet in place of a sliding one does away with the necessity for doubling its length.

Now let us examine carefully Fig. 89, with its two examples of decipherment. At (a) of this figure, a short cryptogram fragment, beginning *T I Q. . . . ,* is being deciphered with the original key-word, BED, and is bringing out the message, SEND SUPPLIES. . . . . This, of course, is to be expected of any cipher. But at (b), it is this *message fragment*, SEND SUPPLIES, which is acting as a *trial key;* exactly the same process is being used as if applying the true key, and this decipherment is bringing out the original key, repeating over and over. The Vigenère cipher, then, works equally well in reverse, and in this respect it differs from some of its kindred ciphers. To understand this peculiarity, we have merely to consider the tableau. Concerning this we have said that the horizontal alphabet which stands across the top is the plaintext alphabet, and that the vertical one at the left is merely a list of keys. Suppose we decide to look at it the other way round, and say that the vertical alphabet at the left is the plaintext one, and that all 26 of the cipher alphabets are standing on end with their key-letters at the top, so that the horizontal alphabet, written across the top, is merely a list of these keys. Will there be any difference in the encipherment? Might the slide, also, be prepared in a vertical position? Does it make any difference in the results whether we encipher plaintext *SEN* by key BED, or encipher plaintext BED by key *SEN?* One road to decryptment, then, is clearly indicated. If we have a probable word, we may use this word exactly as if it were the key, and, if it is actually present, it will bring out the true key. Or, if we have no probable word, we may try probable sequences, or make use of the trigram list. Here, however, we have two separate cases: The simplest, in which the probable word is long enough to bring out the key-word *repeating;* and the most difficult, in which the sequence, or probable word, is very short, and will bring out only a short fragment of the key-word.

The simpler case is readily explained. We have, say, a cryptogram beginning *U S Z H L W D B P B G G F S.* . . , in which we suspect the presence of the word SUPPLIES. We decipher the first eight letters, *using this probable word as a trial key,* and obtain a jumbled series of letters *C Y K S A O Z J,* which is not satisfac-

Figure 89

(a) **Deciphering with the KEY:**

Key:	B	E	D	B	E	D	B	E	D	B	E	D.......
CRYPTOGRAM:	T	I	Q	E	W	X	Q	T	O	J	I	V.......
Plaintext:	S	E	N	D	S	U	P	P	L	I	E	S.......

(b) **Deciphering with the MESSAGE:**

Trial Key:	S	E	N	D	S	U	P	P	L	I	E	S.......
CRYPTOGRAM:	T	I	Q	E	W	X	Q	T	O	J	I	V.......
True Key:	B	E	D	B	E	D	B	E	D	B	E	D........

tory. We leave off the first cryptogram-letter, *U,* and decipher the next eight, obtaining another jumbled series of letters *A F S W L V X X.* We start again at the third letter, then at the fourth letter, and still there is no information. But at the fifth trial, beginning at the fifth cryptogram-letter, we obtain a series *T C O M E T C O,* and this is satisfactory, not necessarily because we have recognized the word COMET, though this, of course, is a very desirable happening, but because the last three letters, *T C O,* are repeating the first three. *The series is beginning over.* The student should practice doing this, using both the tableau and the slide (or disk), until he is sure that he understands the process. The exact details of his work are immaterial; if he is sure that his key will be a recognizable word, it will be satisfactory to make decipherments directly on the cryptogram, erasing as he goes. Sometimes, however, the key is incoherent, or apparently so, and a jumbled series like *C Y K S A O Z J* might actually be the correct key; for this reason, it is well to follow a routine of some kind which will preserve all of the decipherments. One such plan is illustrated in Fig. 90.

Here, the cryptogram, or a substantial portion of it, would be written across a sheet of quadrille paper, and the probable word would be written at one side, where each of its letters will govern one row of decipherments. The first letter, *S* in the figure, has been used to *decipher the whole row of cryptogram-letters,* giving every possible key-letter which can produce *S.* The second letter, *U,* has been used to decipher them all again (except the very first letter; we do not expect a word UPPLIES). The third letter, *P,* has been used to decipher them all a third time; and so on. The resulting rows of decipherment include all key-letters which could have produced *S,* then *U,* then *P,* and so on. To read them consecutively, beginning at any cryptogram letter, start immediately below that letter, and read diagonally downward to the right. The first diagonal gives key *CYK*. . ., the second gives *AFS*. . ., and so on to the fifth diagonal, showing the key as *T C O M E T C O*. (If it is desired that these possible keys should come out standing in a horizontal position, then the *decipherments* may be made diagonally.) F. R. Carter, the originator of this scheme, does not necessarily make all of the decipherments which are included in the figure. He begins with the assumption that his key will be a recognizable word; having deciphered in full the first three rows, he abandons all of those diagonals which cannot develop into words. If, in the end, he is forced to conclude that his key was incoherent, *no decipherments have been erased;* he may still go back and develop the rest of his diagonals, in the hope that one will begin repeating.

The more difficult of our two cases, that in which we have no probable words other than *the, and, which, that, have, but,* etc., can follow exactly the routine out-

Figure 90

Deciphering with the Probable Word SUPPLIES - Routine of F.R.CARTER

Cryptogram fragment:	U	S	Z	H	L	W	D	B	P	B	G	G	F	S	....
Probable word: S	C	A	H	P	T/E	L	J	X	J	O	O	N	A	....
U		Y	F	N	R̄	C/J	H	V	H	M	M	L	Y	....
P			K	S	W	H̄	O/M	A	M	R	R	Q	D	....
P				S	W	H	Ō	M/A	M	R	R	Q	D	....
L					A	L	S	Q̄	E/Q	V	V	U	H	....
I						O	V	T	H̄	T//Ȳ	Y	X	K	....
E							Z	X	L	X̄	C//C	B	O	....
S											Ō//			....

(Key: COMET)

lined in Fig. 90; but in this case there must be two separate work-sheets. Here, it is usually better to forget words and start at once with the list of normally frequent trigrams, *THE, AND, THA, ENT, ION, TIO,* etc. The key-fragments which are deciphered by these will be very short, and very numerous; a great many of them will be very good usable sequences, and perhaps the correct key-sequence will not look quite so inviting as others which are incorrect. It becomes necessary, then, to have a second work-sheet on which we may take these fragments one by one and try them as keys. If any one of them is a fragment of the original key, *it must bring out fragments of plaintext, and must bring them out at some regular interval.* If the scheme of Fig. 90 is the one preferred, the second work-sheet may be prepared exactly like the first, and used in the same way. The only difference is as follows: On the first work-sheet, where the figure shows the word SUPPLIES, a supposed trigram (*THE, AND,* etc.) will have been used to bring out supposed key-fragments; on the second work-sheet, one of these supposed key-fragments will have been used. These new rows of decipherment may then be examined to find out whether any of the new diagonals contain apparent plaintext fragments, and, if so, whether these occur at a regular interval.

For this kind of work, however, Ohaver has offered us another routine which requires somewhat more preparation than Carter's but which is well worth the extra trouble, especially if it be remembered that a trigram-search is never necessary except with the shortest of cryptograms. For the longer cryptograms, we have easier methods. Ohaver's plan can be examined in Fig. 91.

The cryptogram, shown at the top of this figure, contains 26 letters; therefore, remembering that each letter, except the final two, may begin a cipher-trigram, it contains 24 trigrams. The preparation of the two work-sheets requires that these 24 cipher-trigrams be written out in full on both sheets. This work should be done in ink, or on the typewriter. Then, too, for a reason which will be explained in a moment, it is well that the first of these work-sheets be prepared with a great deal of space, say seven or eight lines, between its rows of trigrams. Now, considering the first work-sheet, shown at (a) of the figure: The upper row shows the 24 cipher-trigrams as originally written out. We have been working down the trigram list, using every normally frequent trigram as a trial key, and have failed to find *THE*, *AND*, *THA*, or *ENT*, which means that we have done quite a lot of tedious work. We have now reached the normally frequent trigram *ION*, and this we have ap-

Figure 91

        L N F V E   O L N V M   R N G Q F   H H R N H   I R V F E   B.

                      (a)   Trial Sheet No. 1

ION
<u> </u>
      LNF   NFV   FVE   VEO   EOL   OLN   LNV   NVM   VMR   MRN   RNG   NGQ
      AZS   FRI   XHR   NQB   WAY   GXA   DZI   FHZ   NYE   EDA   JZT   FSD

      GQF   QFH   FHH   HHR   HRN   RNH   NHI   HIR   IRV   RVF   VFE   FEB
      YCS   IRU   XTU   ZTE   ZDA   JZU   FTV   ZUE   ADI   JHS   NRR   XQO

                      (b)   Trial Sheet No. 2

EDA
<u> </u>
      LNF   NFV   FVE   VEO   EOL   OLN   LNV   NVM   VMR   MRN   RNG   NGQ
      HKF   JCV   BSE   RBO   ALL   KIN   HKV   JSM   RJR   ION   NKG   JDQ

      GQF   QFH   FHH   HHR   HRN   RNH   NHI   HIR   IRV   RVF   VFE   FEB
      CNF   MCH   BEH   DER   DON   NKH   JEI   DFR   EOV   NSF   RCE   BBB

                      (c)   Testing out the Period 5

          D A   E D A   E D A   E D A   E D A   E D
          L N F V E O L N V M R N G Q F H H R N H I R V F E B
          I N . . A L L . . I O N . . B E H . . D F R . . A Y

                    (TION?)   (FRIDAY?)

plied as a trial key, assuming one by one that each of the 24 trigrams represents *ION*. We have, then, 24 decipherments on the second row, and *any one* of these 24 de-ciphered trigrams might be a fragment of the original key. However, it is natural to assume that a trigram *FRI* or *WAY* is more likely than one such as *XHR* or *NQB*, and those fragments which look like usable sequences have been underscored in the figure. These are to be tested first. At (b), we have the other work-sheet, the upper row, as before, showing the 24 possible cipher-trigrams. Here, we have already failed in our tests for key-fragments *FRI*, *WAY*, *DZI*, *NYE*, which means that we have done some more tedious work, and we have now arrived at the pos-sible key-fragment *EDA*. If this sequence, *EDA*, is actually a portion of the orig-inal key, it must not only bring out fragments of a plaintext message, but must bring them out at some constant distance apart. The point at which we found this is the tenth trigram, and here it may be advisable to remind that this begins at the tenth cryptogram letter; that is, *every trigram presents only one new letter*, so that to find a completely different trigram in either direction, we must count backward or forward a distance of three trigrams.

Beginning, then, at the tenth trigram, and examining every third trigram in both directions, we find that our key-fragment has·given us the following decipherments: *HKF, RBO, HKV, ION, CNF, DER, JEI, NSF.* These are largely incoherent; but, in addition, it must not be overlooked that on the continuously-written cryptogram, these would be *consecutive,* giving us a message *H K F R B O*. . . Applied at interval 3, then, our key-fragment *EDA,* will not decipher us a message; therefore, the period of this cryptogram, using this key, cannot be 3.

To examine for the possibility of a period 4, we start again with our tenth trigram, and examine every fourth decipherment in both directions; our series, this time, is *JCV, KIN, ION, MCH, NKH, NSF.* Most of these are usable, and the first one might be due to nulls, initials, and so on; but here again we have the reminder that with each trigram representing only one new letter, these are *almost consecutive,* starting at the second cryptogram letter, so that our message, with each fourth letter missing, will be as follows: * *J C V * K I N * I O N.* . . . Unless we can think of some letters which would fill these gaps and provide plaintext, our period is not 4.

Trying again, however, beginning at the tenth trigram and examining each fifth decipherment, we find something more satisfactory: *ALL, ION, BEH, DFR.* If these are correct, the period is 5. At (c), we have gone back to the continuously-written cryptogram in order to try these in their places; and since a period 5 would mean that each of the letters *E D A* is used regularly to encipher each fifth letter, we are able to include two shorter decipherments at the two ends of the cryptogram. The next step in logical order is to try deciphering *T* in front of *ION,* since the trigram *TIO* would have been the next one on our trigram list. This brings out key-letter *C,* which, if correct, will decipher correctly at each interval 5, and which extends our key-letters to *C E D A.* We can see, too, that this is not the beginning of the word; the sequence we have is *D A * C E.* In the given example, it is not difficult, also, to guess a probable word, FRIDAY. Now, having twice called attention to the fact that the trigram-search can grow quite tedious, we hasten to point out that it need not be made more so by deciphering each trigram individually. If your trial key is *THE,* set your slide at the *T*-alphabet (or point this out on the tableau), and decipher every first letter on the sheet. Then set the *H*-alphabet in position, and decipher every second letter on the sheet. Finally, set the *E*-alphabet in position and decipher all of the remaining letters.

The foregoing few paragraphs have illustrated the worst case in almost its worst form, but will show the principle. Now let us consider this work in a much more usual case. As mentioned earlier, the first of the two work-sheets will be prepared with a great deal of space between the rows of trigrams. The full number of decipherments will be made for the first trigram *THE,* but *not erased.* Just below these, a second row of decipherments will be made for *AND,* and these, too, will be left standing. (*THA* can be omitted.) A third row of decipherments is made for *ENT,* a fourth row for *ION,* and so on down the list, until there are six or eight rows of possible key-fragments. These are all examined and compared with one another, in the hope of finding duplications. Perhaps *THE* and *AND* have *both* brought out a key-fragment *EDA,* or one has brought out *CED* and the other *EDA,* having *ED* in common. It is far from unusual, in some of these cases, to find a whole series of these overlapping key-fragments, for instance, *CON, ONS, NST.* This will explain why many persons consider the trigram-search the simplest and most direct way of attacking a Vigenère cryptogram.

For the benefit of the novice, we end the chapter at this point in order that he may have some practice. Example 104 comprises a thrilling serial with all the trimmings, gripping and original title, smashing climax, and a brave hero, John Miller. The key to the title is STRANGE. Part *I* repeats a word found in the title; part *II* repeats a word of part *I;* and somewhere are the trigrams *NOT, CON, YET, ING, TEN, THE.* We have heard, too, that an amateur encipherer will occasionally encipher the nulls which he adds in his final group. Example 105 is easily investigated through short common words. As to the remaining examples, while it is true that they can be attacked by the trigram method, the student will probably prefer to leave them until he has seen the methods outlined in Chapters *XIV* and *XV.*

104. By PICCOLA. (For trigram practice. A new key for each fragment).

Title of Serial: S L K R N   T K W W Z   S N V T W   T I A A I   I X X X X.

Part I: R I G Z V   Z K I U O   M H J L B   W F P K S   R Z T R H   E J T W I

O S W I O   S G Q I I.   Part II: H H T X T   N E O L V   R M T U L   C L P P X

T Y R X K   U K B U W   U O J Z H   X M Z K H.   Part III: S Y Z Y R   T N F U R

K C U S I   I R Q U X   W U F K C   J N R L Q   N F O K V   X M P U O   N H J A X

J H V O P.   Part IV: X B V P Y   S X C J J   Y U R X O   T S P I N   Y I L U P

A V M X M   M F C I B   S T I T O   O T B R O.

105. By PICCOLA. (For investigation of short words. - Still Vigenère!)

V Y I   D J G I E J S   N V R J H J   F J   D B   G E K O W U Y   A R F F   Z W

V O K U   X R   P G   R   J U O E K M R B   U Y S U H   Q W   J L J G   C I W H G I W.

106. By NEON. (Any repeated trigram is worth watching!)

P Q X E J   F V E G Y   M N Y N Y   I U F R D   S G V R I   L P S G Z   T M E S I

R K N Y I   G P E R W   G R R N D   L O J N T   Y I D X O   T Y C I P   C R E V C

E S G O I   R L I S I   R Z Q E U   C G L T C   I X H Y I   X H E L E   K Y J E K

P X I E Y   R R S L H   D L I F Y   G P R J G   S D I C E.

107. By THE ADMIRAL. (Numbers are always possible!)

L V P R V   S F P T Y   J S P H L   F R C E U   S B O S Z   P H J F Z   N S O A P

K T T V V   Z C F R J   X C C T P   W W R H K   E W Y U K   W G L N U   X C C T P

X W G E R   F R Z N V   Z O W F J   W Q Z N U   K W Y O E   W M P A I.

108. By NEON. (This cryptogram, circulated in April, 1935, caused great consternation among solvers. Do you see any reason why?

T W G J C   N I U J X   C S L S K   K B N V G   W I P S U   Q I U J A   U L J U Z

H B E V J   V M A O H   G G L T P   D G L E Y   S S L A F   I M J S W   Q I U M O

N N F L V   H I U I Z   D Q K V Y   R T W H I   M R F E U   K P N O V   Y T K E F

N V Q N O   T.

109. By PICCOLA.

A X S E H   G O I W W   F O I A L   G E M Q W   E E N B W   R E I K L   S H Z Z Q

X L G A H   V P Z K L   D L G G D   W T C M H   Q D J N W   K E H M V   V A B M A.

CHAPTER XIII

The Gronsfeld, Porta, and Beaufort Ciphers

Now let us have a brief look at other classic ciphers of the multiple-alphabet type, and see to what extent these will differ from the Vigenère. The Gronsfeld cipher, as may be seen from the specimen encipherment of Fig. 92, uses a number-key. Its ten alphabets are governed by the ten digits. To encipher S, using key-digit 2, simply begin at S and count forward 2 in the normal alphabet; the substitute is U. To encipher E with key 8, begin at E and count forward 8 in the normal alphabet; the substitute is M. For decipherment, count backward in the alphabet. A very superficial investigation will show that the Gronsfeld key of the figure, 28105, and the Vigenère key $CIBAF$ will produce identically the same cryptograms. The key-digit *zero* governs the A-alphabet of the Vigenère, the key-digit 1 governs the B-alphabet, and so on to the J-alphabet. If it is found convenient to use a tableau (as it may be for the decipherment), the first ten cipher alphabets of the Vigenère

Figure 92

GRONSFELD Encipherment

Key:	2 8 1 0 5	2 8 1 0 5	2 8...
Plaintext:	S E N D S	U P P L I	E S...
Cryptogram:	U M O D X	W X Q L N	G A...

tableau can be ruled off from the rest, and the key-digits, in the order o to 9, can be added beside the key-letters A to J. Or, if the slide is the preferred method, these digits can be written beneath the first ten letters of the sliding alphabet; it is then possible to slide them into position below the index (the stationary A), in the same way as the letter-keys. The Gronsfeld cipher, then, is no more than a minor variation of the Vigenère, and requires no separate discussion other than a simple reminder that its possibilities are far more limited than those of the Vigenère proper. That is, it covers a range of only ten cipher alphabets where the Vigenère covers 26, and this limitation more than compensates for the fact that its key is not a plaintext word (presuming, that is, that we know what cipher has been used). Otherwise, the difficulties are about the same for both). To understand how this limitation may modify the case, let us examine the work-sheet shown in Fig. 93.

Here, we have exactly the routine of Fig. 90, except that our search must be made for probable trigrams, and not for a probable word. We have begun with the most likely trigram, THE. But here we do not find it possible to do as we did in Fig. 90; that is, *decipher every letter*, first as T, then as H, then as E. Of the twelve cryptogram-letters present, only seven can be deciphered as T; the rest are too far away from it in the normal alphabet, and would require keys larger than 9. Of the six letters which immediately follow the possible T's (the seventh is not shown), only three can be deciphered as H. And of the three letters which immediately follow a possible TH, only two can be deciphered as E or as A. It is often possible, in these ciphers, to investigate simultaneously the trigrams THE and THA. So far as the cryptogram is shown, then, there are only two points at which a trigram THE can be present, while a Vigenère cryptogram of the same length would have presented ten possibilities. Thus, we have no real need for a second work-sheet;

Figure 93

Decrypting a Known Gronsfeld

Cryptogram Fragment: X U I I A Q E U U Y J W.......

Trigram tried: T   4 1/   7/   1 1 5/   3
                   H   1/   9/   2/
                   E   4/ 0/

The sequences U I I and A Q E are the only points at which the trigram T H E could possibly be present, so that only the key-sequences 1 1 4 and 7 9 0 are to be tried. The digram T H alone may be present at Y J.

the only possible key-fragments, 114 and 790, can be tested by any hit-or-miss method which happens to be quickest.

This cipher is often decrypted in much the same way as a " Caesar " simple substitution (shown in Fig. 61). The cryptogram, or a convenient portion of it, is copied on a single line of writing; then, with each letter as a point of beginning, a series of alphabets is extended (written in reverse order), but only for a distance which includes ten letters. That is, the ten possible decipherments for each cryptogram-letter are written in the form of a ten-letter column. The decryptor may then inspect the ten rows of decipherment to see what he can find. At any point where it is possible to find T, H, and E in three consecutive columns, the correctness of this possible THE can be checked by finding out whether or not it has a series of companion-trigrams standing at some regular interval on exactly the same three rows.

In Fig. 94, we have the tableau of Giovanni Battista della Porta, adjusted to suit the modern 26-letter alphabet. Here we have only thirteen cipher alpha-

Figure 94

The PORTA Tableau

AB	A B C D E F G H I J K L M N O P Q R S T U V W X Y Z		
CD	A B C D E F G H I J K L M O P Q R S T U V W X Y Z N		
EF	A B C D E F G H I J K L M P Q R S T U V W X Y Z N O		
GH	A B C D E F G H I J K L M Q R S T U V W X Y Z N O P		
IJ	A B C D E F G H I J K L M R S T U V W X Y Z N O P Q		
KL	A B C D E F G H I J K L M S T U V W X Y Z N O P Q R		
MN	A B C D E F G H I J K L M T U V W X Y Z N O P Q R S		
OP	A B C D E F G H I J K L M U V W X Y Z N O P Q R S T		
QR	A B C D E F G H I J K L M V W X Y Z N O P Q R S T U		
ST	A B C D E F G H I J K L M W X Y Z N O P Q R S T U V		
UV	A B C D E F G H I J K L M X Y Z N O P Q R S T U V W		
WX	A B C D E F G H I J K L M Y Z N O P Q R S T U V W X		
YZ	A B C D E F G H I J K L M Z N O P Q R S T U V W X Y		

bets, each of which may be governed by either of two key-letters; these pairs of keys may be seen at the left of their respective alphabets. In all thirteen of these cipher alphabets, the encipherment is *reciprocal*. In the AB-alphabet, for instance, which is the first one on the chart, the substitute for A is N, and the substitute for N is A. The Porta cipher, the oldest known of its kind, employs a key-word, applied as in Vigenère. If the key-letter in use is either A or B, the topmost alphabet is the one to be used; if the key-letter is either C or D, the second alphabet must be used; and so on. Where this encipherment is illustrated in Fig. 95, it may be of some interest to observe that it is not totally impossible for two different key-words to produce identical cryptograms. As to decipherment, we have already mentioned the fact of reciprocal substitution. Whenever the alphabets are reciprocal (in any cipher), the decipherment is identically the same process as encipherment.

The Porta tableau, being smaller than the Vigenère, is not at all inconvenient to prepare and use as it stands. It can be made still more compact: The upper half being alike for all thirteen cipher alphabets, this half can be written *once only,* at the top of the chart. The lower halves can be written below this on thirteen parallel lines, with their pairs of keys at the left. A ruler may then be used, as suggested for Vigenère, to point out any given lower half. But when it is noticed that these lower halves are identically the same series of letters, with its

Figure 95

Porta Encipherment

```
Keyword:    E A S T E A S T
Plaintext:  S E N D S U P P...
Cipher:     D R E Z D H G G...
```

(Compare:)

```
Keyword:    F A T S F A T S
Plaintext:  S E N D S U P P...
Cipher:     D R E Z D H G G...
```

point of beginning shifted one letter at a time, it is promptly seen that a slide is possible, on which the *N*-to-*Z* half of the normal alphabet, if written twice in succession, could be placed in 13 different positions with reference to the *A*-to-*M* half; and a slide is more convenient still. The slide shown in Fig. 96 is another of Ohaver's devices. The only new feature in connection with the Porta slide lies in the handling of the key-letters, which, in this cipher, are no longer the first letters of their cipher alphabets. Mr. Ohaver has added them on the sliding portion of the device, each pair of keys being placed directly below the letter which must stand beneath the index (*A*) whenever one or the other of the pair is the key-letter in use.

The Porta cipher, aside from its purely historical interest, provides a most interesting decryptment study in the formation of its alphabets. Notice that because of the encipherment scheme itself, it becomes totally impossible that the substitute for any letter, in any cipher alphabet, can ever be taken from its own half of the normal alphabet. This limitation is far more visible than that of the Gronsfeld. We have, say, a cryptogram sequence *H E P*. Can this represent the trigram *THE?* No, because *E* cannot represent *H;* for the same reason, it cannot represent *THA.* Can it represent *AND?* No, because *H* cannot represent *A.* Can it represent *ENT?* No, because *H* cannot represent *E.* Can it represent *ION? TIO? FOR? NDE? HAS?* It is not until we reach *STH* that we find a normally frequent trigram which could have the substitutes *HEP.* But to gather the full significance of this Porta limitation, and also a suggestion concerning the detail work when taking advantage of it, let us picture the case of a probable word: INFANTRY.

Using digits 1 and 2 to mean, respectively, the first and the second half of the

Figure 96

A Slide for PORTA - Devised by OHAVER

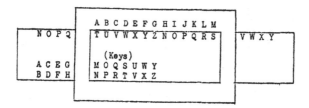

normal alphabet, this probable word INFANTRY has the alphabetical pattern
1 2 1 1 2 2 2 2. And, since every substitute must have been taken from the other
half of the normal alphabet, it will certainly be represented in any Porta cryptogram
by eight letters having the opposite alphabetical pattern: 2 1 2 2 1 1 1 1. Moreover,
a pattern as long as this is not going to be found very often in any one cryptogram.
The decryptor, then, may proceed as in Fig. 97. Each cryptogram letter is marked
1 or 2, or imagined to be so marked, and this series of digits is examined in the hope
of finding a sequence 2 1 2 2 1 1 1 1. If it cannot be found, the word is not present;
if it is found, it can be assumed to represent the word INFANTRY. Here, we
meet with a slight difference between the procedure for Vigenère and the procedure
for Porta.

Figure 97

THE PROBABLE WORD METHOD IN PORTA

```
Pattern of word INFANTRY:   1 2 1 1 2 2 2 2
Pattern of substitute:      2 1 2 2 1 1 1 1
```

The cryptogram, with pattern:

```
F J I D T U V S S L F F I T X M S T M E D L
1 1 1 1 2 2 2 2 2 1 1 1 1 2 2 1 2 2 1 1 1 1
```

Determining the KEYWORD:

```
.....X  M  S  T  M  E  D  L.....
     I  N  F  A  N  T  R  Y

     E  C  A  M  C  E  C  A
     F  D  B  N  D  F  D  B

     D  A  N  C  E
```

In Vigenère, we found it possible to discover the key by simply taking the
probable word and deciphering with it. In Porta, we cannot do this. We must first
pair the two letters, that is, a supposed substitute with its supposed original, and
then find out what key would cause this. In the figure, for instance, we have a
sequence X M S T, assumed to represent I N F A. The first corresponding pair
is X = I. If we are using the tableau of Fig. 94, one of these letters, I, is never
found anywhere except in the 9th column. We find the I-column, and trace down
until we find X; the key, in this case, must be E or F. The next corresponding pair
of letters (M representing N) demands that we find the M-column and trace down
to N; key C or D. The third pair (S representing F) demands that we find the
F-column, and trace down to S; key A or B. The fourth pair (T representing A)
demands that we find the A-column, and trace down to T; key M or N.

Using the slide of Fig. 96: Place X and I together, and note that the key-letters
standing below the index (stationary A) are EF. Place M and N together, and note
key-letters CD. Place S and F together, and note key-letters AB. Place T and A
together, and note key-letters MN. From the recovered pairs of key-letters, we are
to select one each in order to recover the key-word, using somewhat the logic we
might apply in dealing with a key-phrase cryptogram. In the given case, where we
need the two vowels to form any word at all, it is not difficult to surmise that the
key-word was DANCE. It might not be so easy to decide as between EAST and
FATS; but key-words, as a rule, are seldom so short as those we have been using,
and the longer the word, the fewer the possibilities. Concerning keys, however,
there is one contingency which may have to be considered: The various modernized
versions of this tableau are not always duplicates. The cipher alphabets will be the

same as those given here; but where we have caused these to shift in the normal direction, another tableau may show them shifting in reverse. The first alphabet will be the same as here, but the second, still showing key-letters *CD*, will show its lower half beginning *Z N O P*. . . ; the third, still showing key-letters *EF*, will show its lower half beginning *Y Z N O P*. . . ; and so on. The recovery of the key-word, of course, is not vital.

Coming now to the two ciphers which are called Beaufort, we return to a tableau so closely resembling Vigenère's tableau that the two can be used interchangeably. Fig. 98 shows only enough of the Beaufort tableau to bring out the difference in form. Here, we find no separate plaintext alphabet and no separate key-alphabet. Those which form the square have been lengthened by repeating their first letters;

Figure 98

Upper Portion of the BEAUFORT Tableau

```
A B C D E F G H I J K L M N O P Q R S T U V W X Y Z A
B C D E F G H I J K L M N O P Q R S T U V W X Y Z A B
C D E F G H I J K L M N O P Q R S T U V W X Y Z A B C
D E F G H I J K L M N O P Q R S T U V W X Y Z A B C D
E F G H I J K L M.... (Etc.)  ....W X Y Z A B C D E
```

There are no external alphabets. The four outer alphabets of the

square are exactly alike, with **A** in each of the four corners.

TRUE BEAUFORT Encipherment	VARIANT BEAUFORT Encipherment
Key: C O M E T C O M E T C O	Key: C O M E T C O M E T C O
Plaintext: S E N D S U P P L I E S	Plaintext: S E N D S U P P L I E S
Cipher: K K Z B B I Z X T L Y W	Cipher: Q Q B Z Z S B D H P C E

and a 27th alphabet, added at the bottom of the tableau, repeats the alphabet shown at the top. In this way, we have a 27 x 27 alphabet square in which *all four of the outside alphabets are exactly alike*. These ciphers, also, make use of a key-word, applied as in Vigenère and in Porta. As Sir Francis Beaufort himself is said to have used the tableau, the encipherment of a given plaintext-letter, using a given key-letter, was accomplished as follows: To encipher plaintext *S* with key *C*, find the letter *S* in any one of the four outside alphabets, trace into the square along the *S*-column (or row) as far as the key-letter *C*; at that point, turn a right angle, in either direction, and trace outward along that row (or column), emerging from the square at the substitute, which, in the given case, is *K*. Or: To *decipher K* with key *C*, begin with *K*, and *follow identically the encipherment process*, emerging this time at the plaintext letter, *S*. This process we have called the *true Beaufort* cipher. Notice that we have *reciprocal encipherment;* encipherment and decipherment are identically the same thing.

As to the companion cipher, the student will promptly have guessed this for himself: Instead of starting with the plaintext-letter, *S*, and tracing inward to the key-letter, it is entirely feasible to begin with key-letter *C* and trace inward to the plaintext-letter *S*, emerging at *Q* instead of at *K*. This cipher, too, is called Beaufort, since its method of accomplishment is Beaufort's method. But there is a difference in the two resulting ciphers; notice here that the encipherment is no longer reciprocal; should we start at key-letter *C*, trace inward to the new cipher-letter, *Q*, and then trace outward, we do not emerge from the square at the plaintext letter *S*, but at *O*, an entirely new letter. In order to distinguish the two ciphers, we have re-

ferred to this second process as the *variant Beaufort,* or sometimes, more briefly, as
" the variant." There is some justification, also, for calling it the " Vigenère-Beau-
fort." To see why, the student may turn back to his Vigenère tableau, and actually
perform the encipherment, using only the two sides of this tableau in which the alphabets run from *A* to *Z.*

In applying the variant encipherment, in which key-letters are found first, he
need find a given key-letter but once, then lay a ruler along the row (or column)
indicated by that key-letter, and encipher at a single writing all plaintext letters
which are going to have that particular key. But if, as previously recommended, he
has familiarized himself with the use of the Vigenère tableau, he will see instantly
that the operation which, in the variant Beaufort he is calling *encipherment,* is identical, in every particular, with the operation which, in Vigenère, he would have
called *decipherment,* and that, in order to decipher the variant, he must perform the
operation which, in Vigenère, is called encipherment. Neither of these operations

Figure 99

How to find the C-alphabet of each Beaufort

TRUE BEAUFORT		VARIANT BEAUFORT	
Key:	C C C C C C C	Key:	C C C C C C C
Plaintext:	A B C D E F G H...	Plaintext:	A B C D E F G H...
Cipher ALPHABET:	C B A Z Y X W V...	Cipher ALPHABET:	Y Z A B C D E F...

provides a reciprocal substitution; instead, they are reciprocal to each other. Once
it is seen that this is true, it becomes equally plain that the Saint-Cyr slide serves
just as well for the variant as for the Vigenère. To make use of it in applying the
variant encipherment, set key-letters below index-letter *A,* exactly as if making
ready to encipher in Vigenère, but reverse the functions of the two alphabets; that
is, find all plaintext letters in the lower one, and take their substitutes from the upper one.

Now, consider the true Beaufort cipher: Here, plaintext letters are found first,
and keys are found by tracing into the square, so that encipherment is more or
less a letter-by-letter process, and hardly so convenient as in the other two ciphers.
It is true that every ascending diagonal in the tableau is made up of only one key-
letter, so that a ruler, laid diagonally across this tableau, will point out a whole
line of *C*'s, or *O*'s, or *M*'s. But practically every one of these diagonals is broken
into two portions, so that in attempting to encipher by one key-letter at a time, we
find it rather confusing to make the necessary adjustments. Is there not, then, a
more convenient method for applying the Beaufort? Every cipher of this family,
remember, provides a certain number of individual simple substitution cipher-alphabets. For every key (whether it is a letter or a number) there is some kind of
cipher alphabet showing a substitute for *A,* a substitute for *B,* a substitute for *C,*
and so on. To isolate one of these cipher alphabets, and find out what it is like, we
have merely to take some one key-letter (or some one key-number) and discover
what these substitutes are, and what their order is; that is, we need merely *encipher
the normal alphabet,* using this one key. This is true of every cipher of the multiple-
alphabet type. The process can be seen in Fig. 99, where the *C*-alphabet (that is, the
alphabet governed by key-letter *C*) is being isolated for each of the Beaufort ciphers.

In the Beaufort proper, we find that the *C*-alphabet will begin with *C* and come
out in the order *C B A Z Y X. . . . ,* which is merely the normal alphabet reversed.
Should we investigate the *D*-alphabet, we should find that this begins at *D* and comes
out in the order *D C B A Z Y. . . . ,* again the normal alphabet reversed; or, investigating the *E*-alphabet, we should find *E D C B A Z. . . . ,* always the normal

alphabet written backward, and always beginning with whatever letter is called the key. This being the case, it becomes quite evident that a slide is possible, and the formation of this slide is clearly indicated in the left-hand tabulation of the figure: Its upper alphabet must run in one direction and its lower alphabet in the other; if one of the two is made of double length, it becomes possible to place any one of the 26 key-letters in juxtaposition with index *A*, thus bringing into position any one of the 26 cipher-alphabets which are governed by these keys. Nor does it make a particle of difference which of the two *A*'s, the upper or the lower, is regarded as the index-letter; when *C* is standing below *A*, then *A* is also standing below *C*. We saw, in the tableau itself, that the true Beaufort encipherment gives reciprocal substitution. This, however, was not our first meeting with one of the Beaufort alphabets; in Chapter *IX*, we met the *Z*-alphabet. We saw there that whenever a cipher alphabet is merely the plaintext alphabet written backward, it makes no difference which of the two is called a cipher alphabet; we may see here that this fact is not

Figure 100

A Pair of COMPLEMENTARY Alphabets:

```
A B C D E F G H I J K L M N O P Q R S T U V W X Y Z
A Z Y X W V U T S R Q P O N M L K J I H G F E D C B
```

By doubling the length of one or the other of these

two alphabets, we may use them to form a slide which

will encipher and decipher the true BEAUFORT.

altered by shifting one of the alphabets. Since a slide is possible, it follows that a disk is also possible. This particular cipher disk, on which one alphabet runs forward and the other backward, was used long ago in our own army, and is widely known in this country as " The United States Army Cipher Disk." Most persons, apparently, prefer the slides, on which the letters are always right-side up, and the preparation of which does not involve the division of a circle into 26 equal arcs. Of those who prefer the disks, practically all will make the smaller disk *reversible*, with the normal alphabet on one side and the reversed alphabet on the other.

Now, returning to our Fig. 99, and examining its right-hand tabulation: We find that, in isolating the *C*-alphabet of the variant Beaufort, we have merely reproduced the *Y*-alphabet of the Vigenère. Should we now isolate its *Y*-alphabet, we should find that we have obtained the *C*-alphabet of the Vigenère. Further investigation will show that the *D*-alphabet of one is the *X*-alphabet of the other, that the *E*-alphabet of one is the *W*-alphabet of the other; and so on. Only their *A*-alphabets and their *N*-alphabets are keyed alike. Thus we seem to have here a case of "reciprocal" key-letters. These particular pairs of corresponding letters, *B* and *Z*, *C* and *Y*, *D* and *X*, and so on, are called *complements*, one letter of each pair being *complementary* to the other. Since the letters *A* and *N* have no complements (or serve as their own complements), the normal alphabet will furnish only twelve such pairs, and these are shown complete in Fig. 100. In this same set-up, it can be seen that the *A*-alphabet of the Beaufort cipher is the complement of the normal alphabet. Thus, having provided ourselves with a Beaufort slide (or disk), we have always at hand a means for finding out the complements of letters. Once it is clearly understood that the chief difference between a Vigenère cryptogram and a variant cryptogram lies in the names of their respective cipher alphabets, it becomes evident that we might decrypt a variant, believing it to be a Vigenère, and have no trouble whatever in reading its message, though finding that it has an *incoherent key*. Vigenère keys, of course, can be incoherent; occasionally they are based in some way on numbers, following the Gronsfeld scheme. But usually, this is not true; the incoherency is only apparent, and a little investigation will discover what the trouble is. In the case just mentioned, the variant key-word COMET will come out in Vigenère as *Y M O W H*, or vice versa; all that is necessary, in order to discover the original key-word, is to set the Beaufort slide at the *A*-alphabet, and perform a bit of simple substitution. Another cause for the apparently incoherent key lies in the

Figure 101

Applying a PROBABLE WORD to BEAUFORT

(a)

Cryptogram, TRUE BEAUFORT: K K Z B B I Z X T L Y W T Q

Probable word.........	S	C	C	R	T	T	A	R	P	L	D	Q	O	L	I
	U		E	T	V	V	C	T	R	N	F	S	Q	N	K
	P			O	Q	Q	X	O	M	I	A	N	L	I	F
	P				Q	.	.	.	M	I	A	N	.	I	.
	L									E					
	I										T				
	E											C			
	S												O		

Use the word SUPPLIES as a trial key, exactly as in Vigenère, but make use of the VARIANT method, and not the TRUE BEAUFORT.

***
***

(b)

Cryptogram, VARIANT BEAUFORT: Q Q B Z Z S B D H P C E H K

Probable word............	S	Y	Y	J	H	H	A	J	L	P	X	K	M	P	S
	U		W	H	F	F̄	Y	H	J	N	V	I	K	N	Q
	P			M	K	K	D̄	M̲	O	S	A	N	P	S	V
	P				.	.	.	.	O̲	S	.	N	.	P	.
	L									W̲					
	I										H̲				
	E											Y̲			
	S												M̲		

This was deciphered as a Vigenère, and showed the repeating of a scrambled key: Y M O W H. Had it been deciphered with the BEAUFORT SLIDE, suggested in Figure 100, it would have reproduced the plaintext keyword, C O M E T.

use of some other index-letter than the stationary *A*. Say, for instance, that the encipherer has used the key-word COMET, but has placed his key-letters beneath index *D*. The key recovered by the decryptor is *Z L J B Q;* to find the original key-word, he need merely " run it down the alphabet."

Of the ciphers we have seen, then, those three which are complete, that is, which employ a full 26 alphabets, are curiously interrelated to one another. In the matter of substitution (encipherment and decipherment), the Beaufort stands alone, in that it is reciprocal, while the other two ciphers are reciprocal to each other in this respect. But in the matter of keys, it is the Vigenère which stands alone, in that it can be deciphered indifferently by key-letter or message-letter, where this is not true of either Beaufort. *In this respect, these two ciphers are reciprocal.* To see this plainly, we may examine our three encipherments, each one showing a different cryptogram obtained from the plaintext fragment SEND SUPPLIES, using key

COMET. The Vigenère version was seen in Fig. 90. If this be *deciphered with its message*, SEND SUPPLIES, the result is a repeating key-word COMET COMET CO. The other two cryptograms were those of Fig. 98. Here, the Beaufort cryptogram, beginning *K K Z B B*, if deciphered with the key COMET, gives the message-letters *S E N D S*. But when we attempt to decipher it using *S E N D S* as our key, we obtain: *I U O C R*. It becomes necessary, in order to find out our key-letters, that we proceed as we did for Porta: Assuming that the slide is being used, place message *S* beside cipher *K*, and find out what key-letter is standing beside the index *A*. Place *E* and *K* together, and find the next key, and so on. That is, change the position of the slide for every decipherment.

In this same figure, the variant cryptogram begins *Q Q B Z Z*. If it be deciphered with the correct key-word COMET, we obtain the correct message-letters, *S E N D S*. But if we attempt to decipher it with a key *S E N D S*, we obtain the same series as in the other case: *I U O C R*. To decipher it as a variant, we must again proceed letter by letter. How, then, are we going to apply a probable word as we did with the Vigenère in Fig. 90? How are we going to decipher a whole row of letters, first as *S*, then as *U*, then as *P*, and so on? Must we do this letter by letter, shifting the slide for every letter on every row? And suppose it is a page of trigrams, where we wish to decipher every trigram on the page as *THE?* Is there no way in which we can decipher all first-letters as *T*, all second letters as *H*, and all third letters as *E*, with only three settings of a slide? The answer is simple. *Switch the slides.* We have said (and shown) that in this respect the two Beauforts are reciprocal. Where the cryptogram is true Beaufort, and you desire to use your probable word as a trial key, do this with your Saint-Cyr slide (used in reverse, that is, as if enciphering in Vigenère). If your cryptogram is variant Beaufort, use the Beaufort slide (or treat it as a Vigenère, and obtain the key later). Both cases can be looked at in Fig. 101. The cryptogram at (a) is our same Beaufort cryptogram; that at (b) is our same variant. In another chapter, we shall look a little more closely into this odd triangle of Vigenère-variant-Beaufort. Meanwhile, the interested student might like to investigate for himself a few of the curious angles:

Would it be possible to prepare a tableau for the true Beaufort, and use it in exactly the manner described for Vigenère? Recalling the appearance of the Vigenère tableau (Fig. 85): Suppose we should add to this another vertical alphabet, this time on the right-hand side, causing this new alphabet to begin at *A* and run backward, *A Z Y X.* . . . Could this new alphabet be made to serve any useful purpose? More than one? What about the reversible cipher-disk? Is there any way at all in which it would be possible to encipher and decipher Vigenère cryptograms with a Beaufort slide, or Beaufort cryptograms with a Vigenère slide? Could you make a cipher disk for the Porta?

110. By NEON. (Gronsfeld).

```
J Q Q Y P   L R S F Q   Y J N E U   R U V E F   V W P E B   Q F G T E   M K U K G

R W E T Z   I D V I Q   Q S Z I H   K W M C E   K B F J Q   Q X T R F   V R J K O

A T E E N   J U M S N   G L P I B   S O A S R   Y S A X R   U O J G W   M V R U S

V D Q Q R   D P P K P   L I C
```

111. By B. NATURAL. (Gronsfeld).

```
        L N P L G   S Y R U A   I R I Q X   R E N D I   U U N H D

        Y M S U U   O Q N S T   I T U G L   W R E R V   B Z D U Q
```

```
            S I C T U   Q B T F X   J F E H J   W N I K U   N H A Y H

            I E P R G   X K W M P   U K U L F   N G Q P R   B X Z R E

            T E U U W   T R X J F   N H J Y O   J U V S P   N W O Z G

            S O Q C J   N W K G E   B X Z R I   P U N X B   N A W O -
```

112. By B. NATURAL. (Porta).

```
I O U K J   G F Y S M   Q S X H W   W D P K M   M J E S P   Y W Y L B   X B V U D

X T V L V   O G Q K S   L W W Q S   E U D K W   J I A M G   W Z C W F   O U I M M

V Z F U Q   K S O X D   S E L E E   P T I O T   U L U L W   W P K Q K   S Z E U.
```

113. By KRIS KROST. (Beaufort. Probable word: AMERICA).

```
N D L H T   I E Y R K   F M F H L   C S Z Q A   H B H T Y   H A F P I   V I D C S

X P Z E X   N K W Q R   M S A H E   Q X G R E   H A U H G   D S O O A   G X U G D

W G T I L   S A P D V   H A Q W E   W Z M I M   Y Y Q O B   F E K C M   M T F N E

V H W Z Y   B G P W V   E H R Z V   U O O N B   K X F O Z   J A Z I Q   N Z T T O

P R V I T.
```

114. By WHOSIT. (Variant Beaufort.

```
K O A S Y   B B S G P   A R Y A T   F R F D U   L W H J A   R G H S G   U W D B C

J R V M C   U P S T Q   W M B Y S   I W Y I F   H B A A F   I A N Y H   J L S B T

J O C Z E   E N N R U   A S R U I   E J N O E   P S G C G   W V U M E   A K W R L

Y H N S R   G H B A H.
```

115. By PICCOLA. (Short Simple Substitution. - No keyword).

```
O F   T D A F   F B E H Z H W U   W F O M ;   M F W R   J D E D N V F P   Z K

W F D Y F M Z   Q K K Z T.
```

CHAPTER XIV

The Kasiski Method for Periodic Ciphers

Prior to the 1860's, the ciphers of the past two chapters had been regarded as entirely safe. A radical change of opinion took place in 1863, when Major F. W. Kasiski, a German cryptanalyst, was so indiscreet as to publish certain of his observations. The student will surely have noticed, among the examples of Chapters *XII* and *XIII*, the happening which is suggested in Fig. 102. Some sequence, usually a digram, is repeated in the plaintext, and happens to be enciphered more than once by exactly the same few key-letters; the result is a *repeated sequence in the cryptogram*. What he may have failed to notice is the *periodicity* of such repeated sequences. In order that the same few key-letters be used again, *the key-word must have been repeated an exact number of times*, so that, in these cases of repeated cryptogram-sequences, the distance from first-letter to first-letter is *evenly divisible by the key-length* — or period (in the figure, the distance from V to V is 10,

Figure 102

A common happening in all PERIODIC ciphers:

```
Vigenère key:      C O M E T C O M E T C O M E T C O M
Plaintext:         T H E R E I S A N O T H E R Q U E S
REPEATED SEQUENCE: V V Q V . . . . . . V V Q V . . . .
```

which is twice the key-length, 5). This does not mean that all repeated sequences found in Vigenère cryptograms are periodic. Often, they are purely accidental; oftener still, they will be due to the repetition of alphabets in the key itself, especially if it is such a word as CORCORAN or DESDEMONA. But a distinct majority of them, according to Kasiski, are caused by periodicity; and if all of the repeated sequences found in a given cryptogram be examined to find what the separating interval is in each case, and if all of these intervals be factored, *the factor which predominates will betray the period of the cryptogram*.

In order to have a look at the Kasiski method, we will consider the cryptogram shown in Fig. 103; and, to approximate a more troublesome case, we will assume that no repeated sequences can be found except those few which have been underscored in the figure. With the cryptogram-letters serially numbered, in the manner shown, the distance apart of any two of them is readily learned by subtraction. The digram *CH* is found beginning at the 1st letter and again at the 46th letter; 46 minus 1 equals 45, their distance apart. Thus, if *CH* is one of the periodic repetitions, the period could be 15, 9, 5, or even 3. The trigram *UBF*, 8th and 63d letters, shows an interval 55; here, the period could be 11 or 5. Notice that a period 5 has been indicated by both.

Now let us look at Fig. 104, where the method of presentation is once more a debt to M. E. Ohaver. In this figure, the repeated sequences have been listed, and each one is accompanied by the two serial numbers of its two first letters, together with the interval which was obtained by subtraction. Ohaver's process provides a column for each possible factor, beginning with 2 and carried as far as desired. Opposite each interval, its various possible factors may then be noted in their correct columns. In the average case, the correct period will be pointed out by *the column showing the largest number of entries*. But in this connection, it must be taken

Figure 103

```
      5          10          15          20          25          30
C H G S L   F A U B F   X U P H S   J D A G Y   X M N Z U   W W J P D

     45          40          45          50          55          60
J S U P L   G C G F K   R N I M F   C H K O A   Q A V X O   N N U I L

     65          70          75          80          85          90
N S U B F   N D V P K   A I P L S   N M Q O H   M E U I L   B L K Q W

     95         100         105         110         115         120
N D V I Y   X U I I A   Q E U U Y   J W C O K   O E N M P   W W J J J

    125         130         135         140         145         150
Q I U O V   C M W D O   X F C O L   F S K U L   V B W U N   R V G T B

    155         160         165         170
B S Q N L   U E P H A   Q T Q X V   A K Q O E
```

into consideration that *small* factors like 2 and 3, and even factors 4 and 5, are usually present in considerable numbers, partly as accidentals, but also because they are factors of the period itself; that is, if the period is 6, there will surely be factors 2 and 3 for every factor 6, and there will usually be a few extra appearances due to accidental repetition.

Now, considering our tabulation, and ignoring the fact that short periods like 2 and 3 are seldom encountered, we find that factors 3 and 5 are present in equal numbers. Often, we are faced with exactly this problem. Here are two factors which have appeared in approximately equal numbers. Which one of these actually represents the period? Ohaver's recommendations include these: Where two factors seem almost equally prominent, select the larger if it is a multiple of the smaller. If one factor is not a multiple of the other, try to select a period which is a multiple of both (as 15 here, includes both 3 and 5). He points out also that the factor which is the correct key-length will usually be accompanied, in the tabulation, by quite a number of its own multiples, growing gradually fewer and fewer as their size increases. In this respect, our factors 3 and 5 are both disappointing. If we consider factor 5, we find factors 10 and 15, but not growing fewer; instead the number increases. We find no factor 20, but we do find a factor 25; another increase. Or, if we consider factor 3, we find factors 6 and 9, but no factor 12, and then a sudden increase in the number of factors 15. This is a case in which the decryptor would play safe by selecting the period 15.

The student who cares to examine this matter more closely may do so by pre-

Figure 104

Tabulation for Finding Period   M.E.OHAVER

Repeated Sequence	Positions - Intervals	POSSIBLE FACTORS of INTERVALS							
C H	46 - 1 = 45	3	5		9			15	
U B F	63 - 8 = 55		5			11			
U P	33 - 12 = 21	3		7				21	
S U	62 - 32 = 30	2 3	5 6		10			15	
P L	73 - 34 = 39	3					13		
W W J	116 - 26 = 90	2 3	5 6		9 10			15 18	
N D V	91 - 66 = 25		5					25	

The factors found in the **largest number of DIFFERENT intervals** are 3 and 5.

paring for himself a less haphazard listing of the cryptogram's repeated sequences. Perhaps the most satisfactory way of doing this is to begin by making a general frequency count. Then, in order to have the more reliable information at once, start the tabulations by examining those letters whose frequency is only 2; follow this with an examination of those having a frequency of 3, and so on. The theory is that letters of these frequencies are much more likely to belong to only one alphabet, while the letters of higher frequency have probably been enciphered in several different alphabets, so that their repeated sequences are not so sure to be periodic

Figure 105

Individual Frequency Counts - PERIOD 5

	Alphabet 1	Alphabet 2	Alphabet 3	Alphabet 4	Alphabet 5
A	11	11	1		111
B	11	1		11	1
C	111	1	11		
D		111		1	1
E		1111			1
F	11	1		1	111
G	1		111	1	
H		11		11	1
I		11	11	1111	
J	111		11	1	1
K		1	111		111
L		1		1	11111 11
M	1	111		11	
N	11111	11	11	1	1
O	1			11111 1	11
P			111	111	1
Q	1111		1111	1	
R	11				
S		1111		1	11
T		1		1	
U	1	11	11111 11	111	1
V	1	1	111		11
W	11	111	11		1
X	1111			11	
Y					111
Z			1		

For other cases in which there may be some doubt, the writer's advice is to select *large* factors in preference to small factors. Or, if the decision must be made between two factors such as 6 and 7, where a period of 42 would be necessary in order to include both, simply select the handiest and give it a trial. With the longer cryptograms, as we shall see in a moment, an error in the choice is very speedily discovered; as to the shorter cryptograms, there is one rule which invariably holds good: *If you meet with any resistance at all* in dealing with the kind of ciphers which were shown in the past two chapters, you have probably selected the wrong period.

Often, however, where one clue is missing, there will be another present to take its place. Repeated *trigrams* are less likely than repeated digrams to be accidental, and longer repeated sequences are still less likely to be so. In the present tabulation, we find that three of the repetitions are trigrams; in all three cases the period 5 is suggested, while only one suggests also a period 3. That is, if we use a period of 15, two of these trigrams will have to be considered accidental.

If the period here is 5, then we are dealing with *five simple substitution alphabets.*

These five alphabets have been used over and over again, always in a given rotation; therefore, if the cryptogram be rewritten into *five columns* (it is already conveniently grouped), the letters in each column will belong to one same alphabet, and it becomes possible to *take a separate frequency count on each one of these five alphabets.* These individual frequency counts may be seen in Fig. 105. Originally, we had a length of 170 letters, and, if the student desires to take a frequency count on the complete cryptogram, he will find that he has no truly predominant letters which could represent some of the letters *E T A O N I R S H.* Instead, he has a series of frequencies which are all fairly close to 4% of the text (6 or 7), and which, should he rearrange them in decreasing order, would have somewhat the following appearance: 10-10-10-9-9-9-8-8-8-7-7-7-7. . . . . .3-2-2-1. He will probably find, also, that every letter of the alphabet has been used at least once, something which would be very rare indeed in any normal English text of 170 letters. But in these five individual frequency counts, each belonging to a separate alphabet, matters are different. Here, the alphabets represented have a length of only 34 letters each, and yet, in the third, fourth, and fifth alphabets, there is one predominant letter, which could represent *E*, or some other letter which has taken the place of *E*, while, in the first and second alphabets, there are some few letters distinctly more prominent than others. Also, each alphabet has shown some gaps in sequence, where letters of the class *J K Q X Z*, and possibly also some letters like *B P V W*, would surely be missing in a normal text of only 34 letters.

A frequency count made on columns is not, of course, normal. We saw this in dealing with transpositions, when we considered vowel-distribution. Yet, as length increases, we find that the letters present in columns begin to approach more and more the proportions found in normal text; here, with only 34 letters, it would be possible, in any one of these frequency counts, to assign the letters to groups of high, moderate, and low frequencies. *Whenever our frequency counts do not have this general aspect, the period cannot be correct.* (There are, of course, the very short cryptograms, in which the actual frequencies are not apparent.) So far, we are dealing with any cipher whatever of the periodic type, and many of these ciphers do not make use of simple shifted alphabets, or even of alphabets which are in any way related to one another.

Now let us consider the one case in which the alphabets are all "Caesars." In this case, whether the cipher is Vigenère, Beaufort, or Porta, we have only to identify one letter in order to identify a whole alphabet. Suppose we examine, first, alphabet 5, in which the one outstanding letter, *L*, has appeared 7 times. Does this letter represent *e?* If *L* of alphabet 5 represents *e*, then, counting backward (that is, upward), we find that the letter *a* will have to be represented by *H; this* alphabet, then, will be the *H*-alphabet if the cipher is Vigenère. The letter *H* has a frequency of only 1, which, in normal text, is not particularly satisfactory as the frequency of *a*, but this frequency count has not been taken from normal continuous text; suppose we examine the rest of the alphabet, and find out what the frequencies would be for other letters. Beginning at *H*, and calling letters in the order *a, b, c,* we find that this fifth alphabet, provided it is the *H*-alphabet, will contain: 3 *d*'s, 7 *e*'s, 2 *h*'s, 2 *l*'s, 2 *o*'s, 3 *r*'s, 3 *t*'s, and 3 *y*'s. That is, each letter present which shows a frequency greater than 1 will represent some plaintext original which, normally, is of some frequency, the only exception being *y*, which is a vowel. This is the best we can expect of any columnar frequency count made on only 34 letters; but more convincing still, and more reliable, is the fact that out of the entire group *j k q x z* we find only *x*, represented once. Alphabet 5, then, is entirely acceptable as the *H*-alphabet of the Vigenère cipher.

Let us see what we can find out about alphabet 3. Here, the strongly predominant letter is *U*. But when we attempt to identify this as *e*, we find that we should have to accept an alphabet containing 3 *q*'s, 2 *x*'s, and 3 *z*'s, all occurring in only thirty-odd letters of text. We meet with similar trouble when we attempt to identify *U* as *t*, as *a*, as *o*, and so on. It is not until we try it as *s* that we have good luck, finding only a series of blanks to represent the letters *b*, *j*, *k*, *q*, *v*, *w*, *x*, and *z*. And if *U* represents *s*, this alphabet begins at *C*. Alphabet 3, then, is entirely acceptable as the *C*-alphabet of the Vigenère cipher, and we have two of the key-letters: * * *C* * *H*.

In alphabet 1, the leading letter, *N*, is not so strongly predominant, and yet, when we assume it as the substitute for *e*, we find that the rest of the count is satisfactory. Alphabet 1, then, is acceptable as the *J*-alphabet of the Vigenère cipher and we have three of the key-letters: *J* * *C* * *H*.

In alphabet 2, we find no one leading letter, but the two most prominent frequencies are standing opposite *E* and *S*, as if this count might represent the normal alphabet itself. The absence of *O* and the presence of only one *T* is hardly significant in a columnar count; but further examination shows an excess of *M*'s and *W*'s, and this is more disturbing. However, a single *K* has appeared as the only representative of the group *J K Q X Z;* the low-frequency letters *B* and *V* have appeared but once each; and there is an absence of *Y*'s to counterbalance those which were too numerous in one of our other alphabets. So that a detailed examination, and the failure to identify this as any other alphabet, will lead to its tentative acceptance as the *A*-alphabet of the Vigenère cipher. (We can know definitely when we attempt to decipher with it.) With alphabet 2 accepted as the *A*-alphabet, we now have four of the key-letters: *J A C* * *H*. We shall return in a moment to consider the one which is still missing; but according to those present, it does not look as if our key is going to develop into a recognizable word.

Alphabets of the kind we saw in No. 2 can be much more satisfactorily identified by means of a *graph*. This graph, when the cipher is Vigenère, is no more than a picture of the normal frequency table. Ordinarily, it will be a strip of paper on which the normal alphabet has been written twice in succession, with a straight line standing at right angles to each letter, this line being long or short according to the normal frequency of its accompanying letter.

A description of one such graph, suggested by L. H. Patty, will serve to explain them all: Assuming that the several frequency counts are standing in a vertical position, as we see them in Fig. 105, and that the work has been done on quadrille paper, the graph will also be prepared vertically, and the strip of paper will be quadrille paper with squares of the same size, so that the spacing, vertically, will be the same for graph and frequency counts. The graph, however, will be twice the length of the frequency counts, and will carry the normal alphabet written twice in succession (except that the final *Z* can be omitted). The basis for frequencies can be 200, 100, or any other basis desired. If the basis is 200, each small square might represent a frequency of 5, so that a horizontal line placed beside *E* (frequency 24), would have a length of nearly five of the small squares. Or, if the basis is 100, each small square might represent a frequency of 2, and the horizontal line placed beside *E* (frequency 12), would have a length of six of the small squares. Or, if this same graph is being made on a typewriter, we might dispense with the horizontal lines and use a series of diagonals (or l's, or asterisks), after the manner of tally-marks, using whatever number of these is the actual frequency of the letter per 200, or per 100; this will give a good clear picture of the normal frequency count. It is understood that the upper and lower halves of the graph are to be prepared exactly alike, and that there is to be no skipping of extra spaces between them. Thus the graph, being twice the length of the frequency counts, and spaced to match them, can be moved up and down beside each one of these until some point is found at which the *pattern* of the given frequency count bears some resemblance to a pattern found somewhere on the graph. If no such pattern can be found, the conclusion is that the frequency count was not made on one of the simple shifted alphabets; however, due allowance must be made, as in the case of our alphabet 2, for the difference in length and for the fact that frequency counts of this kind have been made on columns. Patty's graph, so far, is representing only the shifted normal alphabet; that is, the cipher alphabets belonging to Vigenère, variant, and Gronsfeld ciphers. If its horizontal lines be made very heavy, and retraced on the opposite side of the strip, and if the letters be written on that side, opposite exactly the same horizontal lines as before, the reverse side of the strip will furnish another graph for identifying the reversed alphabets of the Beaufort cipher. Other graphs can be prepared for other kinds of alphabets. For instance, a graph suitable for examining a series of Porta frequency counts could be made in two halves, each of double length;

Figure 106

Another Tabulation for Finding the Period   EDWIN LINDQUIST

Repeated Sequence	Interval	List of all PRIME Factors.....				
		2	3	5	7	11....(Etc.)
J C V	24	111	1			
C V	13					
D D V	36	11	11			
D S	12	11	1			
S S	8	111				
D T J	60	11	1	1		
T J	48	1111	1			

This was based on a cryptogram whose period was 12. The PRIME FACTOR 2 is obviously included **twice,** and the PRIME FACTOR 3 once.

the A-to-M half would serve for comparison with the N-to-Z halves of the frequency counts, and vice versa.

The Vigenère cipher, and, in particular, the Kasiski method of solution, have given rise to much research among members of the American Cryptogram Association. We doubt that any of this research has ever resulted in any new or valuable discovery. Yet it is interesting in that it shows a body of amateurs arriving at devices which are fully as effective or convenient as those proposed by seasoned cryptanalysts. Carter's " discovery," for instance, which we saw in Fig. 90, was purely his own device; at that time, he had never heard of the " probable word method " proposed by Commandant Bazeries, one of the greatest of modern cryptanalysts. A great many of the first suggestions were directed at methods for making the trigram-search less tedious; these were largely duplications of a same idea, involving the use either of a tableau or of a slide; one example will be shown in the next chapter. The use of graphs, also, was a sort of simultaneous " invention." As to Kasiski processes, while Ohaver's tabulation had been published, it had been out of print and was not available for several years. The only information to be had was the fact that a period could be discovered by factoring intervals between repetitions, and Edwin Lindquist, finding this rather vague, devised for his own use the tabulation which is shown as Fig. 106. This tabulation was made from a cryptogram in which the period was 12. Lindquist, instead of preparing columns for all possible factors, prepared them only for *prime factors*, the repeated sequences and their separating intervals being listed in about the same way as in Ohaver's tabulation. Now, taking one of the intervals, as 24: Tally in column 2, and the interval is reduced to 12. Tally again in column 2, and the interval is reduced to 6. Tally again in column 2, and the interval is reduced to 3, which is itself a prime factor. Tally a final time in column 3, and the interval 24 has been reduced to its prime factors. This process is almost entirely mental, and *very rapid*. Examining the results: Columns 2 and 3 are very full, indicating that prime factors 2 and 3 are both included in the period. But in column 3, the tallies are largely single, indicating that this factor is included only once in the period; while, in column 2, the tallies are largely in pairs, indicating that this factor is probably included twice in the period; had it been included three times, it would have shown up oftener in three's. Conclusion: The period is 2 x 2 x 3, which is 12. This tabulation will be found fully as convenient as Ohaver's, and its results fully as accurate.

Mr. Lindquist also developed his own method for identifying alphabets. This method, which, in theory, is *graphic*, is not particularly applicable to the kind of

Figure 107

The "SHIFT" Method for Identifying Alphabet 4						EDWIN LINDQUIST		

Letters apparently of the high-frequency class: I   O   P   U

Their possible originals................	E	T	A	O	N	I	R	S	H
Amount of SHIFT if I represents..	4	15	8	20	21	0	17	16	1*
" " " " O " ..	10	21	14	0	1*	6	23	22	7
" " " " P " ..	11	22	15	1*	2	7	24	23	8
" " " " U " ..	16	1*	20	6	7	12	3	2	13

A SHIFT of 1 (the B-alphabet) makes all four of these letters the

substitutes for high-frequency originals. It is almost certainly

the shift which was made.

alphabets we have been considering; that is, it would not be needed when there is so much material. But for shorter examples, where alphabets contain only ten or fifteen letters each, it comes close to being that magical thing referred to by Lamb, a "mechanical crypt-solver." This method can be examined in Fig. 107, where it is being applied to our so-far unidentified alphabet 4. An examination of this alphabet 4 (of Fig. 105) shows that it has four letters of more prominence than the rest: *I, O, P, U*. These letters, or most of them, should represent high-frequency originals; and our method consists in examining them collectively in order to find out what amount of " shift " must have taken place in order that some four of the letters *E T A O N I R S H* would have resulted in these four particular substitutes. The word " shift " is best understood by picturing the movement of the lower alphabet on a Saint-Cyr slide. If the two *A*'s are together, this is the starting position, and the " amount of shift " is zero. If the *B*-alphabet be moved into position, we have a *shift of 1;* if the *C*-alphabet be moved into position, we have a *shift of 2;* and so on. These " shift-numbers," o to 25, can be written below the letters of the sliding alphabet.

Now, considering only one of our letters, *I*: If this is the substitute for *e*, the normal alphabet was shifted 4 positions; if it is the substitute for *t*, the amount of shift was 15; if it is the substitute for *a*, the amount of shift was 8; and so on through the rest of the nine letters belonging to the high-frequency group. Finally, having considered our letter *I* as the substitute for all nine of these possibilities, we arrive at a *series of nine shift-numbers:* 4-15-8-20-21-0-17-16-1. And unless one of these is the correct shift, the cryptogram-letter *I* does not represent a high-frequency letter at all. In the figure, this examination has been made for all four of the letters *I, O, P,* and *U*, and opposite each of these we have the resulting series of nine shift-numbers. A comparison of the four series of numbers will show that *each one includes a shift of 1*. A shift of 1, then, that is, the B-alphabet, would have caused all four of our cryptogram-letters to become substitutes for high-frequency originals. This is almost certainly the shift which was made; but should the assumption prove incorrect, then a shift of 7 has appeared in three of the lines, and the H-alphabet would be the next choice. Lindquist's method was found so effective for cases of scant material, that two members of the Association, M. R.

Figure 108

Tableau Showing SHIFTS for Each Letter of the Alphabet - (MORRIS R. COLLINS)

For VIGENÈRE   For BEAUFORT

E	T	A	O	N	I	R	S	H		E	T	A	O	N	I	R	S	H
22	7	0	12	13	18	9	8	19	A	4	19	0	14	13	8	17	18	7
23	8	1	13	14	19	10	9	20	B	5	20	1	15	14	9	18	19	8
24	9	2	14	15	20	11	10	21	C	6	21	2	16	15	10	19	20	9
25	10	3	15	16	21	12	11	22	D	7	22	3	17	16	11	20	21	10
0	11	4	16	17	22	13	12	23	E	8	23	4	18	17	12	21	22	11
1	12	5	17	18	23	14	13	24	F	9	24	5	19	18	13	22	23	12
2	13	6	18	19	24	15	14	25	G	10	25	6	20	19	14	23	24	13
3	14	7	19	20	25	16	15	0	H	11	0	7	21	20	15	24	25	14
4	15	8	20	21	0	17	16	1	I	12	1	8	22	21	16	25	0	15
5	16	9	21	22	1	18	17	2	J	13	2	9	23	22	17	0	1	16
6	17	10	22	23	2	19	18	3	K	14	3	10	24	23	18	1	2	17
7	18	11	23	24	3	20	19	4	L	15	4	11	25	24	19	2	3	18
8	19	12	24	25	4	21	20	5	M	16	5	12	0	25	20	3	4	19
9	20	13	25	0	5	22	21	6	N	17	6	13	1	0	21	4	5	20
10	21	14	0	1	6	23	22	7	O	18	7	14	2	1	22	5	6	21
11	22	15	1	2	7	24	23	8	P	19	8	15	3	2	23	6	7	22
12	23	16	2	3	8	25	24	9	Q	20	9	16	4	3	24	7	8	23
13	24	17	3	4	9	0	25	10	R	21	10	17	5	4	25	8	9	24
14	25	18	4	5	10	1	0	11	S	22	11	18	6	5	0	9	10	25
15	0	19	5	6	11	2	1	12	T	23	12	19	7	6	1	10	11	0
16	1	20	6	7	12	3	2	13	U	24	13	20	8	7	2	11	12	1
17	2	21	7	8	13	4	3	14	V	25	14	21	9	8	3	12	13	2
18	3	22	8	9	14	5	4	15	W	0	15	22	10	9	4	13	14	3
19	4	23	9	10	15	6	5	16	X	1	16	23	11	10	5	14	15	4
20	5	24	10	11	16	7	6	17	Y	2	17	24	12	11	6	15	16	5
21	6	25	11	12	17	8	7	18	Z	3	18	25	13	12	7	16	17	6

Collins and Helen S. Pearson, decided, independently of each other, to set it up in permanent form, so as to avoid fresh computations for each new cryptogram.

Collins' device took the form of a tableau, as shown in Fig. 108. In this figure, the vertical alphabet running through the center is a list of possible cryptogram-letters. On the side marked " Vigenère," the four lines of numbers standing beside the letters *I*, *O*, *P*, and *U*, are the same as those included in Fig. 107. It will be noticed that only the first line of numbers (opposite *A*) need be found from the slide; after that, each column is a series o to 25. The same is true with reference to the Beaufort shifts. These, incidentally, were computed on the assumption that the Beaufort keys, *A, B, C, D.* . . . . . . are passing in their normal alphabetical order beneath the stationary *A* (as most of us prepare the Beaufort slide, this is backward). Fig. 109 shows a similar tableau prepared for the Porta shifts. The zero-position here is the *AB*-alphabet, a shift of 1 is the *CD*-alphabet, and so on. Collins, however, did not use the shift-numbers. *He increased these by 1*, using numbers 1 to 26, which represent the 26 positions of the slide, or, better, the serial positions in the normal alphabet of the 26 key-letters. Others who have since prepared similar tableaux have dispensed altogether with numbers, and have used the key-letters themselves. Doing this, the first row of the Vigenère portion will show the nine key-letters *W H A M N S J I T*, the second row will show key-letters, *X I B N O T K J U*, and so on. If the letters appearing on the slide have been numbered, one method is fully as convenient as the other, though in dealing with a plaintext key one would probably prefer the letters. In any case, where some four letters, such as our *I O P U* of the foregoing alphabet, have been found more than once in a given frequency count, it is merely necessary to find these four letters one by one in the vertical alphabet and *copy* their accompanying numbers. It is even possible, having these three tableaux, to decide whether the frequency counts taken

Figure 109

Tableau Showing SHIFTS for PORTA

E	A	I	H			T	O	N	R	S	
9	0	5	6	N		6	1	0	4	5	A
10	1	6	7	O		5	0	12	3	4	B
11	2	7	8	P		4	12	11	2	3	C
12	3	8	9	Q		3	11	10	1	2	D
0	4	9	10	R		2	10	9	0	1	E
1	5	10	11	S		1	9	8	12	0	F
2	6	11	12	T		0	8	7	11	12	G
3	7	12	0	U		12	7	6	10	11	H
4	8	0	1	V		11	6	5	9	10	I
5	9	1	2	W		10	5	4	8	9	J
6	10	2	3	X		9	4	3	7	8	K
7	11	3	4	Y		8	3	2	6	7	L
8	12	4	5	Z		7	2	1	5	6	M

from a periodic cryptogram represent the alphabets of the Vigenère, the Beaufort, or the Porta.

Miss Pearson's device took the form of *strips*, a set of 26 for each of the three ciphers. Fig. 110 shows the first five of her Vigenère set as she originally prepared them, using the " position-numbers," which are all larger by 1 than those of the tableau. Aside from this, each strip represents one row from the Vigenère half of Collins' tableau. But where Collins had arranged his numbers according to the frequencies of the nine possible originals (so that possibilities found on the left might have more significance than others found on the right), Miss Pearson arranged hers in straight numerical order, and spaced them in such a way that No. 1 is always in the first column, No. 2 is always in the second column, and so on. Had she used key-letters, all *A*'s would have been in the first column, all *B*'s in the second column, and so on. As to the use of these strips: Presuming that the four leading cryptogram-letters are the same as before, simply pick out the four strips which are headed by the letters *I, O, P,* and *U*, and set them together. If any of the numbers are duplicated, *you will find them standing in the same column.* These, remember, are the devices of amateurs, and both will be found very effective. It will be noticed that the basis is the finding of key-letters (or numbers) and not the identification of cipher alphabets.

Now compare these devices with a method proposed by an expert, in which the basis is the identification of cipher alphabets, and not their keys: With this method, a tableau is prepared (which could be arranged like the one of Fig. 85) in which the only letters shown on any one line are the substitutes for the nine high-frequency letters. If, for instance, the tableau is intended for the Vigenère cipher, the top row will contain only the letters *A E H I N O R S T, and the other 17 positions will be left blank.* The second row will contain only the letters *B F I J O P S T U,* the third will contain only the letters *C G J K P Q T U V,* and so on. Or, if the tableau is intended for the Beaufort cipher, the top row will contain only the letters *A W T S N M J I H,* the second row only the letters *B X U T O N K J I,* and so on. Thus, after having taken a series of frequency counts, we may find out, in each of these frequency counts, which are its leading letters, then consult the prepared tableau to find out which of its alphabets will show these same leading letters. An added suggestion is as follows: Prepare the tableau, as described, using black ink. Then, using red ink, add to each alphabet the substitutes for *J K Q X Z* (perhaps, also, for

Figure 110

Strips for Determining SHIFTS HELEN S. PEARSON

SET FOR VIGENÈRE

A	1	-	-	-	-	-	-	8	9	10	-	-	13	14	-	-	-	-	19	20	-	-	23	-	-	-
B	-	2	-	-	-	-	-	-	9	10	11	-	-	14	15	-	-	-	-	20	21	-	-	24	-	-
C	-	-	3	-	-	-	-	-	-	10	11	12	-	-	15	16	-	-	..	-	21	22	-	-	25	-
D	-	-	-	4	-	-	-	-	-	-	11	12	13	-	-	16	17	-	-	-	-	22	23	-	-	26
E	1	-	-	-	5	-	-	-	-	-	-	12	13	14	-	-	17	18	-	-	-	-	23	24	-	-

NOTE: The numbers here are POSITION-numbers, instead of SHIFT-numbers. A shift of zero is "position 1" of a slide. This is also the numerical, or serial, position of A in the normal alphabet. Most members of the American Cryptogram Association prefer to dispense with numbers, and use key-letters.

B P V W); that is, the substitutes for those letters which ought to be largely *absent.* This makes it much easier to decide between two alphabets in which the more frequent letters have made it seem that one is as likely as the other. It will be found that letters of low or moderate frequency are ordinarily as helpful in these ciphers as those of high-frequency; an instance has been pointed out in which those of the cryptogram can be more so: Where the question is one of deciding between two possible periods, a new tabulation can be made using only the sequences found in connection with those letters which are less frequent in the cryptogram than others, and thus not so sure to belong to more than one alphabet.

We have seen, then, what can be done in place of the trigram-search in the case of those longer cryptograms. Having one of only 170 letters, we first found out its period, and then (presuming that we accepted the *B*-alphabet in the case of alphabet 4), found out all five of its key-letters *J A C B H,* and even the type of encipherment (obviously Gronsfeld), *without having deciphered a single letter of its message.* We are now in a position to go back and investigate any which are still unsolved. With Vigenère methods and principles thoroughly understood, the student is fully in possession of methods for dealing with any periodic cipher whatever *in which he knows what the cipher alphabets are.* All that remains, then, is to pick up a few loose ends, and observe a few variations from the strictly periodic encipherment, after which we may consider the case of the unknown cipher alphabets.

116. By NEMO. (A Vigenère? Or a snare and a delusion?)

```
W L P C V   M O G K E   E I F M U   R W W F H   V M F F W   E Y X A V   U B I C Z

O J M L C   H V I Y F   K S C U S   X I L M G   B Q I D B   W I F G B   I Q Z G Z

H F J Y P   M K I G V   P T W Y K   W Z H W M   Z H W I F   A P S D N   W F H E D

S C X A V   O E B Y Y   O K C O Y   U I H U J   L H U D X   P P W V V   H P F W Y

L G F B V   E J M A A   G B P I E   B A V U V   Q L Z N L   P W A J W.
```

117. By NEON. (U.S.Army Cipher Disk. Surely not an advertisement?)

```
D J T X J   M H L M K   O M F D T   F N E U I   G D D N A   A U S N S   A C F G Y

M Z Y A Q   A N M W U   W S R B R   F J J Q S   K A Y B A   N B L T O   J E R K S

N W X A G  T J L Z Y  S T V A R  B X L K N  R L V D U  U F O F A  K Z L W Y  T E E W.
```

118. By TITOGI. (What! Another Vigenère? Some collusion here!)

```
D W P W Z   T C G H H   Z B B V W   F B H I F   W Q B L L   J D Z R G   U M M E S

W B D W L   J K X I F   Y Z D G K   Y I O I K   D W P M F   H C M S F   Q G C E L

J I I H W   A M I W L   J Z I W S   W K V W E.
```

119. By THE ADMIRAL. (Vigenère).

```
N S R V K   D K S I W   J W Y C E   C E G K C   E B D K N   Q Y S J U   L X Z O L

X P S U V   U T F B S   O I N P C   R R E U Y   O N U F K   H K Z D D   O J P Q Z

C K J I E   N A F J D   W B U S J   U R C L C   J C E P C   O K T V F   A F P Y X

G K K Y Z   V.
```

120. By THE ADMIRAL. (Beaufort).

```
Z N J L N   Y H C Z D   A U D D Z   I N H R C   Z Y Z K H   G B P E C   L M L W Y

R O I J Q   D T L Q O   Z H Q S N   D V E S E   P E J O Y   L S Z O J   U P G T K

J F K C U   W N S H G   W F D T M   G K K D W   E H L Z R   N S B G V   E S R A U

K K U M J   Z M T K N   K F Q L G   K C U P Z   U S D L W   D E Z U B   D Y F O D.
```

121. By DOR. (Another "Aristocrat." - Not hard. No keyword).

```
A B C D E F G C   H G I J A   K G F D J F B L M   E D M M I M G B A   N F L C

L O G J P N F   D R F C L N.   O G P I M   S D A N   T D L I F U.   F C B G

N B P J   B G J F C L E F,   K C G A I E D   V B F.
```

CHAPTER XV

MISCELLANEOUS PHASES OF VIGENÈRE DECRYPTMENT

When a Vigenère cryptogram is very short, its alphabets are no longer readily identified by their graphic appearance. But its period, in the majority of cases, can still be determined, and it still remains true that the identification of one letter identifies a whole alphabet. The example of Fig. 111 contains only 30 letters. With this cryptogram in the form shown at (a), we are still dependent upon the search for trigrams and short words, but the case is modified by the presence of a repeated trigram. Unless this repetition, *ZIL*, is accidental, it indicates a maximum period of 12, and the cryptogram is long enough to provide another interval 12, with another trigram, *EUK*, upon which any key-fragment brought out at *ZIL* can be tested in order to see whether or not it will bring out another good sequence. When it finally does, the intermediate trigrams (those at intervals 6 or 4) can be tried, in the hope of finding a shorter period.

Figure 111

(a)		

```
(a)
  Z I L T F   R U I Y T   J R Z I L
    x           x           x

  K A R O I   E A O A E   U K L W K.
    x                      x
```

(b)	1	2	3	4	5	6
	Z	I	L	T	F	R
	U	I	Y	T	J	R
	Z	I	L	K	A	R
	O	I	E	A	O	A
	E	U	K	L	W	K

But assuming a case in which we have no repeated sequences at all, we almost never meet with a Vigenère cryptogram in which there are no *repeated single letters belonging to a same cipher alphabet*. These repeated single letters can be tabulated with their separating intervals, *and these intervals factored in exactly the same way as intervals between repeated sequences*. The evidence, perhaps, will be less clear, and less reliable, than that obtained through repeated sequences; as with sequences, the less frequent letters will usually be more informative than those which are leaders. To illustrate, with our given example, the single letter *I* has shown the interval 6 three times, the single letter *R* has shown it twice, and the single letters *L* and *Z* have shown its multiple. In the average case, the period will not be so clearly evident as here; however, the example was not in any way manipulated in order to produce this evidence.

Once the cryptogram of (a) can be rearranged as at (b), we no longer have before us the piecemeal decipherments and piecemeal tests which are necessary where a period is likely to be anything at all. Whatever key-fragments can be brought out at *ZIL*, or on another trigram, need be tested only on the three columns which contain the trigram. Even presuming that the evidence has been inconclusive between two or more periods, the cryptogram, necessarily a short one, can be written into each of these probable periods, and the two or more resulting blocks, standing side by side, can be considered more or less simultaneously. Here, with our period determined as 6, the columns of (b) are very short, and the number of trials and erasures should not be many.

For this kind of case, however, many solvers have a preference for the purely mechanical method which is detailed in Fig. 112. *Sheet 1* of this figure has been prepared from the first column of our cryptogram, which included the letters *Z U Z O E*. *Sheet 2* has been prepared from the second column, which included the letters *I I I I U;* and *sheet 3* has been prepared from the third column, which included the letters *L Y L E K*. In each case, the column of cryptogram letters, as it first stands, is also the *A*-decipherment. With each letter used as a point of beginning, a series of normal alphabets may be laid out, as in the figure, and the resulting 25 new columns on every sheet will show the other 25 possible decipherments. But if these decipherments have been caused to progress in the normal alphabetical direction,

Figure 112

Sheet No. 1 (For Column 1 of b, preceding figure)

KEYS:

```
a z y x w v u t s r q p o n m l k j i h g f e d c b
Z A B C D E F G H I J K L M N O P Q R S T U V W X Y
U V W X Y Z A B C D E F G H I J K L M N O P Q R S T
Z A B C D E F G H I J K L M N O P Q R S T U V W X Y
O P Q R S T U V W X Y Z A B C D E F G H I J K L M N
E F G H I J K L M N O P Q R S T U V W X Y Z A B C D
```

Sheet No. 2 (For Column 2 of b, preceding figure)

KEYS:

```
a z y x w v u t s r q p o n m l k j i h g f e d c b
I J K L M N O P Q R S T U V W X Y Z A B C D E F G H
I J K L M N O P Q R S T U V W X Y Z A B C D E F G H
I J K L M N O P Q R S T U V W X Y Z A B C D E F G H
I J K L M N O P Q R S T U V W X Y Z A B C D E F G H
U V W X Y Z A B C D E F G H I J K L M N O P Q R S T
```

Sheet No. 3 (For Column 3 of b, preceding figure)

KEYS:

```
a z y x w v u t s r q p o n m l k j i h g f e d c b
L M N O P Q R S T U V W X Y Z A B C D E F G H I J K
Y Z A B C D E F G H I J K L M N O P Q R S T U V W X
L M N O P Q R S T U V W X Y Z A B C D E F G H I J K
E F G H I J K L M N O P Q R S T U V W X Y Z A B C D
K L M N O P Q R S T U V W X Y Z A B C D E F G H I J
```

and if the cipher is Vigenère, the key-letters which produce these deciphered columns will have to run backward in the alphabet. These can be added at the tops or bottoms of their columns, and can, if desired, be written in red ink, or otherwise distinguished.

Fig. 113 shows what modifications would be necessary if the sheets were being prepared for one of the Beauforts. For the variant Beaufort, the only difference lies in the fact that key-letters must progress in the same alphabetical direction as their decipherments. With the true Beaufort, however, the making of an *A*-decipherment does not mean a simple copying of cryptogram letters, as in the other two ciphers; this *A*-decipherment must first be made; after that, the series of normal alphabets can be extended as before, and the key-letters will progress in the same alphabetical direction as their deciphered columns.

Now, assuming that these sheets have actually been prepared, say on quadrille paper, the various columns of decipherment may be examined, and a check-mark placed beside each column in which the series of letters appears to represent a "good" decipherment. With longer columns, those may be checked which contain the largest percentages of letters *E T A O N I R S H*, without too many of the letters *J K Q X Z;* with shorter columns, perhaps those are "best" in which any repeated letters are chiefly vowels, it being remembered that when the cryptogram contains repeated sequences, as well as repeated single letters, the possible identity of these repeated diagrams or trigrams must also be taken into consideration. With all of the apparently good columns checked for attention, *sheet 1* may be creased vertically so as to place any desired column on the extreme right, and this column may then be laid directly against any desired column of *sheet 2* for an observation of the resulting digrams. If these appear to be satisfactory, then *sheet 2* may also be creased vertically, and the series of apparently good digrams may be laid directly against any desired column of *sheet 3* for an observation of the resulting trigrams. And so on, if desired, to a possible *sheet 4*, or *5*, or *6*, though, as a rule, the first three sheets will be found sufficient. While the method, as indicated, is intended to be mechanical, that is, largely visual, it would be possible, where uncertainty exists between two given combinations, to copy these and subject them to a digram test. But this should not be necessary in a case where key-letters, as well as their de-

Figure 113

If column Z U Z O E were VARIANT	If column Z U Z O E were BEAUFORT:
KEYS: a b c d e f g	KEYS: a b c d e f g .....
Z̄ Ā B̄ C̄ D̄ Ē F̄	Z - B̄ C̄ D̄ Ē F̄ Ḡ H̄ .....
U V W X Y Z A	U - G H I J K L M .....
Z A B C D E F	Z - B C D E F G H .....
O P Q R S T U	O - M N O P Q R S .....
E F G H I J K	E - W X Y Z A B C .....

ciphered columns, are expected to set up good combinations in order to form a plaintext key-word.

An interesting version of this method, as shown by Admiral Elliott Snow, included the following variations: To begin with, in extending the alphabets, the decryptor omits altogether the letters *J K Q X Z*, and perhaps one or two others of extremely low frequency, simply leaving the blank spaces which indicate their alphabetical positions. This makes the work more rapid, and, in addition, the presence of these blank spaces in any column of decipherment, advertises at once that the column is probably not a very good one. But Admiral Snow's columns were not columns; they were *rows*. A given series of letters, as *Z U Z O E* of our foregoing *sheet 1*, is laid out horizontally, and its decipherments are extended vertically. The spacing on each row is arranged to correspond with the period; that is, the letters *Z U Z O E*, instead of being continuous, are spaced six columns apart if the period is 6, and their decipherments, of course, are spaced in the same way. The sheets may now be creased horizontally between rows, and one sheet placed against another in such a way that the resulting digrams are all standing on diagonals, but have appeared at exactly their cryptogram distance apart. The student should experiment with both arrangements and decide which one he likes.

It has been pointed out by C. A. Castle, another of our members, that the foregoing method will find its chief application, not on a single cryptogram, but as applied to a case which, so far, we have not considered in connection with the substitution ciphers: One in which the decryptor has in his possession five or six cryptograms, all very brief, but all enciphered with the same key. Here, we have the common practical case, to be handled in somewhat the same way as the last of our transposition examples; the cryptograms can be written one below another, thus forming a series of columns in which every column has been enciphered with the same cipher alphabet. If this case happens to involve also a comparatively short period, it is possible to take intervals between repeated sequences found in two different cryptograms, using the intervals indicated by the number of columns between the first letter of one sequence and the first letter of its repetition. Castle's example, however, was not based on a short key, but upon an extremely long one, and his five or six messages were merely fragments, each one of which was *known to be the beginning of an English sentence.* In the English language, about half of all initial letters used are found in the group *T A O S H I* and more than another one-fourth are found in the group *W C B P F D M.* Thus, having a series of beginnings in which the first column will include only initial letters, the number of truly acceptable decipherments on any *sheet 1* will usually be quite limited. In addition, with vowels known to have a fondness for second and third positions in words, there should be little difficulty in selecting decipherments from *sheets 2* and *3.*

While we have described this device as having been written out on sheets of paper, there are many persons who prefer to have at hand a series of cardboard strips which will set up the "sheets" mechanically. If each of the strips carries

Figure 114

One Form of "DECRYPTING SLIDE"   C. STANLEY LAMB

For VIGENÈRE, the "Decrypting Alphabet" runs backward:

As this is shown, it has been set for the decipherment of a trigram H D G, and every possible decipherment can be read from the slide without changing its present adjustment. The entire list of frequent trigrams can be used as trial keys:

Trial Keys: T H E   A N D   T H A   E N T   I O N   T I O   F O R   (Etc.)
                     H D G
Fragment of True Key: O W C   H Q D   O W G   D Q N   Z P T   O V S   C P P   (Etc.)

the normal alphabet written twice in succession, it is possible to adjust five of the strips so as to place the letters *Z U Z O E* one below another in the form of a column and automatically set up the other 25 columns. The strips can be loose, or may form part of a slide. Slides, in fact, may be used for many purposes, and are well worth preparing for any kind of cipher which the decryptor expects to encounter a great many times. The members of the American Cryptogram Association, who solve a great many Vigenères, Beauforts, and so on, as a matter of recreation, have practically all "invented" slides (or tableaux) which will, to some extent, do away with the irksome task of carrying out a trigram-search. These are prepared in various ways, and variously used, though the principle for all is about the same as that indicated in Fig. 114. They are usually referred to as *decrypting slides,* and the single stationary alphabet, sometimes a list of key-letters and sometimes not, will be called "the decrypting alphabet." C. Stanley Lamb, who is by no means the only "inventor" of the device illustrated, has this in several different forms, according to the purpose for which he intends to use it. Notice that the card, as we have placed it, shows the stationary single alphabet running contrary to the others, for use on the Vigenère cipher, and that this card need merely be reversed in order to have a single stationary alphabet running parallel to the others, for use on the two Beauforts. As to the sliding double alphabets, there may be as many of these as the operator feels like setting up; if the device is being used to assist in the trigram search, three will be needed. To explain its use: The decryptor here is dealing with a sheet of trigrams. Each one of these trigrams is to be deciphered as *THE, AND, THA*, and so on, following the list of normally frequent trigrams, and the resulting key-fragments are to be written down for comparison with one another, in the hope that some two or more will be duplicates, or will contain overlapping letters. The first of these cipher trigrams is *HDG*. These three cipher-letters, found on the three slides, are placed, in order, below *A*. Now, on the first of the slides, every possible decipherment for *H* is standing opposite its key-letter, found in the " decrypting alphabet "; on the second slide, every possible decipherment for *D* is standing opposite the the proper key-letter; and on the third slide, every possible decipherment for *G*. To know, then, what key-letters will be deciphered by *THE*, find *T* on the first slide and note key-letter *O;* find *H* on the second slide and note key-letter *W;* find *E* on the third slide and note key-letter *C;* the complete key-fragment is *OWC*. This may be written down. Then, *without changing the adjustment of the device:* For *AND*, key-fragment *HQD*, and so on down the list.

Where the cipher is Vigenère, the text-letters may be found in the " decrypting alphabet " and their keys on the slides, without changing results. But with either of the Beauforts, a key is specifically a key and not a text-letter. Thus, when the card is reversed, and the same process applied for one of the Beauforts, the student must be careful as to where he finds his letters *T H E* in each of the two ciphers. This peculiar relationship of Vigenère-variant-Beaufort is not hard to untangle if all three of the encipherments are considered to be purely mathematical operations of addition and subtraction. If we must add two numbers, as 5 and 10, it makes no difference whether we call it the sum of 5 plus 10 or the sum of 10 plus 5. But where we must perform a subtraction, there are two separate cases.

In straight Vigenère encipherment, the process is *addition,* in which text-letters may be considered to have the values 1 to 26 (their serial positions in the normal alphabet), while key-letters may be considered to have the values 0 to 25 (the amount of alphabetical shift represented by each one). Thus, the encipherment of *J* by *P* (10 plus 15) will not result differently from the encipherment of *P* by *J* (16 plus 9); in both cases, we obtain *Y*, alphabetical value 25.

In variant Beaufort, we have one of the *subtractions: Message minus key,* with the occasional necessity for " borrowing " 26 in order to make a subtraction possible. Thus, *J* enciphered by *P* (10 minus 15) does not give the same result as *P* enciphered by *J* (16 minus 9). In the first case (after " borrowing " 26), we obtain *U*, or 21, while in the other case we obtain *G*, or 7.

In the true Beaufort, we have the other *subtraction: Key minus message.* This time, we value the key-letters 1 to 26, and the text-letters 0 to 25. Thus, *J* enciphered by *P* (9 taken from 16) results in *G*, or 7, while *P* enciphered by *J* (16 taken from 9) results in *U*, or 21. Our results, then, are exactly the reverse of those obtained in the other subtraction.

If these mathematical comparisons be understood, or simply kept in mind, it will always be possible, whenever a decryptment process has been explained in connection with only one of the encipherments, to examine its "mathematical" details and learn from these in just what respects it would have to be modified in order that it may be applied with equal success to the other two encipherments. There is another interesting possibility which may have escaped the student's notice. If he will turn back to Fig. 98, in which the same message, using the same key, was enciphered in both of the Beauforts, one encipherment coming out as *K K Z B B I Z.* . . . . and the other as *Q Q B Z Z S B.* . . . . , he will notice that these two cryptograms are complementary from beginning to end. If we saw any reason for doing so, we might convert either one of the Beaufort cryptograms to the other form, and apply its probable word with its own slide.

Now, having seen the great vulnerability of the famous " indecipherable cipher," suppose we glance at some of the devices which have been used for doing away with its periodicity. One such device, that of *auto-encipherment* (*autokey, autoclave*), has been given its own separate chapter (the one immediately following), not because of its value as a cipher, but because of the very interesting decryptment problem it presents. A second device, the details of which may be examined in Fig. 115, consists in the use of a very long nonrepeating key, the popular name for which is " running key." The value of such a key, for practical purposes, we have already seen; it was a key of this kind which Castle had used on his five or six cryptogram-beginnings. In single examples, however, it gives more trouble. Unless there is a probable word, its message and key must be dug out bit by bit, and if the encipherment is Vigenère, any recovered fragments can belong equally well to the

Figure 115

Vigenère with a "Running Key"

Key-letters:	M Y C O U N T R Y T I S ...
Plaintext letters:	S E N D S U P P L I E S ...
Cryptogram:	E C P R M H I G J B M K ...

message or to the key. However, with its key known to be purely plaintext, no fragments need be considered except those which are usable combinations, and since the " running key cipher " makes a fascinating puzzle, a specimen has been included among the practice cryptograms. The original of this, apparently, was the Hermann cipher. This employed a slide which was identical with the Saint-Cyr slide except that the stationary alphabet carried an extra cell (position) marked " index " to be used instead of the Saint-Cyr index *A*. As the writer saw this, the index-cell was standing just ahead of *A*, so that the resulting encipherment would have been that of a Saint-Cyr slide on which the letter *Z* was serving as index-letter.

Of other devices aimed at destroying periodicity, quite a few have been based in some way on *key-interruption*. A key-word is selected, as INDEPENDENCE, but the encipherer breaks off before completely using his rotation, so that the completed cryptogram will be enciphered very irregularly by such a key as INDEP INDEPEND I IN INDEPENDENC IND INDEPEN. . . . . . Sometimes this is found as a word-spacing device, the key beginning over with each new word, though naturally not with word-separations showing in the cryptograms. But in the average case, the key-interruption takes place at the discretion of the encipherer; sometimes the agreement with his correspondent allows him to break off as he pleases without any sort of signal, leaving the decipherer to discover the interruptions through the fact that he can no longer decipher; again, he may use an indicator, as *J*. In the latter case, he must encipher any *J*'s which may happen to occur in his message by using the *I*-substitute; then, whenever he decides to break the key, he first enciphers a *J*. Thus, whenever the decipherer brings out the letter *J*, he knows that his key is to begin over with the encipherment of the next letter. It will be noticed that in all of these cases, the decipherer will have to do his work one letter at a time.

There is another of these devices which apparently destroys periodicity and is aimed at throwing all of this onerous work upon the shoulders of the decryptor without at the same time punishing the legitimate decipherer. This consists in shortening the two alphabets of the key, so as to leave some extra letter, which will never be used in any cryptogram. Encipherment, in this case, is accomplished in the regular way, producing a periodic cryptogram. The extra letter may then be inserted at points throughout the cryptogram wherever it can do the most harm. The decipherer, knowing that this one letter is always null, need merely erase it. But if this device is to be really useful, the omitted letter must not be always the same, and this trouble can be overcome as follows: In the shortening of the plaintext alphabet, we omit always the unwanted letter, as J. But in shortening the cipher alphabet, we omit first one letter and then another, according to agreement, and insert J in its place. The decipherer, knowing what letter is null, erases it; but the decryptor, granting that he knows what the process is, will still have to experiment with various letters before he learns which one (or more) of the 26 is the null of the moment.

Shortened alphabets are not uncommon in ordinary use. We meet with 25-letter alphabets in European examples, the letter W having been omitted for telegraphic reasons. This case can usually be distinguished from the one which precedes by the fact that the letter W is never found in a frequency count, and it presents only the minor trouble that the ordinary 26-letter slide will not make the decipherments, so that it becomes necessary to prepare another on which the letter W is not present. This case can, of course, be simulated by making use of a 24-letter alphabet.

These devices, taken as a whole, have added little, if at all, to the security of the straight-alphabet ciphers, though, for the most part, they have succeeded admirably in rendering their ciphers totally unfit for general purposes. Considered as single examples, they can, of course, prove troublesome. We trust that this will not be the case with some one or two of the appended practice cryptograms, but if so, we recommend that the student postpone them for a later investigation. Concerning example No. 122, he may find that some of the material presented in Chapter XVI applies also to the " running key " encipherment; with others, a trigram-search may assist in developing the interrupted key-word; and in one case, a clever decryptor should find a way for applying his Kasiski method.

122. By SABIO. (Vigenère with Running Key. SENT, AGENT, STOP, IMPREGNATED).

```
A R U N N   I N G K E   Y S O Q M   A V Q X K   L U E R S   Z S S R F   A H A I V
X W E T N   K Z Q N V   R A G W V   E T F W N   L K A T A   I B S Z U   H P E X U
B W W A S   P N F F C.          (These are a trifle tedious, but not inhuman).
```

123. By NEON. (Porta, with key-interruption. Plenty of trigrams!)

```
A P V K W   T P K P V   Y G Q P G   A K J Z W   J N I X J   U Q O U K   P V W F U
R F X N K   C K P R K   Q K W F U   R G J O V   Z O K G X   J V Q S W   T F K D L
L Y Q L X   Z E F L Y   U J V Z C   X G Q L J   M T X W K   K P V T V   B Y K X P
F J Z Q X   B V C O V   V H X Z K   J Z U Y.
```

124. By WHOSIT. (Beaufort, with key-interruption. THEY, WHEN, IN, ON, UP, etc).

```
M X Y F U   H P M J B   C X O C K   A L Q E D   B Q A E P   R B Z L G   L W M J B
Z Z C S A   A L A O E   K K C W L   L J B P H   U W B L F   Q O R B Z   L A O E M
A L O K F   P V H Y U   Y H Y J L   X O L X Z.
```

125. By B. NATURAL. (Gronsfeld, with key-interruption).

```
S O W H Z   G H O C V   V W L F F   F X O F H   H X Q S I   H S O Y P   P H K T Q
H Z F Y J   Q G Q H O   B X V X O   F L R J L   F W E A E   F H O G G   V O F E T
Y M U X O   F T H S N   F B U A O   B W H V C   V V H V A   O F Q M A   G V N H S
S C F U X   O F V H E   L O A O J   O E C V V   E Y F A V   S N I P L   E O U P W
T A G P Q   K E T.
```

126. By TRYIT. (Gronsfeld, with interruptors. MY, TO, THE, OF, IS, BE, WHICH).

```
R H X G A   P A S R E   C Z T R T   W Z A J Z   S G Q A Z   M T P E A   U X G K Y
Z F W Z S   G Q Y O E   Y F C T P   W B G K O   D P W N D   X Z A W F   O W H T Z
B M O H K   Q P K V K   S Q N D J   Z S L Z X   L C R T T   N H S H W.
```

127. By B. NATURAL. (Vigenère. One letter reserved as interruptor. Look out!)

```
P N B Y C   A N D V N   P N F Y Z   G V N W E   J N S I T   T T Z B L   N O S L N
X R N I L   Z H N H M   D X D X B   Z N B I K   W Z H N D   J N B M D   T N O I K
N E I I H   T W Q M F   A T N P Q   U N T J W   D C X N G   I C X P Z   B L N O S
L N O I J   N O S L G   N H S C K   T Q D N X   W N R I I   I L M J T   R N U M D  T.
```

CHAPTER XVI

AUTO-ENCIPHERMENT

The term *autokey* (*autoclave;* " the autokey cipher "), as commonly used, refers to the kind of encipherment shown in Fig. 116, in which a message becomes its own key for applying some one of the multiple-alphabet ciphers — usually the Vigenère. It will be noticed from the figure that the auto-encipherment must be " primed " with a conventional key; and whenever the words *key-length, period,* and so on, are used in connection with auto-enciphered cryptograms, their actual reference is to the short initial key. A more accurate term would seem to be *group-length.* But that a term is needed for referring to something akin to the period of the ordinary Vigenère cryptogram can be seen when we consider the mechanics of decipherment: Our present initial key, COMET, *key-length 5,* serves to decipher only one *group* of that length. The five key-letters obtained from this first decipherment will serve to decipher only one more *group;* from this, another five key-letters are obtained, and will decipher a third *group,* and so on. But our *group-length,* some-

Figure 116

Vigenère Autokey:	C O M E T/S E N D S U P P L I E S T O M O R L E Y S
Plaintext:	S E N D S U P P L I E S T O M O R L E Y S S T A T I
CRYPTOGRAM:	U S Z H L M T C O A Y H I Z U S J E S K G J E E R A

times referred to as " period," includes five individual series of letters, any one of which can be enciphered and deciphered independently of the rest. That is, beginning with *C,* or *O,* or *M,* or *E,* or *T,* and taking each fifth letter, it is possible to proceed straight through to the end, enciphering or deciphering only this one series, or " column." It will be noticed from the foregoing that the decipherer gets the short end of the bargain. The encipherer knows in advance what the key is, and, to some extent, can apply one cipher alphabet at a time; the decipherer knows only the key to the first group; the rest he must ferret out for himself.

There is, however, a second form of autokey encipherment in which the respective difficulties of encipherer and decipherer would be reversed. This form of auto-encipherment, which can be seen in Fig. 117, makes use of a preliminary key, as in the regular form, but follows this with the enciphered text instead of with the plaintext. Such an encipherment results, occasionally, from the mechanical construction of a cipher machine, and in this case, where the 26 cipher alphabets are in mixed order, and unknown to the decryptor, may present an interesting decryptment problem. But where the cipher is Vigenère (or any other in which the decryptor possesses the full set of cipher alphabets), it can hardly be argued that there is any great problem about a cryptogram which carries its key in full view. We will confine ourselves, then, to the usual form of autokey, as first explained, beginning our studies with a brief glance at the two common practical cases, that of accumulated cryptograms, and that of probable words. Procedure, in the former case, is self-evident. Possessing several cryptograms all initiated with the same preliminary key, we may write their beginnings one below another to form columns, and the first few of these columns will constitute an ordinary case of Vigenère in which every message is known to be the beginning of a sentence. With beginnings discovered, a little industry accomplishes the rest.

The case of probable words, on the other hand, presents some interesting possibilities inherent in the auto-encipherment itself. When the probable word is short (or if a search is to be made for normally frequent trigrams), the task of bringing out and testing the possible key-fragments is made much less onerous by the fact of the purely plaintext key. Being sure of an abundance of excellent sequences, we need consider none but the very best of the deciphered fragments; and for any one considered, the trials need be made only within a very short range of the spot at which it was found. All of this work may be done directly on the cryptogram. A correct sequence, correctly applied, can be followed out in both directions, and will yield, in full, several of the " columns," and several consecutive letters of the initial key. But if it so happens that the probable word is longer than the initial key, *its first few letters must become the keys for enciphering its last few.* Consider, for instance, the word SIMPLICITY, which has a length of ten letters. If the preliminary key contains only five letters, then, beginning at -*ICITY*, the keys *SIMPL*- will begin to encipher, causing a certain long cryptogram-sequence which, for Vigenère, will always be *A K U I J.* If the preliminary key has

Figure 117

```
Key:  C O M E T/  U S Z H L   O H O S T   .....
      S E N D S   U P P L I   E S T O M   .....
      U S Z H L   O H O S T   ....
```

Note that the cryptogram itself is the key, except that the
first five letters are missing. To decrypt, with any known
alphabet, we need merely find where to begin using it!

six letters, the same word causes a sequence *U Q F N* when the cipher is Vigenère; if it has seven letters, the cryptogram-sequence will be *A B K;* and even an eight-letter key brings out one certain digram, *L G.* Thus, knowing what the cipher is, and having at our disposal any comparatively long probable words, we may write out these sequences *in advance* and be ready to look for them in the cryptograms. In addition to whatever words we consider probable, it is obvious that any other long word may encipher itself in the same way, and, if it is one important to the subject matter, is likely to be repeated, causing the cryptogram to show a *long repeated sequence.* Thus, if we find a long repeated sequence in a cryptogram, we are able to try this as a common suffix, *TION, MENT, ENCE, ABLE,* etc., in the expectation of bringing out some common prefix, *CON, PRE,* etc.

More fascinating, by far, than its practical aspects, however, are the possibilities presented by the autokeyed cryptogram for analytical attack. The devices immediately to follow are described by General Givierge in his *Cours de cryptographie,* and are credited by him to Commandant Bassières.

First, it is possible to discover the length of the short preliminary key, or, at any rate, to confine this to certain definite probabilities. This key, as we have seen, governs a definite group-length, or " period." If this group-length, say, is 5, then, barring the first and final groups, every plaintext letter will be enciphered by the letter standing five positions to its left, and will, in its own turn, serve to encipher the one standing five positions to its right. Since all plaintexts are filled with repeated letters, roughly half of them separated by even intervals, it stands to reason that there will be many occasions on which the letter standing five positions to the left and the one standing five positions to the right will be the same letter. That is, we must often find the encipherment pattern of Fig. 118. Some one letter, as *S*, is repeated at an interval of exactly twice the group-length, with some other letter, as *R*, standing at exactly the group-length interval from both of the *S*'s. The first

S enciphers *R,* and *R* enciphers the second *S.* Or, if the repeated letter is *T* and the intermediate one is *L,* then *T* enciphers *L,* and *L* afterward enciphers *T.* Where the cipher is Vigenère, the result, in the cryptogram, is *a repeated letter standing at exactly the group-length interval.* If the cipher is one of the Beauforts, the same pattern produces *a pair of complementary letters separated by exactly the group-length interval.*

Figure 118

```
           S . . . . R              T . . . . L
  S . . .  R . . . . S      T   .  L . . . . T
           J . . .  J              E . . . . E
```

Now, in order to consider the value of this observation, let us examine the cryptogram of Fig. 119, an autokeyed Vigenère, which, for convenience, is presented in groups of the correct length, 7. According to Bassières, should we inspect this cryptogram for repeated single letters, noting, in each case, the interval of separation, the correct group-length, 7, will be present among those intervals which are noted oftenest, and, in many cases, will be the one which predominates. For making such an examination, perhaps the simplest plan would be that of listing the possible group-lengths at the tops of a series of columns, beginning with group-length 1 and carrying them as far as desired. The counts could then be made by placing a tally mark in the proper column for each time that a given interval is noted. The results of this examination, as compared with the Kasiski examination for a period, may be studied in Fig. 120 At (a), where the leading intervals of our cryptogram have been listed with their frequencies, it is noticeable that the correct group-length, 7, is not represented by the predominating interval or even by the one which is second in frequency; it is merely present among the five leaders. But we find other cryptograms, not necessarily of great length, in which some one letter, as *V,* will be repeated five or six times in succession at exactly the group-length interval, and its evidence amply confirmed in other repetitions. Then, as at (b),

Figure 119

```
L C N D M E K    L C N O Y G T    B G X V N D G    S S H W A W J    Q E V L H O W

Y I J W L E X    A P V E C L B    H D Q E K U W    W G R H X J F    B D Y P I P K

Q D W A R G U    W R L G N I Q    S L V L E S P    H E U T X B O    N D H V X D C

O U D S J T F    J N U Q N Q L    A A I L M Z U    X I E W O B Y    I W E H P·D Q
```

we may find some fairly good clue, leading us to give the first trial to the correct group-length; and again we are left, clueless, to try out five or six different group-lengths before striking the correct one. Results, then, are variable, and the only certainty, at any rate in a short cryptogram, is that of being able to limit the group-length to a given few. With the group-length determined, or with one selected for trial, we may take our choice of two processes.

Process 1 (Bassières). With group-length 7, as we have seen, our cryptogram includes seven independent series, or " columns," of letters. By beginning at the 1st letter, and taking the 1st, 8th, 15th, 22d, etc., letters, we may decipher *series 1* independently of the others; or, by beginning at the 2d letter, and taking the 2d, 9th, 16th, etc., letters, we may decipher *series 2;* and so with the other five series. Many persons, before doing this, will rewrite this cryptogram into seven *columns,* which permits that the decipherment of a series be done straight down its column,

and for that reason the word " column " is sometimes used to describe what we
have called here a " series." In order to understand the first of the Bassières
processes, we need consider only *series 1*, it being understood that whatever applies
to any one of the seven series applies equally well to the other six.

Figure 120

(a)   (b)

Interval 8, found 8 times   Possible Reason for L C N

"   16,   "   8   "

"   4,   "   6   "   T H E o r e m/G E T t i..

"   5,   "   6   "   G E T t i n g T H E b a..

"   7,   "   6   "   Z L Y . . . . Z L Y . .

Now, considering Fig. 121: If the unknown first key-letter was *A*, then the first
plaintext letter, found by deciphering with key *A*, was *L*, and this became the key
for enciphering the eighth letter. If the key which enciphered the eighth letter was
L, then the eighth letter, found by deciphering with key *L*, was *A*, and this became
the key for enciphering the fifteenth letter. Following out this decipherment to the
end of *series 1*, we find that the plaintext letters must have been *L A B R Z Z B*,
etc., as given in full in the figure. A glance at the complete series will show that
this decipherment is not a particularly good one. If another decipherment be carried out, on the hypothesis that the original first key-letter was *B*, we obtain the
series *K B A S Y A A*, etc., which starts out fairly well, but which, when completed,
will contain two *K*'s, one *Z*, two *B*'s, and one *P*. If a third decipherment be carried out, on the hypothesis that the original first key-letter was *C*, we obtain the
series *J C Z T X B Z*, etc., which is a poor decipherment from the beginning. A
trial and error method might consist in making these decipherments one at a time
directly on the cryptogram, erasing one when it is obviously poor, and trying to
add the next series whenever one proves acceptable.

Figure 121

Keys: A   L   A   B

          L C N D M E K   L C N O Y G T   B G X V N D G   S S H W A W J......

Plaintext: L   A   B   R

Series 1, (Key A):   L A B R Z Z B G Q L F R B G H H C Y Z J.

The Bassières process, however, consists in setting up the entire 26 possible
decipherments as these are shown in Fig. 122. In this figure, the original cryptogram-letters of *series 1* are standing in a column at the extreme left. The 26 possible decipherments are also standing in the form of columns, each decipherment
headed by the key with which it was initiated. If the group-length 7 is correct,
then one of these 26 columns shows the original plaintext letters.

Now let us examine, not the columns, but the rows, of this tableau, and find out
just how troublesome it is going to be to prepare tableaux of the same kind for
series 2, *series 3*, and possibly others. The key-letters, across the top, constitute a
normal alphabet, and below this each row contains the 26 decipherments for some
one letter of *series 1*. On the odd-numbered rows, the decipherments for the odd-
numbered letters are alphabetically arranged, but progressing in a direction contrary
to that of their keys, as if these odd letters represented Vigenère encipherment. On
the even-numbered rows, the decipherments for the even-numbered letters are also
alphabetically arranged, but are progressing parallel to their keys, as if these even-
numbered letters might represent variant Beaufort encipherment. Evidently, then,
the *A*-decipherment is the only one which must actually be carried out; afterward,

the preparation of the tableau is a matter of extending alphabets. With similar tableaux prepared for the remaining six series, we have seven sheets, and on each one of these there is one column showing the correct decipherment of the series, headed by the correct key-letter. Thus, our solution is to be the mechanical one of the preceding chapter. On each one of the tableaux, the apparently "good" decipherments may be checked for attention; the sheets may be creased between columns, and the "good" decipherments of one tableau may be placed directly in contact with those of another.

Figure 122

SERIES No. 1, Prepared as a Tableau.   (Corresponds to SHEET No. 1 of Figure 112).

THE CIPHER LETTERS	The 26 Decipherments, with Keys																									
	A	B	C	D	E	F	G	H	I	J	K	L	M	N	O	P	Q	R	S	T	U	V	W	X	Y	Z (Keys)
L	L	K	J	I	H	G	F	E	D	C	B	A	Z	Y	X	W	V	U	T	S	R	Q	P	O	N	M ←
L	A	B	C	D	E	F	G	H	I	J	K	L	M	N	O	P	Q	R	S	T	U	V	W	X	Y	Z →
B	B	A	Z	Y	X	W	V	U	T	S	R	Q	P	O	N	M	L	K	J	I	H	G	F	E	D	C ←
S	R	S	T	U	V	W	X	Y	Z	A	B	C	D	E	F	G	H	I	J	K	L	M	N	O	P	Q →
Q	Z	Y	X	W	V	U	T	S	R	Q	P	O	N	M	L	K	J	I	H	G	F	E	D	C	B	A
Y	Z	A	B	C	D	E	F	G	H	I	J	K	L	M	N	O	P	Q	R	S	T	U	V	W	X	Y
A	B	A	Z	Y	X	W	V	U	T	S	R	Q	P	O	N	M	L	K	J	I	H	G	F	E	D	C
H	G	H	I	J	K	L	M	N	O	P	Q	R	S	T	U	V	W	X	Y	Z	A	B	C	D	E	F
W	Q	P	O	N	M	L	K	J	I	H	G	F	E	D	C	B	A	Z	Y	X	W	V	U	T	S	R
B	L	M	N	O	P	Q	R	S	T	U	V	W	X	Y	Z	A	B	C	D	E	F	G	H	I	J	K
Q	F	E	D	C	B	A	Z	Y	X	W	V	U	T	S	R	Q	P	O	N	M	L	K	J	I	H	G
W	R	S	T	U	V	W	X	Y	Z	A	B	C	D	E	F	G	H	I	J	K	L	M	N	O	P	Q
S	B	A	Z	Y	X	W	V	U	T	S	R	Q	P	O	N	M	L	K	J	I	H	G	F	E	D	C
H	G	H	I	J	K	L	M	N	O	P	Q	R	S	T	U	V	W	X	Y	Z	A	B	C	D	E	F
N	H	G	F	E	D	C	B	A	Z	Y	X	W	V	U	T	S	R	Q	P	O	N	M	L	K	J	I
O	H	I	J	K	L	M	N	O	P	Q	R	S	T	U	V	W	X	Y	Z	A	B	C	D	E	F	G
J	C	B	A	Z	Y	X	W	V	U	T	S	R	Q	P	O	N	M	L	K	J	I	H	G	F	E	D
A	Y	Z	A	B	C	D	E	F	G	H	I	J	K	L	M	N	O	P	Q	R	S	T	U	V	W	X
X	Z	Y	X	W	V	U	T	S	R	Q	P	O	N	M	L	K	J	I	H	G	F	E	D	C	B	A
I	J	K	L	M	N	O	P	Q	R	S	T	U	V	W	X	Y	Z	A	B	C	D	E	F	G	H	I

Process 2 (Bassières). Fig. 123 shows the second of the Bassières processes. With 7 decided upon as the group-length, we make up a *trial key* having the right number of *A*'s, and decipher the cryptogram. The new cryptogram, produced in this way, is *periodic*, and its period, for Vigenère, will be twice the group-length, in the present case 14. In Fig. 124, where this new cryptogram has been repeated, written into its period, it is possible to check its periodicity: It has two repeated sequences, *C J B* and *W G*, at suitable intervals, and while these are very few, their evidence is amply supported by the fact of repeated single letters in every column. When the periodicity is not confirmed in this way, it can be assumed that the chosen group-length was not correct.

The make-up of this new cryptogram is not hard to understand if it is noticed that what we have done is to carry out simultaneously the seven *A*-decipherments of seven tableaux like that of Fig. 122. We saw there that the odd-numbered letters of a series react as Vigenère encipherment and the even-numbered letters as variant Beaufort. With seven *A*-decipherments made at once, the same will apply to odd-numbered and even-numbered *groups*. Thus, our new cryptogram has seven columns enciphered in Vigenère and another seven enciphered in variant Beaufort. The original seven-letter initial key-word will decipher both sets of columns; for the first seven, it must be applied in the Vigenère manner, and, for the other seven, in the variant Beaufort manner.

Figure 123

```
a a a a a a a    L C N D M E K    A A A L M C J    B G X K B B X    R M K M Z V M
L C N D M E K    L C N O Y G T    B G X V N D G    S S H W A W J    Q E V L H O W
L C N D M E K    A A A L M C J    B G X K B B X    R M K M Z V M    Z S L Z I T K

Z S L Z I T K    Z Q Y X D L N    B Z X H Z A O    G E T X L U I    Q C Y K M P X
Y I J W L E X    A P V E C L B    H D Q E K U W    W G R H X J F    B D Y P I P K
Z Q Y X D L N    B Z X H Z A O    G E T X L U I    Q C Y K M P X    L B A F W A N

L B A F W A N    F C W V V G H    R P P L S C J    B W G A M Q G    G I O T L L I
Q D W A R G U    W R L G N I Q    S L V L E S P    H E U T X B O    N D H V X D C
F C W V V G H    R P P L S C J    B W G A M Q G    G I O T L L I    H V T C M S U

H V T C M S U    H Z K Q X B L    C O K A Q P A    Y M Y L W K U    Z W G L S R E
O U D S J T F    J N U Q N Q L    A A I L M Z U    X I E W O B Y    I W E H P D Q
H Z K Q X B L    C O K A Q P A    Y M Y L W K U    Z W G L S R E    J A Y W X M M
```

New Cryptogram: L C N D M E K A A A L M C J - B G X K B B X..........(Etc.)

As to why this encipherment reduces to alternate Vigenère and variant Beaufort groups, this is best understood by resorting once more to the "mathematical" aspects of the Vigenère cipher. In a previous discussion, we have said that Vigenère encipherment consists in the " addition " of key to message, and that variant Beaufort encipherment (which, in Vigenère, would be *decipherment*), consists in the " subtraction " of key from message. In the beginning, our plaintext is a series of groups, as *A, B, C, D, E*, etc. and the first encipherment operation consists in the *addition* of a key, as *X*, but only to the first group, *A*. To encipher group *B*, we add *A;* to encipher group *C*, we add *B,* and so on, so that when the auto-encipherment is complete, we have a cryptogram in which the groups are made up as follows:

1st:	*2d:*	*3d:*	*4th:*	*5th:*
A plus X	*B plus A*	*C plus B*	*D plus C*	*E plus D.* . . . . . (etc.)

Figure 124

The New Cryptogram from Figure 123

```
L C N D M E K A A A L M C J
B G X K B B X R M K M Z V M
Z S L Z I T K Z Q Y X D L N
B Z X H Z A O G E T X L U I
Q C Y K M P X L B A F W A N
F C W V V G H R P P L S C J
B W G A M Q G G I O T L L I
H V T C M S U H Z K Q X B L
C O K A Q P A Y M Y L W K U
Z W G L S R E J A Y W X M M
```

```
1 2 3 4 5 6 7   1 2 3 4 5 6 7
 (Vigenère)     (Variant Beaufort)
```

Now, remembering what the mathematical values were for key-letters, the trial key, made up entirely of *A*'s, is made up entirely of *zeros*. When we subtract zero from the first group, we leave it unchanged, that is, the first cryptogram group is still *A plus X* (plaintext *plus* key, or Vigenère). When we subtract *A plus X* from the second group, this cancels the *A* of both, and leaves *B minus X* (plaintext *minus* key, or variant). When we subtract this from the third group, we cancel the two *B*'s, leaving C *plus* X, again Vigenère. When we subtract this from the fourth group, we cancel the two C's, leaving D *minus* X, again variant Beaufort. And so to the end. Always we come out with the original plaintext group plus or minus X, the key. Those groups which are *plus* X are Vigenère, and those which are *minus* X are variant. And X, in all, is the same: the original preliminary key. A comparison

Figure 125

Tables of High-Frequency Co-Efficients　　　PHILLIP D. HURST

VIGENÈRE (Cipher Letters)

Key	A	B	C	D	E	F	G	H	I	J	K	L	M	N	O	P	Q	R	S	T	U	V	W	X	Y	Z
E					a				e			h	i					n	o			r	s	t		
T	h	i					n	o			r	s	t							a				e		
A	a				e			h	i					n	o			r	s	t						
O		n	o			r	s	t							a				e			h	i			
N	n	o			r	s	t							a				e			h	i				
I	s	t							a				e			h	i					n	o			r
S	i					n	o			r	s	t							a				e			h
H	t							a				e			h	i					n	o			r	s
R					n	o			r	s	t							a				e			h	i

6 4 1 - 4 4 4 4 2 3 4 3 2 3 2 1 4 4 2 2 6 4 2 2 4

BEAUFORT (Cipher Letters)
True Beaufort:

Key	A	B	C	D	E	F	G	H	I	J	K	L	M	N	O	P	Q	R	S	T	U	V	W	X	Y	Z
...VARIANT...	A	Z	Y	X	W	V	U	T	S	R	Q	P	O	N	M	L	K	J	I	H	G	F	E	D	C	B
E	e											t	s	r			o	n					i	h		
T	t	s	r			o	n					i	h			e				a						
A	a							t	s	r			o	n					i	h			e			
O	o	n					i	h			e				a							t	s	r		
N	n					i	h			e				a							t	s	r			o
I	i	h			e				a							t	s	r			o	n				
S	s	r			o	n					i	h			e				a							t
H	h			e				a							t	s	r			o	n					i
R	r			o	n					i	h			e				a							t	s

9 4 1 2 4 3 3 2 3 3 3 4 3 3 3 2 3 3 3 2 1 4

PORTA (Cipher Letters)

Key	A	B	C	D	E	F	G	H	I	J	K	L	M	N	O	P	Q	R	S	T	U	V	W	X	Y	Z
E			r	s	t							n	o			a				e			h	i		
T					n	o			r	s	t			e			h	i					a			
A	n	o			r	s	t							a				e			h	i				
O							n	o			r	s	t		h	i					a				e	
N	t							n	o			r	s	h	i					a				e		
I	r	s	t							n	o							a				e			h	i
S					n	o			r	s	t			e			h	i					a			
H		r	s	t							n	o					a				e			h	i	
R						n	o			r	s	t				h	i					a				e

3 3 3 2 4 4 3 2 3 4 6 5 3 4 2 3 4 4 - 2 3 3 3 3 2

of the same kind applied to the two Beauforts (or a few trials made on actual groups, if the student is not mathematically disposed) will show whether or not the auto-enciphered Beauforts can also be reduced to periodic form, and, if so, what their period is likely to be. In the case of the true Beaufort, it may be necessary to straighten out a quirk as to the application of the *trial key*.

While the foregoing methods are intensely interesting as an example of what can be learned by analyzing the structure of a cipher, most members of the American Cryptogram Association, in practical work, prefer methods of their own which are quicker in giving results. These methods, for the most part, have subordinated other considerations to certain original observations concerning the use of the purely plaintext key. Where message and key, as in the case of the autokey and " running key " encipherment, are each made up of normal text, with both members including the normal 70% of high-frequency letters, it becomes inevitable that high-frequency letters in the key and high-frequency letters in the message will be paired again and again as the co-efficients of cryptogram-letters, so that cryptograms enciphered with this kind of key must contain a great many letters caused by this kind of co-inci- dence. For convenience in making use of this fact, each member has his own ideas. Phillip D. Hurst, for instance, prepared a set of tables of about the kind shown in Fig. 125, one table for each multiple-alphabet cipher with which he expected to

Figure 126

Where the KEY is a Segment of Ordinary PLAINTEXT:

Estimated Rank of the Cryptogram Letters and Their Frequencies Per 10,000

Figured by C. Stanley Lamb From Table of Ohaver.

VIGENÈRE

V	A	I	S	ERL WHB XGM FOZ	K	N	T	P	U	J	Y	C	Q	D
344	314	304	296	(Intermediate)	150	112	84	84	84	72	72	64	49	--

BEAUFORT
& VARIANT

A	N	E	W	O	M	Z	BQK JRT HVF GUDX	P	L	S	I	Y	C
480	262	246	246	196	196	191	(Intermediate)	121	121	104	104	57	57

PORTA

K	N	L	E	RMF TWP UYQ XGC AVI BJZ	D	H	O	S
329	300	282	275	(Intermediate)	132	113	97	--

deal. As these are shown, the alphabet across the top of any table is a list of pos- sible cryptogram-letters, each cryptogram-letter heading its own column; and each column contains only those letters which are themselves members of the high- frequency group *E T A O N I R S H,* and which, if enciphered by another letter from the same group, would result in the cryptogram-letter standing at the top of the column. The key, in each case, can be found at the left. Hurst says that he always attacks a cryptogram at the *second letter,* on the theory that this particular letter is likely to have been a frequent one in both the message and the key. He then attempts to follow out *series 2,* or, if the group length has not previously been determined, to find this series. To explain, without going into too much detail, the second letter in our foregoing autokeyed Vigenère was *C.* A glance at the table for Vigenère shows that this letter can result from only one pair of high-frequency co-efficients, *O* enciphered by *O.* Hurst will make his first trial on *series 2,* begin- ning with initial key-letter *O,* and come out with the correct decipherment at his very first attempt! With other letters, as *V* or *A,* it might be necessary to make as many as six trials, but, as we have seen, it is hardly ever necessary to carry a trial very far in order to see that the decipherment is going to be a poor one. The second letter, of course, will not necessarily give results; but the cryptogram, re- member, is filled with these vulnerable letters, and a decipherment may be started with any letter whatever and carried out in both directions.

Another method, originated by C. Stanley Lamb differs from Hurst's chiefly in that his observations were made from *digrams* and not from single letters. Originally, Lamb had been collaborating with Admiral Snow in establishing frequency counts for various kinds of ciphers, so that when the system was unknown, it would be possible to tell one from another. Fig. 126, for instance, gives a rough estimate as to what the rank and frequency should be for each letter in the kind of cipher we have under consideration. Finding a reasonably long cryptogram in which the

Figure 127

(a) Preparation of the mixed alphabet............
```
C U L P E * * R
A B D F G H I J
K M N O Q S T V
W X Y Z
```

```
C  A  K  W  U  B  M  X  L  D  N  Y  P  F  O  Z  E  G  Q  H  S  I  T  R  J  V
1  2  3  4  5  6  7  8  9 10 11 12 13 14 15 16 17 18 19 20 21 22 23 24 25 26
```

(b) ENCIPHERMENT - Auxiliary Key X, or 8:

```
Plaintext:            S  E  N  D  S  U  P  P  L  I  E  S  T  O  M  O  R
FIRST Substitution:  21 17 11 10 21  5 13 13  9 22 17 21 23 15  7 15 24
AUTOKEY (Addition):   8 21 17 11 10 21  5 13 13  9 22 17 21 23 15  7 15
C R Y P T O G R A M...  29-38-28-21-31-26-18-26-22-31-39-38-44-38-22-22-39-
```

```
L  E  Y  T  O  M  O  P  R  O  W  S  T  O  P
9 17 12 23 15  7 15 24 24 15  4 21 23 15 13
24  9 17 12 23 15  7 15 24 24 15  4 21 23 15
33-26-29-35-38-22-22-39-48-39-19-25-44-38-28.
```
xxxxxxxxxx   xxxxx

(c) Detail of DECIPHERMENT:

```
Cryptogram Numbers:   29 38 28 21 31 26 18 26 ...
AUTOKEY (Subtraction): 8 21 17 11 10 21  5 13 ...
PRIMARY CRYPTOGRAM..... 21 17 11 10 21  5 13 13 ...
Re-Substitution.........  S  E  N  D  S  U  P  P ...
```

(d) Vigenere Autokey - What Happens to REPEATED SEQUENCES with a ONE-LETTER KEY:

```
Key...  X/ T  H  E  M  O  N  T  H  E  X  T
Text... T  H  E  M  O  N  T  H  E  X  T  E
           A  L              A  L
```

letters D and Q have ranked among the last, with letters V, A, I, and S ranking among the first, we have a fairly good reason for suspecting that the encipherment was accomplished with a very long Vigenère plaintext key.

But for short cryptograms, Lamb did not find these characteristic frequency counts half so convincing as the presence in a cryptogram of certain *digrams*, which appeared to be characteristic for each cipher, since he was always able to find from 7 to 10 of them in each 100 letters. By making use of the high-frequency digrams (*th, he, er, in, an*, and so on), he then established lists of cipher digrams which were very characteristic indeed for each type of encipherment. Thus, in attacking an autokey, it is possible to make a good beginning with such a digram as VV (*er-re*) or XK (*th-ed*), if the cipher is Vigenère, and work in both directions.

"*Key-Length 1.*" — Many writers are inclined to make a special case of the autokey in which the "priming" is done with a single letter, not that this actually constitutes a different cipher, but because of the decryptment curiosities which can be brought to light in connection with it. For instance: Having a cryptogram fragment ......*W S Y Q L A H T G B.* .... known to be Vigenère autokey, initiated with a single letter, can you find instantly the trigrams *SAY* and *HAT?* Would you have any reason for trying the word *WAS?* Of the many interesting observations which have come the writer's way with reference to the one-letter initial key, only one has seemed to present the germ of an additional decryptment method. This observation was one made by Ohaver in connection with a cipher in which the substitutes were numbers. The cipher itself can be examined in Fig. 127.

The first step, (a), consists in the preparation of a simple substitution key in which the plaintext alphabet is in mixed order and the cipher alphabet is made up of the numbers 1 to 26. The encipherment, shown at (b), involves two steps. First, there must be a simple substitution, using the key of (a), and this results in a *primary cryptogram*. Afterward, this primary cryptogram, preceded by an in-

Figure 128

A TRIAL-Decipherment (M. E. OHAVER)

```
The Cryptogram:   29 38 28 21 31 26 18 26 22 31 39 38 44 38 22 22 39
                   9 20 18 10 11 20  6 12 14  8 23 16 22 22 16  6 16
                  20 18 10 11 20  6 12 14  8 23 16 22 22 16  6 16 23

                  33 26 29 35 38 22 22 39 48 39 19 25 44 38 26
                  23 10 16 13 22 16  6 16 23 25 14  5 20 24 14
                  10 16 13 22 16  6 16 23 25 14  5 20 24 14 14
```

itial key-number, is *added to itself.* In the discussion to follow, our objective will be that of *recovering the primary cryptogram* (and not the plaintext, which would have to be found later by simple substitution methods). Decipherment, indicated at (c), consists in reversing the two steps of the encipherment: A series of subtractions restores the primary cryptogram, and is followed by the resubstitution of letters. At (d) we have a Vigenère fragment for comparison. The essential fact to be noticed in (d) is the behavior of repeated sequences when the group-length is 1. Any repeated sequence in the plaintext continues to show a repetition in the cryptogram which is shorter by one letter than the original. Even the repeated digrams will give repeated single letters.

Now, putting aside the fact of the mixed plaintext alphabet (since we do not intend to recover the letters) we have here a cipher which, to all intents and purposes, is the Vigenère autokey initiated with a single letter. In place of the letters *A* to *Z* we have numbers 1 to 26, and the encipherment is a series of additions. In the corresponding Vigenère case, the group-length 1 will usually show up plainly in the number of doubled letters — "letters repeated at interval 1." And with the group-length determined as 1, it is possible to begin with some given initial key, as *A*, and either reproduce the plaintext or convert the autokeyed cryptogram to a periodic one in which the period is 2 (twice the group-length). Considering the analogy between the two cases, it should be possible to do the same thing here. That is, it should be possible to take the autokeyed cryptogram of (b), initiate its decipherment with some number chosen between 1 and 26, and either reproduce the primary cryptogram or convert the autokeyed cryptogram to a periodic one in which the alternate numbers will belong to two cipher alphabets. Where this reduction has been carried out in Fig. 128, the initial decipherment was made with key 9 in order to avoid a discussion of negative numbers. Also, the fact of numbers will usually limit the range of the trial keys: here, the first number, 29, was not enciphered by adding any number smaller than 3.

Now, looking at Fig. 129, let us compare the new cryptogram of Fig. 128 with the primary cryptogram of Fig. 127(b), and see whether or not it has the expected formation. Between the two cryptograms (the supposedly periodic one obtained from the trial decipherment and the one we hope to recover), there is a constant numerical difference in the pairs of corresponding substitutes, and this difference, throughout, is alternately plus and minus. Further comparisons can be made, if the student so desires, by initiating other partial decipherments with trial-keys 10, 11, 12, etc. Always, the constant numerical difference persists, and always it is alternately plus and minus. Moreover, for every time that the initial key-number increases in size, there is a corresponding decrease in all numbers occupying the odd serial positions and a corresponding increase in all numbers occupying the even positions.

Figure 129

Comparison of TRIAL DECIPHERMENT with TRUE DECIPHERMENT

True decipherment - (See Figure 127):	21	17	11	10	21	5	13	13	9	22...
Trial decipherment of Figure 128:	20	18	10	11	20	6	12	14	8	23...
CONSTANT DIFFERENCE:	1	-1	1	-1	1	-1	1	-1	1	-1

We have, then, a periodic cryptogram whose period is 2, and two cipher alphabets, consisting of numbers, in which the only difference is one of size. But these substitutes, unlike those of the Vigenère, will not be placed in normal alphabetical order; to complete the solution by one of the general methods, it may become necessary to take a number of frequency counts. For instance, considering the first of the two Bassières processes, it would be possible to set up the same tableau (Fig. 122), causing numbers to run alternately backward and forward (and beginning again at 1 whenever the number 26 is reached). In this way, one of the columns would contain the primary cryptogram, and a frequency count taken on the numbers of that column should resemble a simple substitution frequency count.

Considering the second of the Bassières processes, the autokeyed cryptogram is already reduced to a period of 2; the subsequent solution of the periodic cryptogram belongs to the general case of the next chapter; that is, a case in which the cipher alphabets are in mixed order but parallel. But we have, here, a special method, and a short-cut. The only difference between our two cipher alphabets is a matter of size in all corresponding substitutes. If we can find out what this numerical difference is, we have only to increase or decrease the size of the numbers in one of the cipher alphabets and bring it to the level of the other. Our short-cut, as pointed out by Ohaver, lies in repeated sequences (or even repeated single letters) in the autokeyed cryptogram. A glance back at the plaintext of the foregoing example will show that two repetitions were pointed out: STO and TOMOR, and that these were still present in the primary cryptogram as 21-23-15 and 23-15-7-15-24. In the autokeyed version, they were still repeated sequences, but shorter in length: 44-38 and 38-22-22-39.

Had we initiated our trial decipherment with the correct number, 8, these two repetitions would, of course, have worked back to their original length. But where this trial decipherment was made with a different initial key-number (Fig. 128) we find that only one of the sequences, TOMOR, has done this; the other, STO, has disappeared. The explanation for this has been summed up in Fig. 130. One sequence was repeated at interval 8, which is *even*. When the autokeyed cryptogram is converted to one having period 2, any interval which is divisible by 2 will contain a certain number of periods; thus, any repeated sequence at interval 8, will appear in the periodic cryptogram as one of the ordinary periodic repetitions.

The other sequence, *STO*, was repeated at interval 17, which is *odd*, and thus cannot show up as a repetition in any cryptogram whose period is 2.

It is this repeated sequence found at the odd interval which is to give us our short-cut. We have only two cipher alphabets, each one having a substitute for *S*, a substitute for *T*, and a substitute for *O*. When the repetition occurs at the odd interval, we obtain *both* substitutes for *S*, *both* substitutes for *T*, and *both* substitutes for *O*. By subtracting one sequence from the other, we may learn the numerical difference between the two cipher alphabets. Notice that the difference is *constant*, is *alternately plus and minus*, and is *divisible by 2*. (One alphabet is larger than the original, and the other is smaller by the same amount.) Our special

Figure 130

Respective Behavior of the Cryptogram's Two Repeated Sequences

Sequence 38-22-22-39
Repeated at interval 8

Sequence 44-38
Repeated at interval 17

Trial Decipherments:

1st occurrence: 22-15- 6-16-23
2d occurrence: 22-16- 6-16-23

1st occurrence: 22-22-16
2d occurrence: 20-24-14
 2 -2 2

(This interval was EVEN)

(This interval was ODD)

method, then, for a cryptogram known to have been enciphered in this way, is as follows: First, underscore all repeated sequences which occur at odd intervals, or, in their absence, the repeated single letters. Those which are long will almost surely represent repetitions in the plaintext. Then, selecting a suitable number, make a trial decipherment and examine the resulting sequences. If, by any chance, those repetitions found at the odd intervals have worked back to longer repeated sequences, then the trial key and the original initial key must have been the same. If not, try subtracting one result from the other. If both have represented the same plaintext sequence, the result of the subtraction will be a constant difference, alternately plus and minus, and divisible by 2. To restore the primary cryptogram, split this uniform difference, adding half of it to the numbers of one alphabet, and subtracting half of it from the numbers of the other alphabet. This, as mentioned in the beginning, will leave a simple substitution cryptogram still to be investigated.

Our explanation, perhaps, has been a little rapid, but the student who has read carefully will be able to discover the " germ " originally referred to, and to make his own laboratory tests. Also, there may be an interesting answer to the following question: When the cipher is one of the Beauforts (using letters), and the auto-encipherment is initiated with a single letter, does a trial decipherment, initiated with some other single letter, result in a period of 2?

128. By ELIA, JR.   (Variant, Autokeyed).

```
O O U J V   J M K N C   B U Q L P   F U L A S   A Z F T G   M P B V A   Y V S Q J
L F A W S   P C H A E   I U N R S   M F V W S   S O O H M   E B E A M   K F A A X
R H K Z R   J Q A O J   A V M E I   B T O P D   J G P R J   N F R X T   I I G X F
K D H X A   F T H J Q   H L A R K   T G D L P   S B M V Y   E E V A O   A C S M U
V U W C V   C T S K S   M W L O N   P A O O H   M W W P Y   P O H I L   G A Z Q B
Q U Z B Q   P K M B O   V K W J H   P J A G D   C H X G W   Q B K O G   Y A K S I
W N W E X   Q N U S G   C V O E Y   H Y J J C   B T B V J   Q M N S P   A R V P X
O A G T A   V L V C Z   B D I X N   F M W U E   Z L N N N   W B M O X   G T C P K.
```

129. By ELIA, JR.   (Beaufort, Autokeyed).

```
O A N C Q   R O Q N Y   Z G K P L   V G P A I   A B V H U   O L Z F A   C F M A V
Z J H T I   L L X V B   C Z M M T   O W Z W A   O Q V P M   M Q D L Q   K O H K F
G O B T L   R A U X Y   T Y S F N   O C Y G R   P M U U H   T H E W P   O O S R G
R Z Z S L   Y G K I A   N K M M T   O W Z W A   O Q V A B   E U X W T   C T J I O
G L P H T   E F U F B   R X M U Z   V L D B P   K N S Y A   Q B I V M   O H P V L
G Z Y F C   C W C O M   C A W N A   A A E V A   W M P E B   Q X O D O   V P X A T
E M A J A   T P M J E   A Z Z M D   S B B N A   A A F G L   I D N X A   M K H K P
D B B P Q   Y.
```

130. By ELIA, JR.   (St. Cyr, Autokeyed).

```
T B F N Q   X E F D G   F W E A F   X S Q U N   I G A H E   U N B B J   L O B Q P
H F A K A   S N X G B   P E E J W   W L Z J O   M L L A P   R V Y T N   M X H Y V
O S E S Q   V O A Q M   O G V P A   J K P Y I   U Z F Q G   Y J Y T L   D F E L Q
Z L W Y Y   U Y Z N E   P P F W B   R W M E E   F B W X J   W E P R V   Y B U M P
Z Z M T S   B U K K B   A L K Z I   L Q A L Z   K K F S X   Z U S T G   J T H A R
G S B X I   W V L Z B   Z M P I K   Y I U R H   R V W C V   A U F V L   W F Q Z U
D I G F W   H T Z M S   F B K T Z   U T R K I   V F Z X W   L C A U J   P A N V S
E O Z U X   G I X D S   X M G Q E   L Q T V B   L E I D I   A L L A I   N O E N L
V J I O I   S W Q T D   E C T M.
```

CHAPTER XVII

Some Periodic Number-Ciphers

The use of numbers in a periodic cipher does not, in itself, create a problem essentially different from that of the letter-ciphers. Numbers may, in themselves, cause weakness; we saw such a case in the last of our autokey examples, where a complete disarrangement in their order did nothing to conceal their size. But oftener than not, the weakness lies in the construction of the cipher or in the manner of its application, and while this is fully as true of letter ciphers, the numbers, for some reason, appear to be more inviting for certain kinds of misuse.

In order to observe a weakness which need not have existed, let us consider the slide partially shown in Fig. 131. The use of two-digit numbers will furnish a hundred substitutes; but a strip of that length is awkward to handle, and the constructor of the present slide has confined its length to forty numbers. Then, since

Figure 131

A Slide Carrying a NUMBER-Alphabet(and Keys)

			Plaintext Alphabet - Stationary											
			A	B	C	D	E	F	G	H	I	J	K	L	M......
			10	20	30	40	50	60	70	80	90	00	11	21	31	41	51	61	71 .....

Sliding Cipher-Alphabet:
Key-letters may be added:

A	B	C	D	E	F	G	H	I	J	K	L	M	N	O)
*	P	Q	R	*	S	T	U	*	V	W	X	Y	Z	*)

The addition of key-letters makes it possible to employ a keyword. For the present forty-number slide, it was necessary to double them up as in Porta. A slide having fifty-one numbers would have accommodated all twenty-six of the key-letters.

he has only fifteen different cipher alphabets, and wishes to make use of word-keys, he has adjusted his 26 key-letters to fit the number of alphabets. Now if the alphabet of the slide (that is, the *cipher alphabet,* or series of numbers) is written in straight 1-2-3 order, and if it is considered that letters may have two or more values, so that A has the values 1, 27, 53, etc., B the values 2, 28, etc., C the values 3, 29, and so on, a slide of this kind is exactly the equivalent of the Saint-Cyr slide, since any cryptogram accomplished with it could be promptly converted to a Vigenère cryptogram by substituting letters for numbers. The keys, of course, might differ. The constructor of the slide has desired something more difficult. But instead of carrying his forty numbers through a transposition block, and really mixing them, he has been content to group them, in regular order, by their tens. We shall see in a moment what happens to his cryptograms. But he neglects also an opportunity: Presuming that his circumstances are such as to make the use of numbers practical at all, why waste the opportunity to use the full one hundred substitutes? The remaining sixty numbers might have been placed on the next two rows, and thus, in every position of the slide, he could have had two or three optional substitutes for every letter — a much more difficult case than the simple periodic.

The cryptogram of Fig. 132 was enciphered with the slide of the preceding figure, using the key-word CABLO (equivalent to the numerical key 30-10-20-21-51), and its period, 5, can be determined in the usual way. However, we have already seen the Kasiski method; suppose, here, we look at another, originated by Ohaver; and, since Ohaver himself, explaining his method in connection with a number-cipher of much the kind we have here, illustrated with single numbers instead of with sequences, it seems fitting that it be illustrated again in the same way.

As pointed out more than once, those characters having the highest frequencies in periodic cryptograms will nearly always have derived these high frequencies because of their occurrence in more than one of the cipher alphabets; while

Figure 132

Cryptogram Enciphered with the Slide of Figure 133

32 41 31 61 33 12 32 60 91 91 30 81 70 92 92 51 52 61 23 43 71 01 90 61 71

71 41 12 92 51 01 52 12 91 91 80 50 30 92 53 30 81 62 72 62 30 41 00 02 43

71 20 60 41 51 01 81 00 61 81 71 12 12 31 93 61 50 00 32 33 70 41 00 52 33

22 50 20 51 92 80 31 61 92 23 11 91 01 13 92 81 51 12 91 91 01 30 90 21 82

90 50 01 21 23 70 20 60 01 82 90 31 20 51 91 22 51 12 91 32 12 50 51 51 33

71 10 01 13 92 40 50 91 61 51 60 52 42 91 91 61 01 90 61 43 11 31 60 41 92

51 50 01 02 92 81 21 60 21 33 70 21 60 13 72 70 80 60 21 23 01 90 80 91 43

30 32 20 63 32 80 01 90 61 23 70 90 01 21 82 72 51 30 12 91 50 01 00 62 82

40 50 40 21 53 12 50 12 91 32 12 90 01 81 92 11 41 80 13 92 22 10 21 61 43

11 31 60 21 62 60 32 60 51 92 61 01 42 21 82 22 10 51 63 22 11 01 40 91 51

22 01 90 61 62 30 91 12 42 32 61 12 12 61 33.

those having the lower frequencies will more often represent repetitions in some one cipher alphabet. Thus, when we find, in the present cryptogram, that the numbers 02, 53, and 63, have each a frequency of 2, it seems reasonable to suppose, for each number, that its two occurrences were in a single cipher alphabet; that is, that each one is a periodic repetition. Now, considering Fig. 133, and confining our observations, for the moment, to the number 02, we find that this number, in the cryptogram, occupies serial positions 49 and 154. Having first laid out a series of columns headed by the various possible periods, 2, 3, 4, 5. . . . . , we use each possible period in turn as a divisor, first applying them all to the serial number 49, and then applying them all to the serial number 154, each time setting down, in the proper column, *the remainder from the division.* This remainder tells us, each time, into what cipher alphabet the number 02 would fall, should the cryptogram be rewritten into the period indicated at the top of a given column. Still confining our observations to the number 02: It is seen, under possible period 2. that if this were the period, then the two occurrences of the number 02 would be in different alphabets. The same can be seen under possible periods 4, 6, 8, 9, 10. But if the period were 3, both occurrences of our number would fall into alphabet 1; if it were 5, both occurrences would fall into alphabet 4; if it were 7, both occurrences would fall into alphabet 7 (remainder zero indicates the final alphabet of the given period). Here, then, it would appear that possible periods 3, 5, and 7, are more likely than the rest, as far as the tabulation goes. When exactly the same observations are made for the number 53, it appears that the most likely periods are 3 and 5. And when these observations are made again for the number 63, only the period 5 is indicated as a likely one. Since the period 5 has been indicated oftener than any other, this is probably the correct period, as we happen to know that it is. When the same method is applied to repeated sequences, the serial numbers can be those of the repeated first number. And it may, of course, be applied to letters, just as the Kasiski method might have been applied here. As to why Ohaver might have preferred this method in dealing with numbers, let us examine, in the figure, the entire column under possible period 5. The Ohaver method, unlike the Kasiski, not only indicates the period, but, in addition, shows the exact alphabet of that period into which a repeated number will fall. The number 02 is shown as belonging to alphabet 4; the number 53 as belonging to alphabet 5; and the number 63 as

Figure 133

An OHAVER Method for Finding Period

Substitute	Serial Position	POSSIBLE PERIODS 2	3	4	5	6	7	8	9	10 ...
02	49	1	1	1	4	1	0	1	4	9 ...
	154	0	1	2	4	4	0	2	1	4 ...
53	40	0	1	0	0	4	5	0	4	0 ...
	205	1	1	1	0	1	2	5	7	5 ...
63	179	1	2	3	4	5	4	3	8	9 ...
	244	0	1	0	4	4	6	4	1	4 ...

belonging to alphabet 4. It is thus possible to see that the very small number 02 and the very large number 63 belong to a same cipher alphabet; and since a range of over sixty numbers cannot correspond to only twenty-six letters, we may conclude at once that the numbers on the slide were not in consecutive order. Often, our information is exactly the opposite.

Returning, now, to our cryptogram: In the beginning, we probably made a general frequency count; if not, we now have the five individual counts to be taken. And, as previously mentioned, a frequency count made on numbers is much more conveniently accomplished on a 10 x 10 chart than by sorting and listing the numbers. The moment our five frequency counts are made, in the present case, two facts become evident: Each count includes only fifteen or twenty *different* numbers, with about the frequency-distribution of simple substitution; and, while the tens-digits have included a full series, the units have never run beyond 3. The cipher, then, is a simple periodic; had multiple substitutes been used, the frequency counts would have included more different numbers, and with frequencies more uniformly distributed. As to the series of numbers, two probabilities are suggested, and these, in effect, are the same thing: The numbers may have run in straight order into the thirties, and with each number reversed; or: the numbers may have been grouped by tens. It is further possible that the whole series runs backward, or that the tens do, or the units, or sections of a certain length; and some uncertainty·may arise as to the rank, in the series, of the digit zero; this digit is ordinarily last, but occasionally is ranked first. It is, of course, possible that the series of numbers is well mixed, but the chances are that it is merely methodized; the person who uses numbers in a simple periodic cipher is not usually one who knows the dangers of regularity in a cipher alphabet.

We may try, then, to restore his original arrangement (or an equivalent one), placing beside it the five frequency counts in their five columns, as shown in Fig. 134. The probable arrangements are very few, and the placing of tally-marks opposite their numbers is very rapid, since this, at each trial, is a mere matter of

Figure 134

A Series of PARALLEL Frequency Counts Which Can Be LINED UP By PATTERN

10	•	111	•	•	•
20		11	111	•	•
30	11111	1	11	•	•
40	11	•	11	•	•
50	1	11111 1111	•	•	•
60	11	•	11111 1111	•	•
70	11111	•	1	•	•
80	111	1	11	•	•
90	11	111	11111	•	•
00	•	•	11111	•	•
11	11111	•	•	•	•
21	•	11	1	11111 111	•
31	•	1111	1	1	•
41	•	11111		11	•
51	11	111	11	1111	1111
61	1111	•	11	11111 1111	•
71	11111	•	•	•	1
81	11	111	•	1	1
91	•	11	1	11111 111	11111 1
01	1111	11111 11	11111 1	1	•
12	1111	11	11111 111	1	•
22	11111	•	•	•	1
32	1	111	•	1	1111
42	•	•	11	1	•
52	•	111	•	1	•
62	•	•	1	1	11
72	1	•	•	1	1
82	•	•	•	•	11111 1
92	•	•	•	1111	11111 1111
02	•	•	•	11	•
13	•	•	•	1111	•
23	•	•	•	1	1111
33	•	•	•	•	11111 1
43	•	•	•	•	11111
53	•	•	•	•	11
63	•	•	•	11	•
73	•	•	•	•	•
83	•	•	•	•	•
93	•	•	•	•	1
03	•	•	•	•	•

copying them from their charts. Once the correct rearrangement is reached, notice, in the figure, the appearance of the five frequency counts. Insofar as is ever likely to happen with columnar counts, *all five have followed the same graph.* This, of course, is the simplest case; the finding of the encipherer's original order, so that every frequency count has followed the graph of the normal alphabet. Any substitute can be identified, as in Vigenère, by its serial position in its own alphabet; and where numbers are used, there is seldom any doubt as to what number comes first in its alphabet. The shortest road to solution would be as follows: Prepare a temporary slide *exactly like the one which was used* (except that we have no way of knowing what the key-letters were), mark the points at which the five alphabets begin, and decipher with the slide.

There are many other cases, hardly more difficult, in which our rearrangement of numbers results, not in the original order, but in an *equivalent order*. We could, for instance, arrive at a rearrangement in which we have taken each third number, or each fifth number, of the original cipher alphabet, so that our rearranged num-

Figure 135

The LINING UP of the Frequency Counts of Figure 136

1st		2d		3d		4th		5th		TOTALS
30	11111	10	111	20	111	21	11111111	51	1111	23 *
40	11	20	11	30	11	31	1	61		7
50	1	30	1	40	11	41	11	71	1	7
60	11	40		50		51	1111	81	1	7
70	11111	50	111111111	60	111111111	61	111111111	91	111111	58 *
80	111	60		70	1	71		01		4
90	11	70		80	11	81	1	12		5
00		80	1	90	11111	91	11111111	22	1	16 *
11	11111	90	111	00	11111	01	1	32	1111	18 *
21		00		11		12	1	42		** 1
31		11		21	1	22		52		** 1
41		21	11	31	1	32	1	62	11	6
51	11	31	1111	41		42	1	72	1	8
61	1111	41	11111	51	11	52	1	82	111111	18 *
71	11111	51	111	61	11	62	1	92	111111111	20 *
81	11	61		71		72	1	02		3
91		71		81		82		13		** 0
01	1111	81	111	91	1	92	1111	23	1111	16 *
12	1111	91	11	01	111111	02	11	33	111111	20 *
22	11111	01	1111111	12	11111111	13	1111	43	11111	29 *
32	1	12	11	22		23	1	53	11	6
42		22		32		33		63		(V) 0
52		32	111	42	11	43		73		5
62		42		52		53		83		** 0
72	1	52	111	62	1	63	11	93	1	8
82		62		72		73		03		** 0
										265

bers are following plaintext letters in the order *A D G J. . . .* or *A F K P. . . .* ; thus, all of our frequency counts would be following one same graph, though not the graph of the normal alphabet. The problem here is to make sure that their graphs are all the same graph, and then subject them to the process called " lining up."

To show the handling of all such cases (which would include our final autokey example), let us assume that the five frequency counts of our figure, though still following a common graph, are not following that of the normal alphabet. In this case, granting that all fifty-letter frequency counts will vary considerably from the normal, it is not quite so obvious that their pattern is the same; we shall have to cut them apart (preferably having copied numbers beside their frequencies) and place them side by side for a comparison of their graphs. Where this has been done, in Fig. 135, their similarity is plain in spite of some discrepancies, and the moving up or down of any one or more of the counts (which could be done so as to include another position, since the range of the numbers is only 25 per alphabet) does not result in greater similarity. If the alignment of this figure is correct, then all numbers found on any one row are substituting for one same original; thus, the added frequencies on any one row will be the total frequency of some one letter in a 265-letter text, and all of these totals, collectively, should resemble a frequency count taken on a simple substitution cryptogram of that length. To just what extent this is true may be seen at the right side of the figure. The nine leading letters have totalled 74%, where we normally expect 70%; but any single example can provide its surprises, and the excess 4% is not on the wrong side of the ledger. The other end of the count, as would be expected of the group *J K Q X Z*, is comparatively blank.

Our substitutes, remember, are assumed to be in mixed order. We do not know what letter is represented by the five numbers of the top row, or by the five numbers of any other row. To proceed with solution, we shall have to assign ar-

Figure 136

The NIHILIST Number-Substitution

The "Checkerboard" Alphabet:

```
        1 2 3 4 5
    1   A B C D E         13 = C
    2   F G H I K         34 = O
    3   L M N O P         32 = M
    4   Q R S T U         15 = E
    5   V W X Y Z         44 = T
```

Encipherment, with Keyword COMET:

	S	E	N	D	S	U	P	P	L	I	E	S	T	O	....
Text...	43	15	33	14	43	45	35	35	31	24	15	43	44	34	....
Key....	13	34	32	15	44	13	34	32	15	44	13	34	32	15	....
	56	49	65	29	87	58	69	67	46	68	28	77	76	49	....

This cryptogram is usually seen without grouping: 56-49-65-29-87-58.....

bitrary values, calling the top row *A* (or 01), the second row *B* (or 02), the third row *C* (or 03), and so on; and when all of these substitutions have been made on the cryptogram, *the case has been reduced to one of simple substitution.* The mechanics by which the substitutions are made can be exactly those of the other case: Prepare a temporary slide, on which the numbers run in the order decided upon, and slide this against the normal alphabet (or any other); the result is a simple substitution cryptogram which can be solved by simple substitution methods. This case, first in one form and then in another, is encountered again and again; and however it may seem that its cause, in some one example, is a different one, yet the fault in all such examples is the same: The basic cipher alphabet (the primary one from which others are derived), either by its actual construction or by the method of its application, was not truly a mixed alphabet.

In some of the periodic ciphers, the basic cipher alphabet is a " checkerboard " of the kind we saw in Chapter *XI*, the substitutes being two-digit numbers which will point out the columns and rows of their originals. This primary alphabet, however, seldom appears unchanged in the cryptograms, as " position 1 " often does when a slide is used, or as the *A*-alphabet often does in the Vigenère cipher. Instead, we find a series of secondary cipher alphabets all of which have been derived from the primary one according to a mathematical process.

In view of the fact that any cipher which will necessarily double the lengths of messages is of doubtful value, it seems inadvisable here to do more than mention the infinite multiplicity of processes which would be possible; but with checkerboards, it is difficult to imagine any usable process which would not result in parallel frequency counts; that is, counts which all follow the same graph and thus are capable of being " lined up." With most of these, in fact, the difference between any two of the (secondary) cipher alphabets will be a difference in *size* which is uniform from *A* to *Z*. (Often, the same result is produced with slides.) Here, then, we may content ourselves with a glance at one such cipher which is interesting rather than important. In Fig. 136, we have another of the Nihilist ciphers. Its primary alphabet is that most famous of checkerboards, the *Polybius square*, said to have been the invention of the ancient Greek historian, and certainly well known in his era as the basis for a signalling system — a capacity, incidentally, in which it still serves. We are showing it here in what seems to be the favorite version: The alphabet of the square is the normal one, normally arranged, with *J* the missing letter; and the order of reading for the two digits is row-column. It should be understood, however, that these details, in practice, are quite variable.

For the Nihilist encipherment, the message is first subjected to a simple substitution, using the checkerboard key. A key-word, treated in the same way, is repeated often enough to pair one key-number with each message-number, and the final cryptogram is formed by adding these pairs of numbers. Decipherment, of course, will be the subtraction of key-numbers from the finished cryptogram and the resubstitution of letters. We have, then, another periodic cipher, not essentially different from those already seen. Any number in the checkerboard can become a key, to be applied periodically at some given interval, and thus may govern one of the 25 possible cipher alphabets. It would be possible to lay out any one of these cipher alphabets, simply by adding a given amount to each number of the primary one; if all of them were written one below another, and if the primary alphabet were written across the top and along one side, we should have a tableau which could be used in identically the manner described for the use of the Vigenère tableau.

Decryptment, too, can parallel that of the Vigenère: The period of a cryptogram can be found through repeated sequences, or, in their absence, through repeated single numbers, and individual frequency counts can be taken on the several alphabets of the period. If the arrangement of letters in the checkerboard is that of the figure, or any other strictly alphabetical one to which the order of the numbers can be adjusted, these frequency counts will all follow the graph of the normal alphabet, with allowance made for the missing letter. Or, if the arrangement of letters in the checkerboard is not strictly alphabetical, then the several frequency counts, no matter how badly mixed, will still be parallel; they will all follow one graph, and thus can be " lined up." Very often, however, given the opportunity to examine and analyze a cipher, it becomes possible to formulate for it a special method which is much more rapid than the general one; Ohaver, who first published a special method for the Nihilist, has compared this cipher to a leaky boat in the open ocean.

Notice that its primary alphabet contains only the digits 1-2-3-4-5. The maximum difference among these is 4; and the addition of any same number to all of them does not change this fact; the maximum difference between any two of the sums would still be 4. But the number which is added during encipherment is also a number containing no digit other than 1-2-3-4-5; thus any number found in a cryptogram can be considered as carrying two separate additions, one for tens and one for units. Even when two 5's are added together, the result is an all-revealing zero; the " carried " digit 1 can be mentally " borrowed " back, causing the zero to become 10, and decreasing by 1 the size of the digit which precedes the zero. Specifically: Finding in a cryptogram the number 40, we may regard this as having only 3 tens, with 10 units; or finding the number 110, we may regard it as having 10 tens and 10 units. Thus, there is never a time when it is impossible to see the tens and units as having been separately added; if we find, in a Nihilist cryptogram, the two numbers 29 and 87, with a difference greater than 4 in their respective tens-digits, we may say promptly that they were not enciphered with the same key; no digit whatever added to any two digits of the original square can produce a difference greater than 4. But if the two cryptogram numbers are 30 and 77, where the difference in the tens-digits appears, at first glance, to be only 4, the presence of the zero must be taken into account; thus, the number 30 has only 2 tens, and the difference between 2 and 7 is greater than 4; therefore, the numbers 30 and 77 could not have been enciphered with the same key. It is interesting, also, to note that the

Figure 137

Cryptogram by EDWIN LINDQUIST:

24-66-35-77-37-77-55-59-55-45-55-88-28-66-46-

88-37-67-33-59-58-65-45-66-67-58-44-55-34-79-

44-59-55-45-42-87-28-76-43-78-46-86-26-67-24-

85-26-67-28-76-26-78-46-65-65-88-36-49-54-67-

28-65-42-88-36-49-44-89-57-58-54-66-47-67-26.

Final Investigation of
Supposed Period 4

24	66	35	77
37	77	55	59
55	45	55	88
28	66	46	88
37	67	33	59
58	65	45	66
67	58	44	55
34	79	44	59
55	45	42	87
28	76	43	78
46	86	26	67
24	85	26	67
28	76	26	78
46	65	65	88
36	49	54	67
28	65	42	88
36	49	44	89
57	58	54	66
47	67	26	

digit 2, found in a cryptogram, can have been produced in only one way: the addition of 1 and 1; and that the digit 0, found in a cryptogram, can only have been produced by the addition of 5 and 5. Either one of these digits gives away its key; but, further than this, the cipher provides four "give-away" numbers, 22, 30, 102, and 110, the presence of any one of which in a cryptogram will give away the key to a whole cipher alphabet.

(Acceptable throughout)

Now, to look at Ohaver's special method, let us consider the cryptogram of Fig. 137, prepared by another "inventor" of exactly the same method. It can be noted, first, that this cryptogram has not resulted from the addition of a single number throughout, since it contains pairs of numbers like 24-88, 42-87, and so on, which have a greater difference than 4 in either their tens or their units. Now, using a bit of scratch-paper, we may, if we like, scribble down a series of possible periods, 2, 3, 4, 5, 6, and so on, to be crossed off as fast as we eliminate them. Considering these, one by one:

Period 2: With a thumbnail on the first number, 24, and another on the third number, 35, we may run quickly through the cryptogram comparing numbers found at interval 2; that is, the first and third numbers, the second and fourth, the third and fifth, and so on, until stopped by the two numbers 33 and 38, whose difference, in the units, is greater than 4, showing that their key was not the same. Period 2, then, is eliminated.

Period 3: Here we are stopped short at the very first comparison. The numbers 24 and 77, found at the first interval 3, have a difference greater than 4 in their tens, and thus cannot have been enciphered with the same key. Period 3 is also eliminated.

Period 4: Starting again, and comparing numbers taken at interval 4, we are able to go all the way to the end of the cryptogram without finding any two numbers whose difference, either in tens or in units, is greater than 4. The numbers compared, however, included only those which would have been adjacent in their columns. To make sure that period 4 is possible, we must see numbers collectively in each of the four columns, and this is best done by recopying the cryptogram into its apparently possible period 4. Further examination, made individually on each column, still shows no two numbers in any one column whose difference, either in tens or in units, is greater than 4. It is possible, then, that each of the four columns was enciphered with a single key; and while this is not absolute proof that the period 4 is correct, those cases are extremely rare in which a period found in this manner is not the correct one. With period 4 accepted, and given as much material as we have, perhaps we can also discover just what key-number was added to primary numbers in order to produce each of the four alphabets. Considering alphabets one at a time, and examining separately the tens and the units:

Alphabet 1: The tens-half of the first column contains a digit 2; and since this can only have been produced by the addition of 1 and 1, the only possible key-digit here is 1. (We have already ascertained that all digits in this column could have had a same key.) The units-half has a range of 4-5-6-7-8, the maximum range possible. The smallest digit which can result in 8 is 3, and the largest which can result in 4 is 3; that is, the only digit which can result in *all* of the digits 4-5-6-7-8 is 3, so that the only possible key-digit here is 3. Conclusion: The key which produced the first cipher alphabet must have been 13, *since it cannot possibly be anything else.*

Alphabet 2: The tens-half of the second column ranges over the full five digits 4-5-6-7-8 (key 3), and the units-half ranges over the digits 5-6-7-8-9 (key 4). The key which produced the second cipher alphabet is 34.

Alphabet 3: The tens-half of the third column contains the " giveaway " digit 2, and the units-half contains this digit also. The key which produced the third cipher alphabet is 11.

Alphabet 4: The tens-half of the fourth column ranges only over the digits 5-6-7-8, with nothing to indicate whether the missing one is 4 or 9. Thus, the key to the tens might have been either 3 or 4, though it could not have been anything else. The units have the full range of digits, 5-6-7-8-9, key 4. In the fourth cipher alphabet, then, we cannot tell immediately whether the key is 34 or 44. Granting, however, that the arrangement of letters in Lindquist's key-square was the same as that of Fig. 136, the substitution of letters for numbers may suggest which of the two numbers, 34 or 44, is the correct key. With one of these we obtain letters C O A O, and, with the other, C O A T, a word (The student might find it of interest to decipher this cryptogram and learn what the minister had to say).

Any sufficiently long cryptogram, then, will reveal both its period and its key, and this regardless of how the letters were arranged in the encipherer's checkerboard. It may then be deciphered with its own key, and the case, at worst, becomes one of simple substitution. With shorter cryptograms, we often find, as here, that some one or more of the cipher alphabets could have had two or more possible keys. This happening, presuming that the alphabetical arrangement of the square is a known one, or one easily reconstructed, presents no real problem; a little experimentation on the cryptogram will show which keys bring out a message. When the alphabet of the square is an unknown mixed one, the problem may vary according to length, and the number of key-combinations which are found to be possible. If, for instance, the case resembles that of our preceding cryptogram, where only one alphabet out of four was in doubt, then, remembering that the Nihilist cipher alphabets are of a kind whose frequency counts can be " lined up," we might take frequency counts on the several alphabets, and supply the missing numbers of the doubtful one by making its pattern match that of the rest. With several alphabets in doubt, which could only happen when frequency counts are too scant to betray their graph, it might become necessary to decipher the periodic cryptogram with each possible combination of key-numbers, each time obtaining a new cryptogram, and accept, among these new cryptograms, the one whose general frequency count seems most likely to be that of a simple substitution. The correct cryptogram, in this case, should also contain some fresh repetitions; that is, repetitions which were not present in the periodic one. As to the three examples which follow, there should be little difficulty in deciding whether or not the Nihilist cipher is represented.

131. By B. NATURAL.

45 68 48 46 60 78 45 78 24 59 35 67 50 75 38 58 53 60 65 26 54 46 68 55 38 67 42

69 56 59 24 59 70 54 30 85 32 90 44 46 45 56 79 54 30 86 22 78 27 26 44 49 78 75

38 54 55 78 47 27 45 49 89 44 49 88 42 59 56 49 42 86 50 52 26 55 42 60 47 36 22

50 78 65 50 76 35 78 28 59 26 50 68 54 60 76 25 87 28 29 55 58 59 73 59 97 54 69

66 57 26 46 78 65 48 76 45 57 47 29 65 79 77 55 30 57 35 89 45 49 53 46 66 75 57

97 55 68 28 47 22 66 66.

132. By PICCOLA. (Keyword, CRYPT. Fifth alphabet contains Q. But: Can you rearrange the numbers on the strip before taking frequencies?

15 20 23 18 03   15 26 12 26 25   03 30 40 14 20   09 20 25 11 15   17 25 16 02 29

30 25 21 18 03   11 16 27 30 26   10 02 21 17 01   06 25 13 01 25   03 30 23 26 23

06 27 12 11 20   12 22 16 18 03   29 20 19 01 19   17 19 12 12 20   02 11 14 18 19

13 20 38 11 23   19 01 19 01 27   30 16 21 01 23   17 24 22 25 03   19 26 21 11 28

11 17 16 21 03   13 20 28 05 20   06 26 13 11 26   11 16 27 26 16   02 26 18 05 25

06 03 16 03 03   30 26 16 27 28   10 02 16 02 29   06 26 27 11 24   15 20 23 13 15

11 25 13 05 24   28 20 40 27 19   19 30 27 19 19   13 02 23 21 28   11 30 14 28 03

18 26.

133. By PICCOLA. (If you recognize this gem of literature, you are beyond the draft age. It got around the censor in 1918).

20 08 17 29 15 09 01 05 08 29 24 11 06 05 10 26 13 22 06 01 18 19 05 03 16 24 13

16 04 08 07 19 12 18 24 11 17 09 07 27 26 22 01 15 21 21 10 03 06 22 03 18 04 22

20 06 07 24 12 19 10 19 10 30 10 19 16 24 13 16 04 08 23 01 10 10 23 10 09 05 08

17 21 22 09 15 21 21 10 03 06 06 21 20 12 22 21 08 18 19 23 05 02 01 11 34 19 27

12 06 02 15 10 22 03 03 02 11 12 19 10 11 19 27 13 12 18 24 19 13 24 15 07 16 16

16 26 20 04 05 11 29 26 20 03 10 19 10 23 11 16 19 13 16 04 08 25 17 05 24 20 20

23 09 10 25 20 25 02 05 07 16 26 20 04 05 11.

134. By DAN SURR. (Should you be worried at finding this in Daughter's boudoir?)

A B C D   E F G   E H D G   E F J E   K H D   L J D G   J M M J   D G J M E

E F J E   O J E L F   A C B   D G. - P G M G.

CHAPTER XVIII

PERIODIC CIPHERS WITH MIXED ALPHABETS

Periodic cryptograms in which the cipher alphabets are mixed are nearly always produced by means of slides. Before discussing these ciphers, it may be well to clarify a few terms which otherwise could leave room for uncertainty. We have, for instance, two, and sometimes three, key-words. There is a primary one (sometimes two) used in the preparation of the slide, and a secondary one, often called the " specific " key, which is used, as in Vigenère, for the encipherment of cryptograms. Since we shall have practically no occasion to mention the primary key-word (or words), any references which are made here to a key-word, unless clearly seen to refer to the preparation of a mixed alphabet, can be understood as meaning the secondary one, that is, the specific key which selects the cipher alphabets. Perhaps it is also advisable to call attention once more to the existence of a primary cipher alphabet (the basic one which is written twice in succession on the slide) and of the 26 secondary cipher alphabets which can be derived from it by placing it in its 26 possible positions. These are usually referred to simply as " the alphabets," while the basic one is more commonly called " the sliding alphabet." All, of course, are the same alphabet except for their points of beginning.

To see clearly what is meant by an " equivalent slide," the student may make an experiment: First, form a temporary slide, using any two 26-letter alphabets, and use the slide to encipher a short message. Now form another temporary slide on which the two alphabets of the preceding slide (both treated by exactly the same plan) have been rearranged so that their letters are taken at every interval 3 (or at every interval 5, or 7, or 9 — any interval whatever that is not divisible by 2 or 13), and with care taken always to maintain this constant interval even when the 26th letter is reached and the 1st reappears. Then, using this new slide in the same way as before, encipher the same message with the same key, and compare this new cryptogram with the first. Finally, an *alphabetical* interval (or distance) between two letters will mean their distance apart in the normal alphabet, while a *lineal* interval (or distance) will mean their distance apart in any alphabet whatever. That is, the *alphabetical* distance from A to B is invariably 1 (position), while their *lineal* distance apart on a slide, or in the rows or columns of a tableau, could be anything from 1 to 25. Where these intervals must be mentioned often, the distance from A to B will be referred to more briefly as " the distance AB."

Now let us consider the four slides of Fig. 138, which are being designated (arbitrarily) as belonging to *Types I, II, III,* and *IV,* in what would seem to be the order of their potential resistance to decryptment. Their actual resistance, however, might depend largely upon the manner of their use, and we are assuming throughout the chapter that the encipherment process is identically that described for the Saint-Cyr cipher: The upper alphabet, in all cases, is to be the plaintext one; the index-letter is always the initial one of this plaintext alphabet; and, for the encipherment of cryptograms, the letters of the chosen key-word are to be found in the lower alphabet and brought one by one to stand below the index-letter in order to set up their cipher alphabets. Also, for our immediate purposes, we are neglecting certain precautions the advisability of which will be seen later: First, the mixed

Figure 138

SLIDE - TYPE I.

```
Plaintext:  C U L P E R Z Y X W V T S Q O N M K J I H G F D B A
CIPHER:     A B C D E F G H I J K L M N O P Q R S T U V W X Y Z A B C....
```

```
                        a b c d e f g h i j k l m n o p .......

            Key A:  Z Y A X E W V U T S R C Q P O D .......
            Key B:  A Z B Y F X W V U T S D R Q P E .......
            Key C:  B A C Z G Y X W V U T E S R Q F .......
```

SLIDE - TYPE II.

```
Plaintext:  A B C D E F G H I J K L M N O P Q R S T U V W X Y Z
CIPHER:     C U L P E R Z Y X W V T S Q O N M K J I H G F D B A C U L.....
```

```
                        a b c d e f g h i j k l m n o p .......

            Key A:  A C U L P E R Z Y X W V T S Q O .......
            Key B:  B A C U L P E R Z Y X W V T S Q .......
            Key C:  C U L P E R Z Y X W V T S Q O N .......
```

SLIDE - TYPE III.

```
Plaintext:  C U L P E R Z Y X W V T S Q O N M K J I H G F D B A
CIPHER:     C U L P E R Z Y X W V T S Q O N M K J I H G F D B A C U L.....
```

```
                        a b c d e f g h i j k l m n o p .......

            Key A:  B D A F P G H I J K M U N O Q L .......
            Key B:  D F B G L H I J K M N C O Q S U .......
            Key C:  A B C D E F G H I J K L M N O P .......
```

SLIDE - TYPE IV.

```
Plaintext:  D A M S C U B E F G H I J K L N O P Q R T V W X Y Z
CIPHER:     C U L P E R Z Y X W V T S Q O N M K J I H G F D B A C U L.....
```

```
                        a b c d e f g h i j k l m n o p .......

            Key A:  C R P A Z Y X W V T S Q U O N M .......
            Key B:  A E L B R Z Y X W V T S C Q O N .......
            Key C:  U Z E C Y X W V T S Q O L N M K .......
```

alphabets have all been left undisturbed with their primary key-words (CUL-PEPER, DAMASCUS) and their alphabetical sequences in plain view; in practice, such alphabets ought to be carried through a transposition block, or otherwise made to appear incoherent. Second, the index-letter should never be *A* (or any other frequent letter) unless the details of encipherment are varied. (We might, for instance, consider that the index-letter is in the sliding alphabet and that keys are in the upper.)

In the *Type I* slide, the cipher alphabet is in normal order, and " slides against " a mixed plaintext alphabet. In *Type II*, we find a mixed cipher alphabet " sliding against " the normal one; in *Type III*, we find this mixed cipher alphabet " sliding against " itself; and in *Type IV*, we find it " sliding against " another, and different,

Figure 139

```
        5           10          15          20          25          30
Y V N G K   Y E G D P   Z E A Y K   H S M D Q   K K W S J   I Q C I O
    P         E I         T E A         v   c     I c         c c   v

        35          40          45          50          55          60
K C F K Q   J P M L B   J X G K C   Z D B G N   G Q B D Q   M E O N K
I     T c         v         I T H   T H E P     E c E     c     E

        65          70          75          80          85          90
X T Y A D   D D G J R   X R X F W   G D A Y T   Q S G G C   G P B Y O
    H         H I                   E H A             I P H   E   E v

        95         100         105         110         115         120
C L W K C   B I C F E   Z D G J W   K U F K C   B U I Z Y   B K E K C
    T H     A             T H I     I c   T H   A c   E     A c   T H

       125         130         135         140         145         150
G K T A O   Q C B Y Q   U U F Z G   G Z Y F N   F M J V Z   B L Q J U
E c   H v         E   c     c E     E                 v       A

       155         160         165         170         175         180
V M M J T   A E F V S   M E N K Q   J E I Z Y   A L Q Y R   X R X F R
    v       W E   v       E   T c     E   E       W

       185         190         195         200         205         210
O U F V S   V V V V P   K T B K C   G O M I K   B Q V Z N   B I N A O
c   v           c v       I   E T H   E   v     A c c E     A     H v

       215         220         225         230         235         240
C E V V J   F V U Z S   B K M K C   G P M D T   K K Y A D   D D Y Z C
E c v             E       A c v T H   E   v       I c   H       H E H

       245         250         255         260         265         270
B T K V S   G Q W I T   Z D A K P   G W B I O   N D G R C   H P B H U
A   M v     E c           T H A T   E   E   v     H I   H       E

       275         280         285         290         295         300
G K T Q H   G U V Z N   Y X M L H   F S M D Q   K K W Z Q   U D A M T
E c         E c c E           v           v   c     I c   E c     H A

       305         310         315         320         325         330
Z D B J O   P E U L R   Y U G K U   Z E U S J   Z D B O D   R E S I O
T H E   v         E           c I T   T E         T H E           E   v

       335         340         345
R L A B L   J R S Z Q   Y Q V F L
    A L           E c         c c
```

mixed alphabet. Every slide, used in any manner, has an *equivalent tableau* and
while tableaux are seldom used, it is very important that we carry in mind a clear
picture of their appearance; otherwise we shall find it difficult to understand how
slides can be restored with only partial information. The imaginary tableau which
is to serve this purpose, using any one of the four slides in the manner specified, is
formed as follows: The plaintext alphabet, *with letters in exactly the order of the
slide,* appears at the top. The 26 cipher alphabets, standing below and parallel to
the plaintext one, are all seen in exactly the order of the slide, *and are shifted, one*

letter at a time, exactly as the normal alphabet is shifted in the Vigenère tableau. Thus, exactly as in Vigenère, *the columns of this imaginary tableau are duplicates of the rows.* Keys, if considered, would repeat the first column of such a tableau. This tableau, as mentioned, is imaginary. Should the encipherer or the decipherer actually desire to make use of a tableau in preference to the slide, he would probably prefer one in which both his plaintext alphabet and his key alphabet are running in normal order, so that letters are easier to find. To form this tableau, he would begin by laying out, in normal order, his plaintext alphabet and his key-alphabet, and then lay out his 26 cipher alphabets in the manner explained in connection with the Beaufort alphabets. Each of the four slides of the figure is accompanied by a partial tableau of this kind, and it will be noticed there that we have only one case in which the (secondary) cipher alphabets bear any resemblance to the primary one. This tableau, too, should be well understood, since the cipher alphabets recovered from cryptograms will be like those of the figure.

Of our four slides, only the *Type I* is radically different from the rest. Since its basic cipher alphabet is not a mixed one, it makes little difference what has been done to its plaintext alphabet. Notice, in the partial tableau which accompanies it, that the difference between one cipher alphabet and another is purely a matter of alphabetical shift (or of " size," if we wish to replace all of these letters with numbers). Properly speaking, this cipher belongs to the case of the preceding chapter; it is presented here largely as a warning of what could happen through misuse of the *Type II* slide. In the remaining three cases, the sliding alphabet is a mixed one; a series of frequency counts taken from cryptograms cannot be " lined up " unless letters can be placed in the right order before these frequency counts are taken. The " right " order may be the original one of the cipher alphabet, or an equivalent order in which the original letters are taken at a constant interval. In these cases, as with any other periodic cipher, the period is found in the usual way. Individual frequency counts are then taken on the several cipher alphabets, and these are examined in the hope of finding a known alphabetical graph; that is, the graph of some mixed alphabet recovered from previous decryptments — (but notice also the *C*-alphabet under the *Type III* slide!). It can also be ascertained whether or not the frequency counts have followed one common graph, whether any two or more have followed one graph, and so on. But when it is found that the frequency counts are those of unknown mixed alphabets, then each alphabet is to be treated by simple substitution methods. Here, the principles will still be those of Chapter *IX*, and we will examine, as briefly as possible, the mechanical phases of their application.

Our cryptogram, shown in Fig. 139, is already written into its correct period, 5, with a few substitutions already made, and a few letters noted as vowels or consonants (*v-c*). With the period determined as 5, and alphabets found to be in an unknown mixed order, our next step is the preparation of a contact sheet (contact chart, contact count) for each one of the five alphabets, the usual form being that shown in Fig. 140. The necessary number of sheets is prepared in advance by writing the normal alphabet through the center, and each is numbered to show what alphabet it represents. It may also carry the numbers of the two contacting alphabets (those in parentheses in the figure). Then, if the cryptogram is properly grouped, so that all first letters of groups belong to alphabet 1, all second letters to alphabet 2, and so on, the putting down of contact letters is very rapid.

Illustrating with alphabet 2: Start with its first letter, *V;* find *V* in the prepared alphabet numbered 2; place on its left side the *Y* of alphabet 1; place on its right side the *N* of alphabet 3. Pass on to the next letter, *E:* contacts are *Y-G.* Pass on to the third letter, another *E:* contacts are *Z-A.* And so on to the end of alphabet 2. Each contact chart, of course, will serve also as a frequency count and as a

Figure 140

(5)	1	(2)
YT	A	EL
CSNKZYCC	B	IUKLQIKT
OO	C	LE
DD	D	DD
	E	
HJN	F	MVS
HUPSCCGCCWN	G	QDPKZOPQWKU
CK	H	SP
J	I	Q
LQBQ	J	PXER
QTPWOQ	K	KCUTKK
	L	
SQ	M	EE
O	N	D
R	O	U
O	P	E
OT	Q	SC
OD	R	EL
	S	
	T	
QQ	U	UD
SU	V	MV
	W	
RRK	X	TRR
QRNK*	Y	VEXUQ
JUTTECP	Z	EDDDDED

(1)	2	(3)
	A	
	B	
QK	C	FB
ZZUNZDZGDZ	D	BGAGYAGABB
RZPCJMAMZY	E	GAOFNIVUUS
	F	
	G	
	H	
BB	I	CN
	J	
KGKBGBK	K	WETMYTW
RABC	L	WQQA
VF	M	JM
	N	
G	O	M
HGGJ	P	MBMB
YGBGI	Q	VBVWV
JXX	R	XXS
FQH	S	MGM
BKX	T	YBK
YGOUBK	U	FIFFVG
FVY	V	NVU
G	W	B
YJ	X	GM
	Y	
G	Z	Y

(2)	3	(4)
LDDDE	A	YYKMB
DDPWTCPQD	B	GDYYKIHJO
I	C	F
	D	
K	E	K
UEUUC	F	KKZVV
UDDSDXE	G	DKJGJRK
	H	
EU	I	ZZ
M	J	V
T	K	V
	L	
SXPKOMPS	M	DLJIKDLD
IEV	N	GKA
E	O	N
	P	
LL	Q	JY
	R	
RE	S	IZ
KK	T	AQ
EEV	U	ZLS
QUEQVQ	V	IVZVZF
KQLK	W	SKIZ
RR	X	FF
DKZT	Y	AFAZ
	Z	

(3)	4	(5)
YNTY	A	DOOD
A	B	L
	C	
MMBMG	D	PQQTQ
	E	
VXYCX	F	WENRL
GBN	G	KNC
B	H	U
SBWMV	I	OKTOO
BMQGG	J	RWUTO
GAMBMEFWGF	K	QCCCQCCPU
UMM	L	BHR
A	M	T
O	N	K
B	O	D
	P	
T	Q	H
G	R	C
UW	S	JJ
	T	
	U	
KVVFFJ	V	ZSSPJS
	W	
	X	
QBBAA	Y	KTOQR
SWVYUVIFI	Z	YGYNSCNQQ

(4)	5	(1)
	A	
L	B	J
RZKKKKKGK	C	ZGBBGGGBH
OAA	D	DDR
F	E	Z
	F	
Z	G	G
LQ	H	GF
	I	
SVS	J	IFZ
INYG	K	YHXB
FB	L	J*
	M	
ZZFG	N	GPBY
IJIAAYI	O	KCQCNPR
KVD	P	ZKG
ZZDKYDKD	Q	KJMUJKUY
LFYJ	R	XXOY
VZVV	S	MVBG
MIDJY	T	QAKZZ
KHJ	U	VGZ
	V	
JF	W	GK
	X	
ZZ	Y	BA
V	Z	B

graph. The five graphs should now be compared with one another in the hope that some two or more may represent the same alphabet. Such a key-word as DENSE, for instance, makes use twice of the E-alphabet, thus doubling the amount of material in one of the alphabets. In our present case, it is found that the five alphabets are all different. Now, just as in simple substitution, we wish to determine, for each of the five alphabets, what letters are apparently representing vowels, and what letters are more likely to be consonants. For this purpose, some of our " pointers " are still available, and are just as valid as in Chapter *IX*.

In Fig. 141 we may see some data and probable conclusions concerning alphabet 1. By frequency alone, the four letters *B, G, K, Z*, of this alphabet might all be vowels. When variety of contact is considered in conjunction with frequency, it is noted that *Z* shows no variety on its right. And when contacts with low-fre-

Figure 141

Consideration of Alphabet No. 1

Letter:	Frequency:	LOW-FREQUENCY CONTACTS			VARIETY OF CONTACT		
		Left	Right	Total*	Left	Right	Total *
B (v)	7	2	3	5	6	6	12
G (v)(= E?)	11	5	3	8	8	8	16
K (v)	6	2	1	3	5	4	9
Z (c)	7	4	-	4	6	2	8

(*) These observations are not absolute, as in simple substitution.

quency letters are also considered (from information present on sheets 5 and 2; in the figure, frequencies of 1, 2, or 3 were considered to be low), it is found that in this respect, too, the letter *Z* stands apart from the others. These observations, usually, are mental, and conclusions for any one alphabet must often be modified by what is seen in other alphabets. It may be found satisfactory to begin by selecting only the *most obvious* vowel, or vowels, in each alphabet, and to circle these, or otherwise indicate them, not only on their own sheets, but also on the two adjacent sheets where they are found again as contact letters. When this has been done, the less obvious vowels may be considered again with an additional " pointer," whether or not they show too much contact with the more obvious vowels. Fig.

Figure 142

Conclusions for the Five Alphabets

Alphabet No.	Vowels	Consonants
1	B G K *	Z
2	E	D K Q U
3	B G M *	V
4	V Z	K
5	O	C Q

(*) When B and G appear as vowels in two different alphabets, the graphic appearance of these two alphabets (1 and 3) should be given another inspection. It happens they are not the same.

142 shows, for each alphabet, the probable conclusions which would be reached after examining the contact sheets of Fig. 140, and before any confirmation is attempted. The next step in order is that of indicating them on the cryptogram itself, and the examination of long segments in which no vowels have been marked. At this stage, too, the total number of spotted vowels may be computed to find out how much of the expected 40% is still missing. Up to this point we have nothing new, and nothing particularly difficult. Whether or not the subsequent work is to become difficult depends chiefly upon the amount of material per alphabet, though granting that the presence of probable words materially alters the case of the shorter cryptogram.

If the most frequent of the spotted vowels in each alphabet can be safely assumed as *e*, the establishment of other vowel-identities can follow the rules of Chapter *IX:* The high-frequency vowel which practically never touches *e* is *o;* and the one which follows it is *a;* vowels of lower frequency may precede or follow *e*, but no vowel should touch it very often. And if, in addition, the most frequent of the spotted consonants in a given alphabet can be safely assumed as *t*, then *h* of the next alphabet will seldom be out of reach. A very material aid here is found in those *repeated digrams* (and trigrams) whose letters are already labeled as vowels or consonants. We find, for instance, *ZD*, alphabets 1-2, occurring five times, and with both letters already spotted as consonants. This is very likely to represent *th*, especially when further examination shows it continued as a repeated *ZDB*, with *B* already quite likely to represent the *e* of alphabet 3. Then the contacts of *D*, alphabet 2, supposed to represent *h*, have also pointed out a probable new vowel, *A*, in alphabet 3. Again, we find *KC*, alphabets 4-5, occurring six times, and with both letters already spotted as consonants — another probable *th* — followed three times by *G*, alphabet 1, already likely to represent *e*, and twice by *B*, which could thus represent *a* (the famous English *the, tha*). And similarly we might continue with a long demonstration.

Returning, now, to our mechanical operations: Dealing, as we are, with five different alphabets, it becomes imperative that we keep track of substitutes; otherwise, with all of our numerous trials and erasures, it is almost impossible to know what substitutes have been identified and what substitutes are still available for identification. Also, totally apart from this matter of convenience, we shall probably want these five lists of substitutes for use on future cryptograms. This applies to any series of cipher alphabets, whether or not they are in any way related to one another. But it is very seldom indeed that a series of cipher alphabets used in the same cryptogram will be unrelated alphabets. Nearly always, they will have resulted from the use of a slide, and when this is true, the recovery of alphabets and parts of alphabets enables us to reconstruct the slide. The usual plan for recording substitutes is to lay out a plaintext alphabet in *A B C* order and then, directly below it, to rule off several rows of cells, one row for each cipher alphabet. Thus, any substitute, identified in any alphabet, may be written directly below its presumed original and on the row which corresponds to its particular cipher alphabet. We sometimes speak of such a set-up as a " key-frame " or " key-skeleton," though a better name, probably, would be " partial tableau." (Every row, if completed, will show one cipher alphabet of the kind we saw in the partial tableaux of Fig. 138.) Such a " key-frame " for our present cryptogram can be seen in Fig. 143. At (a) of this figure we have the first tentative identifications. The most frequent vowel in each of the first four cipher alphabets has been assumed as *e* (in practice, the *O* of alphabet 5 would also be assumed as *e*). The *ZD* of alphabets 1-2 and the *KC* of alphabets 4-5 have both been assumed as *th*, and after each *th*, we are trying one letter as *a*. The five rows of this set-up we may now speak of as " alphabets." At (b) we are beginning to speculate as to what kind of slide has been used.

Suppose that the cryptogram has been enciphered with a *Type II* slide. If so, our plaintext alphabet, in the key-frame, is already arranged like the one on the slide; and when this is true, as may be seen by glancing back at Fig. 138, the recovered cipher alphabets will also build up with their letters in exactly the same order as that of the slide, and, in the end, if fully completed, will show a picture of the original sliding alphabet taking five of its possible positions.

Examining the first cipher alphabet of (a), we note that the *lineal* distance from *B* to *G* is 4 positions. If our hypothesis is correct, then the lineal distance *BG* will have to be 4 positions in all of the other alphabets. The third alphabet con-

tains a *B;* measuring 4 positions to the right of this letter, we find that *G* of the
third alphabet would fall below *i,* and thus would be the substitute for *i* in the
third alphabet. To see whether or not this is likely, we return to the contact sheet,
where we find that *G* has already been spotted as a vowel (see the list in Fig. 142).
So far, so good. Then, the first cipher alphabet of (a) shows the lineal distance *BZ*
as 19 positions. Returning to the third alphabet, and measuring 19 positions to
the right of *B,* we find that *Z,* in this alphabet, would fall below *x.* Examination
of the contact chart shows that *Z* has not been used in the third alphabet, making
it satisfactory as the substitute for *x.* Still good. Again, the third alphabet shows
the distance *AB* as 4 positions. Still pursuing our hypothesis, the first alphabet
must also contain an *A* standing 4 positions to the left of *B.* If so, it will fall below *w,* and the frequency of *A,* in the first alphabet is found to be 2, which is sat-

Figure 143

(a)

```
        a b c d e f g h i j k l m n o p q r s t u v w x y z
1 -     B       G                                   Z
2 -             E   D
3 -     A       B
4 -             Z                                 K
5 -                 C
```

(b)

```
        a b c d e f g h i j k l m n o p q r s t u v w x y z
1 -     B       G       K                       Z   A
2 -             E   D
3 -     A       B       G   K                           Z
4 -             Z   A       B   G       K
5 -                 C
```

isfactory as that of *w.* With *G* and *Z* added to alphabet 3, and with *A* added to
alphabet 1, we may now turn our attention to alphabet 4, which contains a *Z,* and,
by making similar observations there, we may add to the 4th cipher alphabet the
letters *A B G,* and, to the 1st and 3d alphabets, the letter *K.* Thus we arrive at (b)
through what is ordinarily referred to as the " symmetry of position " existing among
the several cipher alphabets.

But the second and fifth alphabets cannot yet be combined with the other three,
since neither of these contains any letter in common with them, and thus we have
no point from which to measure lineal distances. We know, however, that if our
hypothesis is correct, the letters *A B G K Z,* in these alphabets also, will be found
at exactly the same lineal distances as before. It would be possible to prepare a
sort of slide on which these letters, written twice in succession, are spaced as in the
other three alphabets, and use this in experimenting with alphabets 2 and 5.

The cryptogram, as we first saw it, showed all substitutions which are possible
from (b) of Fig. 143, together with a few *v-c* notations which were listed in Fig.
142 but not further investigated. In case the student cares to complete solution,
he might refer to certain precautions mentioned at the beginning of the chapter.
Notice, in the last figure, the lineal distance from *G* to *K;* what letters would you
feel inclined to try in the three intervening positions? Or notice the distance *BG.*
What letter is very likely to have been taken here for use in the key-word, and where
is it likely to stand in that word? If the index-letter was *A,* does it seem possible
that the *a*-substitutes could all be selected in advance directly from the contact
sheets? Would this be possible if the encipherment process were varied so that an
index, selected in the sliding alphabet, were brought to stand below keys in the

stationary one? The cryptogram is known to contain the word SUPPOSE, and the period is 5. Is there any room here for *pattern* methods?

Our *Type II* slide, then, unlike the remaining three, builds up automatically in the key-frame, *owing to the simple fact that we are able to set down the plaintext alphabet in the encipherer's original order.* The method of solution, so far as we know, was first published (1883) by Auguste Kerckhoffs, who seems to have originated the term " symmetry of position." The invention of the cipher is credited to " a member of the (French) Commission on Military Telegraphy."

If these parallel cipher alphabets are to be avoided in the key-frame, but still using a *Type II* slide, General Sacco has suggested that the encipherment process be altered as follows: Let the index-letter and the key-letter both be found in the upper alphabet. Slide the plaintext letter to stand below the index-letter, and use the substitute which will then be standing below the key-letter. This, of course, would have to be letter-by-letter encipherment, and represents one of those rare cases in which a slide is less convenient and rapid than its equivalent tableau. If this tableau be laid out in full, as explained for Beaufort alphabets, it shows, on its 26 rows, 26 cipher alphabets not one of which appears to be at all related to the others. One of these (the one in which index-letter and key-letter are the same) will be the normal alphabet. We may find the original sliding alphabet, however, by looking at *columns.* Such a tableau is exactly equivalent to the *Delastelle tableau* if the Z-alphabet be made the normal one. Delastelle's tableau was described as follows: Using the mixed alphabet, fill in the tableau *by columns,* beginning each column with whatever letter, in the mixed alphabet, follows the plaintext letter shown above the column. This causes the final alphabet to come out in *A B C* order. The Delastelle tableau is not nearly so easy to reconstruct as that of the ordinary *Type II* slide; the method, however, will be plain enough when we have understood the reconstruction of *Types III* and *IV*.

The *Type I* slide, as pointed out in the beginning, is somewhat out of place in the present chapter; every frequency count will follow the graph of the mixed plaintext alphabet, so that all can be " lined up " by their common pattern. Having letters, and not numbers, the " top " of a frequency count may be anywhere; it is usually best to prepare at least one of the frequency counts of double length in order to effect the alignment. Granting, however, that for some reason the common pattern of the frequency counts has not been recognized, then the method of decryptment would be exactly the same as for any other case of mixed alphabets. Fig. 144 shows the development of the key-frame in this case. At (a), some substitutes have been correctly identified in each of four cipher alphabets. But long before reaching this stage, the most careless of decryptors must have noticed that the difference between any two cipher alphabets is purely a matter of alphabetical shift. This is particularly visible as between alphabets 3 and 4, where the alphabetical interval is only 1; examination of alphabets 1 and 2 shows that wherever both substitutes are present, their alphabetical difference is 14; and further examination shows that the alphabetical distance from alphabet 2 to alphabet 3 is 17. The use, here, of a Saint-Cyr slide enables us to arrive very quickly at (b). The alphabets of (b) are, of course, secondary cipher alphabets, and the primary one obviously runs in normal order (or, at worst, in a strictly methodized order which is easily obtainable from the normal one). What we still lack, in order to reconstruct the slide, is the mixed plaintext alphabet, and this can be recovered as at (c). Write out the normal alphabet (known to be the original cipher alphabet), then, using any one of the secondary alphabets, place originals above their substitutes wherever these are known. In the given example, all missing letters can be filled in by alphabetical sequence; and even though the index-letter was one of low frequency, and thus was not used in the message, the student should have no trouble whatever in discovering the key-word which governs the four cipher alphabets.

In considering the reconstruction of the remaining two slides, we shall have to keep clearly in mind the *imaginary tableau* on which *the plaintext alphabet has exactly the order of the one on the slide,* so that cipher alphabets, also, have exactly the order of the one on the slide, and are shifted one letter at a time, as in the Vigenère tableau. For one thing, we are going to call some of these alphabets by numbers, or refer to them as odd-numbered and even-numbered alphabets. Thus, with

Figure 144

The Alphabets from a TYPE I Slide:

(a)

```
           a b c d e f g h i j k l m n o p q r s t u v w x y z

    1 -    L . . J Q . H G F . . . . B A . . R Y X . . . . . .
    2 -    Z . . . E . . . T . . C Q . O . . . . . B . . . . .
    3 -    Q P . O V N . . . . I . . G F U . . D C . B A . Y .
    4 -    R . . P W . . M L . J . . . G . . . . D . . . . . .
```

(b)

```
           a b c d e f g h i j k l m n o p q r s t u v w x y z

    1 -    L K . J Q I H G F . D O C B A P . R Y X N W V . T .
    2 -    Z Y . X E W V U T . R C Q P O D . F M L B K J . H .
    3 -    Q P . O V N M L K . I T H G F U . W D C S B A . Y .
    4 -    R Q . P W O N M L . J U I H G V . X E D T C B . Z .
```

(c) **Alphabet No. 1:**

Plaintext: o n m k . i h g r d b a . u l p e r . y . w v t s .
CIPHER (Rearranged):   A B C D E F G H I J K L M N O P Q R S T U V W X Y Z

the alphabet we have been using, the *first* alphabet in the imaginary tableau is position 1 of the slide: *C U L P E R Z Y X W V T. . . . . .*, the *second* alphabet is position 2 of the slide: *U L P E R Z. . . . . . .*, the *third* alphabet is position 3 of the slide: *L P E R Z Y. . . . .*, and so on to the *26th* alphabet, which is the final position of the slide: *A C U L. . . . .* But over and above this, it must be remembered that *the columns of this imaginary tableau are duplicates of the rows,* just as they are in the Vigenère tableau. We do not, of course, recover any of these alphabets in the order mentioned, since our plaintext alphabet of the keyframe must necessarily be arranged in its *a-b-c* order. For instance, the *fourth* alphabet, which, in the imaginary tableau, begins with its key-letter, *P,* and runs in the order *P E R Z Y X W V T. . . . .*, comes out in one of our examples (*Type III* slide) as *L U P C Y A B D. . . . .*, and in the other (*Type IV* slide) as *E W Y P V T S. . . .*

The *Type III* slide is, in many respects, the most interesting member of its family. With every alphabet taking exactly the same order (that is, the plaintext alphabet, the key-alphabet, and all cipher alphabets in the imaginary tableau), it parallels the Vigenère in every particular except the order of the 26 letters. It has a corresponding Beaufort form, and a corresponding variant in which complementary keys are based on the order of the mixed alphabet. Its 14th alphabet, like the *N*-alphabet of the Vigenère, is reciprocal throughout. And its first alphabet, like the *A*-alphabet of the Vigenère, is a duplicate of the plaintext alphabet. This was pointed out in connection with the slide of Fig. 138, where key-letter and index-letter were both *C*. There are two ciphers, then (the *Type III* slide and the Dela-stelle tableau), in which we are sometimes able to find, among a number of mixed

Figure 145

The Alphabets from a TYPE III Slide:

Behavior of an EVEN-NUMBERED Alphabet

```
1st Alphabet (Always normal):  A B C D E F G H I J K L M N O P Q R S T U V W X Y Z
4th Alphabet:                  L U P C Y A B D F G H R I J K Z M X N O E Q S T V W
```

For an EQUIVALENT SLIDE, follow the chain AL-LR-RX-XT-TO......

```
        A L R X T O K H D C.P Z W S N J G B U E Y V Q M I F
        L R X T O K H D C P Z W S N J G B U E Y V Q M I F A
(1)..........  =                 =
(2)...............  ==           ==        ==        ==       ==
```

To find the ORIGINAL SLIDE from the EQUIVALENT one:

(1) Either take letters constantly at interval 9, which is the interval V-W-X:

```
        R Z Y X W V T S Q O N M K J I H G F D B A C U L P E (R)
        X W V T S Q O N M K J I H G F D B A C U L P E R Z Y (X)
```

(2) Or: Spread the letters apart so that the alphabetical sequences K(JI)H, Z(YX)W, etc. are standing at the right interval, always maintaining the alphabet-length, 26, and intertwine. Both alphabets are the same in this slide:

```
(The intervals    A . . L . . R . . X . . T . . O . . K . . H . . D .
are always odd,   . C . . P . . Z . . W . . S . . N . . J . . G . . B
3, 5, 7, etc.)    . . U . . E . . Y . . V . . Q . . M . . I . . F . .
```

Behavior of an ODD-NUMBERED Alphabet

```
1st Alphabet:   A B C D E F G H I J K L M N O P Q R S T U V W X Y Z
3d  Alphabet:   U C L A Z B D F G H I E J K M R N Y O Q P S T V W X
```

```
        1st HALF-CHAIN:                    2d HALF-CHAIN:
   A U P R Y W T Q N K I G D (A)      B C L E Z X V S O M J H F (B)
```

Spread the letters of each half, trying interval 2, interval 4, interval 6, and so on, treating both halves alike, until the intertwining of the two will set up some alphabetical sequences:

```
        . A . U . P . R . Y . W . T . Q . N . K . I . G . D
        B . C . L . E . Z . X . V . S . O . M . J . H . F .
```

frequency counts, a single one which follows perfectly the graph of the Vigenère *A*-alphabet. Concerning the 14th alphabet, however, we are dealing altogether, here, with a 26-letter alphabet; and some of what follows is being explained on the theory that the number 26 contains no factors other than 2 and 13. If the student will give his careful attention to *reasons*, as well as to methods, he will be able to adjust these methods to alphabets of other lengths, as, for instance, the very common 25-letter alphabet met with in foreign texts. The first alphabet, of course, duplicates the plaintext alphabet regardless of what alphabet-length is being considered, and thus, whenever a *Type III* slide has been used, we are always in full possession of one of the cipher alphabets.

Now, granting that we have completed the decryptment of a message, we have before us a key-frame in which several cipher alphabets are at least partially recovered. With one alphabet fully known in advance, the recovery of another full alphabet usually enables us very quickly to restore the original slide, or an equivalent slide. The ideal case is that in which we recover one of the even-numbered alphabets (except No. 14). The recovery of an odd-numbered alphabet will, at times, leave us with thirteen possibilities; while the recovery of the 14th alphabet could be useless, provided we have no other information. The method of reconstruction can be followed in Fig. 145.

First, we have the perfect case, one in which an even-numbered alphabet (the 4th) has been recovered in full. We begin by writing this recovered cipher alphabet letter for letter below (or above) the one which is always known to us; thus the two substitutes for *a* are in a same column, the two substitutes for *b* are in a same column, the two substitutes for *c* are in a same column, and so on. The columns themselves are not in their original order, but the two alphabets, throughout, are running parallel, just as they would in the imaginary tableau, and thus the *columnar distance is uniform* which separates each pair of substitutes; that is, the *vertical* distances *AL, BU, CP, DC, EY*, etc., are all equal in the imaginary tableau. If these be rearranged in such a way that the last letter of each pair is the beginning letter of the next, we have a chain *AL-LR-RX-XT-TO-OK*. . . . . made up entirely of equal vertical intervals, from which the repeated letters may be dropped: *A L R X T*. . . . . , leaving us a series of 26 letters known to be equally spaced in the columns of the tableau. Then, remembering that the columns of this tableau are duplicates of its rows, we have also a series of 26 letters known to be equally spaced on the rows. That this series of letters, *A L R X T*. . . . , *sliding against itself,* produces exactly the results of the original series, the student may ascertain for himself; also that a number of other *equivalent slides* can be formed by taking letters of this series at any constant interval which is not divisible by 2 or 13. The total number possible is eleven, of which one was the original. An equivalent slide, of course, is all that we actually need for enciphering and deciphering cryptograms. But where alphabetical sequences existed in the original alphabet, two methods are shown for obtaining it without writing out the entire eleven possibilities: (1) Find, at some constant interval, the letters of an alphabetical, or nearly alphabetical, sequence, as the (reversed) *V W X* of the figure, standing at interval 9; the taking of all letters at this interval brings back the original order. (2) Find pairs of consecutive letters, as the (reversed) *HK, WZ, GJ,* which, if all spread apart to the same extent (some odd interval, as 3 of the figure), would then be standing at their normal alphabetical intervals, or nearly so. Lay out the 26 positions, and spread the entire alphabet, maintaining the common interval even after the 26th position is reached. The figure shows this on several rows; in practice, there is only one.

If the recovered alphabet is an odd-numbered one, the same plan is followed, but results in a chain of only 13 letters; it is necessary to begin with some other letter, not included among the first 13, and form another 13-letter chain. Having absolutely no additional information, we cannot combine these two halves with certainty unless the original alphabet contained some alphabetical, or nearly alphabetical sequences. Presuming that it did, the method ordinarily described for combining the two halves is that of the figure. Spread the letters of the two halves (plan 2 of the preceding case), treating both halves exactly alike, until a point is found at which the two halves can be intercombined to show alphabetical sequences.

For this case, however, George C. Lamb, the author of Chapter *X*, suggests another plan which would seem to be more direct and less troublesome than the standard one. Lamb, incidentally, is to be congratulated here for his entirely new observation: If the two half-chains can be properly adjusted with reference to each other, *each pair of letters, regardless of the order, will be a digram belonging to the original mixed alphabet.* The reason for this division into halves, of the odd-numbered alphabets, is probably self-evident: One half contains only odd letters (1-3-5-7-9. . . . .) and the other contains only even letters (2-4-6-8-10. . . . . .). If both halves were recovered in this order, and if one half were written directly below the other with letters 1-2 standing together, then the other pairs would also be standing together: 3-4, 5-6, 7-8, and so on. We seldom recover them in straight order; but whatever rearrangement has taken place in one of the halves has taken place, also, in the other half; should one be recovered with letters in the order 1-7-13-19-25-5-11. . . . (each third letter in a series 1-3-5-7. . . . .), then the other will be recovered with letters in the order 2-8-14-20. . . . . . (each third letter in a

<u>Figure 146</u>

<u>Another Method for Combining the two Half-Chains of an Odd-Numbered Alphabet</u>

(Originated by GEORGE C. LAMB)

With a Type III slide, based on the key-word EXCORIATE, the 7th alphabet, as recovered from a cryptogram would come out as shown: H K B L A M N P........

```
A B C D E F G H I J K L M N O P Q R S T U V W X Y Z
H K B L A M N P G Q S U V W D Y Z F E J X C O T R I
```

The second half-chain, started with <u>D</u>, must be re-adjusted so as to place in correspondence the alphabetical sequences PQ, YZ, FG, MN, etc.

1st HALF-CHAIN:		A H P Y R F M V C B K S E
2d HALF-CHAIN:	(d l u x)	T J Q Z I G N W O D L U X

Each corresponding pair of letters was a digram in the original cipher alphabet. Taking some two letters, as FG, which form an alphabetical sequence, look for another pair, such as HJ, which may be its continuation. HJ having been found at the interval 9, try taking <u>pairs</u> at the interval 9:

FG HJ KL MN PQ SU VW YZ <u>EX CO RI AT</u> BD (FG)

series 2-4-6. . . . . .), though neither half necessarily begins with the first letter of its series. If, then, we are able to place together letters 1-2, the other pairs will also be adjusted, perhaps in the order 1-2, 7-8, 13-14, 19-20, and so on. These pairs may then be taken at some regular interval and will bring back the original order 1-2, 3-4, 5-6, and so on.

Lamb's method, applied to an actual cipher alphabet, can be seen in Fig. 146. The first half-chain, if started at *A*, will include the letters *B* and *C*, so that the second half-chain would probably have been started at *D*. But *AD* will not be a correctly adjusted digram. It is necessary to look for one which forms an alphabetical sequence, as *FG;* and when the two halves are adjusted so that *F* and *G* are together, other alphabetical, or nearly alphabetical, sequences are also found to be adjusted, as *MN, VW, BD, KL,* making it likely that we have found some digrams belonging to the original mixed alphabet. With this adjustment reached, it is found that pairs can be taken at the constant interval 9, *AT-BD-FG-HJ.* . . . . , thus bringing back the original cipher alphabet.

Presuming that the original alphabet did not contain these alphabetical sequences, then there are thirteen possible adjustments for the two half-chains, and any one of these could be the original alphabet (or its equivalent). But it must not be forgotten that in an actual case our key-frame always contains portions of other cipher alphabets; and if the foregoing principle has been well understood, it may be readily seen how we could make use of these in order to determine which of the thirteen possible adjustments is correct. Even the recovery of the 14th cipher alphabet (which results in thirteen 2-letter chains), would not be useless with this other information present always in every key-frame. The *Type III* slide, in fact, can often be reconstructed without possessing any fully recovered cipher alphabet. This cipher is very popular with members of the American Cryptogram Association, and is usually known, for no very good reason, as " the Quagmires cipher."

In the case of the *Type IV* slide, we do not begin reconstruction with one complete cipher alphabet already in our possession. It becomes necessary that we recover two, the perfect case being that in which one is an odd-numbered alphabet and the

Figure 147

The Alphabets from a TYPE IV Slide:

Plaintext letters: a b c d e f g h i j k l m n o p q r s t u v w x y z

(1) 4th Alphabet: E W Y P V T S Q O N M K R J I H G F Z D X B A C U L

(2) 7th Alphabet: Y S V Z Q O N M K J I H X G F D B A W C T U L P E R

A CHAIN Started with ab

ab ys vd qx nt jp gl bi sf du xm tz pw lr io fk uh me zo wa ry ov kq hn ej og (ab)
EW UZ BP GC JD NH SK WO ZT PX CR DL HA KF OI TM XQ RV LY AE FU IB MG QJ VN YS

REARRANGEMENT of this CHAIN:

ab bi io ov vd du uh hn nt tz zo og gl lr ry ys sf fk kq qx xm me ej jp pw wa
EW WO OI IB BP PX XQ QJ JD DL LY YS SK KF FU UZ ZT TM MG GC CR RV VN NH HA AE

A Reconstructed EQUIVALENT Slide:

     Plaintext: a b i o v d u h n t z o g l r y s f k q x m e j p w

     CIPHER: E W O I B P X Q J D L Y S K F U Z T M G C R V N H A

ORIGINAL Slide, Found by Taking Letters at the Interval 5:

           b u o s m a d z y x w v t ....
           W X Y Z R E P L U C A B D ....

other an even-numbered one. We will follow this case in Fig. 147, where the two recovered alphabets are Nos. 4 and 7. This tableau, like the preceding one, has columns which are duplicates of its rows, and to see our preceding case again (with its one modification), let us begin by looking only at the three alphabets immediately below the heading. One of these, the plaintext alphabet, shown in lower-case letters, we will disregard for a moment, giving our attention only to the two cipher alphabets.

These two alphabets, like the two from the *Type III* slide, are running parallel in the imaginary tableau, so that we have, as before, a series of 26 *vertical* distances, *EY, WS, YV,* and so on, all known to be equal in the columnar direction and therefore known to be equal distances on any row. A chain may be started, exactly as in the other case, *EY, YV, VQ, QM, MI. . . . ,* resulting in a series of equally-spaced letters *E Y V Q M I F A L R. . . . .* which is either the original cipher alphabet, or the original one with letters taken at some odd interval other than 13. It is, however, only the *cipher alphabet;* the mixed *plaintext alphabet* must still be found. This may be done, as in the case of the *Type I* plaintext alphabet, by using either of the two cipher alphabets which were first recovered and setting originals above their substitutes. If this is done with our cipher alphabet in the order *E Y V Q M I F A L R. . . . . ,* then the plaintext alphabet comes out in the order *a c e h k o r w z m.* . . . . . ., and we have an equivalent slide. If we first rearrange the sliding alphabet (each 9th letter of the series *E Y V Q.* . . .), we obtain the plaintext alphabet also rearranged.

Continuing, now, with the rest of our figure: The method we have just seen was based on a tableau, and our equal intervals were all vertical. In the figure, we are dealing purely with horizontal distances, and our method is based, not on a tableau, but on a *slide* (as it was with the *Type II*). Our 4th and 7th (secondary) cipher alphabets, after all, are merely two different positions of the same slide. If we select any two letters, as *a* and *b* of the plaintext alphabet, and find that their substitutes are, respectively, *E* and *W,* in alphabet 4, then the lineal distance *ab* in the stationary alphabet must be exactly equal to the lineal distance *EW* in the sliding

Figure 148

Some EXERCISES in the RECONSTRUCTION OF ALPHABETS

Plaintext		A B C D E F G H I J K L M N O P Q R S T U V W X Y Z
Exercise 1:		Q * Z A X B O C N * E R F P V G * Y M U I * W * T L
Exercise 2:		U V D W S X K Y H Z C F R J Q L I N G P T O M E A B
Exercise 3:		H J G K F P E Q O R S T D M B U V W X A Y Z C L I N
Exercise 4:	(1)	V N U X J Y Z D Q E M P O W C K R I A T L S B F G H
	(2)	H S G J R K L N F P Q B U I V A W C X Y T Z D E M O
Exercise 5:	(1)	G X Y Z M H A F T R L K E V Q U O J W I P N S B C D
	(2)	E * G J I K * L B * * U T C V W * Q D X S * * * * *

The keywords, all selected by Mr. A. F. SEMPER, do not contain any repeated letters. The TYPES of slide, respectively, are: I, III, III, IV, and III. In the 5th exercise, the completely recovered alphabet is a "number 14." (See also practice-cryptogram No. 46).

one; if this were not true, the letters could not have coincided as they do. Then, if we find the same substitutes, *E* and *W,* in alphabet 7, and note that, in this position of the slide, they have coincided, respectively, with plaintext letters *y* and *s,* then the distance *EW* in the sliding alphabet must be exactly equal to the distance *ys* in the stationary one. It follows from this that *ys* and *ab* are equal in the stationary alphabet. If we begin again with the lineal interval *ys,* we find that this is equal to *UZ* of alphabet 4, and that *UZ,* found again in alphabet 7, is equal to *vd.* Here, then, is another interval, *vd,* which is equal to both *ab* and *ys.* And so we may continue, forming a chain made up of these known equal intervals, *ab, ys, vd, qx,* etc., for the plaintext alphabet, and *EW, UZ, BP, GC,* for the cipher alphabet. Sometimes we return to *ab (EW)* without having included all 26 letters, and in that case (unless the number of letters included is a divisor of 26), it becomes necessary to abandon *ab,* and try starting with some other interval, as *ac.*

Here, as in the case of the *Type III* slide, we sometimes obtain two 13-letter chains; but in the fortunate case of having recovered in full both an odd-numbered and an even-numbered cipher alphabet, we end the chain with every letter represented twice, both in the stationary alphabet and in the sliding one. Pairs of letters (representing horizontal intervals) can then be rearranged as in the other case, the second letter of one becoming the first letter of the next (in both series), and the dropping out of duplicated letters gives us an equivalent slide. In the figure, starting with *ab (EW),* we find a plaintext alphabet *a b i o v d u.* . . . . . and a cipher alphabet *E W O I B P X.* . . . . . This, as mentioned, is one of eleven possible equivalent slides, of which one is the original. Here, the original can be found by taking letters at interval 21. In the figure, letters were taken at interval 5, a result of observing the sequence *W X Y Z* standing at that interval in the lower alphabet, and the slide comes out in reverse order. This is still an equivalent slide, and the decryptor may or may not care to decide which alphabet runs backward.

Since the reconstruction of these mixed-alphabet slides is probably the most fascinating subject in the whole field of cryptanalysis, several problems are being appended in Fig. 148. In all of these, Semper has selected key-words or phrases to contain no repeated letters. With reference to the practice cryptograms, only one of those submitted was thought to have enough alphabet-length for purely analytical attack. The others, even with their probable words or partial translations, will still require some work. The periods of these examples are said to be, respectively, 6, 7, 8, 3, and (?).

135. By NEMO. (Type II. Partial solution: WHEN JACK BOOMER,GREEN RIVER,WYO,B..)

```
TERPJ  YDBNQ  SAIMB  XBLYM  DOBIT  ZPTIH  KOKAG

MYQRX  TDWUU  XBOBQ  YDBWZ  SVZGC  UPRZS  WVODM

TQZCA  TSMYQ  FDBHZ  QUTIH  FSVSY  NFULZ  GLBGD

MTRMU  CNAJM  IYNQO  FBDPQ  LGXUY  WUIPC  AYNJN

XSBKW  IJGRL  GIB.
```

136. By NEMO. (Type III. Partial solution: ALOIS STEPHEN,YOUNG VIENNESE CHARGED W..)

```
HGKST  ILOYD  BOLEG  AZNGP  DUWPB  DRVZQ  YZXFL

QSBHS  LTUQP  SZGXV  AYTGB  CBXKH  URIED  MDXBT

OEPSA  RINKX  KJBIT  PYIXR  IUZYO  MIMHP  HBEJD

NEBSE  FLBFD  BHFJB  FNLGP  LJMIB  OGTAW  DUEQE

ZTYUS  I.
```

137. By THE SQUIRE. (Type III. Probable words: AMERICAN CONSTITUTION. GLADSTONE).

```
HTFMR  SRTYE  OVPDS  ZLAXB  ACNTN  AKXRC  SZKGO

QUOFA  ZRETD  SVIWK  WTELK  FRPRB  IHINA  SWRRS

BOHTF  LADDL  UBUFM  QOJAG  ILIDW  TZIMM  RHLLV

KWUJS.
```

138. By ALII KIONA. (Is this a diplomatic telegram?)

```
LLDRK  YCRFA  SEVSU  KTDUL  XVKFV  CABLY  UPYMR

KBEXU  BTELW  PJFPT  IIUQQ  KTFCT  PSKQL  WNDAP

BFAES  NMPRK  APTTS  HFKBZ  RMGPP  YVMSA  IFNPZ

ALTSU  SAUDN  LXAAZ  YPUCH  KNPYV  MSIAX  KKDBE

TPSAT  PKPSY  VTAYE  APBTE  LWPJF  PTAXN.
```

139. By PICCOLA. (This is a straight-alphabet cipher. Won't tell which one!)

```
ANDNY  LMYXN  KDLRP  GCXGQ  NAARZ  LDEPL  GIAWQ

NEIOG  AGPQG  ZVDEI  EZRHA  YPLBP  NAGEL  NVAGT

DHOKH  VGTIN  DOLSF  CPLRT.
```

CHAPTER XIX

POLYALPHABETICAL ENCIPHERMENT APPLIED BY GROUPS

Any one of the multiple-alphabet ciphers may change keys at each new group instead of with each consecutive letter. As a rule, this kind of encipherment is never found except in connection with very simple ciphers, and the intact plaintext groups, each one standing on its own key-line, are readily discovered by the decryptor who takes the precaution of cutting out a segment from his cryptogram and "running down the alphabet," first treating the original letters and then, if necessary, their complements. Porta encipherment, in any form, is rare, but its cryptograms can be subjected to the same process, provided the letters of the tested segment are first enciphered in the AB-alphabet, and the subsequent extensions properly carried out.

Figure 149

The "PHILLIPS" Cipher

1	C U L P E*	2	R Z Y X W	2	R Z Y X W	2	R Z Y X W
2	R Z Y X W	1	C U L P E*	3	V T S Q O	3	V T S Q O
3	V T S Q O	3	V T S Q O	1	C U L P E*	4	N M K I H
4	N M K I H	4	N M K I H	4	N M K I H	1	C U L P E*
5	G F D B A	5	G F D B A	5	G F D B A	5	G F D B A

	(1)		(2)		(3)		(4)
Plaintext:	T R Y M A........	C D O N A........		L D O N T........		H A T M U..	
CIPHER:	K T Q D C.......	T X N F R.......		I X C F L.......		C R K L D..	

2	R Z Y X W	3	V T S Q O	3	V T S Q O	3	V T S Q O
3	V T S Q O	2	R Z Y X W**	4	N M K I H	4	N M K I H
4	N M K I H	4	N M K I H	2	R Z Y X W**	5	G F D B A
5	G F D B A	5	G F D B A	5	G F D B A	2	R Z Y X W**
1	C U L P E*	1	C U L P E*	1	C U L P E*	1	C U L P E*

	(5)		(6)		(7)		(8)
......	R P H Y P.......	R O P O S.......		I T I O N.......		C U R L Y.	
......	T W G Q W.......	M R O R X.......		W K W N Z.......		T S U Q P.	

With mixed alphabets of any kind, a number of cases may arise, according to whether groups are of uniform length, or of varying lengths, or, in fact, represent word-lengths; or, in the one case of uniform groups, according to the length of these groups, or the amount of material available, or as to how much is known in advance, and so on. From among so many possibilities, suppose we select the case of accumulated short messages, and, at the same time, take a brief look at a cipher which, according to its description, was actually intended for group-by-group application. This cipher, which may be examined in Fig. 149, was described in an early issue of *The Cryptogram* as having been used for military purposes, and was called the "Phillips" system. The text of the figure "Try Macdonald on that Murphy proposition. Curly" includes eight five-letter groups, thus requiring eight cipher alphabets. The key, as originally prepared, is a mixed 25-letter alphabet written into a 5 x 5 square, of which the five rows can be cut apart to form five horizontal strips. It may also be set up with anagram blocks. This is alphabet 1 (or block 1), and serves to encipher the first five-letter group. The method of substitution will be explained in a moment. Alphabet 2 (block 2) is derived from the first by moving line 1 so that it stands between lines 2 and 3. Alphabets 3, 4, and 5 are derived by continuing to move the original line 1 so that it stands, successively, between lines 3 and 4, between lines 4 and 5, and at the bottom of the square. Alphabets 6, 7, and 8 are derived by moving the original line 2 according to the same plan. For puzzle purposes, these movements may continue as they apparently began. Line 2 may be given its one remaining shift, which places it at the bottom of the square, and lines 3, 4, and 5 may then be moved downward in the same way as the first two; some puzzlers, in fact, will afterward continue by treating columns. But according to the description (the only one the writer has ever seen of this cipher), the eighth cipher alphabet is the last. For the encipherment of the next eight groups, either the square is restored to its original set-up and the same eight alphabets used again, or the first key is abandoned altogether in favor of an entirely new one.

Now, considering any one block, as No. 1, the method of substitution is as follows: Each letter is to be replaced by the one standing immediately to its right on the descending diagonal. If the given letter happens to stand at the extreme right side of the square, it is to be replaced by one standing at the extreme left and on the next line below. If it happens to stand on the bottom row of the square, it is to be replaced by one standing on the top row and in the next column to the right. One letter, in fact, requires both of these (mental) adjustments; the letter which occupies the lower right-hand corner is to be replaced by the one occupying the upper left-hand corner. If the foregoing is well understood, is is quite obvious that our key-square is, to all intents and purposes, a rhombus formed with five diagonals. One diagonal is complete, as *C Z S I A* of block 1. The other four break off at the right and are continued from the left, as *L X O N F* of block 1; or, if you prefer, break off at the bottom and are continued from the top, as *N F L X O* of block 1. It should be obvious, also, that any one of these five diagonals can be considered as beginning with any one of its five letters without in the least changing the encipherment. Thus, each diagonal furnishes what is called *cyclical encipherment*. But, as a matter of fact, the entire square involves cyclical encipherment: The placing of line 1 at the bottom of the square, or of column 1 on the right side of the square, or the transfer of several lines or columns, or of both, will not have any influence whatever on substitutes; for this, it is necessary to alter the 1-2-3-4-5 order of these rows or columns. Alphabet 5, then, will be the same as alphabet 1; and if the plan of the puzzlers be followed, this same alphabet continues to reappear for the encipherment of each fourth group, blocks 1, 5, 9, 13, 17, and so on, of a long cryptogram eventually giving a great deal of material in one cipher alphabet. Moreover, groups having a length of five letters will carry some very visible simple substitution patterns. Now suppose we look at Fig. 150.

These eight cryptograms have all come from one source. The general frequency count has shown a missing letter, *J*, suggesting the use of a square, and we have suspected the cipher as " Phillips." With cryptograms arranged one below another, as shown, the first five columns are presumably enciphered with block 1 of that cipher, the next five columns with block 2, and so on; thus, we presumably have 40 letters each belonging to alphabets 1, 2, and 3, and almost that number belonging to alphabet 4, that is, enough material for frequency counts which will show whether or not they have been taken on simple substitution alphabets. While 40 letters of text are very few, we could, eventually, solve any simple substitution cryptogram of that length, or any mixed-alphabet periodic whose alphabets have furnished 40 letters each. In the present case, our first alphabet has furnished eight known word-beginnings; we have one column known to contain only initials, and followed by two others which are very likely to be the hiding-place of vowels. This does not mean that we should have no preliminary struggles, but in the end there are plenty of clues to set us on the right road: The predominant letters of alphabet 1 are *A, B, O, K, U* (practically sure to contain *e, t,* and one of the vowels *a* or *o*). The column of initials repeats both *A* and *T* (to be compared against a list *t s a.* . . .). The second and third columns, combined, include *B* and *O*, three times each, with *O* found in the initial column also (both could be vowels, and *O* probably represents *a*, though *i* is also frequently found as an initial). If *A*, by frequency and initial position, be tried as *t*, then the other repeated initial, *T*, can be tried as *s*. This assumption brings out, in the fourth message, a pattern *s - t t -*, in which the second letter, *B*, would have to be a vowel, either *e* or *o*, since it has been doubled, with *e* appearing more likely in the given pattern and also in that of the sixth message, *s - - - s.* The letter *O*, which under the encipherment scheme could

Figure 150

1. A F S X O S G Y F O N P Y O A K O A D G F Z K S Z O Y Z Y L A W A C F.

2. H O U A L H L E D H D L Y G A V D W A K.

3. K O N B K A X U O N H I Q P L B A Z F F S Y F D R R L Y F.

4. T B A A M A F Q E Z U M A I X G F S K B.

5. D K O A C Y B Y E N I M O W D L E G A D O H C Y U U R G.

6. T B B X T O M M D A S I A A Y D Z.

7. O U S U B U L O I Y G A K X M A K W E L.

8. A K R U W A N A L O N N F M S K A X E U.

General Frequency Count:

A	B	C	D	E	F	G	H	I	J	K	L	M	N	O	P	Q	R	S	T	U	V	W	X	Y	Z
25	8	3	10	6	11	7	5	5	.	11	10	7	7	15	2	2	4	8	3	10	1	5	6	12	6

Frequency Count on Alphabet 1, Only:

A	B	C	D	E	F	G	H	I	J	K	L	M	N	O	P	Q	R	S	T	U	V	W	X	Y	Z
6	5	1	1	.	1	.	1	.	.	4	1	1	1	5	.	.	1	2	3	4	.	1	2	.	.

not possibly be its own substitute, can be assumed, by frequency, as *a*, rather than *i*.

These first correct substitutions are all shown on the left side of Fig. 151, on the lines marked (a). Surely the next identification would be the *m* of *seems*, and probably, too, the *l* of *settl.* . . With the vowel *a* already identified, the repeated *OU* would be tried as *an*, and the repeated *KO* as *ha*, using the digram list. These are the substitutions marked (b), and from this it is but a step to the assumptions marked (c). On the right side of this figure, we are proceeding into alphabet 2. A frequency count here has shown that the leading letters of this alphabet are *A, O, Y*, two of which, *A* and *O*, were also leaders in alphabet 1. It is one peculiarity of the " Phillips " cipher that a change in alphabets means a change in only fifteen of the substitutes, the remaining ten continuing to represent the same originals as in the preceding alphabet. Concerning *A*, we can see, from the third and fourth messages, that it has not continued to represent *t*; but *O*, in the sixth message, has rather suggested the word *all* and even the expression *all right*, which would carry us on into the third alphabet. From this point onward, then, we are in the same fortunate position as the decryptor who intercepts his message partly in cipher and partly in plaintext. With the context as a guide, we need not worry as to what happens at the ninth group.

Presumably, during all of this time, we have been recording substitutes in a

Figure 151

First Alphabet	Second Alphabet
1. **A F S X O**	**S G Y F O** ...
(a) t . . . a	. . . n a
(b) t . . m a	. . o n a
(c) t r y m a	. . o n a (Try ma...)
2. **H O U A L**	**H L E D H** ...
(a) . a . t .	. . . . .
(b) . a n t .	. s u r .
(c) c a n t .	e s u r e (Can't be sure...)
3. **K O N B K**	**A X U O N** ...
(a) . a . e .	i . . a .
(b) h a . e h	i m . a t
(c) h a v e h	i m . a t (Have him ...)
4. **T B A A M**	**A F Q E Z** ...
(a) s e t t .	i . g . a
(b) s e t t l	i n g u .
(c) s e t t l	i n g u p (Settling up ...)
5. **D K O A C**	**Y B Y E N** ...
(a) . . a t .	. . . . .
(b) . h a t .	o y o u t
(c) w h a t .	o y o u t (What do you t...)
6. **T B B X T**	**O M M D A** ...
(a) s e e . s	a l l . i
(b) s e e m s	a l l r i
(c) s e e m s	a l l r i (Seems all ri...)
7. **O U S U B**	**U L O I Y** ...
(a) a . . . e	. . a . .
(b) a n . n e	. s a . o
(c) a n y n e	w s a . o (Any news abo...)
8. **A K R U W**	**A N A L O** ...
(a) t	i . i . a
(b) t h . n .	i t i s a
(c) t h i n k	i t i s a (Think it is a...)

Frequency Count on Alphabet 2, Only:

```
A B C D E F G H I J K L M N O P Q R S T U V W X Y Z
5 1 . 2 3 2 1 2 1 . . 3 2 3 5 . 1 . 1 . 2 . . 1 4 1
```

key-frame. We have recovered fifteen of these in alphabet 1, and also a number in alphabet 2. Those recovered from alphabet 1 are shown at the top of Fig. 152. *O* is the substitute for *a*, *A* is the substitute for *t*, *T* is the substitute for *s*, and *S* is the substitute for *y*. Thus, if the cipher is " Phillips," then, in the original key-square, the two letters *A O* were consecutive on one of the diagonals, the two letters *T A* were consecutive, the two letters *S T*, and the two letters *Y S*, so that the complete diagonal must have been *Y S T A O*, and even though the letter *o* was not used at all in alphabet 1, we know that its substitute must have been *Y*, since these diagonals may be considered to begin with any one of the five letters. By beginning at *c-H*, and following out another such chain, we may find another complete diagonal, *C H K W D;* and, in addition, we may find parts of diagonals. All of these are shown at (b).

Whether or not we can go further than this, without consulting other cipher alphabets, depends upon whether or not the original key-square contained some of those alphabetical, or nearly alphabetical, sequences which so often betray the poorly-mixed alphabet; usually, these are most easily found toward the *X Y Z* end

Figure 152

An Alphabet No. 1 - Taken from a Key-Frame:

```
Plaintext:   a b c d e f g h i . k l m n o p q r s t u v w x y z
SUBSTITUTES: O . H . B . . K R . W M X U . . . F T A . N D . S .
```

```
(a)
        A       T       S       Y           Y
      O       A       T       S           S
                                            T
                                          A
    (b)                                     O
 *Y        C       E     I     L     *V
   S         H       B     R     M     N
     T         K         F     *X      U
   A         *W
     O         D
```

```
(c)           (d)                    (e)
N D . S      S . N D .    S I N D E    . N D . S    I N D E S
  U C . T    . T . U C    B T R U C    T . U C .    T R U C B
  . H L A    H L A . .    H L A F .    L A . . H    L A F . H
  . K M O    . K M O .    . K M O .    K M O . .    K M O . .
  V W X Y    . V W X Y    . V W X Y    V W X Y .    V W X Y .
```

of the normal alphabet. In the given case (b), we are able to find the letters *V, W, X,* and *Y,* each standing on a separate diagonal; thus, by readjusting the beginning-points of their diagonals so as to place these letters at the bottom, we are able to set together four of these diagonals in the order shown at (c), leaving only the part-diagonals *E B* and *I R F* still to be added. Their length will show that *I R F* belongs to the missing diagonal, but *E B,* by its length, could belong to any one of three diagonals. Further developments can be carried out with the rhomboid adjustment of (c), or, if this is confusing, the conversion to a square can be made immediately. The student may decide for himself which he prefers of the two developments marked (d) and (e). Notice that this restoration of the key-square can take place not only from a single alphabet, but with only 15 substitutes known in that alphabet. But without the aid of alphabetical sequences, we must, in the first place, have 20 substitutes, four for each diagonal, in order to recover the full diagonals, after which, each one is entirely independent of the other four, so that they cannot be adjusted and combined without consulting one or more of the other alphabets. Here, the method varies a little, according to just what we can recover, though a hasty glance at the perfect case will serve to show the general path for all. To see this as rapidly as possible, we will assume that we have recovered from alphabet 1 the full five diagonals, and that, in alphabets 2, 3, and 4, we have discovered the substitutes for *e*, and also the originals for which *E* has been the substitute.

A careful consideration of the cipher itself will show that no letter can have more than four different substitutes: the four letters in the next column to its right which are not on the same line with itself. Also, that no letter may act for more than four different originals: the four letters in the next column to its left which are not on the same line with itself. Any letter, in order to take all four substitutes and act for all four originals in four successive alphabets, must have started on the top line, which is the moving one.

Now, considering Fig. 153: Our five recovered diagonals are imagined to be those of a well-mixed square, so that we have no discoverable sequences. It has

Figure 153

Five Complete Diagonals Recovered From Any Alphabet No.1

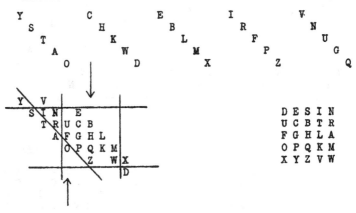

been found that the letter *e*, in alphabets 1, 2, 3, and 4, has taken, successively, the substitutes *B, H, Q,* and *Z*, and that the cipher-letter *E* has served, successively, as the substitute for *x, u, f,* and *o*. The four letters *B H Q Z*, then, must all have stood in a single column *in exactly the order named;* and the four letters *X U F O* must have stood in another column, two positions to the left of the first, but with a minor difference in the order: some other letter (the one on the same line as *E*) must have intervened between *X* and *U*. The order in this column, then, must have been *U F O X*. Our first step toward combining the five diagonals is that of adjusting four of them so as to set up the column *B H Q Z*. This automatically sets up four letters of the other column *U F * X (D)* — in the figure, the *X D* is present, but has not been adjusted to the *U F ** — after which, the fifth diagonal can be added to the others by placing the *O* of the column *U F O X (D)*. Now, since the letter *E* has taken, successively, all four of its substitutes and all four of its originals, it must, in alphabet 1, have been standing on the top row. Two parallel lines (if desired) can be ruled across the set-up to show the top and bottom of the square, and two others (placed anywhere, so long as they mark a width of five columns) may be ruled to show the two sides. The outside letters, *Y, V,* and *D*, may all be transferred to the opposite ends of their diagonals, after which the rhomboid is easily adjusted to the form of a square.

It will be seen from what precedes that group-by-group encipherment offers little, if anything, that is new, and no problems or theories which the student could not figure out with what he has learned of substitutions. Solving the actual cryptograms, of course, could present some difficulties, according to the individual case.

Of the practice cryptograms to follow, No. 140 follows the plan of the puzzlers, and should not prove very difficult in spite of its brevity. No. 141 is also a " Phillips," while No. 142 has been enciphered with a mixed-alphabet slide applied to five-letter groups.

140. By NEMO. ("Phillips." Probable word: ASSOCIATION)

NDQTF   QZCNG   BUZHX   NLUKY   FTEEW   NRGUR   MOXQX

EQZLB   GXHWF   FNRPX   PXVDD   FITGS   EWRTI   ITZXB

RVWAR   ISPEY   IGRQC.

141. By PICCOLA. (This is the real McCoy - in 1938. But times change).

(a) KGEUH   CKTSX   PCKNC   ADFXQ   CBXT

(b) OUTUI   UBFSB   QAPHN   BYZXX   LRUG

(c) OFUOS   KHQTK   PWQFE   TBWWX   PKBOK   GH

(d) BLAMR   PGXBW   GCWKQ   ZIAQC   UHYRC

(e) GUCOS   BBLPS   BQDKP   GPKDS   RCTBL   I

(f) XROSU   ITTFG   YPCMC   KFTFB   OSRBH   OAGM

(g) BOIBV   BUKEE   BDKBC   OBYWB   TBMUH   OOAB

(h) YCUYU   TBITF   HSANP   HCWT.

142. By PICCOLA. (Direct examination - Snowball vs. Snowball).

(q) HFXLF   MBLRN   INJWP   ZZGIS   BBOZX   SFSHR

HTATM   ROFV?   (a)   SXFUR   RWXIQ   SS.

(q) UFVHC   NTITT   FOEJX   OGNSG   XUSOE   HIVLX

EAT?   (a)   URQQT   WEX·UW   ITOS.

(q) HCWRU   QUITT   FYOQI   UDRSG   XZWHG   FETPC

JEMKQ   FINDO   EEZBL?   (a)   URQQT   W.

(q) URSUF   UGJRE   DVTOV   ECZXZ   UZGXS   DSHCQ

KEXZW   IOVIR   MHDWB   DZRRM?   (a)   URQTD   HTTHI

JSS.

(q) XCQHR   EMZLT   TOPAV   HULEB   OYOGN   UFVXT

ZLEKS   WFAVN?   (a)   XRLLQ   EWLTC   OSPWV   CZLEB

DWYIZ   FISRD   TWCEZ   TTASG   OLE.

143. By PICCOLA. (Can you guess what cipher? "Foregoing" refers to No. 141).

RNNGT   RIOOH   EITTA   FNDEN   OGELG   EYFIR   DAISB.

CHAPTER XX

Vigenère with Key-Progression

Before leaving the study of multiple-alphabet ciphers, we will consider briefly the process which, in its simplest form, would be that shown in Fig. 154. The initial key, in each of three examples, is *A*, and a long key has been formed by causing the initial one to progress in the normal alphabet according to an agreed index. In the first example, the progression index is 1, in the second, it is 2, and in the third, it is 25 (or minus 1). The resulting long key will govern a period, which is 26 or 13, according to whether the progression index is odd or even. This encipherment,

Figure 154

Forms of Key-Progression

Keys:	A B C D E F G...	A C E G I K M...	A Z Y X W V U...
	S E N D...	S E N D...	S E N D...
	S F P G...	S G R J...	S D L A...

This type of key-progression can be decrypted by "running down the alphabet," and watching the diagonals for plaintext.

logically, would be applied with a cipher disk. The initial key, as *A* of the examples, would indicate the starting position of the revolving disk, the first letter being enciphered with the disk in this initial position, after which the disk is made to revolve, so many angles at a time, without further reference to key-letters. For this kind of cryptogram, the solution is purely mechanical. A series of alphabets may be extended, with each cryptogram letter as a beginning, and the message can be found following a diagonal path in the resulting set-up.

A much commoner scheme, when using a cipher disk, is that of following a series of irregular shifts in accordance with a numerical key. If, for instance, the initial

Figure 155

Progressing Key:	C U L P E P E R	D V M Q F Q F S	E W N R ...
Plaintext:	T H E R E I S O	T H E R C A U S	E F O R ...
Partial Encipherment:	V B P G	W C Q H	... I ...

position has been established and the first letter enciphered in that position, and if the numerical key is 3-5-2-1-6, the disk will now be revolved 3 positions for encipherment of the second letter, 5 positions for encipherment of the third letter, 2 positions for encipherment of the fourth letter, and so on, so that the disk must move 17 positions during encipherment of five letters. This can produce a very long period indeed, especially when the collective shifts result in an odd number.

Substantially the same encipherment as the foregoing can be had with a slide and a key-word, as indicated in Fig. 155. The progression index, in this figure, is 1. The preliminary key-word, CULPEPER, enciphers the first eight letters, then moves forward in the alphabet and becomes *D V M Q F Q F S* for the encipherment of the next eight, *E W N R G R G T* for the encipherment of the third eight, and so on. In its practical application, one column could be taken at a time. Notice, however, in Fig. 156, that when a key-letter progresses in the alphabet, the possible substitutes for any one letter will also progress, and to exactly the same extent. If the encipherment is Vigenère or Beaufort proper, this progression is in the same alphabetical direction as that of key-letters, while the variant encipherment causes the substitutes to progress in the contrary direction. Probably, then, the

Figure 156

Vigenere and Beaufort Progression		Variant Progression	
Progressing Key:	A B C D E.....	Progressing Key:	A B C D E.....
Plaintext Letter:	H H H H H.....	Plaintext Letter:	H H H H H.....
Cipher Letter (V)(B)	H I J K L...... T U V W X.....	Cipher Letter:	H G F E D.....

most convenient method of application, and the one least likely to result in errors, would be that of Fig. 157. The cryptogram is first enciphered as an ordinary periodic, and the progression is added later, using group-by-group encipherment. Thus, as we receive the cryptogram, our repeated *ther* has been enciphered once as *V B P G*, again as *W C Q H*, and possibly, later on, as *A G U L*, and the only period we shall be able to find, using the regular methods, will be 26 x 8, or, if the progression index is an even number, 13 x 8. But notice, in the same figure, comparisons (a) and (b).

Vigenère, it will be remembered, has been compared to the mathematical process of addition. If the key-digram *CU* be added to the plaintext digram *TH*, their sum is the cipher-digram *VB*. The alphabetical distance from *C* to *U* is 18, the alphabetical distance *TH* is 14, and the alphabetical distance *VB* is 6 or could be 26 plus 6, 52 plus 6, and so on. It is a fact that when we " add " the two digrams *CU* and *TH*, we actually do add their separating intervals, 18 and 14, since we obtain a sum 32 in that of the cipher digram *VB*. It is also an easily verified fact that the same reasoning applies to the subtractions of the two Beauforts. The student who cares to investigate may make use of the tableau shown as Fig. 158; to find quickly the distance from one letter to another, find the first of these at the left, the second at the top, and the alphabetical interval between the two is shown in the cell of intersection. If it is desired to know the reverse interval, find the first letter at the top and the second at the side. Now notice, carefully, that when any digram progresses in the alphabet, as *CU* would become *DV*, *EW*, *FX*, and so on, in a series of periods, *it does not change its alphabetical interval;* in all of these digrams, the distance apart of the two component letters is still 18. Thus, while our period vanishes, the alphabetical intervals which represent it are still present in the cryptogram; we have only to find these intervals, subject them to a Kasiski examination, and convert the cryptogram to an ordinary Vigenère.

Fig. 159 shows the preparation of the cryptogram: The alphabetical interval

Figure 157

Initial Key-word:	C U L P E P E R	C U L P E P E R	C U L P E P E R
Plaintext:	T H E R E I S O	T H E R C A U S	E F O R T H I N...
PRIMARY Cryptogram:	V B P G I X W F	V B P G G P Y J	G Z Z G X W M E...
Progression Key:	A	B	C
FINAL Cryptogram:	V B P G I X W F	W C Q H H Q Z K	I B B I Z Y N G...

(a)

(b) C U (key)   plus   T H (plaintext)   equals   V B (cipher).

     Interval 18   plus   interval 14   equals   (32 less 26) = 6

Figure 158

Tableau for Finding ALPHABETICAL INTERVALS

	A	B	C	D	E	F	G	H	I	J	K	L	M	N	O	P	Q	R	S	T	U	V	W	X	Y	Z	
A	0	1	2	3	4	5	6	7	8	9	10	11	12	13	14	15	16	17	18	19	20	21	22	23	24	25	A
B	25	0	1	2	3	4	5	6	7	8	9	10	11	12	13	14	15	16	17	18	19	20	21	22	23	24	B
C	24	25	0	1	2	3	4	5	6	7	8	9	10	11	12	13	14	15	16	17	18	19	20	21	22	23	C
D	23	24	25	0	1	2	3	4	5	6	7	8	9	10	11	12	13	14	15	16	17	18	19	20	21	22	D
E	22	23	24	25	0	1	2	3	4	5	6	7	8	9	10	11	12	13	14	15	16	17	18	19	20	21	E
F	21	22	23	24	25	0	1	2	3	4	5	6	7	8	9	10	11	12	13	14	15	16	17	18	19	20	F
G	20	21	22	23	24	25	0	1	2	3	4	5	6	7	8	9	10	11	12	13	14	15	16	17	18	19	G
H	19	20	21	22	23	24	25	0	1	2	3	4	5	6	7	8	9	10	11	12	13	14	15	16	17	18	H
I	18	19	20	21	22	23	24	25	0	1	2	3	4	5	6	7	8	9	10	11	12	13	14	15	16	17	I
J	17	18	19	20	21	22	23	24	25	0	1	2	3	4	5	6	7	8	9	10	11	12	13	14	15	16	J
K	16	17	18	19	20	21	22	23	24	25	0	1	2	3	4	5	6	7	8	9	10	11	12	13	14	15	K
L	15	16	17	18	19	20	21	22	23	24	25	0	1	2	3	4	5	6	7	8	9	10	11	12	13	14	L
M	14	15	16	17	18	19	20	21	22	23	24	25	0	1	2	3	4	5	6	7	8	9	10	11	12	13	M
N	13	14	15	16	17	18	19	20	21	22	23	24	25	0	1	2	3	4	5	6	7	8	9	10	11	12	N
O	12	13	14	15	16	17	18	19	20	21	22	23	24	25	0	1	2	3	4	5	6	7	8	9	10	11	O
P	11	12	13	14	15	16	17	18	19	20	21	22	23	24	25	0	1	2	3	4	5	6	7	8	9	10	P
Q	10	11	12	13	14	15	16	17	18	19	20	21	22	23	24	25	0	1	2	3	4	5	6	7	8	9	Q
R	9	10	11	12	13	14	15	16	17	18	19	20	21	22	23	24	25	0	1	2	3	4	5	6	7	8	R
S	8	9	10	11	12	13	14	15	16	17	18	19	20	21	22	23	24	25	0	1	2	3	4	5	6	7	S
T	7	8	9	10	11	12	13	14	15	16	17	18	19	20	21	22	23	24	25	0	1	2	3	4	5	6	T
U	6	7	8	9	10	11	12	13	14	15	16	17	18	19	20	21	22	23	24	25	0	1	2	3	4	5	U
V	5	6	7	8	9	10	11	12	13	14	15	16	17	18	19	20	21	22	23	24	25	0	1	2	3	4	V
W	4	5	6	7	8	9	10	11	12	13	14	15	16	17	18	19	20	21	22	23	24	25	0	1	2	3	W
X	3	4	5	6	7	8	9	10	11	12	13	14	15	16	17	18	19	20	21	22	23	24	25	0	1	2	X
Y	2	3	4	5	6	7	8	9	10	11	12	13	14	15	16	17	18	19	20	21	22	23	24	25	0	1	Y
Z	1	2	3	4	5	6	7	8	9	10	11	12	13	14	15	16	17	18	19	20	21	22	23	24	25	0	Z
	A	B	C	D	E	F	G	H	I	J	K	L	M	N	O	P	Q	R	S	T	U	V	W	X	Y	Z	

from K to O is 4, that from O to S is 4, that from S to X is 5, and so on. If these numbers are placed directly below the first letter, as shown, the computation of their *lineal* intervals apart is less confusing than when they are placed between the two. As to repetitions, each repeated single number may represent a repeated digram, each repeated sequence of two numbers may represent a repeated trigram, and so on. Only the longer of these possibilities have been underscored.

Figure 159

```
         (5)                    (10)              (15)               (20)
K  O  S  X  M  Y  M  M  Q     Y   T   K   N   G   Z   W   L    T   Z   L
4  4  5  15 12 14 o  4  8    21  17   3  19  19  23  15   8    6  12  22

         (25)                   (30)              (35)               (40)
H  C  G  F  A  P  J  Y  K     W   A   T   Z   P   Q   X   U    J   Z   P
21 4  25 21 15 20 15 12 12    4  19   6  16   1   7  23  15   16  16   6

         (45)                   (50)              (55)               (60)
V  C  Z  Q  A  R  F  P  V     Y   U   Y   C   R   C   X   M    X   G   I
7  23 17 10 17 14 10 6  3    22   4   4  15  11  21  15  11    9   2  21

         (65)                   (70)              (75)               (80)
D  U  X  Q  Y  M  T  E  V     V   S   C   X   J   L   J   D    A   E   Y
17 3  19 8  14 7  11 17 o    23  10  21  12   2  24  20  23    4  20   4

         (85)                   (90)              (95)              (100)
C  S  F  P  J  W  F  V  J     V   Q   V   E   G   A   N   G    K   B   B
16 13 10 20 13 9  16 14 12   21   5   9   2  20  13  19   4   17   o  17

         (105)                  (110)             (115)             (120)
S  C  P  Z  B  H  G  I  D     Z   J   A   N   Z   I   Y   E    Z   P   T
10 13 10 2  6  25 2  21 22   10  17  13  12   9  16   6  21   16   4   -
```

Figure 160

Repeated Intervals		Lineal Interval		Possible Factors						
4-4	KOS-UYC	51 - 1 = 50	2		5		10			
15-12	XMY-JYK	27 - 4 = 23								
21-17-3-19	YTKNG-IDUXQ	60 - 10 = 50	2		5		10			
23-15	ZWL-XUJ	36 - 15 = 21		3		7				
21-15	FAP-CXM	55 - 24 = 31								
7-23	QXU-VCZ	41 - 35 = 6	2	3		6				
16-6	ZFV-IYE	115 - 39 = 76	2	4					19	
17-10	ZQA-BSC	100 - 43 = 57		3					19	
10-17	QAR-ZJA	110 - 44 = 66	2	3		6		11		
15-11	CRC-XMX	56 - 53 = 3		3						
9-2	XGI-VEG	92 - 58 = 34	2					17		
2-21	GID-GID	107 - 59 = 48	2	3	4	6	8	12		
17-0	EVV-KBB	98 - 68 = 30	2	3	5	6	10			
13-10	SFP-CPZ	102 - 82 = 20	2		4	5	10			
20-13	PJW-GAN	94 - 84 = 10	2		5		10			
9-16	WFV-ZIY	114 - 86 = 28	2		4	7				

Fig. 160 shows the application of a modified Kasiski examination. Notice the prominence of small factors 2 and 3, caused, often, by repeated alphabetical intervals in the key itself. In the given case, the period 10 would probably be the choice, though period 5 is correct; in practice, we should probably consider possible digrams as well as longer sequences. Accepting period 10, we have still to learn the progression index, and for this we must consider letters, all of which are shown in the second column of the same figure. Taking the longest repetition, most likely to be reliable, the two first letters are *Y* and *I*; their alphabetical distance apart is 10, and their lineal distance apart in the cryptogram is 50. If the accepted period, 10, is correct, it has taken five periods to produce the alphabetical shift of 10, therefore the shift per period (the progression index) is 10 divided by 5; or 2. This, of course, has taken for granted that the encipherment is either Vigenère or Beaufort. Considered as a possible variant Beaufort, where the progres-

Figure 161

$K_4 \ O_4 \ S_5 \ X_{15}M_{12}Y_{14}M_0 \ M_4 \ Q_8 \ Y_{21}$

$T_{17}K_3 \ N_{19}G_{19}Z_{23}W_{15}L_8 \ T_6 \ Z_{12}L_{22} \ (2)$

$H_{21}C_4 \ G_{25}F_{21}A_{15}P_{20}J_{15}Y_{12}K_{12}W_4 \ (4)$

$A_{19}T_6 \ Z_{16}P_1 \ Q_7 \ X_{23}U_{15}J_{16}Z_{16}P_6 \ (6)$

$V_7 \ C_{23}Z_{17}Q_{10}A_{17}R_{14}F_{10}P_6 \ V_3 \ Y_{22} \ (8)$

$U_4 \ Y_4 \ C_{15}R_{11}C_{21}X_{15}M_{11}X_9 \ G_2 \ I_{21} \ (10)$

$D_{17}U_3 \ X_{19}Q_8 \ Y_{14}M_7 \ T_{11}E_{17}V_0 \ V_{23} \ (12)$

$S_{10}C_{21}X_{12}J_2 \ L_{24}J_{20}D_{23}A_4 \ E_{20}Y_4 \ (14)$

$C_{16}S_{13}F_{10}P_{20}J_{13}W_9 \ F_{16}V_{14}J_{12}V_{21} \ (16)$

$Q_5 \ V_9 \ E_2 \ G_{20}A_{13}N_{19}G_4 \ K_{17}B_0 \ B_{17} \ (18)$

$S_{10}C_{13}P_{10}Z_2 \ B_6 \ H_{25}G_2 \ I_{21}D_{22}Z_{10} \ (20)$

$J_{17}A_{13}N_{12}Z_9 \ I_{16}Y_6 \ E_{21}Z_{16}P_4 \ T_- \ (22)$

Figure 162

(A)	K	O	S	X	M	Y	M	M	Q	Y
(C)	R	I	L	E	X	U	J	R	X	J
(E)	D	Y	C	B	W	L	F	U	G	S
(G)	U	N	T	J	K	R	O	D	T	J
(I)	N	U	R	I	S	J	X	H	N	Q
(K)	K	O	S	H	S	N	C	N	W	Y
(M)	R	I	L	E	M	A	H	S	J	J
(O)	E	O	J	V	X	V	P	M	Q	K
(Q)	M	C	P	Z	T	G	P	F	T	F
(S)	Y	D	M	O	I	V	O	S	J	J
(U)	Y	I	V	F	H	N	M	O	J	F
(W)	N	E	R	D	M	C	I	D	T	X

sion is backward, the alphabetical interval from *Y* to *I* is 16, which is not divisible by 5, the number of periods. But this progression might have covered the entire alphabet and then included 16, or it might have covered the alphabet twice, and so on, before including 16. We must make it divisible by 5, adding 26, then another 26, and so on, until we obtain a total progression of 120. This, divided by 5, gives the progression index as " minus 24 " — the same as a normal progression of 2. In Fig. 161, the cryptogram has been re-written into the accepted period 10, and the figures in parentheses at the right of each group will indicate the amount of alphabetical shift when the progression index is 2. A constant progression of 2 per group would correspond to the application of a Vigenère key *A C E G*. . . . . , so that the Saint-Cyr slide will serve for quickly converting the cryptogram to its

Figure 163

MATHEMATICAL FORMULA - C. H. PRICE

$$X = \frac{AD \times P}{LD}$$

P = Period   AD = Alphabetical Distance
X = Progression Index   LD = Lineal Distance

As Applied to the Supposed Repeated Trigram KOS-UYC, Positions 1, 51:

$$X = \frac{10 \ P}{50} = \frac{P}{5}$$

BUT: P and X must be integers   . . If P = 5, then X = 1
(and P must be a divisor of 50)   ·   If P = 10, then X = 2
(Periods of 25, 50, are unlikely)

periodic form, and this is shown in Fig. 162. The period, as mentioned, is actually 5, though this makes no difference in the final results.

For those who like mathematics, Fig. 163 shows a method used by one of our collaborators for determining both the period and the progression index direct from the cryptogram. Price also preferred to find alphabetical intervals by writing the normal alphabet into a block, five letters to the line, with *Z* standing alone on the last line; thus, except for watching *Z* occasionally, the distance from one letter to another could be counted by fives. It is understood, of course, that we do not accept the evidence obtained from only one of the supposed repeated sequences; too many of these will be accidental, and many of those which are actually periodic have not represented repeated digrams, but merely repeated intervals. Naturally, too, the progression index need not be a small number; the disk encipherment, mentioned in the beginning, showed a progression of 17 for each period 5. This disk encipherment, incidentally, has been dealt with in a most interesting manner in Givierge's *Cours de cryptographie*.

We have seen, then, all of the essentials of polyalphabetical encipherment. With the cipher alphabets known to the decryptor, practically all of the multiple-alphabet ciphers will be solved by suitable modifications of processes described for Vigenère. When alphabets are not known, his problem, always, is that of collecting as many as possible of the substitutes belonging to each alphabet, so that he may determine both the order of the letters and the relationship of alphabets to one another.

144. By THE SQUIRE.

```
S O V F O    G S G U F    V I J R I    F M O U I    C F T T I    K Z Y Z Z    Z U I F Q

Q L O W U    V A F J F    I W W L N    C R G J F    E M V V N    N C D H W    T A J N I

W R D B.                 yallyyayyayalyyaaallayaaaylalllaylyayyallyyayayalalllyyall.
```

145. By NEMO.

```
Y Y I Z C    U O F Y V    H Q Y H T    B E B S X    P T S Y C    R M R X L    X E A G U

Y L P U Q    B U U Q N    Y U S O Q    M O O S P    U G I J I    I F F F A    L I R G G

F G E H H    N T E G Y    Z S M C O    F U D E M    X O G I K    K V B N K    W K P Q X

M G D L A    I F N H M    X T U M E    Z X Y Z G    N A P D W    C D M N C    T T H N Y  F D.
```

146. By PICCOLA. (We wouldn't throw monkey-wrenches for anything!)

```
X E I T B    B B B V M    X R S J P    Y L K E N    Y K S Z K    F R W L G    S A Y E A

V I X I X    D U V D U    R J G E I    B A N Z F    H D C C Y    C O Y R V    A B K W B

R H F K K    F X S E J    Y T F N L    R N I V K    V K Q H I    Q H I J L    P G O U R

V F C F T    S H L I D    V D D M H.
```

147. By DAN SURR. (Might try this without bothering about its progression!)

```
E C G M H    T Y T A J    B T H N G    A W K L I    B E M N R    H T D G N    G P D A O

Q A X R P    Z P F H D    D X I E A    U V S Y C    I X C W V    R H P B O    I X Y D Y

D V W N R    V X O O K    K I H F O    X D S V L    V W W C L    I H Z H V    W R L H W

M M I E E    A H G Q Y    R S R L K    L W Z T J    A Y W F N    S S U C V    Z L P X P

S E E E Y    R T H D H    T Z N U P    U R M G K    Z N T Y E    Q D E Z E    N N H M M

I N R L P    S S W P Y    M C R U B    J Z Y C R    N L M A S    M E U C L    R M D Y R

N E S T O    B V J E U    D V L O T    S Q B J H    B N R L B    V D X J P    X N I G F

I C Q J Y    Q Z X Q G    K B L F Q    U B Q K N    E L S S L    Y G T L F    L T D Z Z

Y K E E R    H K L W L    I M R N J    S O O J P    Q C A U D    M E I B B    Q X A H C

V A J C M    G X B I C    D K V C L    G Q I B S    C F V F W    Q N A X I    D R Z S X

R B I W R    C Q R.
```

148. By PICCOLA. (When is a tramp not a tramp?)

```
E R N I C    D M R A S    T A A P H    T P I L T    Q V A A S    N E A E E    R O O L R.
```

CHAPTER XXI

POLYGRAM SUBSTITUTION — THE PLAYFAIR CIPHER

Polygram substitution contemplates the encipherment of several letters collectively: Digrams are to be replaced with other digrams, or with three-digit numbers; trigrams are to be replaced with other trigrams, or with four-digit numbers; and so on, the substitute for an individual letter being entirely dependent upon the combination in which it happens to occur. Many devices have been contrived for accomplishing this. For pair-encipherment, tableaux of the general kind shown in Fig. 164 are fairly common.

Figure 164

```
    A  M  E  R  I  C  N  B  D  F  G  H  J  K  L  O  P  Q  S  T  U  V  W  X  Y  Z

E   AA BA CA DA EA FA GA HA IA JA KA LA MA NA OA PA QA RA SA TA UA VA WA XA YA ZA
Q   AB BB CB DB EB FB GB HB IB JB KB LB MB NB OB PB QB RB SB TB UB VB WB XB YB ZB
U   AC BC CC DC EC FC GC HC IC JC KC LC MC NC OC PC QC RC SC TC UC VC WC XC YC ZC
A   AD BD CD DD ED FD GD HD ID JD KD LD MD ND OD PD QD RD SD TD UD VD WD XD YD ZD
L   AE BE CE DE EE FE GE HE IE JE KE LE ME NE OE PE QE RE SE TE UE VE WE XE YE ZE
I   AF BF CF DF EF FF GF HF IF JF KF LF MF NF OF PF QF RF SF TF UF VF WF XF YF ZF
T   AG BG CG DG EG FG GG HG IG JG KG LG MG NG OG PG QG RG SG TG UG VG WG XG YG ZG
Y   AH BH CH DH EH FH GH HH IH JH KH LH MH NH OH PH QH RH SH TH UH VH WH XH YH ZH
B   AI BI CI DI EI FI GI HI II JI KI LI MI NI OI PI QI RI SI TI UI VI WI XI YI ZI
C   AJ BJ CJ DJ EJ FJ GJ HJ IJ JJ KJ LJ MJ NJ OJ PJ QJ RJ SJ TJ UJ VJ WJ XJ YJ ZJ
D   AK BK CK DK EK FK GK HK IK JK KK LK MK NK OK PK QK RK SK TK UK VK WK XK YK ZK
F   AL BL CL DL EL FL GL HL IL JL KL LL ML NL OL PL QL RL SL TL UL VL WL XL YL ZL
G   AM BM CM DM EM FM GM HM IM JM KM LM MM NM OM PM QM RM SM TM UM VM WM XM YM ZM
H   AN BN CN DN EN FN GN HN IN JN KN LN MN NN ON PN QN RN SN TN UN VN WN XN YN ZN
J   AO BO CO DO EO FO GO HO IO JO KO LO MO NO OO PO QO RO SO TO UO VO WO XO YO ZO
K   AP BP CP DP EP FP GP HP IP JP KP LP MP NP OP PP QP RP SP TP UP VP WP XP YP ZP
M   AQ BQ CQ DQ EQ FQ GQ HQ IQ JQ KQ LQ MQ NQ OQ PQ QQ RQ SQ TQ UQ VQ WQ XQ YQ ZQ
N   AR BR CR DR ER FR GR HR IR JR KR LR MR NR OR PR QR RR SR TR UR VR WR XR YR ZR
O   AS BS CS DS ES FS GS HS IS JS KS LS MS NS OS PS QS RS SS TS US VS WS XS YS ZS
P   AT BT CT DT ET FT GT HT IT JT KT LT MT NT OT PT QT RT ST TT UT VT WT XT YT ZT
R   AU BU CU DU EU FU GU HU IU JU KU LU MU NU OU PU QU RU SU TU UU VU WU XU YU ZU
S   AV BV CV DV EV FV GV HV IV JV KV LV MV NV OV PV QV RV SV TV UV VV WV XV YV ZV
V   AW BW CW DW EW FW GW HW IW JW KW LW MW NW OW PW QW RW SW TW UW VW WW XW YW ZW
W   AX BX CX DX EX FX GX HX IX JX KX LX MX NX OX PX QX RX SX TX UX VX WX XX YX ZX
X   AY BY CY DY EY FY GY HY IY JY KY LY MY NY OY PY QY RY SY TY UY VY WY XY YY ZY
Z   AZ BZ CZ DZ EZ FZ GZ HZ IZ JZ KZ LZ MZ NZ OZ PZ QZ RZ SZ TZ UZ VZ WZ XZ YZ ZZ
```

The tableau proper includes a full list of the 676 possible two-letter combinations, while two external alphabets will furnish another possible 676 two-letter combinations. With the plaintext marked off into pairs, the encipherment of a pair is usually accomplished by finding its two letters in the two external alphabets, where they act as co-ordinates, and replacing this pair with the one which is found at the cell of intersection. Thus, using the tableau of the figure, and the order row-column, the substitute for *th* would be *LG;* or, using the order column-row, *TN.* With a tableau like that of the figure (notice the straight unshifted alphabets), it is also possible to encipher by what is ordinarily considered the decipherment process, finding the plaintext pair inside the tableau and replacing it with the two co-ordinates. But many of these tableaux are filled in a thoroughly haphazard manner, and when this is the case, only the ordinary encipherment plan is really feasible; in fact, the decipherer has trouble in finding his cryptogram pairs, and it is usually necessary that a second tableau be prepared especially for decipherment purposes. On the other hand, it is very easy to construct a mixed tableau in such a way that all of its encipherment is reciprocal, and in this case there is no need for a second tableau, since encipherment and decipherment are the same process. In most forms of tableau, one or both of the external alphabets may be made to slide and for the most part external alphabets are readily changeable. But the tableaux themselves will have to be of more or less fixed nature. Those which are safest are least readily reconstructed from memory, and even those most easily remembered are not set up very rapidly.

Another common method for pair encipherment can be understood from the following description: Picture a chart of 100 cells which is divided sharply into four quarters; that is, having much the appearance of a 100-cell Fleissner grille. Each of the four quarters is a 5 x 5 square and contains a 25-letter alphabet. At

Figure 165

The "SLIDEFAIR" Cipher -(H. F. GAINES)

Key:	H E R C U L E S

Plaintext:	SE ND DI AM ON DS TO AM
CIPHER:.....	XZ ZR RU KC TI HO KX US

	ST ER DA MM ON DA YW EE
.....	MZ NI JU KO TI PO SC MW

	KW I? HO UT FA IL
.....	PR PM XY RW GZ AT

Cryptogram taken off:
X Z Z R R   U K C T I   H O K X U , etc.

least two of these alphabets are mixed, usually with different keys. To encipher a pair, find its two letters in two different squares, and substitute two others which occupy certain relative positions in the other two squares.

The writer's own contribution, accomplished with a slide, may be examined in Fig. 165; the slide used in the example was the Saint-Cyr, and details are self-explanatory, except for the method of enciphering pairs, which was as follows: To encipher those of the *H*-column, bring the *H*-alphabet into position on the slide; then, for each pair, find its first letter in the upper alphabet and its second letter in the lower one; imagine these to be standing at the two ends of a diagonal, and substitute the two letters from the two ends of the corresponding cross-diagonal, taking the upper one first. Where the two plaintext letters happen to coincide (as would be the case with a pair *EL* using the *H*-alphabet of the Saint-Cyr slide) use the two letters which have also coincided immediately to their right (as *FM* for *EL* in the given case).

Occasionally, such a tableau as that of Fig. 164 is made to serve (not very successfully) for trigram encipherment. A third external alphabet is added beside one of the others, so that the two which are parallel will make provision for the encipherment of a third letter simultaneously with the encipherment of each pair. But for trigram encipherment, another type of tableau is commoner: The tableau proper is not a list of pairs, but an alphabet square such as could be prepared for one of the mixed-alphabet slides of Chapter *XVIII*, and is accompanied by four external alphabets, two on the left and two across the top. The exact details of construction are not always the same, and the methods prescribed for using such a tableau are sometimes quite devious, but results are fairly uniform: We obtain cryptograms in which enciphered pairs have alternated with enciphered (sometimes *not* enciphered!) single letters.

In all of the foregoing, no system has been mentioned which the student will not be able to analyze for himself. At worst, he has a case very much like simple substitution, except that he would require a great deal more material, and would use a digram chart instead of a frequency list. Otherwise, he usually finds that he has merely a variation of pure periodic encipherment. There are, of course, more effective methods. Trigrams, tetragrams, and other polygrams, found in alphabet squares, can always be considered as geometrical figures, and replaced with other series of letters in related geometrical figures; and Lester S. Hill, in the American Mathematical Monthly, has described an "algebraic" method which appears practical, provided a machine is used. These methods, however, even

Figure 166

The PLAYFAIR Cipher

KEY	Encipherment		Some Equivalent Keysquares		
C U L P E	(1) bl = IB		L P E C U	N O Q S T	Y Z V W X
R A B D F	ez = FE		B D F R A	V W X Y Z	P E C U L
G H I K M	(2) ol = UP		I K M G H	C U L P E	D F R A B
N O Q S T	oe = UC		Q S T N O	R A B D F	K M G H I
V W X Y Z	(3) th = OM		X Y Z V W	G H I K M	S T N O Q
	ht = MO				

Example:

SE ND DI AM ON DS TO AM ST ER DA MX MO ND AY WE EK WI TH OU TF AI LX.
TP SR BK FH QO KY NQ FH TN CF FB IZ HT SR DW ZU PM XH OM WA ZM' BH BL.

granting that some are practical and not too unwieldy for use, are entirely beyond our present scope, and we will spend our few remaining pages on a cipher of a less cumbersome nature and presenting far more points of interest.

The Playfair cipher, which may be examined in Fig. 166, requires no apparatus other than pencil and paper. Its key is the usual 5 x 5 square, based on a key-word, and filled in by any agreed plan (preferably not by straight horizontals). For encipherment, the plaintext is marked off into pairs, and these pairs are enciphered according to three very simple rules:

1. If the two letters of the pair are found in the same column in the key-square, replace each letter with the one directly beneath it; and if one letter stands at the bottom of the column, use the one standing at the top of the same column. With the key of the figure, *ha* becomes *OH; wa* becomes *UH.*

2. If the two letters of the pair are found in the same row in the key-square, replace each letter with the one immediately to its right; and if one letter stands at the extreme right end of the row, use the one standing at the extreme left end of the same row (*os* becomes *QT; st* becomes *TN*).

3. If the two letters of the pair have a diagonal relationship in the key-square (and these are usually in the majority), consider them to be standing at the diagonally opposite corners of an imaginary small rectangle, and substitute for each letter that letter of the other diagonal which stands on the same row with itself (*bu* becomes *AL*, not *LA*). The decipherment rules, as usual, are the same rules in reverse.

Notice that this encipherment is *cyclical.* So long as the order 1-2-3-4-5 is maintained in both columns and rows, it makes no difference whatever how many columns are transferred from one side to the other, or how many rows are transferred from top to bottom. This may be investigated in the three equivalent squares of the figure. Notice, too, that our three rules do not make any provision for the case in which the two letters of a pair are the same. If, in marking off the plaintext into pairs, we encounter a pair which is a double, it becomes necessary to dispose of this, usually by inserting a null which will throw the second letter into the next pair. Occasionally we find a sequence such as LESS SEVEN, in which it is necessary to do this twice in succession: *LE Sx Sx SE VE Nx.* An unpaired final letter also requires a null (unless left unenciphered), and when five-letter groups are to be used, it often becomes necessary to complete a final group by adding nulls.

The foregoing description and rules are those of the original Playfair cipher. Many encipherers, however, will vary the rules, especially the one concerning doubles; perhaps one letter will be omitted or replaced with a null; sometimes one double is replaced with another; occasionally an encipherer will separate every doubled letter in the message whether or not this is necessary. We meet, too, with variant forms. A 24-letter alphabet will be used in a 4 x 6 rectangle, or a 27-letter alphabet (with character &) will be used in a 3 x 9 rectangle. One variation, attributed to W. W. Rouse-Ball, uses the standard key-square with the standard rule 3, but varies the two rules for lineal encipherment. Rule 1: If the two letters of the pair stand in a column, use the two letters immediately to their right. Rule 2: If they stand in a row, use the two letters immediately beneath them. In all of these cases, presuming the method to be known, the degree of difficulty would be the same as if the standard system had been used; otherwise, it is only necessary to keep in mind the fact that variations occasionally occur. We will give our attention, then, to the standard encipherment. But before entering into the subject of decryptment, let us look carefully at the system itself.

Primarily, we have a *fixed* substitution. No plaintext pair ever has more than one substitute pair; and no substitute pair ever changes its original. We might say that the Playfair is, in effect, a " simple substitution " based on an " alphabet " of 600 pairs; and, just as in simple substitution proper, the Playfair cryptograms will very often contain long repeated sequences which represent whole words. Again, the reversal of a plaintext pair means the reversal of its substitute pair, and vice versa, so that the discovery of any one equation (as $th = OM$) always means the discovery of another (as $ht = MO$); and if, in addition, the encipherment was a rectangular one (rule 3), we obtain also the two reciprocal equations (as $om = TH$, and $mo = HT$). The two lineal encipherments, however (rules 1 and 2), are not reciprocal. But notice particularly that, in spite of the polygram theory, each letter has its individual substitutes. No letter in the key-square may have more than five of these; the four which are standing on its own line, and the one which stands directly beneath it. It may be learned, too, by writing out the 24 (or 48) possible pairs for any one given letter, that the letter standing immediately to its right in the key-square is twice as likely as any one of the other four to act as its substitute; and, further than this, that any letter which is paired with it will be limited to eight possible substitutes, all of which must be found either in the column or on the row of the letter itself. To clarify this important point, let us assume that the letter in question is E, and that the key-square is that of Fig. 166. The letter E may have only the substitutes C, U, L, P, and F, with C twice as likely to be used as any one of the other four. Any letter which is paired with E must take one of the following substitutes: $U L P E F M T Z$.

Naturally, then, those letters which, in the key-square, are standing on the same row or in the same column with the normally frequent letters will have high frequencies in the cryptograms; in fact, the two or three which predominate in a given cryptogram will practically always be letters which, in the key-square, were standing in the same row or column with E or T (in English). Moreover, if any letter has been identified once as the substitute for *E*, there is a most excellent chance that it can be identified again as the substitute for *E*. Say, for instance, that *CF* has been identified, or assumed, as the substitute for *er*. This means that *C* is individually the substitute for *e*, and when another pair *CT* is found to be of some frequency, it can be tried as the substitute for *en, es, et,* and so on. Single-letter frequencies, then, will play an important part in the decryptment of the Playfair. But the process will rest fundamentally upon the frequencies of digrams, and will follow, in general, three steps repeated over and over in the same rotation:

1. Certain pairs are identified, or assumed, as the substitutes for certain digrams.
2. These pairs and their supposed originals are set together in such a way as to start the reconstruction of the key-square.
3. Substitutions are made on the cryptogram and further pairs are identified.

When probable words exist, the work of solution becomes more or less mechanical, as we shall see. At worst, we may begin at the beginning of the cryptogram and work straight through until we find the word. But very often, a really probable word is repeated, and even repeated more than once. In the latter case, we are sure to find the long repeated sequence in the cryptogram; while a word repeated only once may have been divided into two different sets of pairs, as: *ex-ec-ut-io-n* and *e-xe-cu-ti-on*. But notice, here, what the two encipherments would be, using our key-square of the figure: *LZ CU EO HQ x* and *x ZL UL QM QO*. These two sequences have five letters in common, *L Z U O Q*, and, in addition, when considered together, show the letters *E C U O* of the word "execution." This does not invariably happen, but is far from uncommon. Nor is the word "execution" the only one which produces reversal (*ex* in one sequence, *xe* in the other). Then, too, there are many words like "commission" which, regardless of the point at which the division begins, will always end in the same set of pairs: *mi-s?-si-on*.

Granting an absence of probable words, the difficulties of solution are almost entirely dependent upon the amount of material available. A pair-count will be made in the usual chart-form (but only on the divided pairs, and not "straddling" from one pair to another), and pairs will be identified by frequency, by the frequency with which they are found reversed, by the possibility of their letter-combinations in a key-square, and so on. We will not attempt, here, to go into a detailed demonstration, since every case is individual in its details, and success, in all of them, is dependent largely upon the decryptor's own persistence. But in order to see sketchily what some of the routine might be, we will make use of the very short example shown in Fig. 167.

In the usual case, there has been a preliminary frequency count on single letters in order to find out what the cipher is. The appearance of this frequency count has more or less negatived the possibility of simple substitution, and the next step has been a Kasiski tabulation in the hope of finding a period. This tabulation, in any pair-system, will bring out a predominant factor 2, and, since many of the supposed digram systems actually do produce periods, the two supposed alphabets would have been examined for that possibility. But pair-systems, as a rule, will leave a wide-open trail: Repeated sequences, in the majority of cases, will include an *even* number of letters (that is, an exact number of pairs), and will begin largely at the *odd* serial positions (that is, at the beginnings of pairs). The Playfair shows this a little less distinctly than some of the others, because of the fact that substitutes for single letters are so limited in number.

It is sometimes said of the Playfair that it can be distinguished from other ciphers by (1) the fact that cryptograms contain an even number of letters, (2) the fact that only 25 letters are represented in its general frequency count, (3) the fact that when the cryptogram is marked into pairs, no pair will be a doubled letter, and (4) the presence of long repeated sequences at irregular intervals. As conclusive evidence, these are debatable points, but all are good supporting evidence, provided a proper confession can be extracted from the pair-chart: (5) When the cryptogram has been marked off into pairs, and the pairs counted, the result should bear much resemblance to a count made on the same number of normal digrams. Even on an extremely long cryptogram, over half of the cells will be blank, since a normal text never uses more than about 300 of the possible 676 combinations; there will be a certain group of predominant pairs followed by a group of moderate

Figure 167

HR_5	KY_3	LD	ZX	NQ_2	EO	ND	EC	TC	TI_2	AD	CT	AK	RH	LB_2	GT	SN	AN
UN_2	ON	DR	HX	PE	BN	ZC	DT	KV	EQ_2	HD	AO	HR_5	DU	RP	TQ	OB	DE_2
QD_2	HR_5	KY_3	YA_2	HZ	HB	BU	KZ	EQ_2	XG	TI_2	BI	KY_3	RI	CQ	HR_5	CE	CO
SX	RM	BC	TH	CG	QD_2	RK	NQ_2	IT	DC	WT	FV_2	UB_2	YA_2	GU	HE	CZ	NU_2
LB_2	IQ_2	YK	FV_2	UB_2	IQ_2	WD	QB	UN_2	KM	DE_2	TD	KA	HR_5	NU_2	OU

Frequency Count - Rearranged:

D	H	B	C	N	Q	R	T	K	U	E		A	I	O	Y	Z		G	X	L	V	F	M	P	S	W	J
14	12	11	11	11	11	11	11	10	10	9		7	7	6	6	5		4	4	3	3	2	2	2	2	2	-

List of REVERSALS

HR 5 - RH 1	EC - CE
KY 3 - YK 1	TC - CT
UN 2 - NU 2	AK - KA
UB 2 - BU 1	ZC - CZ
TI 2 - IT 1	DT - TD

"Chart of Probable Position"

```
 E T/ D H  B C N Q R  K U
 D H
B C N Q R
K U
```

frequencies; and, with any appreciable length, there will be a generous sprinkling of reversals. In preparing the cryptogram, a great deal of convenience may be had by placing frequency figures beside their digrams, by marking long repeated sequences, noticeable reversals, and so on; and many persons like to list the most prominent pairs and the most prominent reversals.

The Playfair has also a rather characteristic frequency count. Notice, in the figure, where the general count has been rearranged in the order of decreasing frequencies, that the gradation from high to low is somewhat less even than in a periodic; frequency 8, for instance, is skipped altogether, and we have a sort of modified high-frequency group. Sometimes we find from one to three letters of great prominence before the downward gradation begins.

Concerning the " chart of probable position," most solvers prefer simply to keep this in mind, while others will actually set it down and make it the basis of their solution. With 176 letters of text, the average frequency of letters is about 7 (176 divided by 25). Any letter whose frequency is above that average is very likely to have been standing on the same row or in the same column of the key-square as E or T, and the two or three which lead the list are practically sure to have been substitutes for one of these two letters.

With cryptograms of the present length, or even with those of 400 to 600 letters, it is very uncertain as to whether or not the leading pair will represent th, or the leading reversal *er-re*. Here, in fact, we have no reversal of a definitely frequent character, and our one prominent pair, *HR*, might just as well represent *st, at, it, on, re, se*, or any other normally frequent digram capable of being used at the beginning of a sentence. Presuming, however, that it might represent *th*, we know that this digram is followed almost altogether by vowels, and is followed with remarkable frequency by *e* and *a;* we know also that letters have individual substitutes. Thus, we might begin solution by listing (or noting) those pairs which, in the cryptogram, have followed the supposed *th: KY, DU, KY, CE, NU*, assuming that their first letters, *K, D, C, N*, have probably represented vowels, and that, of these, *D, C*, and *N*, which rank high in the list of single-letter frequencies, are very likely to have represented *e*. We may attempt to identify these five pairs by working down the list of normal digrams, taking only those of *v-c* formation. If, in addition, it is assumed that the key-square has been filled by straight horizontals, certain assumptions can be made through possible alphabetical sequence; for instance, the *U* of *DU* and *NU* may have stood on the same line with *R S T (U)*. There is a further field for suggestions to be found in *patterns*, such as *TI BI*, in which the two *I*'s could represent the same letter. And where the square is filled by straight horizontals, it is often possible to identify such a sequence as *HZ HB* as a " split double," since the null used in these cases is often *X*, and *Z* may well represent *X* by alphabetical position. It is even possible to guess here a doubled *L*, since *H* and *L* are not far apart in the alphabet. (It may be, of course, that the two *H*'s represent two different letters.) The foregoing, then, has indicated the general path. If the student desires to follow out a detailed demonstration made on a cryptogram of only moderate length, a most excellent exposition can be found in the appendix to the Macbeth translation of Langie's " Cryptography " (Dutton). It was written by Lt. Commander W. W. Smith of the U. S. Navy, and generally speaking, attacks the identifications of pairs as follows:

Having placed frequency figures beside their digrams, find those points at which two pairs of high frequency are consecutive (not necessarily a repeated sequence), and attempt to identify these tetragrams as frequent tetragrams of the language: *ther, ered, ened, tion, atio, ment, beca,* and so on. We have one here, provided a frequency of 3 can be considered important: *HR KY*. Since this happens also to be repeated, it probably represents a word, as *that, this, they*.

Another good demonstration, provided the student has access to it in his public library, is found in Colonel Parker Hitt's " Manual for the Solution of Military Ciphers." This manual is an elementary work intended for the preliminary instruction of soldiers, and the attack is made on the assumption of a key-square filled by straight horizontals. With a square of the kind we are using, most of the vowels and high-frequency letters will be standing on the upper two rows, and letters on the first two or three rows will have a much higher frequency than those of the last two or three. In fact, it can often be detected that the letters *V W X Y Z* were standing on the bottom row as an intact alphabetical sequence, for the simple reason that they have no frequency in the cryptogram.

Colonel Hitt's demonstration begins with the usual pair-count, made on a chart. He selects from this chart the (approximately) ten letters having the *widest variety of contact*, including, if necessary, the vowel or so which would have to be present in a key-word; and these letters are assumed to have stood on the upper rows of the key-square. The remaining (approximately) fifteen letters are then set up in their alphabetical sequence and are assumed to have stood on the lower rows in about that order. They are not, of course, known to be correctly placed; the set-up merely gives a concrete idea as to where letters ought to have stood. Then, following the military case of abundant material, it is assumed that the leading pair will represent *th* (sure to be followed often by *e*), or, if *th* is not the leader, then *he* (sure to be preceded often by *t*). With a few obvious identifications made in the usual way, letters begin to arrange themselves on the upper rows, and a gradual adjustment takes place which corrects the few wrong assumptions of the lower rows, so that the key-square is restored far in advance of solution. When a short key-word has been used, it is not impossible, by following Colonel Hitt's suggestions, to pick out all of the key-letters, guess the word, and decipher with the key-square. Other demonstrations, based, respectively, on French and Italian language characteristics, can be found in General Givierge's *Cours de cryptographie* and in General Sacco's *Manuale di crittografia*. (In the French work, the cipher is referred to simply as " orthogonal and diagonal substitution.")

It will be seen from the foregoing that the initial difficulty lies in the correct identification of the first few pairs, and this, in a short cryptogram, is no small difficulty. By whatever means it is found possible to make these first tentative

Figure 168

POSSIBLE RELATIONSHIPS

(a) A 3-letter Equation

Vertical	Horizontal
T	
H	T H R
R	

(b) A 4-letter Equation

Vertical	Horizontal	Rectangular
I		I . K
K		
.	I K . S Y	. .
S		
Y		Y . S

(c) Impossible Equations:

```
co nd em na ti on
EO ND EC TC TI AD
```

(d) Possible Equations:

```
-c on de mn at io n-
EO ND EC TC TI AD CT
```

identifications, the operation which is to admit or disprove their correctness is step No. 2, in which we set them up as equations and then attempt to replace them into their connected relationships in the key-square. If this cannot be done, they cannot be correct; and, on the other hand, it would be an extremely rare case indeed in which we could combine as many as five or six such equations into one framework and then find them incorrectly matched. To understand " equations," suppose we look at Fig. 168.

Assuming that the beginning pairs of our cryptogram, *HR KY*, represent the word *this*, we have two equations, *HR = th*, and *KY = is*. The first of these has only three different letters, since *H* is common to both members, while the second has four different letters. With the first case (a), one of the lineal encipherments must have been used, and the common letter, *H*, must have stood between the other two, with its plaintext partner coming first and its cryptogram partner coming last. We do not know whether these three letters stood in a column or in a row, but we do know that they were consecutive. This relationship may be expressed simply as *T H R*, even though, in the actual square, the letters may have been partly at the end of the row (or column) and partly at the beginning: *H R * * T*, or *R * * T H*. Encipherment, remember, is cyclical, and we may come out with any one of numerous " equivalent squares." With the second equation (b), the positions of letters are not so definite. In either of the lineal encipherments, *IK* must be in direct sequence and *SY* must be in direct sequence; either sequence may have come first, and we do not know the exact location of the fifth letter. Concerning their possible rectangular encipherment, all we know is that there must have been a parallel relationship; their distance apart, laterally or vertically, might have been anything permitted by the key-square. As to the rest of the figure, suppose that we have reason to suspect the presence in this cryptogram of the word " condemnation." The equations of (c) are totally impossible, since, in Playfair, no letter may be its own substitute. Those of (d) are not only possible, but probable, since we find many letters from the word itself.

Figure 169

Equations of (d),(Fig.168)				Possible Combinations			
<u>1</u>	<u>2</u>	<u>3</u>	<u>4</u>	<u>5</u>	<u>6</u>	<u>7</u>	<u>8</u>
O		D		O			
N	O N D	E	D E C	N	O N D	O	
D		C		D	E	N	O N D E C
				E	C	D E C	
				C			

<u>9</u>	<u>10</u>	<u>11</u>		<u>12</u>			
M							
T		M . T		O N D E C			
.	M T . N C	. .		. .			
N		C . N		T	M		
C							

<u>13</u>	<u>14</u>			<u>15</u>		<u>16</u>	
A				O N D E C		O N D E C	
T	A T I			. .		. .	
I				A		A T I M	
				T	M		
				I			

To learn whether or not the word " condemnation " does (or could) occur here, we proceed as in Fig. 169. The first of the five equations may have had either one of the relationships marked 1 and 2, and the second may have had either of the relationships marked 3 and 4. These two equations have a letter *D* in common, and it must not be impossible to form a combination which will represent both. This, as it happens, can be done in four different ways, marked 5, 6, 7, and 8, and we do not know which of the four is most likely. The third equation, which has four different letters, may have had any one of relationships 9, 10, and 11. These, fortunately, show two letters, *N* and *C*, which are also present in combinations 5, 6, 7, and 8, and with two common letters, there will not be so many possible adjustments as when we had only one. Nos. 9 and 10, for instance, cannot possibly combine with any one of combinations 5, 6, 7, and 8; both of these have demanded that the letters *NC* be in direct sequence, where the first four combinations will not permit this. We may begin, then, by discarding Nos. 9 and 10. But No. 11, which we have retained, demands of *C* and *N* only that they be on the same row. This is not permitted by any one of combinations 5, 6, or 7, and these also may be discarded. But No. 8 shows them on the same row; thus Nos. 8 and 11 may be further combined, and we have the combination marked 12. The fourth equation, another lineal one, may have had either of the relationships marked 13 and 14, and both of these will combine easily with the combination marked 12, so that again we have more than one possibility, as indicated under numbers 15 and 16. As to which of these is correct, the fifth equation, *io = AD*, is impossible to one, and has automatically been set up in the other.

We are safe, now, in making substitutions on the cryptogram. This means not only the five pairs originally identified, together with their reversals and possible reciprocals, but all others which can be derived from combination 16, such as

Figure 170

```
O * * E     N * E     DE     EC
•           •         •       •
A           T         I       M
```

om = CA, or *dm = CI*, or *en = DC*, together with their reversals and possible reciprocals. Then, too, there will be many partial equations, such as those indicated in Fig. 170, where one letter of a pair can be identified. Usually time is saved by taking cryptogram pairs just as they come and filling in as many letters as possible; in this way, patterns are sometimes brought out, and thus we come back to step 1: the identification of more pairs. With the key-square beginning to shape up, the " chart of probable position " may be used to good advantage. For instance, what about the letters *H* and *B* which were very high in the frequency list?

Once a beginning is made, the cipher is broken, though just how rapidly we may proceed with the solution depends chiefly upon the manner in which the square has been filled. The presence of alphabetical sequences (either horizontal or vertical) will often enable us to complete the key-square independently of the cryptogram; but the badly mixed square must usually be built up to the very end, and we must sometimes be satisfied with one of the " equivalents " in place of the square originally used. If the student cares to make a fresh beginning of his own, this same cryptogram contains the word RECONSTRUCT.

The Playfair has been, in its day, a very effective cipher, and is still good for many purposes. It can be rendered much safer if subjected to the process called *seriation*. This process may be examined in Fig. 171. Here, the text is " Send

Figure 171

```
S E N D D     D S T O A     R D A M M
I A M O N     M X S T E     O N D A Y
```

diamonds to Amsterdam Monday," and the agreed *seriation index* is 5. The text is written in pairs of five-letter lines, so that each ten-letter segment forms five *vertical pairs*, SI, EA, NM, etc., and these are the pairs which undergo the digram encipherment (notice the treatment of the doubled *S* in the second group). If the key-square is that of Fig. 166, the first ten-letter segment is enciphered QK, UF, TG, SA, RS, and the cryptogram may be taken off in that order, or by taking the upper and lower lines separately: *Q U T S R   K F G A S*. Seriation, it will be noticed, adds a transposition to a substitution, so that what we have here is combination cipher. This case, in short examples, is extremely difficult; it is mentioned only by way of general information, and is not included in the practice cryptograms which follow.

149. By NEMO. (Playfair. Probable words: ENEMY AGENTS).

OS CF WD OG DR AN PO AS OA DH SD EH XK FU CN DR MS UK SD.

150. By NEMO. (Playfair. Probable words: AUTHORIZED, EMERGENCY).

PK HL PG RI YH YN HQ IF YF GY ZL EB YF UK NK NG FL FG OL BD GX GK FC PK HG NV AC ZL

KH PK FG FK RZ FG RQ XO IB PB BD LE MV KG GY OL AD FK OR FC LK YN HL LK KZ IF EF AX

NG ON BV IK BI PK IO HQ IF AG LX YA FK AD YG KO AK EG TO OH BI RB OL ON KM FO PK KY

PR EF DZ IF AY QH CZ OK IQ WP FG LF DM CA VO GW PK NG KX KO LH AG NB RT NG KO KH HK

OX ML GP ML PB QD RB OH EB LH NK NG FC PK KY QS LH NE IQ WP FG.

151. By PICCOLA. (Figure 164; new external alphabets. THE, THIS, CHARACTER).

NF BJ HT MD NF·WJ GD UC HN FW QI CE HP NF IA SE HS HS LG QA IY QD HV CC LB NF IA IA

CL GA RJ BD NM MA SY KU RD FT HC US HN GH VJ UA SY UL HN XJ EG QQ CJ LB NF KJ CN CS

UK GJ MD NF IA FK NQ GJ XX.

152. By PICCOLA. ("Slidefair." Probable word: DESCENT).

AA FS AF XY GJ BD UI AA PW GN IV QZ RC NK CC WA FT QQ PR GP TT WF PS JS QC HM DI XC

AH JP FB DC EW OX UG GP UI US CV GP MH QR OG JI ZR.

153. By DAN SURR. (Playfair. History: Detective Gettamann, investigating the
murder of Franois V. Bacon, well-known traveler, explorer, and
connoisseur, has found this message in an envelope addressed
to Wm. K. Pierce, former traveling companion of the deceased.
Death had occurred during sleep; caused by strangulation with
red silk thread. Only clues found: a few grains of sand on the
kitchen floor and what appears to be an oriental turban).

YG NG CR FV FZ RI OU KZ CW OW BQ GQ IH HL YW EG NG QM WX RT KP VE CA IG QI VD QI GN

GZ IZ QY QR HY NG XN AB AK OX NY WC WC TN OX DH NE IH IH YR IS QY WC HI UI UI IR QE

WS RW LG WR AB GW VW CA RQ XM ER QM RE CW ZI RQ XW QW GH YC AY YO VO NE RL PG CG WI

NX VW CA NX QM LH IG RQ WT GO UI GZ EG XN IW OU XT WO LH IG RQ XM WS QY TX IR IQ XM

OG DU AB RM AK UM RG ZR XA PM RW LD KG HI XK LC RT KP VE FO NX XK WR WS QY UR ZX YL

AT UI RH TR AV WS DH WQ PM AK IW OU WT DE IR WX RQ XZ SI GU QN IR XN IR YN IG GY TR

ZX YU RU YL IQ YA RU KG QM PD QM IY HA WS FE RW GH RB HA QI QM GI QC QR UL WV AB NX

GO HA FR IY QY BN QM YH NG IQ RU YL IQ BL PK QM RU GU IR TX SI GQ LQ DX XO EV BM CR

FV GV AB GE RZ GQ YH HA RW YM NE YM BL VW PS.

CHAPTER XXII

HIGHLIGHTS OF FRACTIONAL SUBSTITUTION

Fractional substitution requires a cipher alphabet of the " multifid " type; that is, one in which the symbols are composed of two or more units, as in the Bacon and Trithemius alphabets (Chapter *II:* Figs. 3 and 4), the various " checkerboards " (Chapter *XI*), and so on. Polygram " alphabets " are also of this type, and seriation is a form of fractional substitution.

Among the older fractionals, we find a system called the " Pollux," in which the basis was the Morse telegraphic alphabet. There were three units, the dot, the dash, and a separator (made necessary by the irregular lengths of the substitutes). There

Figure 172

Delastelle's "BIFID" Substitution -(Keyword Feature Added by M. E. OHAVER)

Preparation of Alphabet:

```
G E N * R A L
B C D F H I K
M O P Q S T U
V W X Y Z
```

Checkerboard Key:

```
      1 2 3 4 5
  1   G B M V E
  2   C O W N D
  3   P X F Q Y
  4   R H S Z A
  5   I T L K U
```

Substitutes:

```
S = 43
E = 15
N = 24
D = 25
```

Preliminary Substitution:

```
S E N D S U P    P L I E S T O    M O R L E Y S    R I G H T A W    A Y.
4 1 2 2 4 5 3    3 5 5 1 4 5 2    1 2 4 5 1 3 4    4 5 1 4 5 4 2    4 3
3 5 4 5 3 5 1    1 3 1 5 3 2 2    3 2 1 3 5 5 3    1 1 1 2 2 6 3    5 5
```

Re-Substitution:

```
41 22 45 33 54 53 51    35 51 45 21 31 53 22    12 45 13 43 21 35 53
R  O  A  F  K  L  I     Y  I  A  C  P  L  O     B  A  M  S  C  Y  L

45 14 54 21 11 22 53    43 55     Transmitted:
A  V  K  C  G  O  L     S  U.     R O A F K   L I Y I A   C P L O B, etc.
```

was a first substitution in which the letters of the text were replaced with their Morse symbols, including the space. The resulting cryptogram, composed entirely of the units dot, dash, space (. — x), was then subjected to a second substitution, using a small cipher alphabet (either digits or letters) in which each one of the three units might have any one of several different substitutes, chosen at will. For instance, a dot might be replaced with any one of digits 1, 8, 5, 6, a space with any one of digits 3, 9, 0, and a dash with any one of digits 2, 4, 7.

We find also a number of systems called " Collon " in which the basis is some one of the " checkerboards." The text is subjected to a simple substitution in the agreed alphabet, and the resulting cryptogram is then subjected to a transposition, usually seriation, this being the final operation.

A similar system called the " Mirabeau " uses an alphabet of the same type as that of the *Polybius square,* in which only the digits 1-2-3-4-5 are significant. The remaining digits are all null, and numbers like 67 or 88 may be inserted at will. Numbers are written vertically (tens below units); then, in the taking off of the cryptograms, the whole series of units is taken first, and the second half of the cryptogram includes all of the tens-digits. In all of these forms, the undesirable features are self-evident. The later devices have added another operation: the regrouping of the scattered units, and their reconversion into letters.

Classic examples are those described by Delastelle as "bifid" and "trifid" (terms, incidentally, which some of our own writers find objectionable, as they do also the term "multifid"). Delastelle's "bifid" cipher was of the kind shown in Fig. 172. A two-unit alphabet must be used, and all possible two-unit combinations must be convertible into letters. Any desired seriation-length may be agreed upon,

Figure 173

A Fractional Substitution Based on Morse Symbols - M.E.OHAVER

The Alphabet, Arranged by Group-Lengths:

E .	S ...	H	B -...
T -	U ..-	V ...-	X -..-
	R .-.	F ..-.	C -.-.
	W .--	ü ..--	Y -.--
I ..	D -..	L .-..	Z --..
A .-	K -.-	á .-.-	Q --.-
N -.	G --.	P .--.	ö ---.
M --	O ---	J .---	ch ----

S	E	N	D	S	U	P							
...	.	-.	-..	...	..-	.--.		Reverse digits, and re-group:					
3	1	2	3	3	3	4		4	3	3	3	2	1	3
								....	-.-	...	...	.-	.	--.
								H	K	S	S	A	E	G

though it should not be divisible by 2. In the figure, the key-word GENERAL, 7 letters, governs the seriation-length as well as the mixing of the key-square, a feature suggested by Ohaver. The substitution is identical with that of the Polybius square, except that the two units of the substitute are written vertically below the original. Digits are then grouped horizontally in pairs, treating one seven-letter group at a time (if the seriation index is 7), and these pairs are replaced with letters from the same key-square. It will be noticed that we have here a form of polygram substitution, in which one seven-letter group has been replaced with another. Also, that possible errors have been confined by the seriation feature to their own seven-letter group.

Delastelle's "trifid" cipher was of the same kind, except that a three-unit alphabet was required, resulting in three rows of units. It would have been the same as that of Fig. 4, Chapter II, but with the French accented E replacing the character &. All combinations of three units must be re-convertible into letters.

Fig. 173 shows a form of "mutilation" cipher once published by Ohaver. Beyond stating that its only key is the group-length (7 in the example), we leave the student to figure it out for himself.

As an example of recent use (1918), we are told on excellent authority that the Germans, for quite a long time during the World War, used a field cipher of the following description: There was a preliminary substitution using a key-square of the Nihilist type, except that the external co-ordinates were letters, and not digits, and were chosen in such a way that the five or six letters used were letters having very distinctive Morse symbols; this was for the avoidance of telegraphic errors.

In some cases a 5 x 5 square was used, containing only a 25-letter mixed alphabet, and in others a 6 x 6 square containing a 26-letter mixed alphabet and all of the digits. The preliminary cryptogram obtained from this first encipherment was then written into a transposition block and taken off by columns, using key-word columnar transposition. The cryptograms were not afterward shortened by resubstitution, but were always twice as long as their messages, and never contained any other letters than the five (or six) originally used as co-ordinates. This German Field Cipher proved very effective until finally broken by the great French analytical genius, Georges Painvin.

We shall make no attempt, here, to go into the decryptment of these ciphers. The Delastelle " bifid " is, perhaps, a practical cipher, and the student may try his own hand at analyzing the example. The other examples should give no trouble.

154. By PICCOLA. (Delastelle's "Bifid." - Repeated words: AMERICA(N), ATTEMPT, REPORT, THAT, THE, OF, TO. Other short words: FROM, WITH, BEEN, HAVE. Likely words: REPORT, AGENT, CONFIRM, CABLE, etc).

```
Q I N H P    R M L M G    R N B M A    H G T O L    O O E L O    A O D R I    N H W R O

A A B M M    I M M W I    B M D A B    T H D I L    T H T H I    N T L A Q    M C A M F

I V N K Y    N O F H B    I I T R F    Q L A D K    V Q I N H    P R M R B    H S L L U

A B M E T    S O A A B    M M I M M    I B P I V    R Q F T K    H I R D F    G N I E M

A B E N I    L M M P A    S I F I O    P L Y C C    R C I T W    I V W M F    G I O O S

O E R O I    K Q I E F    O V N V M    Q T D R S    I O E R I    B U Q C D    O A L L A

P L A A O    O C A Q O    M E I D C    N T I U L    O L Z D G.
```

The mixed alphabet here was placed in the square by straight horizontals. History: Message intercepted following a report that on the tenth of August an attempt had been made to enter the American embassy in a country where Royalists are opposed to a group of radicals.

155. By PICCOLA. (Fractional. - Not so hard).

```
3 3 3 2 3    1 1 1 2 3    2 2 1 3 1    1 1 1 3 1    3 3 1 1 3    2 2 1 2 2    1 1 2 3 1

2 3 3 2 1    2 3 3 1 1    3 2 1 1 2    1 2 2 2 3    1 2 2 2 3    1 1 2 2 1    2 3 2 3 2

2 1 2 3 1    3 3 2 3 1    1 2 2 1 3    2 1 2 2 3    2 1 3 1 2    2 2 2 3 2    3 2 2 2 2

3 1 1 1 3    1 2 3 2 1    1 2 2 2 3    2 3 1 3 2    2 2 2 1 2    3 1 2 2 1    2 1 2 2 1

1 2 2 3 2    3 2 2 3 2    2 2 3 2 2    3 3 1 2 2    3 1 2 1 3    1 1 1 1 2    1 3 3 3 3

1 2 3 3 3    2 1 3 3 1    1 1 1 2 2    3 1 1 3 1    1 1 1 1 1    1 1 3 2 2    1 2 3 2 2

2 1 2 1 2    1 2 2 2 3    3 2 2 1 3.
```

156. By PICCOLA. (Fractional. - Nor is this very hard).

```
EDCYB   AZCBZ   AVWXC   XBAEY   DCBVA   EDWBX   AEYZD

AEZVW   DCAED   XCBYD   YZVCB   WBAZV   EWXBX   AEYDC

BVAEW   DCXAE   YZDCE   ZVDWC   BEDXC   BYAZD   CBVWA

AEDCB   AEEWD   CBXYD   CYZBV   ABAZV   EWXAE   WDCXY

EDYZC   BVEDC   WBAXE   DZVCB   ACBVW   AXYXB   YAEDZ

EYZDV   WCWED   XCBAD   YZVCB   ADCWB   AXEED   CBAVE

DCXYB   ZAEDC   BAEWD   YZCVB   ABAZV   EWXED   VWCXY

XDCYB   AZCZB   AVEWB   AEWDX   YEDXY   CZVVE   DWCBA.
```

CHAPTER XXIII

INVESTIGATING THE UNKNOWN CIPHER

When the type of encipherment is unknown, the decryptor's first problem may concern the probable language used in the plaintext, and this he is usually able to determine from the source and history of the cryptogram.

His second problem is the major classification, and this, too, is usually simple, since transposition, as a rule, can be recognized by its appearance. It must, however, respond to a group-test, and for cases in which this is needed, the approximate percentages for English can be taken as follows:

Vowels, with or without Y,	about 40%	(Variation limits: 35% to 45%)
Consonants L N R S T	about 30%	(Variation limits: 25% to 35%)
Consonants J K Q X Z	about 2%	(May be influenced by nulls).

The 5% variation is suggested in the Parker Hitt Manual. In this connection, it should be pointed out that an apparent transposition with exactly 40% of vowels and 100% evenness in their distribution is suspicious. Many of the checkerboard systems result in this way, and also some of the codes based on pronounceable five-letter groups. Then, too, it is easily possible to construct a simple substitution cipher in such a way that the resulting cryptograms will resemble transposition, and even respond satisfactorily to a group-test. It should be carefully ascertained that a supposed transposition cryptogram does not contain the many repeated sequences which belong to simple substitution. As to those transpositions which do show an appreciable number of repeated digrams, they will probably have undergone one of the route transpositions, especially one in which columns were taken off in alternating directions.

Concerning the characteristics of simple substitution, these have been seen throughout the text; we have normal frequencies attached to the wrong letters, and we have those numerous repetitions of various lengths, occurring at all kinds of intervals, which are never found in a transposition. Here, too, we may apply a group test, based only on the relative frequencies of letters. The five most frequent are supposed to represent the letters $E\ T\ A\ O\ N$ or their equivalents, and should total about 45% of the text. The nine most frequent should total about 70%; the eleven most frequent well over 75%; the five of lowest frequency (which would include all of those totally absent) should correspond to the normal behavior of the group $J\ K\ Q\ X\ Z$.

If the simple substitution frequency count is present without the repeated sequences, then we probably have a combination of simple substitution with transposition. It becomes necessary to rewrite the cryptogram into various new arrangements until one is found which will bring back the repeated sequences. Ordinarily, the simplest kinds of transposition will have been used; sometimes the transposition will have taken place in a complete-unit block, and there will be a clue in the total number of letters present in the cryptogram.

When all letters are present in the frequency count (or all but one or two in the possible cases of 25-letter and 24-letter alphabets), a period-investigation is usually indicated. The case of periodics has been seen at considerable length, though a final hint might be added for the detection of a possible Porta encipherment. One of our many collaborators, F. R. Carter, suggests that any Porta cryptogram, periodic or otherwise, ought to show from 52% to 53% of letters N to Z — the opposite of normal.

The characteristics of digram-encipherment have been mentioned. Other polygram ciphers show corresponding characteristics, according to the polygram length, though the trail grows fainter as polygrams grow longer. A trigram-system, for instance, might be present when the cryptogram is evenly divisible into three-letter groups; it might suggest period 3, and might even show repeated sequences whose length is a multiple of 3 and which begin at serial positions such as 1, 4, 7, 10, which are the beginnings of trigrams. A great many of the trigram systems will show only repeated digrams beginning at these serial positions, or separated by intervals which are divisible by 3.

A 5 x 5 square is often suggested in the fact of a missing letter; but the fact of 26 letters does not deny one, since the careful encipherer may make use of his missing J instead of using I exclusively. Great evenness in frequencies may suggest one of the key-lengthening devices, such as autokey and progressing key; and the practical absence of repeated sequences will usually mean that a transposition has been added to a substitution. It is never a bad idea, in a puzzling example, to make the various digram-counts (in chart form): An actual digram count, in which every letter is considered the beginning of a digram; a pair-count on separated pairs, as in Playfair; the two counts which could be made with the cryptogram marked off into three-letter groups; and the kind of pair-count which could be made in Playfair if the first cryptogram-letter were omitted. Many devices, as mentioned, may be uncovered simply by " running down the alphabet." And if the cryptogram has come from an amateur " inventor," it may be a case of digging into one's memory for previous " inventions." With this last case, however, the " inventor " very often fails to submit material in proportion to the amount of complication he has introduced.

Of the examples to follow, there is none in which the system may not be learned through analysis, unless perhaps the final unnumbered cryptogram, and the material, in every case, should be sufficient for solution.

No. 163 follows Mr. Berkley's encipherment plan, illustrated just above it.

No. 164 is said to have been taken from a German spy serving in the American army in France. This applies, however, to the first fifty groups only; the remainder was added to increase the length and to emphasize the plan followed by the spy.

No. 166 was accompanied by a plot:

" Supposed to have been found on the body of a man floating in San Diego Bay. Autopsy shows death by drowning. Victim was a local banker who had disappeared a few days earlier. Wife says no financial worries. No money missing. Banker had prospered during depression. Was yachting enthusiast. Our hero solved the cipher with the unconscious assistance of a radio crooner. Tragedy occurred in *August, 1932.*" The date was doubly underscored, but those who have read the message have found no reason for this and no explanation for the " crooner."

157. By PICCOLA.

```
CSRZV  YPQZJ  KHKVQ  UUCVM  RTWZN  GHQSA  KOXPM
HDRWA  JDFQD  FSRZZ  CGXPA  JJTZU  LHTGS  AEXJJ
LTRNN  ZPBZG  REBNF  YGEJN  MTNJJ  QHPJX  MOBJA
LXIAI  CPFJO  OFRNH.
```

158. By PICCOLA.

```
OCEEA  TTITK  SNDTD  STHOO  YEAOE  EPEBO  TYTAO
ADSEO  ETFTT  THRVW  CTHOY  LTOOH  LRBTT  UHRRV
RAWOB  RUAOY  EHHLA  BNERL  RKVCR  IONSE  IDRUE
RIP.
```

159. By TITOGI.

```
AHYNU  HCEST  ITNDO  RFEHR  WEATF  NRFPA  OTMAT
LHFEI  OTNRL  ODRHE  EATES  CTDIN  WTSTO  EATSI
TECDU  TMSOT  RLDON  GNIIS  OFAET  LITAS.
```

160. By PICCOLA. (Veiled reference to crypt No. 166?)

(a) HZMQL DNNDZ SPRFS KLLLL.　　(b) LILVM STZUG
DHZUQ XLLLL.　　(c) TVIUM FRUOY UQYPS FWXLL.
(d) LILVM FPOEY ZKFDV UELLL.　　(e) GKPVD ZTAYT
BFYYC FIULL.　　(f) QBFPW YCLUD VPZZO SWYNC.
(g) QBRTF FGVTU ENSZH BQERL.

161. By PICCOLA.

```
EGWGW  GEGTU  CLCUO  XGKZT  EGOBG  BYLWM  IQNKQ
YENFS  CLHMN  YBXSE  TNIWO  CEGCB  FCTCS  ZTVGB
EAEGT  URKFK  BEGKX  BCTGZ  YLXCH  YEGCU  OXYTQ
FADQT  TCUNB  OGCOH  XCEWE  CUVEG  COCXY  XGBEA
YTKXF  QCOTB  XNEGT  UCONT  OPELE  KUVUN  TOCNG
NGBKW  CEECS  ZKWNH  EIKCC  REGCT  EGTUR  KFKTB
RGMWX  CFGQN  ICEBP  EEWEN  BKIYF  KFDOF  EGNUC
BGMTZ  TFXCE  WECPV  DTTUZ  TENEG  WGLFM  CTOV1
```

162. By PICCOLA.

```
SPPAS  TASEF  UNMTE  HSOOA  ESLEI  CTRCH  VUGSE
LYREM  ENEER  OSNEH  IRAET  ORNSH  MODRO  PEAOR
POSRY  PDOIN  OCKGT.
```

The "NICODEMUS" Cipher (Harold Berkley) SPECIMEN ENCIPHERMENT

```
Key:   M E T H O D I C      M E T H O D I C      M E T...
       6 3 8 4 7 2 5 1     '6 3 8 4 7 2 5 1      6 3 8...
                                                               Cryptogram:
       T H I S I S E N      A N S P O S E D      E T C...
       C I P H E R E D      U S I N G T H E             PFGVT   VUHDG  LMRIV
       I N V I G E N E      S A M E K E Y F      ZOPUH   MMVNB   FOUDQ  WSURF
       R E A N D A F T      O R B O T H O P      BIOTP   FGHRU   VWHKR  RWEVV
       E R W A R D T R      E R A T I O N S
                                             WULVA MPGWV  MGEAQ   CUYHW  LBFUT.
```

163. By PICCOLA.

```
T Y D Q V   W P A Z O   M B W B I   R K F I O   O G W C O   G E F L T   Q M S R F

X T C J C   M A W P P   Q M E X V   O Q C O C   Z F S F W   V F E V E   R S A B E

C V J J W   S I P P H   M M K O X   V Y I D B   D B C I S   Y N L J C   Y F K C W

E N Z E I   T J V L Z   M I L I I   R W K R O   O S Z A W   E K J V J   G F M Q K

G F N C K   H P B R D   L V I A P   E S L Y M   D J Z Z V   F Z F F R   D B A D P

Q W E N L   A L O E K   M F M F W   X O K D W   D G C K K   K C Q R V.
```

164. By VULPUS.

```
P E N A R   C P F T I   Q E V A T   E N B L A   T K Q F O   A R E N E   U I P E P

F U K X I   L C N F Q   E P C V B   T A W A O   B N C O E   T I N D W   B N A R D

Q F O F N   B V C P E   P G V G P   A V A P B   P F O A O   B S C L B   V B T F W

A N E W B   T C S D N   F M A N A   O E V A R   A R C T K   Q E N B M   B Q F V E

V B X K O   A P E T B   U I P F O   F Q E L E   O B R D R   B Q F U A   W A S C U

K L F P E   W B O C O   D N A M E   L G V F V   A N C N D   M F N B V   D T D L E

P F V I T   I Q E Q F   O C O A U   C L F L A   O B M E P   E N A S D   L B T K L

H N E P D.   .....     U I L A L   B O B M A   V K M G U   K R F P F   U B U D M

F W E T A   T I Q E V   B R C M B   W A N F Z   I L E N A   Q F W B T   C R D T B

T K O E P   E U A V A   O F N B S   C Z K V B   W C U B O   A L F O B   M E X I T

D Q C Q D   W A P F Q   E N A L A.
```

165. By PICCOLA. (Again that No. 166?)

```
R O V L L   A B T L D   L B C Q M   P X L B A   F B T C T   A T C O R   L T O L C

R H P D T   X L Y O A   E L B X P   H L X B T   X X Q L D   R G L T K   X R L G D

B K L D P   P L O H L   Y O A E L   K O M X B   L H O E L   V C R R C   R J L T K

D T L R C   I N X P L   L L T K X   L R C I N   X P L V D   B L V O R   L P O R J

L D J O L   F Y L I O   P O R X P   L M D E N   X E L K C   T T L V K   O L O H H

X E X G L   T O L I O   Q M E O Q   C B X L H   O E L T V   O L I X R   T B L B C

R I X L K   X L V D B   L D F P X   L T O L B   X R G L T   K X L B O   P A T C O

R L F Y L   E X T A E   R L Q D C   P L L B T   C P P L C   T L V O A   P G L F X

L V O E T   K L D R O   T K X E L   R C I N X   P L T O L   H C R G L   O A T L T

K X L N X   Y L L T K   C B L Q A   B T L F X   L T K X L   X W M P D   R D T C O
```

```
RLOHL   TKXLE   XHXEX   RIXLT   OLDLI   EOORX   ELDRG

LTKXL   XQMKD   BCBLO   RLDLG   DTXLL   MLBLT   KXLTV

OLIXR   TBLKD   BLROT   LYXTL   FXXRL   MDCGL.
```

166. By CACHE. (Contributor, C. H. Price, died without explaining his key).

```
03 65 12 45 58 28 06 41 72 14 22 03 02 17 36 88 25 20 55 77 74 51 23 45 41 42 30 24

36 61 96 09 07 78 05 44 08 06 55 92 16 93 02 15 36 37 40 87 42 01 33 77 06 36 27 54

43 29 16 78 92 66 03 10 38 17 45 23 72 96 73 01 49 25 72 38 92 72 24 55 48 08 40 92

28 01 72 96 02 04 74 61 06 99 30 45 72 69 74 93 77 23 55 36 24 93 47 84 76 35 32 89

87 76 77 64 51 96 58 43 76 02 81 38 87 69 89 55 99 23 79 55 51 06 99 71 74 69 89 84

27 25 22 39 42 53 19 93 41 66 09 75 87 37 91 87 90 91 43 19 40 30 38 16 96 22 69 38

78 02 74 92 47 25 77 91 15 40 24 45 07 07 96 48 44 15 12 06 99 44 93 19 25 23 55 30

45 87 96 18 01 78 44 29 45 86 47 69 48 30 66 44 03 41 66 37 38 22 06 42 41.
```
                                                                            59.

Here is one which nobody has ever been able to decrypt:

```
VQBUP   PVSPG   GFPNU   EDOKD   XHEWT   IYCLK   XRZAP

VUFSA   WEMUX   GPNIV   QJMNJ   JNIZY   KBPNF   RRHTB

WWNUQ   JAJGJ   FHADQ   LQMFL   XRGGW   UGWVZ   GKFBC

MPXKE   KQCQQ   LBODO   QJVEL.
```

APPENDIX

ENGLISH FREQUENCY AND SEQUENCE DATA

(Compiled from the MEAKER Digram Chart)

Order and Frequency of
Single Letters

E	1231	L	403	B	162
T	959	D	365	G	161
A	805	C	320	V	93
O	794	U	310	K	52
N	719	P	229	Q	20
I	718	F	228	X	20
S	659	M	225	J	10
R	603	W	203	Z	9
H	514	Y	188		

Group Percentages:

A E I O U	38.58%
L N R S T	33.43%
J K Q X Z	1.11%
E T A O N	45.08%
E T A O N I S R H	70.02%

Order and Frequency of
Leading DIGRAMS

TH	315	TO	111	SA	75	MA	56
HE	251	NT	110	HI	72	TA	56
AN	172	ED	107	LE	72	CE	55
IN	169	IS	106	SO	71	IC	55
ER	154	AR	101	AS	67	LL	55
RE	148	OU	96	NO	65	NA	54
ES	145	TE	94	NE	64	RO	54
ON	145	OF	94	EC	64	OT	53
EA	131	IT	88	IO	63	TT	53
TI	128	HA	84	RT	63	VE	53
AT	124	SE	84	CO	59	NS	51
ST	121	ET	80	BE	58	UR	49
EN	120	AL	77	DI	57	ME	48
ND	118	RI	77	LI	57	WH	48
OR	113	NG	75	RA	57	LY	47

List of Common REVERSALS:

ER RE	ON NO	TE ET	ST TS
ES SE	IN NI	OR RO	IS SI
AN NA	EN NE	TO OT	ED DE
TI IT	AT TA	AR RA	OF FO

Order of the Leading TRIGRAMS
In 10,000 Letters of Semi-Military Text - PARKER HITT

THE	ENT	FOR	NCE	OFT
AND	ION	NDE	EDT	STH
THA	TIO	HAS	TIS	MEN

INITIAL LETTERS OF WORDS:

Order, as found by M. E. OHAVER ... T A O   S H I W C   B P F D M R, etc.

Order, as found by H. O. YARDLEY .. T O A   W B C D S   F M R H I Y, etc.

FINAL LETTERS OF WORDS:

Order, as found by M. E. OHAVER ... E S T D N R O Y, etc.

Order, as found by H. O. YARDLEY .. E T D N S R Y, etc.

NOTE: Lists of terminals (letters, digrams, trigrams); of common affixes,
short words, and common pattern-words, can be found in the booklet
"CRYPTOGRAM SOLVING", obtainable from the author, M.E.Ohaver, at
Columbus, Ohio.

X J M M T   V O Z B N   Q M F B T   F S F N J   U G P S U   I J T B E ?

COMPARATIVE TABLE OF SINGLE-LETTER FREQUENCIES (Per 100)

ENGLISH		GERMAN		FRENCH		ITALIAN		SPANISH		PORTUGUESE	
A	7.81	A	5.	A	9.42	A	11.74	A	12.69	A	13.5
B	1.28	B	2.5	B	1.02	B	.92	B	1.41	B	.5
C	2.93	C	1.5	C	2.64	C	4.50	C	3.93	C	3.5
D	4.11	D	5.	D	3.38	D	3.73	D	5.58	D	5.
E	13.05	E	18.5	E	15.87	E	11.79	E	13.15	E	13.
F	2.88	F	1.5	F	.95	F	.95	F	.46	F	1.
G	1.39	G	4.	G	1.04	G	1.64	G	1.12	G	1.
H	5.85	H	4.	H	.77	H	1.54	H	1.24	H	1.
I	6.77	I	8.	I	8.41	I	11.28	I	6.25	I	6.
J	.23	J	...	J	.89	J	...	J	.56	J	.5
K	.42	K	1.	K	...	K	...	K	...	K	...
L	3.60	L	3.	L	5.34	L	6.51	L	5.94	L	3.5
M	2.62	M	2.5	M	3.24	M	2.51	M	2.65	M	4.5
N	7.28	N	11.5	N	7.15	N	6.88	N	6.95	N	5.5
O	8.21	O	3.5	O	5.14	O	9.83	O	9.49	O	11.5
P	2.15	P	.5	P	2.86	P	3.05	P	2.43	P	3.
Q	.14	Q	...	Q	1.06	Q	.61	Q	1.16	Q	1.5
R	6.64	R	7.	R	6.46	R	6.37	R	6.25	R	7.5
S	6.46	S	7.	S	7.90	S	4.98	S	7.60	S	7.5
T	9.02	T	5.	T	7.26	T	5.62	T	3.91	T	4.5
U	2.77	U	5.	U	6.24	U	3.01	U	4.63	U	4.
V	1.00	V	1.	V	2.15	V	2.10	V	1.07	V	1.5
W	1.49	W	1.5	W	...	W	...	W	...	W	...
X	.30	X	...	X	.30	X	...	X	.13	X	.2
Y	1.51	Y	...	Y	.24	Y	...	Y	1.06	Y	...
Z	.09	Z	1.5	Z	.32	Z	.49	Z	.35	Z	.3

Vowel Percentages:

English	German	French	Italian	Spanish	Portuguese
40%	40%	45%	48%	47%	48%

Percentages for L N R S T:

33%	34%	34%	30%	31%	29%

NOTES: ENGLISH frequencies, which may be compared with those of Mr. Meaker,

(A, 8.05; B, 1.62; C, 3.20; etc.), were taken from M.E.OHAVER.

FRENCH, ITALIAN, and SPANISH frequencies were taken from a count

made by the author. All four counts are based on 10,000 letters

of literary text, and the dropping of the decimal point gives

the actual count. The frequencies given for GERMAN and PORTUGUESE

are approximations, reduced from other texts, probably military.

Chart Showing Normal CONTACT PERCENTAGES – Compiled by F.R.CARTER

(Based on a Digram Chart by M.E.OHAVER)

%V (left)	%C (left)	Left contacts	Letter	Right contacts	%V (right)	%C (right)
19	81	$P_4 L_4 C_5 D_5 M_5 N_6 S_6 W_7 T_8 R_8 E_{11} H_{14}$	A	$N_{21} T_{17} S_{12} R_{10} L_8 D_5 C_4 M_4$	6	94
55	45	$Y_4 B_4 N_5 T_5 U_8 D_9 O_9 S_{10} A_{16} E_{16}$	B	$E_{34} L_{17} U_{11} O_9 A_7 Y_5 B_4 R_2$	70	30
61	39	$U_4 O_5 S_8 N_{13} A_{13} I_{18} E_{20}$	C	$H_9 O_{10} E_{17} A_{13} I_7 T_6 R_4 L_4 K_4$	59	41
52	48	$R_4 I_5 L_6 A_{10} N_{29} S_{39}$	D	$E_{16} I_{14} T_{14} O_8 S_6 U_5$	54	46
8	92	$C_4 B_4 E_5 M_5 V_5 D_5 S_5 L_5 N_6 T_6 R_6 R_{11} T_{24}$	E	$R_{15} D_{10} S_9 N_8 A_7 T_6 M_5 E_4 C_4 O_4 W_4$	21	79
69	31	$S_4 N_5 F_5 D_5 A_6 I_7 E_{12} O_{41}$	F	$T_{22} O_{21} E_{10} I_9 A_7 R_5 F_5 U_4$	52	48
36	64	$O_4 D_4 U_5 R_5 I_9 E_9 A_{10} N_{48}$	G	$E_{14} H_{12} O_{12} R_{10} A_8 T_6 I_5 W_4 I_4 S_4$	42	58
7	93	$F_4 M_4 W_5 E_6 N_6 L_6 D_8 S_8 R_9 H_{11} T_{14}$	H	$E_{50} A_{23} I_{12} O_7$	90	10
13	87	$F_4 M_4 W_5 E_6 N_6 L_6 D_8 S_9 R_9 H_{11} T_{14}$	I	$N_{25} T_{13} S_{10} O_8 C_7 R_4 E_4 M_4 A_4 L_4$	17	83
28	72	$Y_7 W_7 T_7 S_7 N_7 E_7 C_7 B_7 A_{14} M_{29}$	J	$U_{35} O_{29} A_{12} E_{12} M_6 W_6$	88	12
53	47	$V_5 U_5 I_5 N_7 A_{11} R_{13} E_{13} C_{15} U_{18}$	K	$E_{34} I_{21} N_{10} A_9 T_7 S_6$	68	32
52	48	$N_4 P_4 T_6 I_7 B_7 U_7 O_{10} F_{11} L_{11} A_{17}$	L	$E_{19} I_{15} Y_{12} L_{12} O_9 A_8 D_7 U_4$	65	35
69	31	$S_4 D_4 M_5 R_5$	M	$E_{26} A_{17} O_{12} I_{11} P_5 M_5$	71	29
21	79	$S_4 D_4 R_5 I_? A_{13} O_{16} E_{24}$	N	$D_{16} T_{14} G_{12} E_{10} A_7 S_7 O_7 I_6 C_5$	32	68
47	53	$M_4 O_4 D_4 L_4 P_4 H_5 N_6 A_7 G_8 U_{10} R_{20} S_{30}$	O	$N_{20} F_{14} R_{11} U_{10} T_6 M_5 L_5 S_4 W_4 O_4$	18	82
20	80	$P_5 I_5 U_5 T_7 A_{13} O_{16} E_{30}$	P	$O_{17} E_{16} A_{15} R_{15} L_9 P_6 T_5 I_5 S_4$	59	41
70	30	$O_{10} U_{10} O_{10} I_{10} O_{10} R_{20} S_{30}$	Q	U_{100}	100	–
48	52	$P_5 L_5 U_5 T_7 A_{13} O_{16} E_{30}$	R	$E_{23} O_{12} A_{11} T_{11} I_{10} S_7 Y_4$	61	39
43	57	$D_4 T_4 O_6 U_6 R_7 N_8 S_9 I_{11} A_6 E_{18}$	S	$T_{19} E_{11} O_{10} I_9 S_9 A_8 B_6 P_5 U_4$	41	59
35	65	$U_4 O_5 D_6 I_6 R_7 B_7 E_8 I_{10} N_{10} S_{13} A_{14}$	T	$H_{39} I_{10} O_{10} E_8 A_7 T_6 R_4$	38	62
88	12	$R_4 L_4 T_4 N_4 I_4 P_6 M_6 A_7 O_8 U_{10}$	U	$N_{18} S_{13} T_{13} R_{12} L_{10} P_7 B_4 C_4$	8	92
48	52	$R_6 F_5 S_5 B_6 D_8 S_9 O_{30}$	V	$E_{65} I_{14} O_9 A_8$	99	1
95	5	$R_6 U_{10} O_{16} A_{16} E_{20}$	W	$A_{27} H_{16} I_{16} E_{15} O_{11} N_4$	80	20
24	76	$G_4 D_4 I_5 S_{10} I_{11} E_{23}$	X	$P_{29} I_{19} I_{14} A_{14} U_{10} C_5 K_5 O_5$	38	62
88	12	$B_4 N_8 A_8 E_{13} E_{14} R_{15} L_{15} T_{25}$	Y	$A_{15} O_{12} S_{12} T_9 W_7 H_5 I_5 E_5 D_4 M_4 B_4$	38	62
88	12	$O_{12} N_{12} A_{25} I_{50}$	Z	$E_{43} I_{43} W_{14}$	86	14

All figures indicate PERCENTAGES. – Taking any one letter, as A: On the left, it was contacted 14% of the time by H, 11% by E, etc., and 81% of its total contacts on that side were consonants. On the right, it was contacted 21% of the time by N, and 94% of the time by consonants.

Chart Showing FREQUENCIES of English DIGRAMS - Prepared by O. PHELPS MEAKER

(Actual Count, Made on 10,000 Letters of Literary Text).

	A	B	C	D	E	F	G	H	I	J	K	L	M	N	O	P	Q	R	S	T	U	V	W	X	Y	Z	
A	1	8	44	45	131	21	11	84	18			34	56	54	9	21		57	75	56	18	15	32	3	11		805
B	32			18	11	2	2	1	7			7	9	7	18	1		4	13	14	5				11		162
C	39		12	4	64	9	1	2	55			8	1	31	18			14	21	6	17		3	5	10		320
D	15			10	107	1	1	1	16			28	2	118	16			16	6	9	11		4		4		365
E		58	55	39	39	25	32	251	37	2	28	72	48	64	3	40		148	84	94	11	53	30	1	12	5	1231
F	10		1	12	23	14	3	2	27			5		8	94			6	13	5	1		1		3		228
G	18			2	20	1	1		10			1		75	3			6	6	1	12				5		161
H			46	3	15	6	16	5					1	9	3	7		3	30	315	2		48		5		514
I	16	6	15	57	40	21	10	72			8	57	26	37	13	8		77	42	128	5	19	37	4	18	2	718
J		2		1	1	1						1		3				1									10
K	10		8		2				8			3		3	5			11	2								52
L	77	21	16	7	46	10	4	3	39			55		10	17	29		12	6	12	28		4		6	1	403
M	18	1		9	43	3	1	1	32			4	5	7	44			15	14	14	9		1		4		225
N	172			5	120	2	3	2	169		3	1	3	9	145			12	19	8	33		10		3		719
O	2	11	59	37	46	38	23	46	63	4	3	28	28	65	23	28		54	71	111	2	6	17	1	28		794
P	31		1	7	32	3	1	1	3			2	16	7	29	26		8	24	8	17		2	4	7		229
Q	1			1	14							2							2								20
R	101	6	7	10	154	4	21	8	21			2		5	113	42		18	6	30	49		1		5		603
S	67	5	1	32	145	8	7	3	106		2	12	6	51	37	3		39	41	32	42		3		17		659
T	124		38	39	80	42	13	22	88		1	19	6	110	53	14		63	121	53	45		6	1	21		959
U	12	25	16	8	7	11	8	2		4		8	13	12	96	7	20	6	30	22			1	1	1		310
V	24			4	16	1			14			2		4	13			5	2	4			1		3		93
W	7		1	9	41	4	2	7	1		3	5	2	15	36	1		10	27	16			2		14		203
X					17				1					1							1						20
Y	27	19		6	17	1	1	1			3	47	3	14	4	2		17	4	21	1						188
Z	1								4						2						1					1	9
																											10000

To learn the frequency of any digram, find its first letter at the top, find its second letter at the side, and observe the figure in the cell at which the column headed by the first letter crosses the row headed by the second. Frequency for EA, 131; for AE, zero.

SOME FOREIGN LANGUAGE DATA

NOTE: Frequencies of letters, and their order, are not fixed quantities
in any language. Group frequencies, however, are fairly constant
in every language. (These may be computed from the Comparative
Table for any desired group in the languages given.) Of the material
which follows, portions came from Lange and Soudart, and from Valerio,
but exact sources were not in every case furnished to the author.

G E R M A N

Order of single letters: E N I R S A D T U G H O L B M C F W Z K V P (J Q X Y)

Order of digrams: EN ER CH DE GE EI IE IN NE ND BE EL TE UN ST DI NO UE SE AU RE HE

Order of trigrams: EIN ICH DEN DER TEN CHT SCH CHE DIE UNG GEN UND NEN DES BEN RCH

Order of tetragrams: ICHT KEIT HEIT CHON CHEN CHER URCH EICH DERN AUCH SCHA SCHE

                 SCHI SCHO SCHU (Furnished by JOSEPH ARTHOLD).

Peculiarities:

         C is practically always followed by H (or K), and SC by H.
         Word-length is normally greater than in English.

F R E N C H

Order of single letters: E A I S T N R U L O D M P C V Q G B F J H Z X Y (K W)

Order of digrams: ES EN OU DE NT TE ON SE AI IT LE ET ME ER EM OI UN QU

Order of trigrams: ENT QUE ION LES AIT TIO ANS ONT ANT OUR AIS OUS

Peculiarities:

         Q followed by U and a second vowel.
         Four and five vowels may be found in sequence ("J'ai oui dire.."), but
         E seldom touches the other vowels. D and M contact E about 75% of the
         time, and L contacts it over 50% of the time. It is unusual to find
         more than four consonants in sequence; when five are found in
         succession, one is almost surely the final S of a plural word.

Order of doubled letters: S L M R T N P E C F
Order of initials: P A S M C E D T V F R B L G J I Q N O H U Y X Z
Order of finals: E S T R N D A I X Z L C U P F Y

Average word-length: 4.3 letters.
Commonest short words, in order: DE IL LE ET QUE JE LA NE UN LES EN CE SE SON MON
                                  PAS LUI ME AU UNE DES SA QUI EST DU

ITALIAN

Order of single letters: E A I O N L R T S C D P U M V G H F B Q Z   (J X K W Y)

Order of digrams: ER ES ON RE EL EN DE DI TI SI AL AN RA NT TA CO

Order of trigrams: CHE ERE ZIO DEL ECO QUE ARI ATO EDI IDE ESI IDI ERO PAR NTE STA

Peculiarities:
> Q followed by U and a second vowel.   H largely preceded by C, in CHE,CHI,
> or sometimes by G in GHE GHI.   Z most often part of ZIO or NZA.
> The frequencies of the vowels E A I O often exchange places.
> Doubling of consonants is very frequent.

Order of doubled letters: L T S C R G P N B M Z F V I D
Order of initials: S P A C D V T M F I G Q R E B L N O U Z H
Order of finals: O E A I   (Others, if used: R L D N)

Average word-length: 4.5 letters.
Commonest short words, in order: LA DI CHE IL NON SI LE UNA LO IN PER UN MI IO PIU
                                              DEL MA SE

SPANISH

Order of single letters: E A O S N I R L D U C T M P B E Q G V Y J F Z X   (K W)

Order of digrams: ES EN EL DE LA OS AR UE RA RE ER AS ON ST AD AL OR TA CO

Order of trigrams: QUE EST ARA ADO AQU DEL CIO NTE OSA EDE PER IST NEI RES SDE

Peculiarities:
> Q followed by U and a second vowel.   The only doubles are
> LL, RR, CC, EE, NN, OO, in the order given, but the latter three
> are very rare.   Group frequencies somewhat less stable than
> in the other languages.

Order of initials: C P A S M E D T H V R U N I L B O F Q G J Z
Order of finals: O A S E N R D L I Z

Average word-length: 4.4 letters.
Commonest short words, in order: DE LA EL QUE EN NO CON UN SE SU LAS LOS ES ME AL
                                              LO SI MI UNA DEL POR SUS MUY HAY MAS

PORTUGUESE

Order of single letters: A E O R S I N D M T U C L P Q V F G H B J Z X   (K W Y)

Order of digrams: ES OS DE AS RO EN CO DO RE ER NT SE AD OR AO SA TE AR EM QU UE OD ST

Order of trigrams: QUE ENT NTE DES EST ODE ADO CON STA MEN ADE DOS ARA COM

> Much like Spanish. Spanish cion becomes cao; ll becomes lh. Articles drop
> the L: os, as, in place of Spanish los, las, etc.

BIBLIOGRAPHY

By W. D. WITT

An extended bibliography of cryptography would fill many pages and is therefore beyond the scope of this work, but it is hoped that the following short selected list will be found useful. Some of these works are out of print or otherwise unobtainable, but may, in some instances, be found in public libraries or in old bookstores. The Riverbank Publications may be consulted at The Library of Congress, Washington, D. C.

MORE OR LESS ELEMENTARY WORKS

BOYER, JOHN Q. " The Cryptogram " in *Real Puzzles* by John Q. Boyer, Rufus T. Strohm and George H. Pryor, pp. 147–154. Baltimore, 1925. (Simple substitution ciphers only.)

BURANELLI, PROSPER, MARGARET PETHERBRIDGE and F. GREGORY HARTSWICK. *The Cryptogram Book.* New York, 1928. (Simple substitution ciphers only.)

HITT, PARKER (Colonel). *The A B C of Secret Writing.* New York, 1935.

LYSING, HENRY, pseud. (John Leonard Nanovic). *Secret Writing.* New York, 1936.

——. *The Cryptogram Book.* New York, 1937.

MANSFIELD, LOUIS C. S. *The Solution of Codes and Ciphers.* London, 1936.

——. *One Hundred Problems in Cipher.* London, 1936.

OHAVER, M. E. *Cryptogram Solving.* Columbus, Ohio, 1933. (Simple substitution ciphers only.)

THOMAS, PAUL B. *Secret Messages.* New York and London, 1928. 2nd printing, 1929.

WINDOLPH, J. FRED (" Phil Down "). " Cryptograms: Their Construction and Solution " in *A Key to Puzzledom,* pp. 53–64. New York, 1906. (Simple substitution ciphers only.)

YARDLEY, HERBERT OSBORNE (Major). *Yardleygrams.* Indianapolis, 1932. (The London edition (1932) bears the title *Ciphergrams.*)

ADVANCED WORKS

FRIEDMAN, WILLIAM F. (Lt.-Colonel). *Elements of Cryptanalysis.* Washington, Gov. Printing Office, 1924. " For Official Use Only." (Contains a bibliography. Out of print and unobtainable.)

——. See also *Riverbank Publications.*

GIVIERGE, MARCEL (General). *Cours de Cryptographie.* Paris, 1st edition, 1925, 2nd edition, 1932.

HITT, PARKER (Colonel). *Manual for the Solution of Military Ciphers.* Fort Leavenworth, Kans., 1st edition, 1916, 2nd edition, 1918.

Riverbank Publications. Papers (except No. 19) by W. F. Friedman. Department of Ciphers, Riverbank Laboratories, Geneva, Illinois.

No. 15, 1917. " A Method of Reconstructing the Primary Alphabet."

No. 16, 1918. " Methods for the Solution of Running-key Ciphers."

No. 17, 1918. " An Introduction to Methods for the Solution of Ciphers."

No. 18, 1918. " Synoptic Tables for the Solution of Ciphers, and a Bibliography of Cipher Literature."

No. 19, 1918. " Formulae for the Solution of Geometrical Transposition Ciphers," by Captain Lenox R. Lohr, with an introduction by W. F. Friedman.

No. 20, 1918. " Several Machine Ciphers and Methods for Their Solution."

No. 21, 1918. " Methods for the Reconstruction of Primary Alphabets."

No. 22, 1922. " The Index of Coincidence and Its Applications in Cryptographic Analysis."

SACCO, LUIGI (General). *Manuale di crittografia.* Rome, 2nd edition, revised and enlarged, 1936. (The first edition was privately printed under the title *Nozioni di crittografia.* Rome, 1930.)

ZANOTTI, MARIO. *Crittografia.* Milan, 1928.

MISCELLANEOUS (Primarily descriptive of systems, historical, special essays, etc., usually with little on cryptanalysis.)

ANON. " Cryptography " in *Encyclopaedia Britannica,* Vol. 6, 14th edition, New York and London, 1929. (Contains a bibliography.)

BALL, W. W. ROUSE. " Cryptographs and Ciphers " in his *Mathematical Recreations and Essays.* 7th edition, 1917 and later. (Latest edition is the 11th, 1939.)

BLAIR, WILLIAM. " Cipher in Diplomatic Affairs " in Rees's *Cyclopaedia.* 1803–1819.

CANDELA, ROSARIO. *The Military Cipher of Commandant Bazeries, An Essay in Decrypting.* New York, 1938.

FRIEDMAN, WILLIAM F. (Lt.-Colonel). " Codes and Ciphers " in *Encyclopaedia Britannica,* Vol. 5, 14th edition, New York and London, 1929. (Contains bibliography.)

——. " Edgar Allan Poe, Cryptographer " in *American Literature, A Journal of Literary History, Criticism and Bibliography,* Vol. 8, No. 3, Nov. 1936, pp. 266–280. Duke University, Durham, N. C.

HULME, FREDERICK EDWARD. *Cryptography, or, The History, Principles and Practice of Cipher-Writing.* London, 1898.

LANGE, ANDRÉ and E. A. SOUDART. *Traité de Cryptographie.* Paris, 1st edition, 1925, new edition, 1935. (Contains an extensive bibliography.)

LANGIE, ANDRÉ. *Cryptography.* Translated from the French by J. C. H. Macbeth, London and New York, 1922.

PRATT, FLETCHER. *Secret and Urgent, The Story of Codes and Ciphers.* Indianapolis, 1939.

YARDLEY, HERBERT OSBORNE (Major). *The American Black Chamber.* Indianapolis and London, 1931. Reprinted, New York, 1933, London, 1934.

THE COMMONEST ENGLISH WORDS

Below are listed the hundred most frequently used words in English. The figures give occurrences in 242,432 words of English text taken from fifteen English authors and many newspapers. Compiled by Frank R. Fraprie, after the rest of the book had been completed.

THE	15568	OR	1101	WHEN	603	ONLY	309
OF	9767	HER	1093	WHAT	570	ANY	302
AND	7638	HAD	1062	YOUR	533	THEN	298
TO	5739	AT	1053	MORE	523	ABOUT	294
A	5074	FROM	1039	WOULD	516	THOSE	288
IN	4312	THIS	1021	THEM	498	CAN	285
THAT	3017	MY	963	SOME	478	MADE	284
IS	2509	THEY	959	THAN	445	WELL	283
I	2292	ALL	881	MAY	441	OLD	282
IT	2255	THEIR	824	UPON	430	MUST	280
FOR	1869	AN	789	ITS	425	US	279
AS	1853	SHE	775	OUT	387	SAID	276
WITH	1849	HAS	753	INTO	387	TIME	273
WAS	1761	WERE	752	OUR	386	EVEN	272
HIS	1732	ME	745	THESE	385	NEW	265
HE	1727	BEEN	720	MAN	383	COULD	264
BE	1535	HIM	708	UP	369	VERY	259
NOT	1496	ONE	700	DO	360	MUCH	252
BY	1392	SO	696	LIKE	354	OWN	251
BUT	1379	IF	684	SHALL	351	MOST	251
HAVE	1344	WILL	680	GREAT	340	MIGHT	250
YOU	1336	THERE	668	NOW	331	FIRST	249
WHICH	1291	WHO	664	SUCH	328	AFTER	247
ARE	1222	NO	658	SHOULD	327	YET	247
ON	1155	WE	638	OTHER	320	TWO	244

ENGLISH TRIGRAMS

The ninety-eight most frequent English trigrams, combining a count of 20,000 trigrams by Fletcher Pratt, in " Secret and Urgent," supposed not to include overlaps between words, and 5,000 by Frank R. Fraprie, including overlaps. This table and the following one are not referred to in the text, having been compiled since the completion of the book.

THE	1182	HER	170	HIS	130	ITH	111
ING	356	ATE	165	RES	125	TED	110
AND	284	VER	159	ILL	118	AIN	108
ION	252	TER	157	ARE	117	EST	106
ENT	246	THA	155	CON	114	MAN	101
FOR	191	ATI	148	NCE	113	RED	101
TIO	188	HAT	138	ALL	111	THI	100
ERE	173	ERS	135	EVE	111	IVE	96

REA	95	INE	73	ORE	65	ART	58
WIT	93	WHI	51	BUT	64	NTE	58
ONS	92	OVE	71	OUT	63	RAT	58
ESS	90	TIN	71	URE	63	TUR	58
AVE	84	AST	70	STR	62	ICA	57
PER	84	DER	70	TIC	62	ICH	57
ECT	83	OUS	70	AME	61	NDE	57
ONE	83	ROM	70	COM	61	PRE	57
UND	83	VEN	70	OUR	61	ENC	56
INT	80	ARD	69	WER	61	HAS	56
ANT	79	EAR	69	OME	60	WHE	55
HOU	77	DIN	68	EEN	59	WIL	55
MEN	76	STI	68	LAR	59	ERA	54
WAS	76	NOT	67	LES	59	LIN	54
OUN	75	ORT	67	SAN	59	TRA	54
PRO	75	THO	66	STE	59		
STA	75	DAY	65	ANY	58		

ENGLISH DIGRAMS

The one hundred and nine most frequent English digrams, compiled from a count of 20,000 trigrams by Fletcher Pratt, in "Secret and Urgent," supposed not to include overlaps between words, and 5,000 by Frank R. Fraprie, including overlaps.

TH	1582	RO	275	WI	188	SA	146	CT	111
IN	784	LI	273	HO	184	NI	142	TU	108
ER	667	RI	271	TR	183	RT	142	DA	107
RE	625	IO	270	BE	181	NA	141	AM	104
AN	542	LE	263	CE	177	OL	141	CI	104
HE	542	ND	263	WH	177	EV	131	SU	102
AR	511	MA	260	LL	176	IE	129	BL	101
EN	511	SE	259	FI	175	MI	128	OF	101
TI	510	AL	246	NO	175	NG	128	BU	100
TE	492	IC	244	TO	175	PL	128		
AT	440	FO	239	PE	174	IV	127		
ON	420	IL	232	AS	172	PO	125		
HA	420	NE	232	WA	171	CH	122		
OU	361	LA	229	UR	169	EI	122		
IT	356	TA	225	LO	166	AD	120		
ES	343	EL	216	PA	165	SS	120		
ST	340	ME	216	US	165	IL	118		
OR	339	EC	214	MO	164	OS	117		
NT	337	IS	211	OM	163	UL	115		
HI	330	DI	210	AI	162	EM	114		
EA	321	SI	210	PR	161	NS	113		
VE	321	CA	202	WE	158	OT	113		
CO	296	UN	201	AC	152	GE	112		
DE	275	UT	189	EE	148	IR	112		
RA	275	NC	188	ET	146	AV	111		

Page 8

1. Open Sesame! (Read initial letters.)
2. Police on trail . . . (Read 2nd letters of words.)
3. Being held . . . (Read every 5th letter.)
4. This is a null cipher. (Progress 1-2-3 etc. within words.)
5. Send supplies . . . (Read every 3rd word.)
6. Why not use . . . (Read every 3rd letter, beginning with 2nd.)

Page 16

7. This is an . . . (Write in columns of 5, normal order.)
8. Three hungry Esquimaux . . . (Box 8 x 8; write in ascending diagonals from upper left corner.)
9. Well, I swan . . . (Box 4 x 8; write in columns, normal order.)
10. Magic squares are simple . . . (Taken out by rows, normal order, from this magic square where plain letters are put ordinally:

20	11	2	49	40	31	22
12	3	43	41	32	23	21
4	44	42	33	24	15	13
45	36	34	25	16	14	5
37	35	26	17	8	6	46
29	27	18	9	7	47	38
28	19	10	1	48	39	30

11. Best trust the . . . (Box 7 x 22; write in columns, normal order.)
12. Art is a bit of . . . (Box 5 x 10; write in columns, normal order.)
13. Fifth battalion . . . (Box 9 x 10; write in columns, normal order.)
14. For some real fun . . . (Box 11 x 6; columns taken out in normal order, but even-numbered columns reversed.)
15. It is not the . . . (Box 7 x 7; taken out spirally counterclockwise from center.)

Page 24

16. Following message received . . . (Box 9 x 8; columns taken out by key NAVAL TOWN.)
17. Research is like . . . (Columns transposed by key 71536248, then taken out by ascending diagonals from upper left corner.
18. The E foot N of T the E rainbow . . . (Transposed by key ENTERPRISE, then taken out spirally counterclockwise from upper left corner.)
19. Man wants but little . . . (Key PATTERN.)
20. The keyword used . . . (Key ADJUST.)
21. Now don't get excited . . . (Key COLUMNARS). Still this example . . . (same key, but all even-numbered columns taken off reversed.)

Page 35

22. The dog insists that the same grille . . .
23. Advance right flank to a point . . .
24. Information about suspected espionage . . .
25. I find the grille very interesting . . . (Four blocks of 6 x 6.)
26. There once was a gal in Ark . . . (Two blocks of 8 x 8.)

27. A grille is easy to solve . . .
28. Honesty is said to be the best policy, but watch out for a dirty trick quite soon. (Four separate grilles used, each twice with a half-turn, for 8 letters at a time.)

Page 52

29. Signal Corps reports . . . (Key SIGNAL CORP.)
30. There was an old gramp . . . (Key DISPIRIT.)
31. Jackson wires that . . . (Key PIN GAME.)
32. See the funny pelican . . . (Key INSUBORDINATION.)
33. To solve this . . . (Key SIMILAR.)
34. Philosopher XX Generally . . . (Key PHILOSOPHER.)
35. Oh yes that dirty trick . . . (Key 539284176.)

Page 66

36. (a) See if you can get in touch with Jimmy.
    (b) All right, tell me what you want of Jim.
    (c) Tell him to be ready for that stickup.
37. (a) The mixing up of words in a plai
    (b) ntext often gives . . .
38. Hollywood is the place . . . (Nihilist; key 3 1 4 10 8 5 2 7 6 9; taken out by rows.)
39. I am not sure this is a good way to write a Nihilist message . . .
40. Enemy will attack . . . (Four blocks of 5 x 5; rows transposed by key FRANK; taken out spirally clockwise from center.)
41. The above message has four completed units and each unit was a five by five square with columns transposed using the keyword DAMON, then taken off from the center in a counterclockwise spiral XX. (Key THE ABOVE MESSAGE HAS FO. This description does not apply to No. 40.)
42. (a) In the past . . . (b) Signals in broad daylight . . .
    (c) Are you clever enough . . . (Key AMIABILITY.)
43. This, my children . . . (Null cipher; read 2nd and 4th letter of each group.)
44. Enny wun hoo tinks he nose awl about sifurs . . . (Periods of 18; odd-numbered letters of each period taken out first, then even-numbered.)

Page 86

45. If you had trouble . . .
46. Davis reported buying . . .
47. The trapdoor spider . . .
48. When a message . . .
49. No, this is not an Aristocrat . . . (Order of words in plaintext is reverse.)

Page 92

50. While boxing with a friend . . .
51. Without having had experience . . .

52. A dog can run only halfway . . .
53. Civilization means concentration . . .
54. Due to refraction . . .
55. Life in a trailer . . .
56. Professions of patriotism . . .
57. Mrs. Apple, serving dinner . . .
58. Package store policy . . .
59. Am sorry to take up . . .
60. Downcast actor complains . . .
61. Social tact is . . .
62. Big oaks from little . . .
63. Trailer home should be . . .
64. Some solving aids . . .
65. Dumb minx knots damp rope . . .
66. At spring moon dog attends . . .
67. Ridiculous usurpation once . . .
68. Couple spread lunch alfresco . . .
69. Chemist experimenting with arfvedsonite . . .
70. Pharmaceutical farmer propagates . . .
71. Awkward madam reverses level kayak . . .
72. Ptarmigan, pschometry, pfennig, phaeton . . .
73. Spry miauling lynx irks . . .

74. Dancing down fairway, madcap ouphe . . .
75. Weird allies, oriental fiend . . .
76. Playful stray angora kitten . . .
77. Chowchow diet with agaragar . . .
78. Glyceryl trinitrate, otherwise nitroglycerin . . .
79. Sentinels, watchful, alert . . .
80. Young nimrod catches tularemic . . .
81. Foxy thug sapt hick dick . . .
82. Zebra yawns, wakes . . .
83. Nymphs waltz, vex frog . . .
84. Phlegmatic lifeguards purchasing . . .
85. Pigmy subkingdom upset when okapi . . .
86. Humpbacked Notre Dame dwarf . . .
87. Ichthyosauri, plesiosauri gambol . . .
88. Holiday crowds watch youths . . .
89. Rapt medico opines zeugma . . .
90. Devout kaik-beclad hadji . . .
91. Ornithorhyncus, pterepod, grysbok . . .
92. Languid, grumach tzigane, zestful . . .
93. Thrasonical yahoo watched xanthous . . .
94. Psychophysic brightsmith hamstrung . . .
95. Mirza, gawky bucko, hides pyxis . . .
96. Oerlax, uhlan, adzing ngaio . . .
97. Itivimiut eskimo behind igdlu . . .
98. Abracadabra cryptogamic cythla . . .
99. Uyezd bans kefir. Kumys-mad muzhik . . .

Page 107

100. Plans are made to attack the city at daybreak . . . (Key HIS MAJESTY THE KING WOULD DINE.)
101. All of the things . . . (Simple substitution, written backwards.)
102. Have Murphy interview . . . (Simple substitution with variants for E T.)
103. From what people say . . . (Checkerboard, with co-ordinates 4 x 1.)

Page 116

104. (Title) A strange disappearance. (Key STRANGE.)
    (I) Miller reports . . . (Key FAVORITE.)
    (II) Latest report . . . (Key WHAT BUNK.)
    (III) News not confirmed . . . (Key FUDGE.)
    (IV) The lost is found . . . (Key EUREKA.)
105. The average length . . . (Key CREDO.)
106. After learning the fundamentals . . . (Key PLEASURE.)
107. There are three hundred . . . (Key SOLAR.)
108. Solving ciphers . . . (Key BIVOUACS.)
109. XXX We do not . . . (Key DAVID.)

Page 125

110. In other men . . . (Key 13258406.)
111. Cipher solving . . . (Key 95042163.)
112. When you get a cipher . . . (Key DOGGEREL.)
113. Crossword puzzles . . . (Key PUZZLES.)
114. For a young girl . . . (Key VARIANT.)
115. We have exciting news . . .

Page 137

116. The idea that one gets . . . (Key DELUSION.)
117. Cipher enthusiasts . . . (Key FRIENDLY.)
118. You should put great men . . . (Key FIVES.)
119. Real optimism consists in . . . (Key WORK.)
120. These also are proverbs . . . (Key SUNDRY.)
121. Director found potential celluloid star . . .

Page 145

122. Sent bias tape by agent three STOP. Complete instructions are impregnated on the strip STOP. Karl. (Key starts INHUMAN OREJONS MURDER . . .
123. When all common trigraphs . . . (Key TRIGRAPHS.)
124. Freckles in profusion . . . (Key ROCHESTER.)
125. Oh say can you see . . . (Key 471302.)
126. My contribution to the unknown cause . . .
127. A mull or quirk has deceived zou . . . (Plain N's replaced by M; cipher N's replaced by O; null N's inserted in wordbreaks in ciphertext. Key PERPLEXITY.)

Page 158

128. To CCC camp educational instructors . . . (Key FAITH.)
129. To CCC camp . . . (Key HOPES.)
130. To CCC camp . . . (Key AND LOVE.)

Page 168

131. Once upon a time . . . (Nihilist; key APPLESAUCE.)
132. Perhaps it should be pointed out . . . (System of Fig. 131.)
133. Sam's girl is tall and slender . . . (Primary alphabet REPUB-
LICAN.)
134. Meet me at three.

Page 184

135. When Jack Boomer . . . (Alphabet WOLF HUNTER; key BOUNTY
under A.)
136. Alois Stephen, young Viennese . . . (Alphabet BIGAMY; key
DOWRIES under B.)
137. The American Constitution . . . (Alphabet ANDROCLES; key
TERMINAL under A.)
138. Recent press dispatches . . . (Type II; alphabet PICOLA; key
KPA under A.)
139. Speaking of secret communications . . . (Type N/-N; key
SCHNITZEL under A.)

Page 191

140. The American Cryptogram Association . . . (Alphabet BLACK-
SMITH.)
141. If you wish more cryptograms . . . (Alphabet WONDERFUL.)
142. How long have you been married . . . (Enciphered by Type II
in groups of 5; alphabet UNCOPYRIGHTABLE; key CROSS under A.)
143. The foregoing is not definitely arranged. (Box 7 x 5; columns
taken out in normal order, but columns, 1, 2, 5, 6 reversed.)

Page 197

144. God made the country . . . (Key MASTODON.)
145. The Man in the Iron Mask . . . (Key FRENCH.)
146. MMBR Pity is one of . . . (Key PITY.)
147. To live content . . . (Key LOVE.)
148. Ever hear a transposition called a tramp Q. (Box 5 x 7; columns
taken out by key 34521.)

Page 208

149. Enemy agents . . . (Alphabet SAN DIEGO.)
150. The Playfair cipher . . . (Alphabet GRAYSON.)
151. The use of the word . . . (Alphabets INDOMITABLE, QUAG-
MIRES.)
152. The trouble with most people . . . (Key HOOEY.)
153. Dear Bill . . . (Alphabet UNWAVERINGLY.)

Page 211

154. Report from agent . . . (Period 7; alphabet IMPOST.)
155. These things are not very hard to solve even when the trinumeral alphabet is in mixed order. (Each period of 25 letters put through normal columnar transposition in box 5 x 5; numerals substituted from Fig. 4, written in column; taken out by rows within each group of 5.)
156. This is the shortest message . . . (Baconian, with each group of 7 in ciphertext reversed.)

Page 215

157. A professor says . . . (Beaufort; key CHINA.)
158. The keyword to this block . . . (Columnar transposition; key PSYCHOPATHIC.)
159. How about releasing Tony . . . (Simple substitution contrived to look like transposition. Plaintext is a null cipher; read every 5th letter: Being held, trail bearer.)
160. Great opportunity . . . (Phillips; alphabet CONTEMPTIBLY.)
161. This is the same key . . . (Playfair; alphabet CONTEMPTIBLY written in a special way stated in the plaintext.)
162. Does the superimposing . . . (Incomplete columnar transposition; key 9 11 6 1 8 3 4 7 5 10 2.)
163. Perhaps it was not obvious . . . (Key CHIKORY.)
164. Tentative date U. S. Attack St. Mihiel salient Sept. 14 . . . (Checkerboard 5 x 7 including nine digits.)
165. Now just a simple substitution . . . (Simple substitution with plain J used as a word separator.)
166. If you don't bring the money tonight, you will soon find that I am not . . . (Mexican Army Cipher Disk with a mixed plaintext alphabet—THEP-ANICLOWS; Key 01, 40, 76, 91.) This solution was given for the first time at the 34th annual convention of the American Cryptogram Association (Montreal, 1967).
167. Unsolved.

INDEX

A CATALOG OF SELECTED
DOVER BOOKS
IN ALL FIELDS OF INTEREST

A CATALOG OF SELECTED DOVER BOOKS IN ALL FIELDS OF INTEREST

100 BEST-LOVED POEMS, Edited by Philip Smith. "The Passionate Shepherd to His Love," "Shall I compare thee to a summer's day?" "Death, be not proud," "The Raven," "The Road Not Taken," plus works by Blake, Wordsworth, Byron, Shelley, Keats, many others. 96pp. 5 3/16 x 8 1/4. 0-486-28553-7

100 SMALL HOUSES OF THE THIRTIES, Brown-Blodgett Company. Exterior photographs and floor plans for 100 charming structures. Illustrations of models accompanied by descriptions of interiors, color schemes, closet space, and other amenities. 200 illustrations. 112pp. 8 3/8 x 11. 0-486-44131-8

1000 TURN-OF-THE-CENTURY HOUSES: With Illustrations and Floor Plans, Herbert C. Chivers. Reproduced from a rare edition, this showcase of homes ranges from cottages and bungalows to sprawling mansions. Each house is meticulously illustrated and accompanied by complete floor plans. 256pp. 9 3/8 x 12 1/4. 0-486-45596-3

101 GREAT AMERICAN POEMS, Edited by The American Poetry & Literacy Project. Rich treasury of verse from the 19th and 20th centuries includes works by Edgar Allan Poe, Robert Frost, Walt Whitman, Langston Hughes, Emily Dickinson, T. S. Eliot, other notables. 96pp. 5 3/16 x 8 1/4. 0-486-40158-8

101 GREAT SAMURAI PRINTS, Utagawa Kuniyoshi. Kuniyoshi was a master of the warrior woodblock print — and these 18th-century illustrations represent the pinnacle of his craft. Full-color portraits of renowned Japanese samurais pulse with movement, passion, and remarkably fine detail. 112pp. 8 3/8 x 11. 0-486-46523-3

ABC OF BALLET, Janet Grosser. Clearly worded, abundantly illustrated little guide defines basic ballet-related terms: arabesque, battement, pas de chat, relevé, sissonne, many others. Pronunciation guide included. Excellent primer. 48pp. 4 3/16 x 5 3/4. 0-486-40871-X

ACCESSORIES OF DRESS: An Illustrated Encyclopedia, Katherine Lester and Bess Viola Oerke. Illustrations of hats, veils, wigs, cravats, shawls, shoes, gloves, and other accessories enhance an engaging commentary that reveals the humor and charm of the many-sided story of accessorized apparel. 644 figures and 59 plates. 608pp. 6 1/8 x 9 1/4. 0-486-43378-1

ADVENTURES OF HUCKLEBERRY FINN, Mark Twain. Join Huck and Jim as their boyhood adventures along the Mississippi River lead them into a world of excitement, danger, and self-discovery. Humorous narrative, lyrical descriptions of the Mississippi valley, and memorable characters. 224pp. 5 3/16 x 8 1/4. 0-486-28061-6

ALICE STARMORE'S BOOK OF FAIR ISLE KNITTING, Alice Starmore. A noted designer from the region of Scotland's Fair Isle explores the history and techniques of this distinctive, stranded-color knitting style and provides copious illustrated instructions for 14 original knitwear designs. 208pp. 8 3/8 x 10 7/8. 0-486-47218-3

Browse over 9,000 books at www.doverpublications.com

CATALOG OF DOVER BOOKS

ALICE'S ADVENTURES IN WONDERLAND, Lewis Carroll. Beloved classic about a little girl lost in a topsy-turvy land and her encounters with the White Rabbit, March Hare, Mad Hatter, Cheshire Cat, and other delightfully improbable characters. 42 illustrations by Sir John Tenniel. 96pp. 5³⁄₁₆ x 8¼.   0-486-27543-4

AMERICA'S LIGHTHOUSES: An Illustrated History, Francis Ross Holland. Profusely illustrated fact-filled survey of American lighthouses since 1716. Over 200 stations — East, Gulf, and West coasts, Great Lakes, Hawaii, Alaska, Puerto Rico, the Virgin Islands, and the Mississippi and St. Lawrence Rivers. 240pp. 8 x 10¾.   0-486-25576-X

AN ENCYCLOPEDIA OF THE VIOLIN, Alberto Bachmann. Translated by Frederick H. Martens. Introduction by Eugene Ysaye. First published in 1925, this renowned reference remains unsurpassed as a source of essential information, from construction and evolution to repertoire and technique. Includes a glossary and 73 illustrations. 496pp. 6⅛ x 9¼.   0-486-46618-3

ANIMALS: 1,419 Copyright-Free Illustrations of Mammals, Birds, Fish, Insects, etc., Selected by Jim Harter. Selected for its visual impact and ease of use, this outstanding collection of wood engravings presents over 1,000 species of animals in extremely lifelike poses. Includes mammals, birds, reptiles, amphibians, fish, insects, and other invertebrates. 284pp. 9 x 12.   0-486-23766-4

THE ANNALS, Tacitus. Translated by Alfred John Church and William Jackson Brodribb. This vital chronicle of Imperial Rome, written by the era's great historian, spans A.D. 14-68 and paints incisive psychological portraits of major figures, from Tiberius to Nero. 416pp. 5³⁄₁₆ x 8¼.   0-486-45236-0

ANTIGONE, Sophocles. Filled with passionate speeches and sensitive probing of moral and philosophical issues, this powerful and often-performed Greek drama reveals the grim fate that befalls the children of Oedipus. Footnotes. 64pp. 5³⁄₁₆ x 8 ¼.   0-486-27804-2

ART DECO DECORATIVE PATTERNS IN FULL COLOR, Christian Stoll. Reprinted from a rare 1910 portfolio, 160 sensuous and exotic images depict a breathtaking array of florals, geometrics, and abstracts — all elegant in their stark simplicity. 64pp. 8⅜ x 11.   0-486-44862-2

THE ARTHUR RACKHAM TREASURY: 86 Full-Color Illustrations, Arthur Rackham. Selected and Edited by Jeff A. Menges. A stunning treasury of 86 full-page plates span the famed English artist's career, from *Rip Van Winkle* (1905) to masterworks such as *Undine, A Midsummer Night's Dream,* and *Wind in the Willows* (1939). 96pp. 8⅜ x 11.   0-486-44685-9

THE AUTHENTIC GILBERT & SULLIVAN SONGBOOK, W. S. Gilbert and A. S. Sullivan. The most comprehensive collection available, this songbook includes selections from every one of Gilbert and Sullivan's light operas. Ninety-two numbers are presented uncut and unedited, and in their original keys. 410pp. 9 x 12.   0-486-23482-7

THE AWAKENING, Kate Chopin. First published in 1899, this controversial novel of a New Orleans wife's search for love outside a stifling marriage shocked readers. Today, it remains a first-rate narrative with superb characterization. New introductory Note. 128pp. 5³⁄₁₆ x 8¼.   0-486-27786-0

BASIC DRAWING, Louis Priscilla. Beginning with perspective, this commonsense manual progresses to the figure in movement, light and shade, anatomy, drapery, composition, trees and landscape, and outdoor sketching. Black-and-white illustrations throughout. 128pp. 8⅜ x 11.   0-486-45815-6

Browse over 9,000 books at www.doverpublications.com

THE BATTLES THAT CHANGED HISTORY, Fletcher Pratt. Historian profiles 16 crucial conflicts, ancient to modern, that changed the course of Western civilization. Gripping accounts of battles led by Alexander the Great, Joan of Arc, Ulysses S. Grant, other commanders. 27 maps. 352pp. 5⅜ x 8½. 0-486-41129-X

BEETHOVEN'S LETTERS, Ludwig van Beethoven. Edited by Dr. A. C. Kalischer. Features 457 letters to fellow musicians, friends, greats, patrons, and literary men. Reveals musical thoughts, quirks of personality, insights, and daily events. Includes 15 plates. 410pp. 5⅜ x 8½. 0-486-22769-3

BERNICE BOBS HER HAIR AND OTHER STORIES, F. Scott Fitzgerald. This brilliant anthology includes 6 of Fitzgerald's most popular stories: "The Diamond as Big as the Ritz," the title tale, "The Offshore Pirate," "The Ice Palace," "The Jelly Bean," and "May Day." 176pp. 5⅜ x 8½. 0-486-47049-0

BESLER'S BOOK OF FLOWERS AND PLANTS: 73 Full-Color Plates from Hortus Eystettensis, 1613, Basilius Besler. Here is a selection of magnificent plates from the *Hortus Eystettensis,* which vividly illustrated and identified the plants, flowers, and trees that thrived in the legendary German garden at Eichstätt. 80pp. 8⅜ x 11. 0-486-46005-3

THE BOOK OF KELLS, Edited by Blanche Cirker. Painstakingly reproduced from a rare facsimile edition, this volume contains full-page decorations, portraits, illustrations, plus a sampling of textual leaves with exquisite calligraphy and ornamentation. 32 full-color illustrations. 32pp. 9⅜ x 12¼. 0-486-24345-1

THE BOOK OF THE CROSSBOW: With an Additional Section on Catapults and Other Siege Engines, Ralph Payne-Gallwey. Fascinating study traces history and use of crossbow as military and sporting weapon, from Middle Ages to modern times. Also covers related weapons: balistas, catapults, Turkish bows, more. Over 240 illustrations. 400pp. 7¼ x 10⅞. 0-486-28720-3

THE BUNGALOW BOOK: Floor Plans and Photos of 112 Houses, 1910, Henry L. Wilson. Here are 112 of the most popular and economic blueprints of the early 20th century — plus an illustration or photograph of each completed house. A wonderful time capsule that still offers a wealth of valuable insights. 160pp. 8⅜ x 11. 0-486-45104-6

THE CALL OF THE WILD, Jack London. A classic novel of adventure, drawn from London's own experiences as a Klondike adventurer, relating the story of a heroic dog caught in the brutal life of the Alaska Gold Rush. Note. 64pp. 5³⁄₁₆ x 8¼. 0-486-26472-6

CANDIDE, Voltaire. Edited by Francois-Marie Arouet. One of the world's great satires since its first publication in 1759. Witty, caustic skewering of romance, science, philosophy, religion, government — nearly all human ideals and institutions. 112pp. 5³⁄₁₆ x 8¼. 0-486-26689-3

CELEBRATED IN THEIR TIME: Photographic Portraits from the George Grantham Bain Collection, Edited by Amy Pastan. With an Introduction by Michael Carlebach. Remarkable portrait gallery features 112 rare images of Albert Einstein, Charlie Chaplin, the Wright Brothers, Henry Ford, and other luminaries from the worlds of politics, art, entertainment, and industry. 128pp. 8⅜ x 11. 0-486-46754-6

CHARIOTS FOR APOLLO: The NASA History of Manned Lunar Spacecraft to 1969, Courtney G. Brooks, James M. Grimwood, and Loyd S. Swenson, Jr. This illustrated history by a trio of experts is the definitive reference on the Apollo spacecraft and lunar modules. It traces the vehicles' design, development, and operation in space. More than 100 photographs and illustrations. 576pp. 6¾ x 9¼. 0-486-46756-2

Browse over 9,000 books at www.doverpublications.com

A CHRISTMAS CAROL, Charles Dickens. This engrossing tale relates Ebenezer Scrooge's ghostly journeys through Christmases past, present, and future and his ultimate transformation from a harsh and grasping old miser to a charitable and compassionate human being. 80pp. 5³⁄₁₆ x 8¼. 0-486-26865-9

COMMON SENSE, Thomas Paine. First published in January of 1776, this highly influential landmark document clearly and persuasively argued for American separation from Great Britain and paved the way for the Declaration of Independence. 64pp. 5³⁄₁₆ x 8¼. 0-486-29602-4

THE COMPLETE SHORT STORIES OF OSCAR WILDE, Oscar Wilde. Complete texts of "The Happy Prince and Other Tales," "A House of Pomegranates," "Lord Arthur Savile's Crime and Other Stories," "Poems in Prose," and "The Portrait of Mr. W. H." 208pp. 5³⁄₁₆ x 8¼. 0-486-45216-6

COMPLETE SONNETS, William Shakespeare. Over 150 exquisite poems deal with love, friendship, the tyranny of time, beauty's evanescence, death, and other themes in language of remarkable power, precision, and beauty. Glossary of archaic terms. 80pp. 5³⁄₁₆ x 8¼. 0-486-26686-9

THE COUNT OF MONTE CRISTO: Abridged Edition, Alexandre Dumas. Falsely accused of treason, Edmond Dantès is imprisoned in the bleak Chateau d'If. After a hair-raising escape, he launches an elaborate plot to extract a bitter revenge against those who betrayed him. 448pp. 5³⁄₁₆ x 8¼. 0-486-45643-9

CRAFTSMAN BUNGALOWS: Designs from the Pacific Northwest, Yoho & Merritt. This reprint of a rare catalog, showcasing the charming simplicity and cozy style of Craftsman bungalows, is filled with photos of completed homes, plus floor plans and estimated costs. An indispensable resource for architects, historians, and illustrators. 112pp. 10 x 7. 0-486-46875-5

CRAFTSMAN BUNGALOWS: 59 Homes from "The Craftsman," Edited by Gustav Stickley. Best and most attractive designs from Arts and Crafts Movement publication — 1903–1916 — includes sketches, photographs of homes, floor plans, descriptive text. 128pp. 8¼ x 11. 0-486-25829-7

CRIME AND PUNISHMENT, Fyodor Dostoyevsky. Translated by Constance Garnett. Supreme masterpiece tells the story of Raskolnikov, a student tormented by his own thoughts after he murders an old woman. Overwhelmed by guilt and terror, he confesses and goes to prison. 480pp. 5³⁄₁₆ x 8¼. 0-486-41587-2

THE DECLARATION OF INDEPENDENCE AND OTHER GREAT DOCUMENTS OF AMERICAN HISTORY: 1775-1865, Edited by John Grafton. Thirteen compelling and influential documents: Henry's "Give Me Liberty or Give Me Death," Declaration of Independence, The Constitution, Washington's First Inaugural Address, The Monroe Doctrine, The Emancipation Proclamation, Gettysburg Address, more. 64pp. 5³⁄₁₆ x 8¼. 0-486-41124-9

THE DESERT AND THE SOWN: Travels in Palestine and Syria, Gertrude Bell. "The female Lawrence of Arabia," Gertrude Bell wrote captivating, perceptive accounts of her travels in the Middle East. This intriguing narrative, accompanied by 160 photos, traces her 1905 sojourn in Lebanon, Syria, and Palestine. 368pp. 5⅜ x 8½. 0-486-46876-3

A DOLL'S HOUSE, Henrik Ibsen. Ibsen's best-known play displays his genius for realistic prose drama. An expression of women's rights, the play climaxes when the central character, Nora, rejects a smothering marriage and life in "a doll's house." 80pp. 5³⁄₁₆ x 8¼. 0-486-27062-9

Browse over 9,000 books at www.doverpublications.com

DOOMED SHIPS: Great Ocean Liner Disasters, William H. Miller, Jr. Nearly 200 photographs, many from private collections, highlight tales of some of the vessels whose pleasure cruises ended in catastrophe: the *Morro Castle, Normandie, Andrea Doria, Europa,* and many others. 128pp. 8⅞ x 11¼. 0-486-45366-9

THE DORÉ BIBLE ILLUSTRATIONS, Gustave Doré. Detailed plates from the Bible: the Creation scenes, Adam and Eve, horrifying visions of the Flood, the battle sequences with their monumental crowds, depictions of the life of Jesus, 241 plates in all. 241pp. 9 x 12. 0-486-23004-X

DRAWING DRAPERY FROM HEAD TO TOE, Cliff Young. Expert guidance on how to draw shirts, pants, skirts, gloves, hats, and coats on the human figure, including folds in relation to the body, pull and crush, action folds, creases, more. Over 200 drawings. 48pp. 8¼ x 11. 0-486-45591-2

DUBLINERS, James Joyce. A fine and accessible introduction to the work of one of the 20th century's most influential writers, this collection features 15 tales, including a masterpiece of the short-story genre, "The Dead." 160pp. 5³⁄₁₆ x 8¼. 0-486-26870-5

EASY-TO-MAKE POP-UPS, Joan Irvine. Illustrated by Barbara Reid. Dozens of wonderful ideas for three-dimensional paper fun — from holiday greeting cards with moving parts to a pop-up menagerie. Easy-to-follow, illustrated instructions for more than 30 projects. 299 black-and-white illustrations. 96pp. 8⅜ x 11. 0-486-44622-0

EASY-TO-MAKE STORYBOOK DOLLS: A "Novel" Approach to Cloth Dollmaking, Sherralyn St. Clair. Favorite fictional characters come alive in this unique beginner's dollmaking guide. Includes patterns for Pollyanna, Dorothy from *The Wonderful Wizard of Oz,* Mary of *The Secret Garden,* plus easy-to-follow instructions, 263 black-and-white illustrations, and an 8-page color insert. 112pp. 8¼ x 11. 0-486-47360-0

EINSTEIN'S ESSAYS IN SCIENCE, Albert Einstein. Speeches and essays in accessible, everyday language profile influential physicists such as Niels Bohr and Isaac Newton. They also explore areas of physics to which the author made major contributions. 128pp. 5 x 8. 0-486-47011-3

EL DORADO: Further Adventures of the Scarlet Pimpernel, Baroness Orczy. A popular sequel to *The Scarlet Pimpernel,* this suspenseful story recounts the Pimpernel's attempts to rescue the Dauphin from imprisonment during the French Revolution. An irresistible blend of intrigue, period detail, and vibrant characterizations. 352pp. 5³⁄₁₆ x 8¼. 0-486-44026-5

ELEGANT SMALL HOMES OF THE TWENTIES: 99 Designs from a Competition, Chicago Tribune. Nearly 100 designs for five- and six-room houses feature New England and Southern colonials, Normandy cottages, stately Italianate dwellings, and other fascinating snapshots of American domestic architecture of the 1920s. 112pp. 9 x 12. 0-486-46910-7

THE ELEMENTS OF STYLE: The Original Edition, William Strunk, Jr. This is the book that generations of writers have relied upon for timeless advice on grammar, diction, syntax, and other essentials. In concise terms, it identifies the principal requirements of proper style and common errors. 64pp. 5⅜ x 8½. 0-486-44798-7

THE ELUSIVE PIMPERNEL, Baroness Orczy. Robespierre's revolutionaries find their wicked schemes thwarted by the heroic Pimpernel — Sir Percival Blakeney. In this thrilling sequel, Chauvelin devises a plot to eliminate the Pimpernel and his wife. 272pp. 5³⁄₁₆ x 8¼. 0-486-45464-9

AN ENCYCLOPEDIA OF BATTLES: Accounts of Over 1,560 Battles from 1479 B.C. to the Present, David Eggenberger. Essential details of every major battle in recorded history from the first battle of Megiddo in 1479 B.C. to Grenada in 1984. List of battle maps. 99 illustrations. 544pp. 6½ x 9¼. 0-486-24913-1

ENCYCLOPEDIA OF EMBROIDERY STITCHES, INCLUDING CREWEL, Marion Nichols. Precise explanations and instructions, clearly illustrated, on how to work chain, back, cross, knotted, woven stitches, and many more — 178 in all, including Cable Outline, Whipped Satin, and Eyelet Buttonhole. Over 1400 illustrations. 219pp. 8⅜ x 11¼. 0-486-22929-7

ENTER JEEVES: 15 Early Stories, P. G. Wodehouse. Splendid collection contains first 8 stories featuring Bertie Wooster, the deliciously dim aristocrat and Jeeves, his brainy, imperturbable manservant. Also, the complete Reggie Pepper (Bertie's prototype) series. 288pp. 5⅜ x 8½. 0-486-29717-9

ERIC SLOANE'S AMERICA: Paintings in Oil, Michael Wigley. With a Foreword by Mimi Sloane. Eric Sloane's evocative oils of America's landscape and material culture shimmer with immense historical and nostalgic appeal. This original hardcover collection gathers nearly a hundred of his finest paintings, with subjects ranging from New England to the American Southwest. 128pp. 10⅝ x 9. 0-486-46525-X

ETHAN FROME, Edith Wharton. Classic story of wasted lives, set against a bleak New England background. Superbly delineated characters in a hauntingly grim tale of thwarted love. Considered by many to be Wharton's masterpiece. 96pp. 5³⁄₁₆ x 8 ¼. 0-486-26690-7

THE EVERLASTING MAN, G. K. Chesterton. Chesterton's view of Christianity — as a blend of philosophy and mythology, satisfying intellect and spirit — applies to his brilliant book, which appeals to readers' heads as well as their hearts. 288pp. 5⅜ x 8½. 0-486-46036-3

THE FIELD AND FOREST HANDY BOOK, Daniel Beard. Written by a co-founder of the Boy Scouts, this appealing guide offers illustrated instructions for building kites, birdhouses, boats, igloos, and other fun projects, plus numerous helpful tips for campers. 448pp. 5³⁄₁₆ x 8¼. 0-486-46191-2

FINDING YOUR WAY WITHOUT MAP OR COMPASS, Harold Gatty. Useful, instructive manual shows would-be explorers, hikers, bikers, scouts, sailors, and survivalists how to find their way outdoors by observing animals, weather patterns, shifting sands, and other elements of nature. 288pp. 5⅜ x 8½. 0-486-40613-X

FIRST FRENCH READER: A Beginner's Dual-Language Book, Edited and Translated by Stanley Appelbaum. This anthology introduces 50 legendary writers — Voltaire, Balzac, Baudelaire, Proust, more — through passages from *The Red and the Black, Les Misérables, Madame Bovary,* and other classics. Original French text plus English translation on facing pages. 240pp. 5⅜ x 8½. 0-486-46178-5

FIRST GERMAN READER: A Beginner's Dual-Language Book, Edited by Harry Steinhauer. Specially chosen for their power to evoke German life and culture, these short, simple readings include poems, stories, essays, and anecdotes by Goethe, Hesse, Heine, Schiller, and others. 224pp. 5⅜ x 8½. 0-486-46179-3

FIRST SPANISH READER: A Beginner's Dual-Language Book, Angel Flores. Delightful stories, other material based on works of Don Juan Manuel, Luis Taboada, Ricardo Palma, other noted writers. Complete faithful English translations on facing pages. Exercises. 176pp. 5⅜ x 8½. 0-486-25810-6

FIVE ACRES AND INDEPENDENCE, Maurice G. Kains. Great back-to-the-land classic explains basics of self-sufficient farming. The one book to get. 95 illustrations. 397pp. 5⅜ x 8½. 0-486-20974-1

FLAGG'S SMALL HOUSES: Their Economic Design and Construction, 1922, Ernest Flagg. Although most famous for his skyscrapers, Flagg was also a proponent of the well-designed single-family dwelling. His classic treatise features innovations that save space, materials, and cost. 526 illustrations. 160pp. 9⅜ x 12¼. 0-486-45197-6

FLATLAND: A Romance of Many Dimensions, Edwin A. Abbott. Classic of science (and mathematical) fiction — charmingly illustrated by the author — describes the adventures of A. Square, a resident of Flatland, in Spaceland (three dimensions), Lineland (one dimension), and Pointland (no dimensions). 96pp. 5³⁄₁₆ x 8¼. 0-486-27263-X

FRANKENSTEIN, Mary Shelley. The story of Victor Frankenstein's monstrous creation and the havoc it caused has enthralled generations of readers and inspired countless writers of horror and suspense. With the author's own 1831 introduction. 176pp. 5³⁄₁₆ x 8¼. 0-486-28211-2

THE GARGOYLE BOOK: 572 Examples from Gothic Architecture, Lester Burbank Bridaham. Dispelling the conventional wisdom that French Gothic architectural flourishes were born of despair or gloom, Bridaham reveals the whimsical nature of these creations and the ingenious artisans who made them. 572 illustrations. 224pp. 8⅜ x 11. 0-486-44754-5

THE GIFT OF THE MAGI AND OTHER SHORT STORIES, O. Henry. Sixteen captivating stories by one of America's most popular storytellers. Included are such classics as "The Gift of the Magi," "The Last Leaf," and "The Ransom of Red Chief." Publisher's Note. 96pp. 5³⁄₁₆ x 8¼. 0-486-27061-0

THE GOETHE TREASURY: Selected Prose and Poetry, Johann Wolfgang von Goethe. Edited, Selected, and with an Introduction by Thomas Mann. In addition to his lyric poetry, Goethe wrote travel sketches, autobiographical studies, essays, letters, and proverbs in rhyme and prose. This collection presents outstanding examples from each genre. 368pp. 5⅜ x 8½. 0-486-44780-4

GREAT EXPECTATIONS, Charles Dickens. Orphaned Pip is apprenticed to the dirty work of the forge but dreams of becoming a gentleman — and one day finds himself in possession of "great expectations." Dickens' finest novel. 400pp. 5³⁄₁₆ x 8¼. 0-486-41586-4

GREAT WRITERS ON THE ART OF FICTION: From Mark Twain to Joyce Carol Oates, Edited by James Daley. An indispensable source of advice and inspiration, this anthology features essays by Henry James, Kate Chopin, Willa Cather, Sinclair Lewis, Jack London, Raymond Chandler, Raymond Carver, Eudora Welty, and Kurt Vonnegut, Jr. 192pp. 5⅜ x 8½. 0-486-45128-3

HAMLET, William Shakespeare. The quintessential Shakespearean tragedy, whose highly charged confrontations and anguished soliloquies probe depths of human feeling rarely sounded in any art. Reprinted from an authoritative British edition complete with illuminating footnotes. 128pp. 5³⁄₁₆ x 8¼. 0-486-27278-8

THE HAUNTED HOUSE, Charles Dickens. A Yuletide gathering in an eerie country retreat provides the backdrop for Dickens and his friends — including Elizabeth Gaskell and Wilkie Collins — who take turns spinning supernatural yarns. 144pp. 5⅜ x 8½. 0-486-46309-5

HEART OF DARKNESS, Joseph Conrad. Dark allegory of a journey up the Congo River and the narrator's encounter with the mysterious Mr. Kurtz. Masterly blend of adventure, character study, psychological penetration. For many, Conrad's finest, most enigmatic story. 80pp. 5³⁄₁₆ x 8¼. 0-486-26464-5

HENSON AT THE NORTH POLE, Matthew A. Henson. This thrilling memoir by the heroic African-American who was Peary's companion through two decades of Arctic exploration recounts a tale of danger, courage, and determination. "Fascinating and exciting." — *Commonweal.* 128pp. 5⅜ x 8½. 0-486-45472-X

HISTORIC COSTUMES AND HOW TO MAKE THEM, Mary Fernald and E. Shenton. Practical, informative guidebook shows how to create everything from short tunics worn by Saxon men in the fifth century to a lady's bustle dress of the late 1800s. 81 illustrations. 176pp. 5⅜ x 8½. 0-486-44906-8

THE HOUND OF THE BASKERVILLES, Arthur Conan Doyle. A deadly curse in the form of a legendary ferocious beast continues to claim its victims from the Baskerville family until Holmes and Watson intervene. Often called the best detective story ever written. 128pp. 5³⁄₁₆ x 8¼. 0-486-28214-7

THE HOUSE BEHIND THE CEDARS, Charles W. Chesnutt. Originally published in 1900, this groundbreaking novel by a distinguished African-American author recounts the drama of a brother and sister who "pass for white" during the dangerous days of Reconstruction. 208pp. 5⅜ x 8½. 0-486-46144-0

THE HUMAN FIGURE IN MOTION, Eadweard Muybridge. The 4,789 photographs in this definitive selection show the human figure — models almost all undraped — engaged in over 160 different types of action: running, climbing stairs, etc. 390pp. 7⅞ x 10⅝. 0-486-20204-6

THE IMPORTANCE OF BEING EARNEST, Oscar Wilde. Wilde's witty and buoyant comedy of manners, filled with some of literature's most famous epigrams, reprinted from an authoritative British edition. Considered Wilde's most perfect work. 64pp. 5³⁄₁₆ x 8¼. 0-486-26478-5

THE INFERNO, Dante Alighieri. Translated and with notes by Henry Wadsworth Longfellow. The first stop on Dante's famous journey from Hell to Purgatory to Paradise, this 14th-century allegorical poem blends vivid and shocking imagery with graceful lyricism. Translated by the beloved 19th-century poet, Henry Wadsworth Longfellow. 256pp. 5³⁄₁₆ x 8¼. 0-486-44288-8

JANE EYRE, Charlotte Brontë. Written in 1847, *Jane Eyre* tells the tale of an orphan girl's progress from the custody of cruel relatives to an oppressive boarding school and its culmination in a troubled career as a governess. 448pp. 5³⁄₁₆ x 8¼.
0-486-42449-9

JAPANESE WOODBLOCK FLOWER PRINTS, Tanigami Kônan. Extraordinary collection of Japanese woodblock prints by a well-known artist features 120 plates in brilliant color. Realistic images from a rare edition include daffodils, tulips, and other familiar and unusual flowers. 128pp. 11 x 8¼. 0-486-46442-3

JEWELRY MAKING AND DESIGN, Augustus F. Rose and Antonio Cirino. Professional secrets of jewelry making are revealed in a thorough, practical guide. Over 200 illustrations. 306pp. 5⅜ x 8½. 0-486-21750-7

JULIUS CAESAR, William Shakespeare. Great tragedy based on Plutarch's account of the lives of Brutus, Julius Caesar and Mark Antony. Evil plotting, ringing oratory, high tragedy with Shakespeare's incomparable insight, dramatic power. Explanatory footnotes. 96pp. 5³⁄₁₆ x 8¼. 0-486-26876-4

Browse over 9,000 books at www.doverpublications.com